Conscience and Slavery

Conscience and Slavery

The Evangelistic Calvinist Domestic Missions, 1837–1861

Victor B. Howard

THE KENT STATE UNIVERSITY PRESS
Kent, Ohio, and London, England

© 1990 by The Kent State University Press, Kent, Ohio 44242
All rights reserved
Library of Congress Catalog Card Number 90-34051
ISBN 0-87338-411-3
Manufactured in the United States of America

Library of Congress Cataloging-in-Publication Data

Howard, Victor B.
    Conscience and slavery : the evangelistic Calvinist domestic
missions, 1837-1861 / Victor B. Howard.
    Includes bibliographical references.
    ISBN 0-87338-411-3 (alk. paper) ∞
    1. Slavery and the church—United States—History—19th century.
2. Slavery and the church—Calvinists. 3. Calvinism—United States—
History—19th century. 4. United States—Church history—19th
century. 5. American Home Mission Society—History—19th century.
I. Title.
E449.H8494   1990
266'.5'097309034—dc20   90-34051
                                            CIP

British Library Cataloging-in-Publication data are available.

For my grandchildren
Victor, Katherine, and David

Contents

Acknowledgments

*R*esearch on this study began after unanswered questions arose that were beyond the scope of my dissertation. At the time I was located in the Chicago area, which was rich in Calvinist church sources. The progress of the research could not have gone forward without the kindness and assistance of Calvin Schmitt, director of the Virginia Library, McCormick Theological Seminary. Schmitt made the seminary library available for my use and arranged for me to use the extensive collection of midwestern Presbyterian records. He also purchased many monographs I needed to use in my research, even though I was not an alumnus or student. The late Joseph King, director of the Hammond Library of the Chicago Theological Seminary, was equally accommodating. He arranged for me to use the extensive collection of American Home Missionary Society (AHMS) Papers on Saturdays and Sundays when the library was closed. During the early period of my research, extensive time was spent in the use of the American Missionary Association (AMA) Papers depositories of Fisk University and in the Presbyterian Historical Society, Philadelphia, using the massive collection of church records, church newspapers, and journals. I owe a debt of gratitude to the librarians of Fisk University and the Presbyterian Historical Society.

I am indebted to James M. McPherson, who read early drafts of my manuscript and offered important suggestions. Fred Hood read the manuscript and pointed out important deficiencies in the narrative, and Joseph Conforti read portions of the manuscript and assisted in strengthening my understanding of the early national period of church history. I am deeply grateful to Guy Smith, who went beyond a scholarly professional courtesy and assisted me with chapter-by-chapter suggestions.

I am grateful to the American Philosophical Society for the Penrose Award and for coming to my assistance with additional funds that permitted research to continue in neglected but important depositories. I wish to express my gratitude to the staff of the Camden-Carroll Library, Morehead State University, particularly to the interlibrary loan librarians, Carol Nutter and Betty Lane, without whose assistance the work could not have gone forward. Carolyn Hamilton and Wilma Howard cheerfully and skillfully typed the manuscript, and Wilma Howard read many drafts of the manuscript and offered suggestions on revision of the narrative.

I owe a debt of gratitude to Margaret King Library of the University of Kentucky; the Berea College library; the Library of Congress; the Historical Libraries of Ohio, Western Reserve, Indiana, Illinois, Wisconsin, and Iowa. I wish to thank the librarians of Wooster College, Hanover College, Beloit College, Grinnell College, Oberlin College, Wheaton College, Randolph-Macon College, Carroll College, Kent State University, Yale University, Harvard University, Princeton University, Miami University (Oxford, Ohio), the University of Virginia, the University of Chicago, Tulane University, Indiana University, and Syracuse University.

I am grateful for the assistance provided by the staffs of the Rochester Public Library, the Detroit Public Library, the Boston Public Library, the New York Public Library, the Chicago Historical Society, the Massachusetts Historical Society, the New York Historical Society, the Indiana Historical Society, the Worcester Antiquarian Society, the Presbyterian Foundation, the Cincinnati Historical Society, and the Georgia Department of Archives and History.

I also wish to thank the Louisville Presbyterian Theological Seminary, and Union Theological Seminaries of New York and Richmond. The Presbytery of Cleveland and the Synod of Indiana kindly made their records available for my use. Finally, I wish to thank Clifton Johnson of the Amistad Library which housed the AHMS Papers and the AMA Papers during the later stage of my research.

The substance of chapter 9 was previously published in *Church History* 41 (1972): 208–24. It is included here by permission of the original publisher.

Introduction

*T*his study examines the significance of evangelical religion as a factor in the events leading to the Civil War. In order to make the subject more manageable, I limited the study to Calvinist churches. The focus is on the Plan of Union adopted by the Calvinist churches to work out a collective endeavor for benevolent enterprises. After the Presbyterian church split in 1837, only the New School Presbyterians remained under the Plan of Union, thus I do not include a detailed treatment of the Old School Presbyterians. Eventually, the collective enterprise was limited to the evangelical (revivalist) Calvinist churches, consisting of the New School Presbyterians, Congregationalists, and some synods of the smaller Calvinist denominations.

As the antebellum period advanced, the North took on a holier-than-thou attitude toward the South, while the South developed a new political and social philosophy that replaced their previous defenses and apologies and boldly asserted that slavery was a positive good. The critical factor for both church and state was the controversy over territorial control. No other religious groups were more committed to shaping frontier communities by group action through domestic missions than the evangelical Calvinist churches. The uncompromisable moral antagonism that developed over free soil in the territories and was a significant factor in the final struggle existed in religion as well as politics. As new western states came into the Union and settlers moved to the frontier, the thorny problem of slavery pricked the national conscience more deeply. This was true despite the fact that the institution neither needed, nor had prospects for, additional territory.

The evangelical view of manifest destiny included the belief in a millennium based on the Revelation of St. John, in which a thousand-year era is prophesied when God will return to the earth for a Second Advent. Some Christians were pre-millennialists who believed that the Second Coming of Christ would occur before the millennium. The pre-millennialists did not expect the world to improve before the Second Coming and usually were not committed reformers or activists. Post-millennialists believed society could be improved according to God's plan and that improving the earth should not be neglected simply because it seemed difficult — or even impossible — to achieve by human efforts. The post-millennialists believed that no matter how difficult a problem seemed, God would aid in creating a better world.[1] Post-millennialists also believed that Jesus would return after a millennium that established the Kingdom of God on Earth. Post-millennialism in the evangelical churches aided in the advancement of abolitionism. The Christian reformer could easily identify the activist post-millennial philosophy with abolitionism, which reinforced the dominance of post-millennialism in the antebellum period. Both movements taught that man had the ability and mandate to abolish slavery and would sin by not doing so.

The Second Great Awakening fostered the growth of all denominations affected by the evangelical movement. Millennialism became intertwined with revivalism, which made both clergy and laymen aggressive proselytizers. Calvinist churches were among the most missionary-oriented churches. The revival spirit also fostered an expansive humanitarian movement. The evangelists were committed to changing the world. Many of these reformers concentrated on abolishing slavery. Some devoted their lives to the cause, to the point of withdrawing from established churches, and started their own denominations.[2] Both the "come-out" churches and the older evangelical denominations envisioned reform as coming from within the church rather than from outside.

Post-millennialism and antislavery sentiment were very strong among Christians of Congregational background. Since the Congregational churches had few Southern adherents and followed a system of government in which the policy-making role was vested in the local churches, their abolition campaigns did not make Congregational churches vulnerable to a backlash.[3]

The Presbyterians were more conscious of collective responsibility and thus more responsive to collective sin, but also less prone to come out of an ecclesiastic body that did not measure up to individual standards at a given time. The General Assembly was the court of final appeal, but the New School General Assembly in 1839 gave the responsibility for dealing with slavery to each presbytery. Since the New School Presbyterians in the North were vulnerable to retaliation not only from the South but also from the northern Presbyterian conservatives, as abolitionism grew in the Congregational churches the two denominations were driven farther apart from their joint benevolent programs formed under the Plan of Union of 1801.

The American Home Missionary Society was the institution of the evangelical Calvinist churches that worked to shape the frontier into the

Kingdom of God as a society with free religion, free schools, and free labor. The concept of millennialism was a powerful belief and very prevalent in the American Home Missionary Society. Missionary work in the West contributed greatly to the concept of American missions. It gave divine sanction to the belief in manifest destiny. The journal of the American Home Missionary Society, the *Home Missionary*, kept the theme of American missions before the Society's patrons. The editor of the *Home Missionary* wrote in 1845: "Vast designs of Providence are fast being accomplished." The editor warned the patrons, "The destiny of our country, and the part which it is to act in the work of a world's redemption, will soon be a matter of unalterable record." The *Home Missionary* agreed with the editor of the Baptist *New York Recorder* when he wrote: "The home missionary will do more for liberty than troops of vaunting politicians."[4]

The belief that America had a special mission in the divine scheme of things to come was generally held by Americans. The concept of America's glorious destiny was taught to each generation by William McGuffey's readers.[5] Laymen in the halls of Congress expressed their faith in the American mission. In the debate on establishing a territorial government for Oregon, Representative Alexander Duncan told his colleagues that "Providence seems to have a design in extending our free institutions as far and as wide as the American continent." It was the duty of every member of society to do his part. He cautioned his fellow congressmen that if they failed, all were "accountable in proportion to their means and influence."[6] New School layman Joshua Giddings warned his colleagues that retribution would be visited on the nation if slavery was expanded by the annexation of Texas. "I feel as confident that chastisement and tribulation for the offences which we have committed against the downtrodden sons of Africa await this people, as I do that justice controls the destinies of the nations."[7]

Christians of the West believed they were destined to lead the nation in the great mission, but to exercise leadership the section must remain free soil. In the contest with slavery for the dominance of the West there could be no compromises. Both Christian laymen and evangelical clergymen believed the West would be the future battleground of good an evil.[8]

After 1846, when the dispute over the extension of slavery became the dominant political issue, Christian antislavery men in the older denominations and the "come-out" churches exerted a powerful influence to move northern religious bodies to an antislavery position. Churches had become sectional institutions. The decisive factor in the posture of the northern evangelical church was not abolitionism's influence outside of organized religion but the political controversies over the issue of the extension of slavery and the contest for the West.

By 1850 the most meaningful vitality of the antislavery crusade survived mainly within the churches,[9] and the influence of the Garrisonians in the churches was limited largely to the liberal churches and to the Progressive Friends. It was not the moral suasion and the American Anti-Slavery Society that drove the churches to action, but the determination of the South for equal treatment in the territories and the open proslavery doctrine that had been developed in the southern churches by their clerical leaders. The controversy over the extension of slavery moved the slavery question from the abstract to a vital issue of everyday life and a living contest between right and wrong.

Opposition to the extension of slavery on moral grounds was the principal unifying force of the early Republican party. In 1961 Don Fehrenbacker put it well when he wrote, "Only the steady growth of a Northern consensus on the moral unacceptability of slavery explains either the rise of Republicanism or its brilliant success in contrast with the disintegration of Whiggery, the failure of Know-Nothingism, and the disruption of Democracy."[10]

No study relating the free soil concept to the idea of post-millennialism and moral sentiments of the evangelical churches has been made; rather, the free soil principle has been treated as an economic and political concept. No writer has previously integrated the political controversy over slavery with the religious dispute concerning servitude to show the interaction of events in church and state that accelerated the development of the political crisis as well as the increased contentions in the church. I have undertaken to do both. Historians have tended to view the concept of free soil too narrowly to mean free labor. Free labor was a part of a concept that also included free religion and free schools unhampered by the institution of slavery. I am indebted to Eric Foner for his clear ideas of the free soil ideology he presents in *Free Soil, Free Labor, Free Men*, but he reveals only the political side of the issue during the antebellum period. I am fully in accord with S. E. Maizlish (*The Triumph of Sectionalism*, 1983) and Dale Baum (*The Civil War Party System*, 1984), but both scholars could have presented a broader view by giving more attention to the moral issues rather than limiting consideration to abstract ideology.[11]

Excellent studies have been published on the position of the evangelical churches on social issues during the antebellum period by John Bodo (*The Protestant Clergy and Public Issues, 1812–1848*, 1954) and Charles Cole (*The Social Ideas of the Northern Evangelists, 1826–1860*, 1954). More recently, Shelton Smith (*In His Image*, 1972) focused entirely on slavery as a controversy that broke up the churches into sectional bodies, but he failed to show the interrelation of the controversy in church and state.[12]

The material on the issues in these masterly monographs is completely divorced from the political events of the period in which they took place.

C. C. Goen has written an excellent study (*Broken Churches, Broken Nation*, 1985), but the thrust of his thesis is that the breakup of churches in the 1840s sealed the doom of the political union and was one of the great causes of political separation of the nation.[13] He does not dwell on the effects of the political episodes that escalated the controversy in the churches during the last twenty years of the antebellum period. I have tried to show how the interaction of church and state led to the acceleration of the controversy in politics as well as in religion, each contributing to the tensions that led to the Civil War.

In writing of the political developments in the slavery controversy, no attempt is made to write a well-rounded political treatment of the Mexican War, the Compromise of 1850, the Kansas-Nebraska Act, and the elections of 1856 and 1860. That has been well done by others. My purpose is to show how church and state interacted to escalate the controversy beyond control in both sectarian and secular institutions.

John McKivigan has made a significant contribution by his recent study (*The War Against Proslavery Religion*, 1984), but to classify the evangelical churches as being proslavery by accepting the partisan Garrisonians view is to ignore the realities of church history.[14] McKivigan's book is a capable study of antislavery literature but he makes no use of church records and does not examine the day-by-day ordeal of the churches in dealing with the problem of slavery. Some of the meetings of the New School presbyteries, synods, and the General Assembly devoted the better part of a week to heated controversy and debate that could not have occurred in proslavery churches. The Congregational associations dealt with the problem of slavery without so much heated debate, but the western associations almost broke off fellowship with the eastern brethren before the western Congregationalists were appeased in 1852 by a stronger position on slavery.

Although each evangelical church had proslavery as well as an antislavery elements, through much of the antebellum period moderates dominated most evangelical churches. The moderates were inclined to place the growth of the church at the top of their list of priorities. With the aggressive posture of slavery in the territories after the Mexican War, many churches came under the control of an antislavery majority. The northern evangelical churches played a significant role in the events leading to the Civil War. Their part in the controversy centered around what they considered to be the moral struggle over the millennial destiny of the free territories.

The Rise of the
Missionary Spirit

*T*he social and economic conditions in New England following the
American Revolution were not conducive to the growth of the Congregational Church. The new Congregational churches that were founded
in Massachusetts hardly replaced those that had ceased to exist in the state.
As a result, the growth of Massachusetts as a state was lower in the decade
after the war than in any other decade in the century. The reasons for the
decline of orthodox religion were changes in philosophy, changes in the
economic and social order, and the rise of religious sects.[1] Economic self-
sufficiency waned with the growth of commercial agriculture, and the vitality of rural New England disappeared. At the same time that the transition from self-sufficiency to commercial agriculture was taking place, the
textile industry was shifting from the farmhouse to the factory, and the
new mill towns were altering the social and economic structure of New
England society. As the population became more mobile, the clergy as well
were less permanent in their tenure. As a result pastors became more identified with their calling and less oriented with their congregation as com-
munal leaders of their flocks.[2]

The ranks of Congregational clergy were alarmingly depleted in several
sections of New England. Many Vermont towns could afford to support
only one church and many more congregations shared a minister with a
neighboring community. Even more appalling was the large number of
towns without any pastor at all. The instability and insecurity was more
pronounced and ministerial tenure less permanent as rural communities
declined.[3]

At the same time, disaffection between the pulpit and the pew began
to develop. The struggle between the New Light and Old Light clergy partially accounts for the apathy among laymen, who had no interest in clerical polemical debates. Added to this was the growth of deism in society,
which made inroads on religious orthodoxy, and the stirrings of Unitarian-
ism in the urban centers.[4] The church leaders undertook to reverse this

trend toward apathy and to restore their power, but without results until the Second Great Awakening burst forth in New England at the beginning of the nineteenth century. The Awakening was crucial for the Congregationalists, providing the impetus for a new direction in social and moral values. The Second Great Awakening "appeared to have stimulated renewed lay interest in and willingness to accept conservative theology and the ecclesiastical policies of the New Divinity men." The Awakening in New England was ultimately used by the clergy to promote the democratization of Calvinism and to create reform agencies as an instrument of social control "to replace the crumbling state-church established church system." The managers of the benevolent societies believed that the religion propagated by them could be an effective means of controlling an increasingly chaotic society.[5]

During the period of the American Revolution, both the Presbyterians and Congregationalists believed God was an active participant in the affairs of men and nations, and it was a common conviction that God had been instrumental in aiding the American cause. After the war, among Presbyterians, the doctrine of providence, which had been such a driving force in the efforts to secure independence, "underwent a marked development from the dynamic concept of God's personal activity in History" to a belief that God worked primarily through immutable natural and moral laws that could be discovered and used by man. Thus God's role in national affairs was seen as working through established laws. Religion became more impersonal and lost much of its dynamic influence.

Presbyterian efforts to revitalize the church were influenced by their commitment to the "natural right" doctrine, which involved a firm belief that most people could be saved in their youth as a result of Christian education. As religious education was accelerated by massive efforts of the leadership, it took on the character of revivals under the guidance of religious instruction. These Presbyterian revivals were confined to middle- and upper-class church members, but the Awakening changed revivals into mass movements and supplanted the former method of converting the youth.[6]

The paternalistic controls of the passing era of handicraft fabrication were replaced by voluntary self-restraint in the new age of free labor, and revivalism furnished a new individualized restraint. But religious humanitarians had little conscious motive to control society or to reconstruct social order in which clerical authority was dominant. There was no radical change in humanitarian benevolence between the 1770s and 1820s, but the humanitarians' "earlier relatively sentimental approach was replaced by a more hard-headed attitude."[7]

In New England the Congregational clergy's response to revival was to channel the enthusiasm into forming missionary societies to carry the gospel to the frontier communities. This marked the birth of the missionary movement. As Bernard Weisberger put it, benevolent societies came about as the "fruit of what were called 'revivals of religion.'" The evangelical movement coincided with, and in part fostered, an expansive humanitarian spirit as a by-product. The humanitarian spirit found expression in benevolent enterprises to aid people who could not help themselves. Revival enthusiasm led many to embrace social activism as a means of bringing about humanitarian change.[8]

The Awakening, however, accelerated the decline of evangelical opposition to slavery by dispelling the apprehension and uncertainty in religious life that had been the driving force in the antislavery work. In their enthusiasm to bring about the millennium, the leaders of the Awakening maintained that slaveholding and Christianity could be compatible if masters displayed Christian piety and slaves served with Christian humility. In the early stage of the mission movement that followed in the wake of the revivals, the evangelists threw all their energy into this undertaking and discouraged young clergy from undertaking benevolence that was completely independent of the church. But out of the continuing social tensions came pressures for more specific goal-oriented movements by humanitarians than was the object of the older leaders of the Second Great Awakening.[9]

The extension of the frontier work, due in large part to the religious awakening of the period, resulted in a call issued on June 22, 1797, by the Congregational Association of Connecticut, for the formation of a voluntary society. The Missionary Society of Connecticut was the outcome.[10] Two years later the Massachusetts Congregationalists formed a similar society.

The New School theology that arose in the Presbyterian Church during the early nineteenth century taught that conversion was a matter of human decision that immediately affected behavior. The change in belief about conversion had significant implications. Mass conversion seemed possible. It did not require literacy and it seemed to require that a massive effort be made to Christianize the slaves, for "it could no longer be asked: 'Does he know about Christian principles? Can he read?'"[11] Increased motivation for the conversion of the slave was the result of this new view.

As the population of the West underwent explosive growth and diffusion, the Presbyterian evangelists discovered that a revival could more rapidly accomplish the same goals pursued by the organized church. The Second Great Awakening led many Presbyterians to consider themselves to be part of a great body of Christians encompassing all denominations, which moved them to support interdenominational missionary societies. While the primary motivation for the formation of missionary societies was the desire to bring Christianity to the unchurched, several other factors contributed to the rise of voluntary societies. At the end of the eighteenth century the frontier had extended so far from established communities that frontier settlements could not be served by local pastors in settled parishes. To continue missionary activity meant the expenditure of more funds than a local church possessed. The churches turned to the state to meet financial demands beyond their ability. In October 1792, the Connecticut legislature authorized contributions to several religious societies and congregations in the state.[12]

The growth of voluntary religious societies was accelerated by the movement to separate state and church. Vermont was the first state to grant full religious liberty when it passed an act abolishing compulsory tax support for religion in 1807. Article seven of the new Connecticut constitution of 1818 allowed all persons to withdraw from an ecclesiastical society merely by registering their intentions with the clerk of the society. In 1819 New Hampshire passed a similar law. With state aid no longer available, the associations had to pool their resources. Needing some other source of funds, the American churches adopted the British system of voluntary societies. The hope that voluntary societies could secure aid from the government soon vanished and self-help became the only solution.[13]

Congregationalists and Presbyterians worked out a plan to cooperate in mission efforts. The General Assembly of the Presbyterian Church in 1801 appointed a committee to "consider and digest a plan of government for the churches in the new settlements agreeable to the proposal of the General Association of Connecticut."[14] The committee's report was approved by the General Assembly on May 29, 1801, subject to approval by the General Association, which it received on June 16. The Plan of Union contained four articles: (1) All missionaries were strictly enjoined to promote a spirit of cooperation between Presbyterians and Congregationalists; (2) a Congregational church in a new settlement might accept a Presbyterian minister and still conduct its discipline according to Congregational principles; (3) by the same token, a Presbyterian church might select a Congregational minister and continue to manage its affairs by a Presbyterian session; and (4) a church composed partly of Congregationalists and partly of Presbyterians could unite and select a minister and appoint standing committees to exercise disciplinary authority. Ministers, however, could belong to only one denomination at a time.[15]

In May 1822, a convention of delegates from various New York domestic missionary associations met and formed the United Domestic Missionary

Society. Four years later the United Domestic Missionary Society called a meeting of Congregationalists, Presbyterians, Reformed Dutch, and Associate Reformed to establish a national society that would represent all Calvinist churches. The new society was called the American Home Missionary Society. The Second Great Awakening and the organization of the Benevolent Empire, as it was called, brought new power and prestige to the clergy. The Calvinist clergy used benevolent associations as vehicles to disseminate clerical wisdom and to exercise social control in the new order.[16]

The benevolent societies moved from indoctrination to salvation by conversion and merged with revivalism. The most obvious indication of the change in benevolence was the organization of the American Anti-Slavery Society in 1833. The leaders of the American Anti-Slavery Society were all revival men and Christian reformers, mostly evangelists but including some liberal Christians. Many of the agents and directors of the antislavery societies gained their early training as assistants and agents in the missionary, Bible, and tract societies.[17] Thus the antislavery movement was "deeply enmeshed in the Congregational-Presbyterian missionary movement," which sponsored the numerous tract, Bible, educational, and Sunday school societies.[18]

The abolition movement owed much to the evangelicals because of their uncompromising moral fervor, their teachings of divine retribution upon the slaveholder, and their insistence that slavery be regarded as a practice devised by an inner corruption of the slaveholder rather than as a social or economic system necessitated by the inferiority of the slave. But important as revivalism was, all abolitionists were not evangelists, and the rise of revivalism does not fully explain the growth of the antislavery movement. Most abolitionists felt a profound sense of alienation from the social order because of the materialism and greed produced by the rapid commercialization and industrialization of society, and slavery seemed the most extreme example of this new order of things, taking on a materialism not present in the ancient institution.[19]

Just as the new breed of Calvinists demanded immediate surrender to God in the revivals, the antislavery men demanded immediate abolition of a system that was contrary to "the laws of God, the spirit of the Gospel, the dictates of humanity and the principles of justice." They attempted to apply Christian ethics to the great moral issues of the day.[20] The man primarily responsible for the change in the nature of revivals and the character of voluntary societies was Charles Grandison Finney. American revivalism had tended to make personal salvation the primary objective of conversion, but for Finney, salvation was the beginning of religious experience, not its end. The emotional impulse that the new Calvinism had concentrated on as a preparation for a safe escape from this life Finney turned into a beginning of life and the pursuit of benevolent activity. "Converts," he declared, "did not escape life; they began a new life 'in the interest of God's Kingdom.'" Instead of withdrawing from worldly affairs, the converts began a new life of greater service to society. The followers of Finney threw themselves into various social movements, such as temperance, penal reform, and antislavery. Theodore Weld was the greatest of Charles Finney's converts, and he preached in the same churches where Finney had held revivals. By 1836 Weld and his associates made antislavery the most powerful force affecting the new converts.[21]

By 1800 changes in childrearing also affected evangelism. Freed from the drudgery of household industries by the Industrial Revolution, mothers devoted more time to the religious training of their children. Instead of relying on shame, humiliation, and physical punishment, they guided their children with love and inculcated a conscience, directing them toward benevolence and piety by example as well as precept. The mothers' work was continued and carried on by ministers, church elders, and college and divinity school faculties. The result was a generation of youth who were prepared for service in benevolence.[22]

The growth of nationalism after the War of 1812 and the new perspective inspired by the Second Great Awakening led the clergy to regard the whole nation as their parish. Before 1780 the average ministerial term of tenure was uniformly long, and many members of the clergy were settled for life. Under such a condition pastors did not see the nation as an area of concern. After 1820, when permanency had all but disappeared and the clergy had become increasingly job-oriented rather than congregation-oriented, and with the rise of national benevolent societies, the clergy became concerned about national sins such as war and slavery that transcended the boundaries of their parishes.

The evangelical movement aimed at reforming individuals, not society, although its leaders insisted that society would benefit indirectly from the reformation of individual conduct. Religious reformers did, however, see the relief of human suffering as part of their ministry, and they often gave powerful testimonies against the evils of slavery.[23] The reformers and abolitionists believed their mission went beyond conversion and insisted that opposition to slavery went beyond empathy for the slave and testimony against the evils of the institution. They asserted that opposition to slavery should become a part of the evangelical witness, and further argued that the churches and benevolent societies could not carry out the preaching mission while they were obstructed by an evil so crippling as slaveholding. The organizers of missionary societies and their supporters, however, looked on the antislavery appeal as a distraction from the primary work of extending the church and saving souls. The adoption of a public stand against slavery would alienate prospective converts. Many of the older evangelicals admitted that slaveholding was inherently evil, but they believed that slavery would be eradicated with the spread and influence of the gospel.

In the 1740s Jonathan Edwards had aroused the belief that the millennium would begin in America. Two generations later the Calvinist community was sure the millennium was at hand. As Reverend Thomas Skinner put it, the new institutions for training clergy "would bring the millennium to the very door." The ministerial students were convinced they were preparing for a great purpose. The fervent young missionaries recruited by Weld felt that God had called them to usher in the millennium, and the belief that they were the agents of this great purpose dominated their subsequent sense of what their life's work should be. Although they were strongly committed to their calling as moral leaders, they saw the traditional churches as repositories of spiritual emptiness, moral cowardice, and materialism, both in the pulpit and pew. They were committed to a new spirit, and felt a higher calling than they had observed among the older practitioners of their profession. Whether they combined pastoral duties with immediatism, that is, advocated the immediate abolition of slavery, or became agents of benevolent societies and pursued their immediatist career from that station, or left the ministry entirely, the young evangelists were convinced that abolitionism afforded a second chance at a calling that offered a closer and more direct service to God.[24]

While the prominent evangelists and benevolent leaders were reluctant to take a firm stand against slavery for fear of dividing the church and diverting attention from their primary mission, which they saw as converting the nation, the young missionaries believed the millennium would be achieved by striking at the great evils of society. Finney expressed the thinking of the evangelical leaders when he said "if abolitionism can be made an appendage of a general revival all is well."[25] But as a by-product of revivalism, the antislavery movement soon became a church by furnishing the young activists with an institution that would permit them to withdraw from clerical domination and sectarian narrowness, while permitting them to hold to the vision of Protestant unity. Much of the appeal of the antislavery movement for the young missionaries lay in the ability "to merge essentially religious impulses and spiritual discontent into a constructive, acceptable social role."[26]

The abolitionists had adopted the voluntary principle to promote a reform that the majority of evangelists saw as creating a controversy that was polarizing the churches and creating bitter confrontation. In the name of missions and harmony of the church the majority of the evangelists rejected their antislavery colleagues' plea to discipline slaveholding churches and exclude unrepentant slaveholders from communion. The evangelical supporters of missions were certain that abolitionism would not only result in the division of the church, but of the Union, and would end in civil war. In their view voluntarism was supposed to unite the republic, but immediate abolition of slavery would destroy it. Ultraism, or a radical and extreme position on slavery, caused many clerics to question the new optimism regarding the millennium, and they hardened their opposition to immediate abolition. Abolitionists, however, considered antislavery work to be a necessary step in the march toward the millennium.[27] The abolitionists reached their zenith in the 1830s and then declined as an organization because they failed to capture and hold enough of America's institutional power.

2

The Search
for a Middle Way

A characteristic of the decades of the 1820s and 1830s was the comprehensiveness of the reform movement. The whole man – no less than the total society – was the objective of the crusade. It was universal in all its aspects. The membership of the national benevolent societies was largely a reshuffling of personnel from one society to another; thus many of the members and officers of the American Home Missionary Society (AHMS) and its auxiliaries were also members and officers of the American Colonization Society (ACS). After the AHMS was reorganized following the separation of the Old School Presbyterians from the Society, no fewer than twenty-two of the vice presidents and directors of the AHMS were holding similar offices in the American Colonization Society.[1] When the National Anti-Slavery Convention met in Philadelphia in December 1833 to organize the American Anti-Slavery Society (AAS), a large number of those present were clergymen, many of whom were supporters of home missions. One of the leading members was Amos A. Phelps, pastor of the Pine Street Congregational Church in Boston. The board of managers of the new society included George Shepard, David Thurston, and William Smith, all Congregational clergy of Maine.[2]

Impatient for immediate results, the abolitionists made a concerted frontal attack on the ACS. William L. Garrison led the abolitionist assault on colonization. In his book, *Thoughts On African Colonization* (1832), Garrison charged that the colonization movement was a proslavery plot, designed to rid the South of the troubling presence of free Negroes. Although Garrison's book was the most celebrated rebuke of colonization, Lydia Maria Child's *Appeal* more effectively proved that the colonization scheme was futile. She accused the Colonization Society of putting public opinion to sleep on a subject where it needed to be wide awake. In operation for more than fifteen years, the society, she insisted, had transported between two and three thousand free people of color. There were in the United States two million slaves and three hundred thousand free blacks with the numbers of free blacks increasing at the rate of seventy thousand annually. "It would cost three million five hundred thousand dollars a year," she informed the money-minded supporters of the Colonization Society, "to provide for the safety of our Southern brethren in this way."[3]

Most of the leading abolitionists originally supported colonization. Gerrit Smith, a director of home missions, left the AHMS and the ACS. The renunciation of colonization by Theodore Weld was one of the most serious blows delivered to the colonization principle. James G. Birney, a prominent Presbyterian layman who had served as an agent, also denounced the principles of the ACS as breeding apathy and indifference and as devoid of moral quality. Furthermore, Arthur Tappan, a wealthy silk importer, withdrew his support from the ACS of which he was a life member. Tappan was one of the largest contributors to the AHMS. Arthur Tappan and his younger brother, Lewis, raised questions about fellowshipping Christians guilty of moral indiscretions such as the use of tobacco and alcohol, and Absalom Peters anticipated the question of whether to allow slaveholders church membership in the rising winds of abolitionism. The conservatives in the AHMS made the abolitionists unwelcome and Arthur Tappan made the break complete in May 1840, when he asked to "not be considered for the office of auditor" of the AHMS.[4]

The break between the supporters of home missions was further dramatized on October 9, 1833, when Abijah Fisher, a member of the executive committee of the AHMS; Jasper Corning, a director and treasurer of the Society; and James Boorman, a life director of the AHMS as well as vice president of the Colonization Society after 1837; and others held a convention of the ACS to raise twenty thousand dollars. The previous week, Smith and the Tappans had joined with the Rev. Joshua Leavitt, editor of the Presbyterian *New York Evangelist*, William Goodell, a Congregational clergyman, and others to organize the New York Anti-Slavery Society. A considerable number of these antislavery advocates had formerly supported colonization. Those who stayed with the colonization movement had stronger traditional political and commercial ties with the South, and they were more conservative. Benjamin Franklin Butler, a director of the AHMS and later Secretary of War in Andrew Jackson's Cabinet, was typical of this group. In 1830 Butler was the author of a memorial that the New York Colonization Society sent to the New York legislature. He wrote that the ACS was "the only neutral ground upon which the northerners can meet the southerners for a candid interchange of Sentiments on the delicate subject of Slavery, and the situation of the free Blacks." On the first of October 1833, the supporters of the colonization movement held a meeting at Albany, New York, and Butler and other home mission patrons were in attendance. The prominent part that Butler and the other AHMS directors took in the proceedings revealed the connection between the Colonization Society and the AHMS.[5]

In New England the dispute between colonization and abolition led to a similar split. Simeon S. Jocelyn, a New Haven engraver turned clergyman, was one of the leading immediatists. Jocelyn pastored a Negro church in New Haven and was the central figure in the dispute concerning the establishment of a Negro school there. The antislavery movement, however, was no match for the colonization society in Connecticut. Leonard Bacon, a director of the AHMS and a leading Connecticut churchman, was the most influential advocate of colonization in that state. In 1828 he drew up an "Address to the People of Connecticut" setting forth the advantages of colonization. The controversy between the abolitionists and the colonizers came to a head in September 1831, when the people of New Haven, led by colonizers and supporters of Yale University, blocked the establishment of the Negro college that was endowed by Arthur Tappan and under the leadership of Jocelyn. In June 1833, a meeting was called in Portland, Maine, to organize a state colonization society. The meeting was presided over by Bennet Tyler, a director and later vice president of the AHMS. A prolonged and spirited discussion ensued between the supporters of the colonization and antislavery movements. Samuel Fessenden, a Congregational layman, led the antislavery forces and Tyler was the leading protagonist for the colonizers. When an antislavery society was organized by the opponents of colonization, the controversy became more heated.[6]

In Ohio the struggle between colonizers and abolitionsts divided the Western Reserve and the college there into two hostile camps. As late as July 4, 1831, Charles B. Storrs, president of Western Reserve College, was fervently in favor of colonization. But by December 1, 1831, an editorial in the *Observer and Telegraph,* of which Storrs was part owner, advocated immediate emancipation. A series of articles appearing in the *Telegraph* from August 2 to November 29, 1832, also advocated immediatism. They were written by Elizur Wright, a professor at the school. These were answered by colonizationists who controlled a majority of the board of trustees of the college and the newspaper.[7] In November 1832, Beriah Green wrote that after "examining the matter in discussion between the abolitionists and anti-abolitionists," Storrs, Professor Wright and his father, and Green himself had yielded to the conviction that abolitionism occupied the only ground that the Bible could "justly be regarded as approving and sustaining." They felt impelled by motives they "would not resist, to give 'arm and soul' to the cause of African emancipation."[8] By this time Elizur Wright had been denied the use of the columns of the *Observer and Tele-*

graph, and after a reorganization of the newspaper, the editor, James B. Walker, was gradually forced out of the *Ohio Observer,* as it was now called, because of his antislavery position. The trustees secured a more conservative faculty and the new president of Western Reserve, George E. Pierce, was given a seat as vice president of the AHMS.[9]

The agent of the Home Missionary Society, D. W. Lathrop, tried to work in harmony with both groups on the slavery question. Yet he had "no confidence in the removal of slavery from the U.S. by the direct tendency of the past operations of the Col[onization] Soc[iety]," and was inclined to favor the antislavery society. The excitement of the controversy between colonization and abolitionism created an apathy toward home missions on the Western Reserve. According to Lathrop's view of the situation the abolitionists felt they had "just discovered a great work to be done. It must be the all engaging object of American Christians till it *is* accomplished." The abolitionists reasoned that since so few supported their movement and it encountered such powerful opposition, they had to give all that was available for benevolence to the cause of the slave. The colonizers, in turn, decided that the greater part of their aid must go to colonization because "so many" had withdrawn.[10] When Lathrop questioned Peters, the secretary of the AHMS, concerning the position of the executive committee and the secretaries on the controversy between the abolitionists and colonizers, he was told that the executive committee was "all very nearly of one mind on this subject. We deeply regret the rash and intemperate measures and discussions of the abolitionists" but "both as individuals and as a committee" the officers of the Society regarded it as their duty to keep aloof, as far as possible, "from the agitation and ill will which they [the abolitionists] have produced." The members of the committee thought "well of the object of the Colonization Society," and most probably aided the society by contributions, he added, but they deprecated agitation from the colonization corner as well as from the other. To reinforce his point, Peters concluded in summary that any member of the AHMS who wished to mingle in the affairs of other public efforts should step aside and let others, who would give the work their full attention, fill the place.[11] In February 1836, Lathrop resigned because of poor health, and the more conservative and diplomatic Myron Tracy became the agent. Tracy, who had spent a few years in northern Ohio, was a native of Vermont. He had served as the agent of the ACS for three years in western Massachusetts and Vermont.[12] He was more in harmony with Peters's viewpoint. Peters, who was a half brother to Ralph R. Gurley, the general agent of the Colonization Society, became an active member of the ACS after he retired as secretary of the AHMS.[13]

From 1834 to 1840 the country witnessed a series of protracted formal discussions between the advocates of abolitionism and colonization. In August 1835, the prolonged argument was climaxed by a debate between Samuel May, one of the leading abolitionists, and Ralph Gurley. When Lyman Beecher, in a speech before the Colonization Society in 1836, insisted that he was a "decided friend of emancipation," Gerrit Smith challenged his right to claim adherence to the principle because it was "a *future* and not a *present* emancipation" that enlisted Beecher's friendship. In 1840, when Benjamin F. Butler and Theodore Frelinghuysen expressed the idea that the free blacks had received the colonization scheme with enthusiasm, Samuel E. Cornish, an Old School Presbyterian clergyman, joined with Theodore S. Wright, another black clergyman, in publishing a pamphlet to refute the claim. As the heat of the debate began to wane, an open letter was sent to the friends of the American Colonization Society residing in New England, requesting that they convene in Boston in May 1841, while religious anniversaries were being held, in order to take measures that they considered expedient concerning colonization. The call was signed by Ralph Emerson, Mark Tucker, and Zedekiah S. Barstow, among others, all officers of the AHMS.[14] But despite the fact that the officers and directors of the AHMS were on the side of colonization, "tend to your own proper work" was the password of the officers of this organization where antislavery principles were involved. Thus Leonard Woods, one of the founders and a vice president of the Society, proudly announced to the *Boston Recorder*, February 3, 1835, that the Andover students had adopted resolutions that they would not form "associated action to agitate slavery because it would interfere with the pursuit of studies."[15]

The AAS was effectively capturing the rural church in areas away from centers of commerce. If this were not enough to disturb the friends of colonization, the loss of some of the leading clergymen of the East to the antislavery cause left the colonizers in distress. Three of the most talented eastern clergymen — Edward M. Kirk, Samuel Cox, and Swan Pomroy — identified with the abolitionists. In time, they turned conservative, but their position in the 1830s alerted the churchmen to the weakening position of the colonization movement. Many churchmen saw the greatest evil of the controversy between the abolitionists and the colonizers to be the devisive tendency it created in the church, and they desired to replace the antagonism with harmony. Lyman Beecher was one of the foremost advocates of the proposal to find a middle ground. In June 1834, Beecher, who was a vice president of the AHMS and president of Lane Theological Seminary, spoke before a colonization meeting in Cincinnati. He condemned and deplored the prejudice against the Negro, but concluded that colonization was the only remedy in the face of the strong bias against Negroes. He tried to quiet the troubled waters by pointing out that it should be possible for the antislavery and colonization movements to exist side by side in harmony.[16]

During the 1830s the sentiment in favor of accommodation between conservative and liberal wings of the benevolent movement grew. The greatest difficulty blocking the path to harmony was the different view that was taken concerning the slaveholder. The radical abolitionists felt that the slaveholder should be condemned and denounced until he was moved to put away his sinful relation with his fellow man. The colonizers and many moderate abolitionists believed that the slaveholder should be pitied and shown sympathy. The sin should be hated but not the sinner. Not only did the abolitionists castigate the slaveholder, but many of them lumped the whole South together in a stereotyped image of a master with a horsewhip in hand, ready to act as Satan's agent in the eternal warfare between evil and good. Hatred of slavery became hatred of the master, and the master became indistinguishable from the Southerner. The abolitionists conjured up an illusion of the "Slave Power" that defied the realities of the political structure of the 1830s and contradicted the true character of the frontier nature of the South of that day. In the end, however, the abolitionists were successful in convincing the North that the image of the "Slave Power" was a reality. Some of the most bitter attacks upon the South came from abolitionist clergy.[17]

The violent attacks by the abolitionists were not only denounced by many northern clergy for failure to observe the "Law of Love" that was considered to be basic to the gospel, but these attacks brought a reaction in the South that sought to cleanse the section from the delusion of fanaticism. The work of home missions in the South was seriously threatened. Since the region was a missionary field, many of the clergy in the service of the AHMS were from the North. All outsiders were natural suspects. The secretary of the Presbyterian Missionary Society in Richmond, Virginia, advised the secretary of the AHMS that northern-born missionaries would have difficulties in the South because of slavery.[18] Other missionary societies throughout the South took a similar stand. A series of meetings was held during the summer of 1835 throughout the South for the purpose of inciting hostility against the abolitionists. In most of these meetings the clergy were conspicuous and outspoken.[19]

The rise of abolitionism divided the church on the question of means and tactics. All agreed that slavery was a problem that the church as an institution must deal with and resolve. The abolitionists alienated a considerable portion of the northern church as well as the entire South. Many moderate colonizers felt that the church in conscience could not divorce itself from what was considered a Christian duty to the slave. But the ebbing fortune of the ACS was the principal reason many Christians began to look for an alternative. Could a way be found to reunite the church in a program that would secure the cooperation of the South in the service of the blacks?

The ACS suffered a serious decline in revenue, and by the end of 1833 it faced a deficit of $46,000. It was suffering from division within its ranks that was also a result of its struggle with the abolitionists. At the annual meeting of 1833 a bitter debate broke out when the northern delegates tried to depose five managers in order to give the North control of the society. An opposition was growing in New England to the colonization of free Negroes, and it was proposed that contributors be given the option of having their funds used only for "the removal of emancipated Slaves to Liberia."[20]

The conservative Federalist and Calvinist forces rejected any alliance with the abolitionists. The colonizers were committed to an elitist organization of society, while the radical fringe of the abolitionist movement envisioned a leveling of the class society. The objectionable nature of the new social structure proposed by the abolitionists was most vigorously expressed in Garrison's attack on the colonizers in his *Thoughts on African Colonization:* "There is power enough in the religion of Jesus Christ to melt down the most stubborn prejudice, to overthrow the highest wall of partition, to break the strongest caste, to improve and elevate the most degraded, to unite in fellowship the most hostile, and to equalize and bless all its recipients."[21] It was this leveling tendency, which entered into the political and social life of America in the early nineteenth century, that was so objectionable to the old Federalist elite who supported colonization. As conservatives, the colonizers believed that whatever was genuinely traditional and deep-rooted should not be changed, and slavery fit into this pattern. Thus, racial prejudice and the lines that separated economic and social classes were considered natural in the legitimate order of society.

The objections heaped upon the American Colonization Society by Garrison were more personal. The society was "a creature without heart, without brains, eyeless, unnatural, hypocritical, relentless, unjust." The leaders were not merely misguided; they were deceitful, evil, odious Christian apologists for the crime of slavery. Since the Colonization Society in New England was dominated by conservative clergy of the commercial centers, Garrison's attack on the clergy and church was still worse.[22]

The real issue was not whether the ACS would succeed or fail, but its basic morality. Many of its leaders were making use of, encouraging, and manipulating negrophobia to serve what it regarded as a larger humanitarian end by advancing the elite. Garrison was correct in charging that the movement actually buttressed the slave system it purported to attack. Contrary to the goals of benevolent institutions, it was attempting to thrive on hate instead of Christian charity and love. Its shortcomings soon touched the conscience of the leaders of the church, and they saw their influence over religious institutionalism slipping from their grasp as the rural parishes recognized the deeply committed Christian objectives of the AAS and joined in its support.

The philosophy of the colonizers clashed with the traditions of New England. The deep commitment of New England to the power of formal education to uplift and improve the Negro was brought to the attention of the public long before the question became a point of contention between the ACS and the AAS. In 1826 the board of the Boston Prison Discipline Society pointed out in its first annual report that Negroes constituted a disproportionately large percentage of the prison population of the northeastern states. The Prison Discipline Society was convinced that an appropriation for black education equal to the cost of maintaining black convicts "would very soon raise their character to a level of that of whites, and diminish the number of convicts among them, about ten fold."[23]

The colonizationists felt that education was wasted on the Negro in America because the races could not live amicably together. Although they professed support for Christian missionary endeavors in Africa, they denied the Christian mission to convert the world and reunite mankind in Christ as brothers. In their commitment to religious education of blacks, religious conservatives recognized the strength and justice of Garrison's criticism of the Colonization Society's tendency to discourage instruction and elevation of the Negro in America. A small but powerful group of conservative clergy within the ranks of the Colonization Society advocated improving the blacks on American soil as a step of first importance.[24]

With the rise of the antislavery societies, which immediately challenged the philosophy as well as the objectives of the ACS, the need for an organization that could occupy a position midway between the ACS and the AAS began to take shape in the minds of many conservatives in New England who were sensitive to criticism by the antislavery societies. They saw the justice of the criticism but rejected the denunciatory language, tactics, and immediatism of the antislavery societies. As early as July 1831, Thomas H. Gallaudett, one of the leaders in the organization of the Massachusetts State Colonization Society, suggested a new organization that would be formed by the recognized friends of colonization for the purpose of answering the criticism of "the fault finders and opposers of the

American Colonization Society." The Christian public must be convinced that the friends of the ACS are ready "in all prudent and practicable ways, immediately and extensively, to promote the intellecual and moral improvement of the free colored populations . . . and also to promote in the same way, the melioration of the condition of the slaves, and their emancipation, as soon and as extensively as it can be done," Gallaudett informed Ralph Gurley, the general agent of the ACS. Gallaudett proposed that a correspondence be undertaken among the friends of the society in all sections so as to "bring to bear the weight of their united *counsels,* upon public opinion." Gurley sent Gallaudett's letter to the influential benevolent planter, John H. Cocke of Virginia, with the suggestion that he correspond with Gallaudett on the various topics contained in the letter.[25]

After much discussion and correspondence among conservative leaders, by July 1834 Gallaudett had formulated plans for "The American Society of Inquiry on the Slave Question." It would first conduct the inquiry and establish a quarterly periodical. The editor would be someone who had the confidence of both the North and the South, and the journal would be open to a discussion and investigation of the moral obligation of the whole nation to pursue such measures as would result in the entire removal of slavery. David Bacon, with the assistance of his brother Leonard, established the *Journal of Freedom* in May 1834 in New Haven, Connecticut, to prepare the ground for the movement in the East. The prime objective of the journal was "the Elevation and Improvement of the Colored People, Bond and Free." Complete freedom was the ultimate goal, but the editors were committed to a plan to reach this goal without inflaming passions against the South.[26]

An informal correspondence committee established in Boston decided to call the organization "the Friends of the People of Color." The new association was seen as necessary to prevent the people of New England from going "in a mass in favor of the Anti-Slavery Society," and "to stem the torrent of Garrisonism!"[27]

By 1834 conservative northern sentiment was dissatisfied with current attempts to deal with the slavery question. On one hand, they did not believe that colonization was an adequate remedy for the evil, and on the other, they viewed the attempt to destroy its influence upon the character and future destinies of Africa as peculiarly unfortunate and ill-judged. They felt the time had come for emancipating the slaves at the earliest possible period consistent with their interest.[28]

This determination was increased by the failure to reform the ACS, which was engineered by Gurley at the annual meeting in order to put the society under Northern control and free it of charges of proslavery domination.

Equally important in creating a feeling that a new society was needed was the fact that many churches in New England had gone over to the abolitionists and many others tended to close their doors to both the ACS and the AAS as the safest way to avoid being involved in interbenevolent warfare and dividing members of the congregations.[29]

Lyman Beecher clearly stated the predicament facing the benevolent supporters of colonization when he addressed the Ohio Colonization Society in the summer of 1834. "Humanity, benevolence, self-preservation, and the providence of God, demand, urgently, a more direct and efficient movement" than any existing society to remove the evil of slavery. The Colonization Society must "bow submissively to the providential will of heaven."[30]

By December 1834, the advocates of a new organization committed to gradual abolition had agreed to undertake the establishment of the new movement. Contacts had been made from Maine to Georgia and from the Atlantic to the Mississippi. It was claimed that the contest between colonizers and abolitionists was retarding the work of religious benevolence to uplift the blacks, and a truly national organization that would include the South was desperately needed to work for an end to slavery. The leaders hoped that General John Hartwell Cocke, an aristocratic slaveholder and temperance leader who had advocated the gradual emancipation of the slaves in Virginia after the Nat Turner insurrection, would come forward and be the Southern advocate and founder of the new movement, but conditions were such in the South that no Southerner took the initiative. There was some sentiment in the South favoring a national organization in behalf of Negro missions. While a student at Princeton Theological Seminary in 1830, Charles C. Jones of Georgia had organized a "Society of Enquiry Concerning Africans," before which he delivered a paper urging the establishment of missions to the slaves of Georgia. Back in Georgia, four years later, Jones was inclined to be satisfied with slow progress. In 1834 Jones wrote to the Reverend William S. Plummer of Virginia deploring the inefficiency of the duplication and multiplication of small ineffective missionary activities among the blacks. But he did not think that a united effort by a national organization was yet advisable. He cited the opposition that would be awakened by the fear that "it would lead to Emancipation, and nobody knows what besides." In the same year the Kentucky Presbyterians proposed a united missionary agency to serve the blacks, but no wide support for the plan materialized.[31]

Many Northerners believed the need for a national organization was so urgent that they decided to take the initiative. While steps were being taken to establish a national organization, on December 16, 1834, delegates from ten congregations in the Middlesex Union Association of Congregational Churches came together at Shirley, Massachusetts, and organized a new society under the name of "The African Friends Society of Middlesex North and Vicinity" to work for the temporal and spiritual improvement of all blacks everywhere and for gradual emancipation.[32] This indicated a grass roots sentiment for the movement.

The organizational meeting for a national association was called by a committee of eight representatives of a much larger body. Three of the eight — Joseph Tracy, Nehemiah Adams, and Hubbard Winslow — were editors of the Congregational journal, the Boston Recorder; all eight were orthodox Calvinists. The notice, which appeared in the religious journals in December 1834 and early January 1835, stated that the meeting was called to consider the expediency of organizing a society, but on further consideration it was decided in later announcements to conclude that the society had already been formed and to invite only those "who entertained similar views." This effectively eliminated the immediate abolitionists. Although most of the leaders in the new movement were active in the ACS, the board of managers of that society refrained from sending an official delegate to the January 14, 1835, meeting.[33]

The leaders of the new movement were men who managed and directed the AHMS and the American Board of Commissioners of Foreign Missions (ABCFM). The new society was called the American Union for the Relief and Improvement of the Colored Race. It was composed of both clergy and lay leaders; and although the Orthodox Congregationalists dominated, the Unitarians, Methodists, Baptists, and Episcopalians were each represented by a board member.[34]

The convention convened under the modified call and membership was open to all who agreed that a new organization was needed. The chairman ruled that the resolutions before the meeting were open to discussion only by members of the private organizational meeting. The half dozen members of the AAS were, therefore, given no opportunity to modify the measures previously adopted by the executive committee. They felt they were treated "with utmost rudeness and even insulted, by men in the station of Christian ministers."[35]

When the constitution was taken up for approval by the meeting it was reviewed clause by clause. Several attempts were made to put the constitution in stronger language, but all failed. The constitution called slavery a "wrong" and effort was made by the more liberal members to change this to read a "sin." A change was rejected by a large majority, and an attempt to insert the word "immediately" in front of "abandoned," so that the constitution would read that slavery "ought to be universally and immediately abandoned" was likewise defeated.[36]

After attending the meeting of the American Union for the Relief and Improvement of the Colored Race, Garrison expressed "utter want of confidence" in the new organization. He was critical of the sectarian character of the American Union and charged that three-fourths of the members of the organizational meeting were Orthodox Congregationalists, and he pointed out that the call had come from only one religious journal, the Congregational *Boston Recorder*. Garrison warned the abolitionists throughout the country against the American Union: "Be not led captive by its specious appearance; it is the old hand-maid of slavery, with her cheeks newly painted, a new set of teeth, false hair, and a new attire!"[37]

The abolitionists had been kept out of the American Union, and the names of known immediatists had been purged from the roll of members because the organizers of the Union were primarily interested in creating a union with the South for the improvement of the blacks, and ultimately abolishing slavery as a means to this end. They hoped to "unite all the best men of the North and many at the South." This could only be done by staying clear of ultraism and immediatism. The conservatives of the North desired to reclaim many influential Northerners who had gone with the abolitionists because they preferred "violent measures to no measures at all." Efforts were made to bring Gerrit Smith into the movement, but he saw that only the AAS was identified with the preservation of freedom of speech and American liberties. He threw his lot with the immediatists.[38]

The conservatives succeeded temporarily with Arthur Tappan, president of the AAS. Tappan had been drawn into correspondence during the planning stage and Lyman Beecher worked to win over Arthur and Lewis Tappan, his brother, to a program for the reunification of the evangelical front on the slavery issue, and at the same time to drive a wedge between them and Garrison. "Get rid of Garrison, and thousands will join," he advised in 1834. After the organizational meeting of the American Union adjourned, Arthur Tappan appeared in Boston and spent a day or so conferring with the organizers of the American Union. The evening before his departure he met with many of the local members of the AAS in their Boston headquarters. He urged them to unite with the American Union to the extent that this society was disposed to cooperate. He questioned the value of endorsing all sentiments put forth by Garrison. Garrison rose and announced that, although he owed much gratitude to Tappan, he could not "compromise principle, and sacrifice what he believed to be his duty to his colored brethren." The meeting continued until near midnight, but Tappan failed to carry the group with him.[39]

Arthur Tappan journeyed on to New Haven where he doubtless conferred with Leonard Bacon, one of the leaders in the new movement. While in New Haven, he wrote the influential general agent of the AAS, Amos A. Phelps, and attempted to win Phelps over to a position of cooperation.[40] On the same day he penned a letter to Joseph Tracy, editor of the *Boston Recorder*. He informed the readers of the *Recorder* that after visiting Boston and talking to the leaders of the American Union and to the leading antislavery men, he was convinced that "on emancipation the two societies meet on common ground and should unite in urging forward the cause of religious philanthropy." To both groups he pleaded, "let us not impugn each other's motives and assume a hostile attitude towards each other before the public." Tappan was critical of Tracy's characterization of antislavery men as "Garrisonites," but he admitted that Garrison had his faults. Tappan appealed to a large group of abolitionists who did not support the position of either Tappan or Garrison concerning the American Union, preferring to let the Union stand or fall on its own without interference.[41] Garrison printed Tappan's letter in the *Liberator* and claimed that the abolitionists unanimously regretted Tappan's actions. He declared that Tappan owed the antislavery men a statement of exoneration from all participation in his attempts to associate the antislavery movement with the American Union. Below Tappan's letter, Garrison printed a letter from Lewis Tappan, a member of the AAS's executive committee, in which Lewis expressed approval of Garrison's opposition to the new society and predicted that his opposition would meet "a hearty response from every true-hearted emancipationist in the land."[42]

Many abolitionists in New England expected the Massachusetts Anti-Slavery Society to separate into supporters of Garrison and followers of Arthur Tappan. Within the loyal Garrison circle there was talk of ousting Tappan from his office of president. By mid-February, however, Arthur Tappan ceased to promote the American Union and no longer urged that the two societies cooperate. In February 1835, when he gave the AAS a thousand dollars, the Garrisonians were sure he had freed himself from conservative influence and regretted his former course, and in March 1835, while attending the executive committee meeting of the AAS, Garrison seemed completely reconciled with Arthur Tappan and regarded him as a "truly noble spirit." When the American Union caught him "it caught a Tartar and will be glad to get rid of him," Garrison informed his wife.[43]

With the danger of a split in the abolitionist ranks removed, the immediatists did not forget the new society. In February, the Vermont Anti-Slavery Society declared that they had no confidence in the American Union because the society "refused to call slavery a SIN," and at its next meeting the New England Anti-Slavery Society passed a resounding vote of no confidence in the American Union. In May 1835, the AAS hailed the advent of the American Union as a sign of victory over the ACS. They felt that colonizers had been forced to strike out in "a middle course of action."[44]

The American Union published its "Exposition" or address to the people in March 1835. As set forth in the "Exposition," the society's objective was the ultimate abolition of slavery. Unlike the AAS the American Union was committed to a policy of gradualism free from "contention or reviling" language. The society would proceed in many respects as the Prison Discipline Society had done by investigation and making facts available. Abolition was not the end but a means to the intellectual and moral improvement of blacks. It would replace the AAS, which was barred from the South, and it would work in harmony with the slaveholder to gradually remove slavery from the South. The American Union announced in its address that slavery was "wrong in every one of its aspects and relations." They disclaimed any hostility toward the ACS or the AAS and appealed to the "professed followers of Christ in the slaveholding states" to aid them in the intellectual and moral improvement of the blacks.[45] The founders of the American Union were convinced that the Christian community demanded the new organization. Daniel Noyes, soon to be a secretary of the AHMS, expressed the sentiment of the majority when he informed Leonard Bacon "that the Northern community required such an organization to furnish a mode of action . . . and thus relieve themselves from the condition of disapproving the conduct of others and doing nothing themselves." The leaders of the AHMS and many organizers of the American Union hoped to see a missionary plan operating among the slaves and masters that would transform Southern society and gradually remove slavery.[46] The controlling influence in their lives was a commitment to natural rights.

In April 1835, the first auxiliary of the American Union was formed in Boston, and others soon followed in Salem and Taunton. The auxiliaries primarily concerned themselves with the moral and physical condition of the local blacks. By September 1835, when an auxiliary was formed for the state of Maine, sectional feeling had grown so bitter, due to the controversy concerning abolitionist literature in the mail, that the Maine convention stressed the protection of American rights as much as it supported cooperation in a program of benevolence to blacks.[47]

Kentucky was the only slave state to organize a branch of the new society. Lyman Beecher and Calvin Stowe spoke before the Kentucky Colonization Society in 1834 for a plan of union with good effect, and Reverend John Young, a Presbyterian clergyman of the Synod of Kentucky, was converted to the plan of action. "Elevate the black character by religious influence and you remove the chief difficulty to their liberation. . . .

If a general system of religious and moral instruction were prosecuted, the masters' sympathies would be excited and public sentiment would then not only tolerate but demand their manumission," Young wrote.[48] The organization of a Kentucky Anti-Slavery Society, auxiliary to the AAS, during the same period probably contributed to the enthusiasm among conservatives for an organization occupying a middle ground. The Presbyterians led the way in the new movement. In 1834, the Presbyterian Synod of Kentucky selected a committee to study the problem of slavery and to draw up a plan to deal with it. At the synod meeting in 1835, the committee recommended a system of gradual emancipation. On July 15, 1835, in Lexington, Kentucky, a convention was held to establish a society called the Kentucky Union for the Moral and Religious Improvement of the Colored Race. The Union pledged itself to have nothing to do with colonization or abolition and to devote itself entirely to religious instruction from the Bible for blacks in such a manner as the master might think salutary. Most of the officers were clergymen, and although the Presbyterians were one of the smallest denominations in the state, a majority of the executive committee was of this denomination.[49] The society's constitution stated that the object of the organization was "the simple evangelization of the colored race."[50]

The Kentucky Union issued its "Exposition" in August, and in November the executive committee sent a circular to clergy and slaveholders urging them to look after and protect the morals and virtues of the female slaves.[51] A convention was held in December 1835 to discuss the best means of giving the slave instruction in religion[52] but the opposition to religious instruction of blacks in Kentucky was so great that their religious meetings were frequently broken up and their Sabbath schools for blacks dispersed.[53] When the Georgia missionary Charles C. Jones inquired about the status of slave missions in Kentucky, John C. Young informed him that the Kentucky Union had not accomplished much.[54]

The American Union held its first annual convention in May 1835. The convention again emphasized that their missionaries would work through the slaveholders by an appeal to their "humane and Christian principles." In answer to the public criticism of the society for not calling slavery a sin, the convention declared the institution to be sinful, but the declaration was softened by emphasizing that it was "Our country's" guilt that was surrounded by difficulties involved in its removal.[55] At a meeting in February 1836, the American Union again emphasized that "the mode of relief for the slave" would be decided by the master.[56] The meeting was adjourned until the May anniversary, at which time the American Union committed itself to "compassion and good will . . . derived from the gospel."[57]

Much had been done in the way of religious instruction for the slaves in the South long before the idea of the American Union came to the Northerners as a means of easing their consciences and filling the gap left by the decline of the Colonization Society in New England. The greatest effort and the pioneer work was done in Liberty County, Georgia, and the surrounding region through the cooperation of several denominations. Charles C. Jones, a Presbyterian, became Georgia's most devoted missionary to the slaves. In 1833 the Presbyterian Synod of South Carolina and Georgia instructed the churches under its care to provide religious instruction for the slaves. The Domestic Missionary Society of East Hanover Presbytery, Virginia, had already invited the AHMS to aid in the cultivation of a missionary field within its bounds which contained "a black population probably larger than the whole population of the Sandwich Islands." The East Hanover missionary secretary admitted that the opportunity among the blacks was limited at the time, but he was convinced that a prudent missionary, by using the progressive influence of the gospel, would have an opportunity to affect existing institutions in the southern states. Cortlandt Van Rensalear, formerly of Albany, New York, and J. W. Philips of North Carolina successfully carried on individual missionary projects among the blacks in the South, and advocates of a mission for southern blacks hoped that Van Rensalear's work would form the nucleus of an expanding program. Van Rensalear taught slaves in more than twenty different locations in Halifax County, Virginia.[58]

In the early stages of the discussion of black missions, the dialogue turned toward the possibilities of an American union working through the AHMS as an auxiliary for Negro missions. Correspondence of this type came to Absalom Peters, secretary of the AHMS, from both the North and South, suggesting that "the zeal which . . . excited . . . the North on behalf of the slave . . . ought to be better directed" than it was under the existing organizations. The editor of the Congregational Vermont Chronicle informed Peters that the northern religious press was waiting to know what it could best do to promote the cause. Peters suggested to a reliable influential friend in the South that he secure the cooperation of others in setting up an auxiliary society to the AHMS to give religious instruction to the blacks. Peters was advised that there was no enthusiasm in the South for new innovations in domestic missions and that missionaries who desired to work among the slaves should put themselves under the supervision of judicatories in the South.[59]

As many in the North began to doubt the feasibility of a separate missionary organization, interest was directed toward a program within the framework of the AHMS. From the West Hanover Presbytery, Peters received information that native-born southern missionaries were not available, and the community was so sensitive upon the subject of slavery that northern men would not be trusted even if they were as "pure as angels."[60] In the Presbytery of Baltimore the feeling of the majority was so strong against the North and the AHMS that there was a formidable bar to a successful operation.[61] In the Piedmont section of North Carolina, inquiry revealed that slaveholders had no objection to oral instruction in religion for the slaves or to the AHMS commissioning a missionary from the North to work in that section giving special attention to the slaves, but not much could be done for the slave without creating opposition because of the excited state of public opinion due to the effects of the abolition movement and the uneasiness left by the Nat Turner revolt.[62]

A Christian slaveholder from South Carolina who abhorred "the whole system of *involuntary* slavery" wrote the *New York Observer* that he hoped the American Union would come up with "something reasonable, practicable and efficient." By steering a middle course, he felt that the American Union could "enlist the talents, and the efforts of all in every section."[63] The discussion led to a plan of action. In March of 1834 some forty or fifty representatives of the synods of Virginia and North Carolina met in convention at Petersburg, Virginia, to consider the question of missionary efforts among the slaves but without adopting a plan of action because of fear of opposition.[64] When Ethan A. Andrews was sent to tour the South in July 1835 to test the public sentiment of education and religion for the slave, he warned his colleagues that there was "such a jealousy of foreign interference" in the South that the missionary work for the present must be left principally to the southern church.[65] A mob even assaulted General John H. Cocke in April 1835, because he had expressed a willingness to support the AHMS in supplying a missionary to his slaves.[66] As a result of the conditions existing in the South, the Union failed to bring religion to the slave.

The goals and objects of the Union included work among the northern blacks that could have resulted in significant accomplishments without any consideration of the South. But the American Union also failed here, largely due to the tendency of the blacks to distrust the organization. In 1837 Samuel E. Cornish, editor of the *Colored American* in New York, warned that the American Union was too full of prejudice to be serviceable. The society would hinder more than it would help until its members had "buried their prejudice of heart," and learned to view blacks "as brethren of the same family and the same blood, with themselves."[67]

The American Union was not only weakened by the lack of cooperation from the South and the black community, but the northern benevolent community was divided and lacked unity on the need for action. The American Union never had the full support of several important leaders in the domestic mission field. Leonard Woods, president of Andover Theological Seminary and a vice president of the AHMS, wrote the editor of the *Boston Recorder* that it was a serious question among those who were called to direct ministerial education whether they could consistently take an active part in any organization formed with reference to slavery. Woods's refusal to cooperate in the work of organizing the American Union was primarily dictated by the fear that active participation by seminarians would lead to a distraction from the scholarly pursuits of the students and professors. Professor Ralph Emerson of Andover, also a vice president of the AHMS, shared Woods's distrust of any organized efforts on behalf of the slave. Emerson declined to join the American Union even though he recognized it as a mild and conservative benevolent society.[68]

The cooling of the ardor of the northern advocates of cooperation with the South in a benevolent program for the blacks was a significant factor in the failure of the society. In the autumn of 1835, the southern states moved to suppress the sending of abolitionist literature to the South through the mail. Early in 1836 a "gag rule" was adopted in the House of Representatives to prevent the reading of abolitionist petitions similar to petitions that had already been considered.[69] A meeting of clergymen of Richmond, Virginia, convened in August 1835 and unanimously resolved that they earnestly deprecated the unwarranted and highly improper interference of the people of the North with the domestic relations of master and slave.[70] In the wake of the aborted Mississippi slave revolt of 1835, a planter in Dallas County, Alabama, recorded in his diary that "the committee of Vigilance" in Benton, Alabama, had tried a minister for favoring abolition. While this minister was found innocent "beyond all doubt," others were summarily and ungraciously forced to leave the South because of their unsuitable attitudes toward slavery.[71] A grand jury in Cass County, Georgia, in 1835 warned all citizens to be watchful over the missionaries and the conduct of all missionary agents passing through the country.[72] The missionary agent of the American Sunday School Union reported that the prejudice against northern men along the southern Atlantic seaboard was so great that southern Christians had barred "the door of access by which spiritual blessings" were to reach them and had rejected all religious measures that were suspected of coming from the North. A wealthy cotton and sugar planter in the Florida parishes of East Louisiana verified the accuracy of the missionary agent when he emphatically warned other planters to "never allow" any missionary to talk to his servants. "Nothing is more injurious," he declared. Even a man as dedicated to missions for slaves as Charles C. Jones of Georgia insisted that "missionaries should be *Southern* men."[73]

The North reacted against these measures as an attempt to suppress the American freedom of the press and petition. The measures taken by the South to defend slavery caused many in the North associated with benevolence to reconsider plans to associate with the American Union, and the attitude of the members of the Union stiffened toward the South. When the Maine Union for the Relief and Improvement of the Colored Race was organized in September 1835, the convention deplored the interference with the United States mail and the denial of freedom of speech when the question of slavery was under discussion. In February 1836, when the American Union met for their annual meeting, the society resolved that it claimed the right of free discussion on the question of slavery. But other factors affected the destiny of the American Union. The Panic of 1837 was fatal for the Union. The panic came at a time when the society was making efforts to establish a financial basis for its work, and the American Union was never put on a sound economic foundation.[74]

The 1837 anniversary of the American Union was the last reported by the press. In May 1841, a group of conservative Christians closely identified with the AHMS issued a call for a meeting to reestablish the Colonization Society in New England.[75] As the abolitionists had predicted, the American Union's ship had run aground on the hazardous course it had undertaken. It was not created to put down Garrison, as he was inclined to think, but to work with the South as the AAS could not do. It was an attempt to combine the basic objectives of both emancipators and colonizers so as to replace both by putting emphasis on religious instruction in the South. The American Union had miscalculated the extent of dissension among the abolitionists. The conservative Congregational clergy had reservations about the movement. Many were in sympathy with sentiment of conservative Reverend Nehemiah Adams when he advised the founders at the annual meeting in May 1836, "Let us not throw ourselves upon the tempest from a mistaken bravery."[76] The advocates of the American Union were motivated by a drive to establish black missions because of an uneasy conscience that sprang from the Calvinist commitment to the Protestant work ethic rather than a desire to erect an anti-Garrison organization.[77] The American Union had fallen apart because it was composed of "incongruous materials, based upon the shifting sand of policy, and cemented with selfishness." With the demise of the American Union, the Massachusetts Anti-Slavery Society declared, "The mourners *do not* go about the streets; there is none so poor as to do it reverence."[78] The mourners, however, would fill the streets twenty-five years later.

The missionary movement to the slaves provided contacts with the South that revealed that much of the abolitionist criticism was uninformed and unfair. Many moderate antislavery men channeled energies into the movement that might otherwise have been directed into radical movements. Southerners were moved to take the initiative to make determined unilateral efforts to promote religion among the slaves.[79] Although it was not realistic to expect the idea of the American Union to succeed, a program of cooperation between the North and South offered the only solution short of war.

3

Antislavery Political Action

*T*he decade of the 1830s was a time of agitation and turbulence. In 1837 the Presbyterian church split into the Old School and New School Presbyterians. The controversy concerned church government, doctrine, and slavery. The New School advocated liberalization along the lines of Congregationalism, voluntary or nondenominational benevolent societies, and revivalism. The Old School retained its strict adherence to Calvinist tradition and established a conformity to Presbyterian particularism that resulted in complete separation from all voluntary societies. The AHMS and the ABCFM became the agents of the New School Presbyterians, Congregationalists, and the smaller evangelical Calvinists at a time when the antislavery movement was greatly agitated. When the AAS met in New York in May 1840, the convention, dominated by delegates from New England and under the influence of William Lloyd Garrison, passed resolutions condemning the creation of an abolitionist political party. These resolutions, and the controversy concerning the participation of women in the meetings of the AAS, split the organization into a New England wing dedicated to nonpolitical principles and the North Atlantic–Northwestern group that organized the American and Foreign Anti-Slavery Society.[1] The American and Foreign Anti-Slavery Society and its supporters remained closely identified with religious benevolence and in friendly relations with some of the religious organizations.[2] While continuing to seek the abolition of slavery by moral suasion, the American and Foreign Anti-Slavery Society became the effective gadfly of organized religion.

During the 1830s the North was swept by a series of acts of violence against antislavery advocates. Elijah P. Lovejoy was murdered in Alton, Illinois. A mob wrecked the press that James G. Birney used to print the *Philanthropist* in Cincinnati. In New York, the home of Lewis Tappan and the church of Reverend Samuel H. Cox were plundered. Pennsylvania Hall was burned because abolitionists dared to raise their voices against slavery in this Philadelphia monument to free speech. The African Hall and a Presbyterian church in Pittsburgh were burned in 1839, following a Negro celebration of the anniversary of emancipation in the West Indies. Mobs destroyed schools in Connecticut and New Hampshire because Negro students were admitted.[3] All of this caused abolitionists to consider political action to protect the rights of free speech, the press, and petition.

The antislavery advocates charged that the mob violence and the muzzling of freedom had been incited by the merchants and supporters of colonization. The New York riots were preceded by a public meeting of opponents of antislavery called by merchants in August 1835. Similar meetings were held in Albany, Boston, and Philadelphia. Garrison charged that many supporters of the meeting had close ties with the South through commerce and marriage. The leaders of business, finance, and government organized a protest meeting against the *Philanthropist* before its press was thrown into the Ohio River. When mobs rioted against the banks in Cincinnati in 1842, Weld observed, "They that sow the wind shall reap the whirlwind." It was charged that Reverend Joel Parker, a life member of the ACS and a vice president of the AHMS, had delivered a speech in Alton before Lovejoy was murdered by a mob. "His injurious remarks in public against the abolitionists were thought to have contributed to exciting the mob to the fatal issue which took place," charged Birney. In the North, colonization had the support mainly of the aristocratic and business community. The ACS became the rallying ground for all the reactionary elements in the slavery controversy.[4]

The violence against the antislavery advocates did not go unchallenged. "The contest is becoming — has become — one not alone of freedom for the *black*, but of freedom for the white. . . . There will be no cessation of the strife until slavery shall be exterminated or liberty destroyed," predicted Birney. Albert Barnes, a Presbyterian clergyman in Philadelphia, denounced the mob rule. "There must be heard but one voice . . . from the pulpit, the press, and from every place of influence" for liberty, urged Barnes. Many Americans who, like Barnes, were not active in the antislavery movement but were sensitive to the threat to American liberties, denounced the violence against the abolitionists. The controversy was seen by Weld as settling down to a clear-cut political issue. "*Events*, the master of men, have for years been silently but without a moment's pause, settling the basis of two great parties, the nucleus of one slavery, of the other freedom," explained Weld.[5]

In the name of freedom of speech and press, and because the arm of the law was on the side of the opponents of abolitionism, the supporters of the American and Foreign Anti-Slavery Society and the friends of the slave were pushed into independent political action. Having found moral suasion ineffective, antislavery Christians were ready to turn to politics.

Beriah Green, an early supporter of the AHMS, was convinced that God was calling the antislavery Christians "into the field of Politics." The abolitionists first tried pressure group techniques, asking opposing candidates questions concerning their position on slavery issues. The politicians soon began to excuse themselves from answering on the grounds that "the abolitionists will generally vote for the candidate of their respective parties regardless of the answer." It was the 1838 gubernatorial election in New York that finally convinced the abolitionists that the pressure strategy was useless. Although in the eyes of the abolitionist leaders William L. Marcy, the Democrat candidate, took a more favorable antislavery stand, the rank and file among the reformers, who had grown up as Federalists and Whigs, preferred William H. Seward. This led Gerrit Smith to suggest a new antislavery organization whose members would be bound to vote only for candidates who would definitely go on record as favoring immediate emancipation.[6]

A national convention called by New York abolitionists met in Albany on July 31, 1839, but the poorly attended affair proved to be a disappointment. A resolution was adopted to "neither vote for n[or] support the election of any man for President . . . who is not in favor of the immediate *abolition of Slavery."* The New York State Anti-Slavery Society called a political convention April 1, 1840, in Albany, as the "National Anti-Slavery Convention for Independent Nominations." Birney was nominated for president and Thomas Earle of Pennsylvania received the nomination for vice president. This movement had distinct religious overtones. Birney wrote to party leaders: "The security of life – of liberty – of civil and religious privileges – of the rights of conscience . . . constitute the highest concerns of government." The new antislavery political party was known as the Liberty Association. The leaders – Myron Holley, Alvan Stewart, Joshua Leavitt, William Goodell, and Elizur Wright, Jr. – were all Congregational and Presbyterian laymen and clergy who had turned to political action after losing faith in the efforts to secure a solution through the church. As Alvan Stewart had expressed it in 1841, "We have no choice . . . left, but by a vigorous use of political power, as a Christian duty, to storm the castle of slavery. The Church has refused the great and immortal honor of over-throwing this horrible power," he argued. The close relationship of the Liberty party to Calvinist religious groups can be seen by examining the Liberty press. To a considerable extent the Liberty party newspapers were in the hands of Presbyterian and Congregational clergymen and active laymen.[7]

The organization of the Liberty party, however, tended to drive a wedge between the cordial relations of the antislavery men and the western church. The Wednesday night monthly concert or prayer meeting for the slave, which had become an institution, now took on the aspect of a political caucus. When the Southern and Western Liberty Convention met in Cincinnati in June 1845, it was resolved that the party was founded "upon the great cardinal principle of true democracy and of true Christianity, the brotherhood of the human family." It thus established itself as a political party while throwing out the challenge that it represented "true Christianity." But the most persistent foe of the political abolitionists was not the rank and file, the pew and pulpit. It was the colonizers in the ranks of the Democrat and Whig parties. "The class of men who now oppose Anti-slavery political action as a great general thing opposed us stoutly at first. . . . They now, very *gravely* and benevolently, tell us that to vote for men who imbibe the great principles for which we plead and pray, will certainly 'wreck our hopes and aims,'" explained an astute observer of the events.[8]

In the presidential campaign of 1844, the Liberty party occupied the position of a balance of power, particularly in New York. Theodore Frelinghuysen was nominated by Whigs for vice president and Benjamin F. Butler was active in the Democratic convention. Both Frelinghuysen and Butler would soon be promoted from directors to vice presidents in the AHMS. In the early 1830s Butler had urged the secretary of the AHMS to use his influence to prevent missionaries from mixing in politics. "May they [the missionaries] be kept from all . . . improper interference with political or other extraneous concerns," advised Butler.[9] Most of the antislavery advocates tended to support the Whig party and Butler desired to keep down the controversy over slavery and to keep the clergy, with their benevolent inclinations, from expressing opinions on politics. Since the friends of domestic missions were deeply involved in both political parties, the secretaries of the AHMS were very interested in keeping the question of slavery as a moral issue from being discussed in relation to politics. But with the rise of the Liberty party this was impossible.

The Liberty party received strong support from black Calvinists in states where they could vote. A National Convention of Colored Citizens met August 15, 1843, at Buffalo, New York. The most sensational part of the convention was the speech delivered as an address to the slaves by Henry Highland Garnet. Garnet urged the slaves to rise up and destroy slavery. "Brethren, arise, arise! Strike for your lives and liberties — Rather die free men than live to be slaves," he thundered. "Resistance to tyrants is obedience to God." A correspondent to the *Buffalo Commercial Advertiser* wrote of the speech: "Here, Mr. Editor, was true eloquence — the ridiculous, the pathetic, the indignant, all called into irresistible action;

and I cannot but think that, had it been one of our white orators instead of Garnet, he would have been lauded to the skies." The convention refused to endorse Garnet's address, but pledged support to the Liberty party as the previous convention had done in 1842.[10]

Samuel R. Ward, a black minister, campaigned widely for the Liberty party, speaking in almost every state of the North. Ward was the pastor of a white Presbyterian church at South Butler, New York, that received aid from the AHMS. When his commission ran out in October 1843, he did not ask for renewal "due to a chronic ailment of his throat" that speaking agitated. But the Society was immediately petitioned by a Free Congregational Church at Geneva, New York, for aid in his support. When the auxiliary agency of western New York was petitioned for a commission, objections were raised because of a charge that he preached political sermons on the Sabbath. Ward defended himself by denying that he pleaded for any party or candidate on the Sabbath. "I call upon the people to do all in their power at the ballot box and elsewhere for the removal of this sin [slavery] or to expect the severe judgement of God," he admitted. In December, the AHMS commissioned Ward to serve the Geneva church.[11]

Garnet did not fare so well with the AHMS. Garnet's address to the slaves had focused attention on him. After the Liberty party convention, Garnet canvassed the state, speaking to groups and urging their support for the party's program. Garnet had been commissioned to serve the Liberty Street Presbyterian Church of Troy, New York, in May 1843. When he applied for a renewal in May 1844, the secretary asked the advice of the mission committee of the Troy presbytery concerning the political activities of Garnet. Hall, the secretary, stated that "ninety-nine in a hundred of the members and patrons of the AHMS judge it inexpedient for ministers to be prominent actors in political matters," and that they would be "unwilling to appropriate the charity . . . to assist in supporting those . . . who thus violate the proprieties of their office." After the matter was presented to the Presbytery of Troy, Garnet withdrew his request for renewal of the commission. He insisted that his only crime was that he had lifted up his feeble voice for his oppressed brethren, and he offered to return the fifty dollars granted to him the previous year. Hall now added the charge that the Society had been recently advised that he was "neglecting" his people "to engage in political action." Since the report had not been received from the presbytery, Garnet was asked not to withdraw his renewal. Garnet's name disappeared from the roll of the missionaries of the AHMS, but he continued as a pastor of the Liberty Street Presbyterian Church until 1857.[12]

The Presbyterian church at Arcade, New York, under the influence of Liberty party politics, voted not to support the AHMS because it sanctioned "that giant sin, and so far winked at it" as to render the Society obnoxious as a channel for the religious contributions of Christians. Other churches that were affected by antislavery politics were considering similar action. John A. Murray, secretary of the agency of western New York, asked Milton Badger to advise him on answering a letter from C. O. Shepard who was the Liberty party candidate for lieutenant governor of New York during the previous election. Shepard had asked for a statement on "the position of the AHMS in regard to Slavery." He informed Murray that several churches were hesitating in their support to home missions because of doubts on this question. Badger advised him to respond to the question by denying that they could take any position whatever on slavery.[13]

While some churches and clergymen were agitated because the missionary societies did not respond to the changing political issues, others were aggrieved by the distracting effects of politics. A missionary at Westfield, New York, complained to the Society of the "injuries" the church had suffered because of "Third Party-isms, etc."[14] A worker in the Michigan field believed "it required the wisdom which cometh from above . . . to steer safely among the whirlpools and eddies and quick-sands" of politics.[15]

Lewis Tappan had refrained from taking part in political abolitionism in 1840, but by the time the Liberty party held its convention in 1843 he felt it his duty to give "all the help" he could. In July 1844, Tappan asked the AHMS a series of questions concerning its relations to slavery. Did the Society accept money from slaveholders without rebuke, did missionaries preach against the sin of slavery, had the executive committee ever refused assistance to a church because it had a slaveholding minister or member? In reply Badger stated that the organization had no soliciting agents in the South and only a small part of its funds came from that section; no special instructions were given to missionaries living in slave states, and the Society had never denied assistance to a church on the ground that its members held slaves, nor because its members opposed servitude. Although Badger did not commit himself to win the favor of Tappan, partially as a result of the impact of politics the Society took a position in advance of that taken by any other benevolent society. In the May 1833 annual report, the Society had reported "an obstacle . . . of increasing magnitude . . . enthralling more than two and a half million souls . . . prevents the most direct and effectual efforts for their salvation."[16]

One of the most important reasons for the strong statement against slavery in the annual report of the AHMS was the influence and effects of an address delivered by Reverend Thomas Lafon in Brooklyn, New York, on September 28, 1843. Lafon had recently returned from the Sandwich Islands where he had served as a physician and missionary under the ABCFM. He became an outspoken opponent of slavery while serving as a missionary. "There is no cause that can have my sympathy more than that of the slave. I do regard it, next to carrying Gospel to every creature, as the most important subject that interests and agitates the world," he wrote Lewis Tappan from his missionary field. Back in the United States, he toured New England delivering lectures and making speeches urging the churches to support antislavery missions. In the Brooklyn address Lafton pointed out that one of the fruits of oppression was its tendency to paralyze conscience. The address was published before the end of the year under the title "The Great Obstruction of the Conversion of Souls at Home and Abroad." It was extremely potent in arousing inquiries concerning the relation of missionary boards to the southern institution.[17]

The statement of the AHMS in May 1844 had the effect of staving off a microscopic examination of the Society's relation to slavery. Gerrit Smith found that the report spoke "honestly and fearlessly of Slavery" and sent the secretary of the central New York agency twenty dollars.[18] Lewis Tappan confided to an English friend that the AHMS had in their annual report spoken "in decided terms against the cruel system." It was the first time any of the benevolent societies had "ever uttered condemnatory language" against slavery, coming as it did before the campaign of 1844. The article, appearing in the annual report of the Society, took considerable pressure off the executive committee during the critical days. The AHMS was obviously moving closer to the position of the political abolitionists.[19]

The Northwest was especially disturbed by the political events of the time. Before the rise of the Liberty party relations between the evangelistic Calvinist churches and the antislavery society in the West were exceedingly cordial and close. The antislavery societies would often hold their convention just before or after the meetings of the Presbyterian and Congregational assemblies. As early as 1838, the Illinois Association of Congregational Ministers resolved that they were obliged to vote according to religious convictions on the slavery question. "We will ever maintain the right of free discussion and petition. . . . We recommend to the community to withhold their support from all candidates for office who deny these rights," the association avowed. The first political convention to nominate an antislavery political ticket was held in Princeton, Illinois, a settlement of Congregational and Presbyterian influence.[20] In May 1842 the Illinois Anti-Slavery Society held its convention in the First Presbyterian Church of Chicago. At least fourteen Presbyterians from Illinois attended and four of their co-workers from Wisconsin sat as corresponding delegates. The next day the Illinois Liberty party was organized in the same church. The Address to the People stated, "First of all we wish distinctly . . . to acknowledge our dependence on God and our amenability to Him." The organizational meeting contained at least seven evangelical Presbyterian and Congregational clergymen and two well-known Calvinist laymen — Philo Carpenter and Zebina Eastmen.[21]

One of the Wisconsin delegates who attended the Illinois antislavery convention was Dexter Clary, pastor of the Congregational Church of Beloit, Wisconsin. On the fourth of July, 1843, he delivered an address at Rockford, Illinois, on "Religion and Politics." While Clary expressed regret that the abolitionists found it necessary to organize a distinct political party, he rejoiced that a party had been created through which Christians could "exert their political influence conscientiously."[22] Several others connected with the AHMS concurred with Clary's opinion. After arriving in Tazewell County, Illinois, one of the missionaries of the AHMS found that the image of the Presbyterians related to the subject of slavery rather than doctrine. "In the public mind," he wrote, "Presbyterians are abolitionists — political abolitionists." M. N. Miles, a missionary in central Illinois, could not secure the full cooperation of the Congregational portion of his church because of their abolitionist feelings even though he had been an abolitionist himself for the past ten years.[23]

A Congregational clergyman, Ichabod Codding, took the message of political abolitionism to the churches. He made a tour of the northern counties of Illinois in 1843 and continued his lectures on slavery and political action for several years. On July 20, 1843, he reported: "The arguments in favor of organized political action are coming to be better understood, and to a good extent appreciated."[24] In June 1844, as the election of that year drew near, the weekly *Herald and Philanthropist*, organ of the Liberty party in Ohio, pointed to the moral purpose of the antislavery party. The editor called on Christians to do battle against all parties who "trample upon morality, religion and virtue. . . . With what consistency can Christians pray to the God of nations to send us righteous rulers, and then go and vote . . . for abject bondage?" queried the editor.[25]

Although most of the churches in the West viewed slavery as a moral issue and had opened the doors of their buildings for antislavery meetings, many religious associations had reservations about cooperating with the antislavery advocates when they organized themselves into a political party. Some churches were even reluctant to continue the regular prayer meeting for the slave. In the territory of Wisconsin, the controversy about political abolitionism became very bitter. A correspondent writing to Stephen Peet, AHMS agent for the territory, charged that the Presbyterian and Congregational convention was the "organ of abolitionists." Peet admitted to the secretary of the AHMS that all the members of the convention were abolitionists, but he denied that any were of the "Garrisonian, no-government" variety. On February 7, 1843, the first anniversary of the Wisconsin Territorial Anti-Slavery Society was held in the Congregational Church at Prairieville (Waukesha), Wisconsin. The roster of the members of the meeting looked like a roll of the Presbyterian and Congregational convention of Wisconsin. Lewis Bridgman, J. J. Miter, Dexter Clary, and Stephen Peet all took an active and leading part.[26] In 1843 the Calvinist churches and the antislavery society in the territory worked together in harmony.

During the heat of the campaign of 1844, an antislavery convention was arranged in Milwaukee for the winter season. Some of the foremost men of the territory met with this convention in "Roger's Hall." Up from Illinois came Ichabod Codding, "one of the most eloquent who had . . . ever spoken" in the region. Many of the clergy participated and John Miter, pastor of the Plymouth Congregational Church, Milwaukee, and Aaron L. Chapin, pastor of the Presbyterian Church in Milwaukee, were leading delegates. After the convention, Codding remained to give six public lectures. The sessions were held alternately in the Plymouth church and the Presbyterian church. Before the snows of winter began to thaw, division began to show itself in the churches of the Wisconsin convention. In February 1845, the Congregational Church of Beloit, Wisconsin, refused to close its doors to lectures on slavery even though some urged this course, but by June of the same year attempts to accomplish this were so persistent that the pastor, Dexter Clary, threatened to resign. For the time the church remained open to Liberty party lecturers. In February 1846, however, the Presbyterian and Congregational district convention of Beloit adopted resolutions of nonfellowship with slavery and the exclusion of its advocates from the pulpits of its churches. Although this was a strong position, it gave no support to the advocates of a commitment to support Liberty party politics. The leaders of the Presbyterian and Congregational convention were determined to prevent the association from being controlled by the Liberty party. Stephen Peet became aware that a plan was afoot to secure the adoption of measures in the Wisconsin convention to pledge the Presbyterians and Congregationalists "to vote for no man for any political office" unless he was "identified with the Liberty party." Peet solicited the aid of Chapin, Miter, and others to take a strong abolitionist stand as the Beloit convention had taken but to beat back the "ultraists" who would commit the convention politically and condemn the benevolent societies.[27]

In August 1846, Codding informed a member of the Presbyterian Church of Milwaukee that he would deliver a series of lectures on slavery in that city. Codding requested that a hall be secured for the lectures. The trustees of the Presbyterian church, in accord with Chapin, the pastor, unanimously rejected the request on the ground that it was "inexpedient to allow . . . any meeting whose action is political." Chapin informed Peet that the facilities were denied to Codding because "his relations and course for the last two years, and his ranging through the territory at this particular juncture were regarded as identifying him and what he does with a peculiarly political movement." The Plymouth Congregational Church took the same stand, and in February 1847 a group withdrew from both churches and organized the Free Congregational Church of Milwaukee.[28]

The Liberty Association of Wisconsin met in January 1847, at Southport, Wisconsin. A committee report was presented to the meeting asking them to censure the AHMS and other benevolent organizations for their position on slavery. Since there were members of the convention who were aided by the AHMS and because of its outspoken statements in the Society's annual report on 1844, a heated debate raged for days in the convention on the question of including the Home Missionary Society in the censure of the benevolent organizations. Codding denounced the AHMS as a proslavery body that should not be fellowshipped by antislavery men, and the measures were adopted.[29]

In February 1847 at a Liberty meeting in Milwaukee, resolutions were adopted informing the faithful that "the first and foremost in the effort for its [slavery] overthrow should be the church, the great instrumentality ordained by God for the destruction of the powers of darkness." The next year the district convention of Beloit resolved that "the position assumed by the Wis[consin] Liberty Association that — 'it is the mission of the association to reform the world and the church' — is unscriptural and unfounded, that Jesus Christ is the chief reformer, and His spirit is the true spirit of reform." The Beloit convention had stated that the church "should exert a leading and controlling influence over the various associations." This was the key to the whole controversy. The Liberty party had set out to reform the church and establish itself as a superchurch. In 1845, the Liberty party of Indiana nominated Stephen C. Stevens, a Presbyterian layman, for governor of the state. During the campaign, Stevens delivered a speech in which he declared: "We must reach the abolition of slavery through the doors of twenty thousand churches. . . . We must bring them on the side of Jesus Christ instead . . . of slavery. But we shall divide the

Church! Sir, division implies separation; and what shall we separate? Why, the sin of slaveholding from Christianity."[30]

The Liberty party had been organized because many antislavery men were convinced that American society could not free itself from slavery through moral suasion alone. They turned to political action or attempted to put morals into politics, but the Liberty party continued to attempt to use the church as an instrument of moral suasion. Thus, during the 1840s, the breach between the church and the advocates of antislavery political action grew progressively wider. The abolitionists failed to convert the church to an antislavery stance because of their individualistic view of social evils. They believed slavery would come to an end when they had converted a sufficient number of individuals and churches to abolitionism. They were naive about the social realities and organic nature of institutional life of which Americans would become aware after the experience of the Civil War and with the later understanding of sociology. Although the abolitionists were unsuccessful in converting the northern church to their view of slavery, their crusade led to a hardening of proslavery sentiment in the South. By 1849 many clergy in the North no longer stressed the connection between a Christian's personal relationship to God and the duties as a citizen. The split between political abolitionism and the church appeared to be settling into a permanent rupture, but political events followed that brought them into complete accord again. This was true because the antislavery fervor was primarily a religious sentiment.[31]

Antislavery Advocates
Besiege the American Home
Missionary Society

*B*y 1842 the antislavery societies and liberty associations had launched a full-scale attack against the benevolent societies to force them to end all ties with slaveholders. While the brunt of the attack was made against the ABCFM, the AHMS cautiously and quietly moved to free the Society of slaveholding officers, agents, and missionaries.

The first test of the new policy came in Kentucky. Although the separation of the New School and Old School Presbyterians took place in 1837, it was not until 1843 that New School sympathizers in Kentucky united with the New School General Assembly.[1] As soon as the Synod of Kentucky was accepted in the assembly, the Kentucky judicatory set up a synodical missions committee and appointed an agent. The committee chairman, Arches Charles Dickerson, asked the AHMS to furnish one-third of the support for the new agent, Jonathan Black.[2] The previous year Black had walked out of a convention of western presbyteries when resolutions were adopted declaring it an "illusion" to "hope that the Gospel" would "remove slavery while the Church sanctions it." Black had cast the only vote against the resolutions on slavery.[3] Milton Badger, the new secretary of the AHMS, had attended the convention at the invitation of the Synod of Cincinnati, and after receiving the request for support of Black, he asked Henry Little, agent at Cincinnati, whether there would be any objections to the appointment "on the other side of the river." Specifically, Badger wanted to know if Black was a slaveholder.[4] Little described the new Kentucky agent as a "northern man with southern principles." Though not a slave owner, Black believed that order would be achieved with Christianized masters in "a slaveholding community." Little felt the abolitionists on the north bank of the Ohio would not object any more to an agent in Kentucky than they would if the Cincinnati agent went into Kentucky for a few weeks each year as had been the procedure.

It should, however, be tried reluctantly for a year only, until the results could be determined, he advised.[5]

In 1844, shortly after Black was approved as an agent, Reverend Issac W. R. Handy, of Berlin, Maryland, asked the AHMS for aid in his own support as a missionary in Indiana, Kentucky, or Missouri. Badger inquired of the secretary of the Philadelphia Home Missionary Society, E. R. Fairchild, about the character of Handy. When he learned that Handy was a slave owner, he turned down the request for aid and suggested that Handy stay in Maryland and follow the maxim that was applicable to missionary arrangements, "let pretty well alone." A month had hardly passed when A. W. Campbell of Paducah, Kentucky, communicated with the AHMS, informing the secretaries that Handy had arrived in Kentucky and asking for four hundred dollars to support Handy as a missionary. In 1843 Campbell had asked the Home Missionary Society to send missionaries into his area. "Send us a devoted, . . . active . . . prudent, and acceptable missionary, who will not, whatever may be his feelings, touch the vexed subject of slavery." Campbell informed the AHMS that he had written to the synod missions board for a commission for Handy who would "be both useful and popular" in his new field.[6]

Badger again inquired about Handy's status as a slaveholder. This the Society must know. Since many were ready to take exception, it was necessary that the Society have all the facts in the case. No reply was received by Badger on the status of Handy in relation to slavery, but in November 1844 the secretary of the missionary committee of the Synod of Kentucky requested that the AHMS supply a missionary for a field in the western part of the state. The parish was the same as that which had earlier been described as the one Handy would occupy. After almost five months had passed with no word from Kentucky on the status of Handy in the Synod of Kentucky, Badger communicated with the secretary of the synodical committee. Speaking as a friend and not as the secretary of the Society, Badger denied that his earlier letter concerning Handy had been intended "to intimate that if he were a slaveholder," a commission would be denied. If Handy were involved with the vexed institution, it would require more correspondence to determine the circumstances of the case. "Our committee has not declined the case, nor was it so stated," but the Society would be placed in a difficult position that might prevent the synod from being properly aided "if you should insist upon our giving a commission to a slaveholder, whose case differed not especially from others," Badger elaborated. Since funds came primarily from the North, it was best that the slaveholding states avoid offense. "Our committee would, I think, desire to be relieved, if practicable, from making a decision," he concluded.[7]

During the next meeting of the General Assembly, Handy made his position clear to the whole church. He defied anyone to point to the scripture in which it was positively taught that slavery was *malum in se.*[8] Handy remained in the church, but did not serve as a missionary in the service of the AHMS.

The course taken by the AHMS was influenced by developments in other benevolent societies and ecclesiastic bodies. In 1844 the Methodist Church had divided after Bishop James O. Andrew of Georgia had been asked by the General Conference to desist from his episcopal labors until he should dispose of the slaves he had acquired by a second marriage. Other religious bodies were suffering from similar disputes concerning slavery. On February 17, 1842, the *Emancipator* carried an article stating that some of the missionaries from the South in the service of the ABCFM were known to be slaveholders.[9] A letter appeared in the *New York Observer* identifying John Leighton Wilson, a Presbyterian missionary in West Africa, as belonging to this class.[10] Wilson, a native of South Carolina, had inherited the servants before he was born and had tried to emancipate them. He had refused to force them to accept their freedom even though the relationship was an economic burden. One servant had refused to depart willingly from him. The ABCFM had informed Wilson that it was desirable that the relation of servant and master be terminated "with as little delay" as circumstance would permit.[11] The ABCFM had later ruled in 1843 that Wilson was justified only if he withheld his sanctions to the system.[12] It was known in religious circles that the ABCFM had lost contributions because of the case. By 1846, Rufus Anderson, one of the secretaries of the ABCFM, reported that this case had cost the society half of its annual contributions.[13] The Baptist Church was suffering from a similar agonizing dispute. Before the end of 1845 the Baptist Church had divided because the Southern Baptists resented the refusal of the national mission board of their church to take slaveholders into their service.[14]

The experience of other religious bodies caused the AHMS to work to avoid the pitfalls of slavery that had split other groups. In February 1845, the agent of the missions committee of the Synod of Kentucky had confessed to Badger that slavery existed throughout the whole state of Kentucky, though in a very limited degree, "which may have an important bearing upon the future . . . of the church."[15] The Calvinist churches and their missionary boards appeared to be rapidly following the course of the Baptist and Methodist churches. But quiet consultations were taking place between the officers of the AHMS and the officials of the agencies and auxiliaries. In November 1845, Dickerson, the secretary of the Kentucky missions committee, informed Badger that the committee would "endeavor to keep clear of any warping influence emanating from selfish considerations. We will recommend, knowingly, no appropriation, not to our judgments justified by the principles and objects of your Society."[16]

Before the Handy case was disposed of, the New York missions office received an application from the Domestic Missionary Society of Richmond, Virginia, for a commission for a missionary understood to be a slaveholder. Badger had previously contacted a representative of the Domestic Missionary Society of Richmond and worked out an agreement that no applications from slaveholders would be submitted to the executive committee for approval. The slaveholders were to be taken care of locally so that the AHMS would be saved from the embarrassment of either approving or rejecting such cases. Badger wrote to the emissary to find out why the plan had gone astray, and in the meantime the appointments for Virginia were delayed. Badger was informed that the plan had not been communicated to the Richmond secretary, and the questionable application was withdrawn. "We duly appreciate the delicacy of your situation," Badger was informed.[17]

Thus the AHMS had avoided the horns of the dilemma that had confronted several religious institutions in 1844 and 1845. The secretaries and the executive committee were influenced in the adoption of their cautious policy by the division taking place in other religious bodies resulting from the slavery controversy. But the Society was also hounded on its course by the zeal and fervor of individual abolitionist Christians and by the action of the Congregational and Presbyterian missionary conventions that were held by enthusiastic antislavery Christians in the West.

In March 1844, Oliver Emerson, an abolitionist missionary in Iowa, asked the secretaries of the AHMS for information on the Society's relations to slavery. Since the organization was forming the future destinies of the country, he wanted to know if any of its officers or missionaries "held or trafficked in slaves," if funds were collected in the South, and if missionaries in the South were required to bear testimony against the sin. Emerson informed the Iowa agent, J. A. Reed, that he was thinking about withdrawing from the AHMS because of slavery. "I have not yet made up my mind that it is wrong to continue my connexion with it," he wrote. When the information was not forthcoming he renewed his request in June.[18]

In July, Badger sent Emerson a copy of the annual report for 1844, with its statement recognizing slavery as a hindrance to the gospel. None of the directors, vice presidents, missionaries, or agents, to Badger's knowledge, were slaveholders. The Society had no soliciting agents in the South, and received no contributions from slaveholders, known to be such, but no inquiry into the sources of funds were instituted. The AHMS could not become an antislavery organization without departing from the cause marked out by its constitution, Badger explained, but "the missionaries have been allowed the greatest freedom of opinion and action in relation to this . . . subject."[19] Emerson rejoiced that the AHMS had been the first to speak up on the southern institution in its annual report. But the Society was giving a "powerful" support to the sinful system by receiving funds from the South in such a way as to recognize the Christian character and standing of the churches, and sending funds to the region to build up slaveholding churches while nothing was done for the slave. Since the AHMS was "conniving with slavery," Emerson withdrew from the Society as a missionary because he could not "eat its bread" under such circumstances. Thus Emerson became the first of a long procession of missionaries to withdraw because of slavery.[20]

While Emerson represented the missionaries' opposition to slavery in relation to the AHMS, George W. Perkins was an example of opposition from the patrons of the Society. Perkins was probably the most tenacious critic of the AHMS. He was born in Hartford, and educated at Yale University and Andover Theological Seminary. He became the pastor of the Congregational Church in Meriden, Connecticut, in 1841.[21] During July 1843, Perkins opened a one-man offense against the AHMS that was to continue for two years. "How happen it that when you are speaking of the causes which threaten the religious interests of the country, and which hinder the usefulness of your missionaries, that you should never happen to mention or allude to slavery, which is the most dangerous and deadly of those causes?" he queried.[22]

After waiting almost three months for a reply, Perkins renewed his request, and in order to strengthen his case before the Society, he took out a life membership.[23] In reply, Badger pointed out that slavery was less in the vision of the missionary association because the AHMS was "almost exclusively" an organization operating in the northern states. The executive committee of the missionary body would review the situation and do what could be done "to remove from the land so dark an evil," but the officers must act consistently with the objective of an institution formed simply to do missionary work. Yet Perkins thought it strange that the missionary organization remained "so silent — profoundly silent — and so far as silence proves it — so unfeeling — in relation to the severe spiritual privations of *three millions* at the South."[24] When satisfaction was not immediately given, Perkins joined with Josiah Brewer, who had spent eleven years in the service of foreign missions, Sherman M. Booth, who later would gain fame in the Glover fugitive slave case, and others, in organizing a convention of clergymen at Middletown, Connecticut, in November 1843 to deal with the problems of slavery and church. A resolution introduced by Perkins was adopted committing the members of the convention to refuse communion or fellowship to such persons "as voluntarily hold slaves, or . . . defend the system."[25]

When the AHMS annual report of 1844 was circulated, Perkins suggested that the references to obstructions to the gospel presented by slavery ought to be given prominence in the anniversary address of 1845. "If no one else will do it, will you allow me to do it?" he added. Before the month was over this persistent clergyman was bombarding the Society with questions about the status of the southern directors, vice presidents, agents, and missionaries in relation to slavery. Did the missionaries admit slaveholders to their churches? Perkins inquired. To the best of Badger's knowledge no slaveholders were officers or missionaries in the service of the missionary organization, and the executive committee made whatever investigations they deemed necessary before commissioning ministers. Badger did not know if slaveholders were admitted to churches supported by the Society.[26] After Badger failed to accept Perkins's offer to speak on slavery before the anniversary meeting, Perkins returned to a discussion of the strong statements concerning the southern institution that were contained in the annual report for 1844. He paid the Society the first and only compliment he would give it. Perkins informed the Society that its remarks were "manly, earnest and direct: neither speaking as if you were afraid, nor turning aside from your object to say it. The only wonder is that you have not said so years ago, and often."[27]

Perkins was not satisfied with the position of the Society and he speedily returned to the offensive against the AHMS. Badger, who obviously wanted to bring the discussion to a close, suggested that the Society would have "to be judged by its deeds" and referred his tenacious critic to the published records and transactions. But the next day the determined reformer wanted to know if any checks were made of possible ties with slavery before missionaries were appointed, and added that the publications were silent on this. "Surely a member and hearty friend . . . has a right to make inquiries . . . and to know on what principles appropriations are made," he persisted. After a second request for an answer, Perkins was told that he certainly had a right to ask, and "we as certainly the right *not to answer.*" As the controversy reached a stalemate, Perkins reminded the officers of the AHMS that he had increased the contributions of his church 200 percent, and he asked if the Society would in any case appoint a slaveholder. Badger would only refer his correspondent to what the AHMS had done in the past.[28] George Perkins finally broke off his efforts to reform the Society from within and shifted his attack to a proposal to create, with others, an organization to compete with the AHMS. But before the new organization had come into existence the AHMS had silently undergone a change of policy without publicizing the change.

The AHMS was confronted with complaints from antislavery patrons in the East as well as antislavery missionaries in the West. It was from out of the West that the greatest threat to the status quo on slavery in the religious organizations came. The challenge was directed mainly at the New School Presbyterian General Assembly, but the American Home Missionary Society also became uneasy about the rumbles of discontent coming from the West. The General Assembly of 1839 asked the presbyteries to take the order best calculated to remove servitude. The presbyteries of the Northwest responded in large numbers by adopting resolutions to deny fellowship to slaveholders and those who defended the institution. In the General Assembly of 1840 the presbyteries were ordered "to rescind such resolutions" that excluded "slaveholders from their pulpits and from their communion."[29] The response of the western presbyteries was to reaffirm their previous testimony, and many additional judicatories in the West joined the ranks of those denying fellowship. The Presbytery of Ripley, Ohio, sent a letter to the other presbyteries asking, among other things, that they join together in denying communion to slaveholders. By 1842, almost all of the judicatories in the Presbyterian Church in the West had committed themselves to this stand.[30]

In 1841 antislavery Christians held the first of a series of conventions concerning benevolent societies. A call was made inviting the friends of the oppressed to attend a Christian Anti-Slavery Convention that would convene in Auburn, New York, in July 1841. Almost half of the 203 who attended the sessions were Presbyterians or Congregationalists. The convention resolved that benevolent societies were "under imperative obligations" to conduct their enterprises in such a manner as not to give "sanction to any iniquitous practice." Benevolent institutions that were strictly voluntary and not interwoven with ecclesiastical policy were "even more without excuse for conniving at slaveholding." The societies were warned that if the remonstrances of Christian abolitionists were not heeded, and the connivance with the sin of servitude continued, it would be the duty of the friends of the oppressed "to open pure channels" for the propagation of the gospel. The convention recommended "a serious inquiry" to determine if missionary societies that elected slaveholders as managers, agents, or missionaries, and solicited funds from those involved in servitude, were not thereby participating "in the sins of oppression and robbery."[31]

In March 1842 the Synod of Cincinnati sent out a call for a convention of the Presbyterian Church in the West to convene at Cincinnati in June.

Since home missions would occupy the attention of the convention, an invitation was sent to the secretaries of the AHMS. When the convention assembled, a committee on slavery was selected under the chairmanship of Calvin Stowe. After the report was made to the full convention, John Rankin and Jonathan Blanchard spoke against servitude. James B. Walker, editor of the *Watchman of the Valley*, in speaking of the cordiality of the meeting, found the unanimity most delightful and encouraging where it was least expected — on slavery. There was only one vote against the resolutions. The measures adopted by the convention "viewed slavery as opposed to the benevolent spirit and designs of Christianity," and regarded those in the church who justified or apologized for it "as in a fearful degree responsible for its continuance." "From all accounts," judged the *Philanthropist*, "they were just such as all abolitionists will approve." Badger, who was there representing the home missionary organization, considered the measures on servitude to be "pretty strong resolutions." The judicatories of the New School Presbyterian Church in the West had responded to church suggestions in the region to discuss the question of missions and the church. But Milton Badger, with the aid of Dr. Samuel Cox, who supported the slavery resolutions, effectively steered the home missions discussion into safe channels.[32]

However, there was resentment in the West against the failure to make a direct connection between the problems of home missions and slavery. Jonathan Blanchard addressed the Literary and Moral Society of Ripley College in September 1842 with words of condemnation for this failure. "One of the secretaries [of a benevolent society] from New York at the ecclesiastical convention in Cincinnati spoke at length . . . on the obstacles to the gospel in the West, and the dangers to our country arising from them, . . . but though he stood on the very confines of slavery, he never once alluded to slaveholding, which every well informed man considered, in point of endangering our country, scarcely inferior to the worst evil which he names." The benevolent societies must have secretaries and agents "who will not, in any place, 'Shun to declare the whole counsel of God,'" warned Blanchard.[33]

The Cincinnati convention initiated a discussion that went beyond a local interest. A letter from "an Eastern Man" was addressed to Lyman Beecher concerning the "Union of the East and West." It implied that missionary aid for the West from the East was conditioned on the willingness of the West to keep quiet on slavery. The writer warned: "The position taken by some of your presbyteries and by the Cincinnati convention is a serious bar to the union of efforts which you invoke for the West. The movement of some of our western brethren to enlist the church in a crusade without and beyond her legitimate province of action . . . impairs confidence at the East." James B. Walker, editor of the *Watchman of the Valley*, pointedly answered, "The desired union is utterly unattainable until this fundamental principle of union is settled, and . . . the only possible way of settling it is to meet the subject openly, freely and candidly."[34]

The Cincinnati convention selected a committee to convene a Presbyterian and Congregational convention in Cleveland in June 1844, restricting delegates to those connected with the General Assembly and associations or consociations of Orthodox Congregationalists who sympathized with the operations of the AHMS and the ABCFM. This action eliminated independent Congregational churches, those who were tinged with Oberlin perfectionism, and those who did not cooperate with the Plan of Union. Individuals who fell in these categories were usually under strong antislavery influence. One of these barred clergymen wrote to the *Oberlin Evangelist* and indicated that those in his group "differed with the neutral policy pursued by the [Home Missionary] Society on the slavery question." He thought the AHMS should have administered reproof to those churches with slaveholding members that were under its jurisdiction. The convention, however, did not avoid the question of servitude. The assembly declared, "It is . . . the imperious duty of all men, in all suitable ways, to make known their hearty disapprobation of American Slavery; specially by avoiding all such fellowship with those who uphold it, as might imply, directly or indirectly, any connivance at its perpetuity or extension." Blanchard was on hand in Cleveland and spoke against slavery in home missions. He charged Badger with skillfully avoiding the slavery problem when he spoke of the obstacles to the gospel at the Cincinnati convention in 1842.[35]

On March 3, 1845, Florida came into the Union as a slave state. Two days before this, President John Tyler had signed the resolution to admit Texas to the Union. Antislavery advocates under the philosophical influence of the Natural Rights philosophy, a doctrine that maintained progress would come in a gradual, unbroken course, viewed these developments with foreboding. Particularly among the Presbyterians in the West, the slow evolutionary extinction of slavery harmonized with their concept of the "Idea of Progress." They had hopes of seeing slavery gradually become extinct in the South as it had in New Jersey and Connecticut. Now, with the further expansion of slavery, their philosophical optimism began to falter; the passage of the Kansas-Nebraska Act in 1854 led to its complete collapse. The changing attitude in the Northwest was reflected in the new attitude that prevailed among those concerned with Christian benevolence. In June 1845, the Third Western Presbyterian and Congregational Convention was scheduled to meet in Detroit. In May, a delegate to the con-

vention served notice "that the time to fix finally our denominational relation to slavery is come. . . . I now contend, distinctly, that it is time our
ecclesiastical relations to slavery should all be reviewed; to wit: our relations to it through the Assembly, and our benevolent Societies; — that every
member of our churches may know precisely on what ground he stands
respecting this national evil."[36] During the same month, the Sand Creek
Presbyterian Church, Decatur County, Indiana, drew up a series of resolutions on the sectional problems. "We cannot cooperate with those Societies . . . [which send] agents into slaveholding churches to receive the
fruits of unrequited toil; who employ slaveholders as agents; or who cooperate with slaveholders in the disbursement of their funds; or who send
ministers to build up slave-holding churches while they continue in this
course. . . . We deem it the duty of all ministers of the gospel, to bear a
decided and unequivocal testimony against this sin." A copy was sent to
the Detroit convention, all benevolent organizations, and the moderator
of the General Assembly.[37]

Charles Hall, the junior secretary of the AHMS, was chosen to represent the Society at the Detroit convention. Stopping in Cincinnati en route
to Detroit, he met an Arkansas Presbyterian who had collected a full quota
of rumors that the abolitionists under the leadership of Blanchard intended to take over the Detroit convention. During the past January the
Arkansas clergyman had asked that a missionary be sent to Arkansas, but
underscored the necessity that *he must not be an abolitionist*. Even though
this was not the best source of information, Hall had enough supporting
evidence to make the story readily acceptable.[38] "The ultra-abolitionists . . .
are exceedingly enraged, and Blanchard, *et id genus*, are rallying for a
grand onset at the Detroit Convention. They say the time has come to
straighten the Home Miss[ionary] Soc[iet]y on that subject [slavery] —
and nothing but a total withdrawing of aid or cooperation from not only
slaveholding ministers but also ch[urc]hs *having slaveholding members* . . .
can satisfy them," he wrote. Hall proposed three courses that he might
pursue. He might hastily return to New York and let them rave alone. He
could go to the convention and deny that he had the power to speak for
the executive committee. He could boldly say that the Society knowingly
appointed no slaveholders, and had no agents soliciting funds in the South,
but did not follow each dollar to its source; that since the missionary
organization was not an ecclesiastic body, it could not discipline slaveholding in the churches. Hall preferred the last course. As the convention
would be highly antislavery in composition, Hall wished Badger were there
instead of himself, and he volunteered to let his fellow secretary exchange
places with him.[39]

Back in New York, Badger submitted only Hall's third proposition to the executive committee and although "no vote was taken" all were "of one opinion and . . . one feeling that the ground" they should stand on ought to be that churches would not be refused aid because they were from slave states. Hall was advised "not . . . to commit the society to any different action" from what they had taken. Badger named the board members who resided in the South and again stated that none of the four surviving members were, to his knowledge, slaveholders. The executive committee had not, to Badger's knowledge, ever appointed a slaveholding agent or missionary. Such inquiries were made by the executive committee in all cases as they deemed important. Whether any slaveholders were admitted to the churches, or what the missionaries preached, the Society was not informed. Hall was reassured that he would not stand alone in the convention; Nathan S. Beman and David H. Riddle, directors of the Society and representatives of the ABCFM, would be there. But these assurances did not relieve Hall's mind. The day after receiving Badger's letter he wrote to his colleague: "I dread that convention what with abolition[ism], Oberlinism, Presbyter[ia]n and Cong[regationa]l Sectarianism — and the blending of these with individual cases of disappointment."[40]

When the convention met, a committee was selected to which the memorials on slavery were referred. The committee was composed of Joel H. Linsley, president of Marietta College, Nathan S. Beman, and George E. Pierce, president of Western Reserve College, all vice presidents and directors of the AHMS. Added to this group was Harvey Hyde, a missionary in Michigan who was a firm supporter of the AHMS. Jonathan Blanchard was the only abolitionist on the committee.[41] On June 20, the day before the committee on slavery made its report, Blanchard informed the editor of the Watchman of the Valley that it was expected that "the Benevolent Associations" would "speedily be brought to a practical conformity to the non-fellowship principle." The convention was "resolved . . . that the . . . Benevolent Societies ought to, and ere long will, recognize that principle in their operations," he optimistically wrote.[42] The same day, Hall wrote to the home office that the meeting on home missions was scheduled for the following day. He had arranged to have Calvin Stowe and Linsley speak for the AHMS. Henry Little, Myron Tracy, and Stephen Peet, agents of the Society, were there and could be relied on to defend the cause. Hall had seen Blanchard, and his physical appearance belied the reputation he had developed as an abolitionist. "I have met Blanchard, and taken his measure and am ashamed that I should ever have felt afraid of him. I think I may safely let him 'say his say,'" Hall predicted confidently.[43]

The committee reported the two resolutions on slavery that were adopted in 1844 at Cleveland but added a third resolving that God had afforded "cheering tokens that He is about to establish the principles here recognized . . . and to work a practical conformity thereto in all benevolent associations and operations." The report had primarily been the work of Blanchard. Linsley reported to the convention that the committee was unanimous on the resolutions, but Blanchard insisted on giving his own interpretation on the floor. He argued that "the language of the report should be clearer and more explicit." According to his interpretation the report indirectly declared that the societies should soon act upon the principle that slaveholding was an un-Christian practice. "May God in His mercy hasten the hour when the American Home Missionary Society sustain no churches at the South but such as propagate a Christianity which does not leave standing the worst institution of heathenism," he beseeched. Although the *New York Observer* charged that Blanchard tried to get the convention to take stronger ground, he denied it. Hall felt that Blanchard was seeeking "to *win* rather than scold, to touch the sympathies, rather than to vituperate," but his efforts were powerless.[44]

The Detroit convention made the secretaries and executive committee aware that the AHMS was extremely vulnerable because Southerners were directors and vice presidents of the domestic missionary organization. This had been one of the points of query by George W. Perkins in the month before the Detroit convention assembled. Badger had also prepared Hall with an answer on this point if it came up at the convention. In September 1843, Thomas Lafon had charged that all missionary boards contained slaveholders on their panel of directors. "Their names are published in the annual proceedings . . . and heralded through the length and breadth of the land, thus showing in a public manner their connection with the institution of slavery, and in that way sustaining it," he charged.[45] The standard answer of the AHMS to questions of whether there were slaveholders on the board had been that "to the best of their knowledge" none were slave owners. This answer was not satisfactory to the abolitionists. Under the new pressures on the AHMS most of the directors from the South were dropped.

In 1841 the roster of officers of the Society contained eight directors and vice presidents from the South. In 1842 the number was reduced to six. Three more were dropped in 1845, one of whom was removed by death. One of those dropped in 1845, Frederick A. Ross of Kingsport, Tennessee, a Presbyterian minister, was a slaveholder. In 1845, Artemas Bullard of St. Louis was added to the list of directors. He was born in Massachusetts, and came to St. Louis as the pastor of a Presbyterian church in 1838. At the time of the Detroit convention, there were thus four southern members on the list of officers. Before the next annual meeting of the AHMS this number had been reduced by two. Thomas H. Cleland of Kentucky and Benjamin M. Palmer of Charleston, South Carolina were dropped from the list. Palmer was a slaveholder at the time of the Detroit convention. When the annual report of 1846 was published, only Bullard and Eliphalet W. Gilbert of Delaware remained on the list of directors as representatives of the South. Gilbert was born in Lebanon, New York, and went to Delaware in 1817 when he was twenty-four years of age. In 1846 he was president of Delaware College, but he would change his residence to Philadelphia in 1847, leaving Bullard as the only director who resided in the South.[46]

After the Detroit convention the attack on the AHMS continued unabated because antislavery Christians desired the church to be completely separated from slavery. In New England the spearhead of the attack on the benevolent institutions was directed against the ABCFM, but there were signs that more attention would soon be directed at the AHMS. In September 1845, a clergyman in Maine was prompted by the 1844 annual report of the AHMS to ask, "If you employ slaveholders — or aid slaveholding churches — or missionaries are allowed to receive slaveholders into churches; then is not this inference [correct] viz.: that the gospel which you are laboring to extend does sanction slavery?" Since the Society had taken a stand that slavery was the most serious obstacle to the gospel, he asked, "Ought not a Society that is laboring to diffuse the pure gospel . . . give the whole weight of its influence against whatever opposes its success? . . . I think I speak advisedly," he warned, "when I say, that if the AHMS is sustaining and fellowshipping slavery, the day is not far distant when it will be shorn of its strength, and will appeal in vain to the opposers of slavery for support."[47]

But it was in Indiana that the first statewide attack was made against aiding slaveholding churches. In October 1845, the Synod of Indiana took up a question posed by Jonathan Cable's church: "Is it the duty of churches who believe slaveholding to be a sin . . . to contribute to the funds of benevolent Societies who employ agents to solicit funds from slaveholders, and employ a portion of their funds in building up and sustaining churches that receive slaveholders into communion and fellowship of the Church?" The synod declared that it could not "approve of the organization of churches, . . . by anybody, on the principle of sanctioning slaveholding." It was hoped that the societies would soon be "conducted . . . so as to be manifestly . . . opposed to all sinful practices, and slaveholding among the rest." But for the time the synod knew "of no better, purer, safer, more intelligent or more efficient agents" than the national societies.[48]

The dissatisfaction in Indiana led to a meeting of ministers and elders of the New School Presbyterian Church of Indiana at Logansport, Indiana, on October 14, 1845. They invited members of other Presbyterian and Congregational groups to join them in Philadelphia two days before the General Assembly to consider the problem of slavery in the church. While slavery continued in connection with the church, stated the call, "it will be a source of continual discord, distract her counsels, divert or dry up her charities." The call for convention was signed by twenty of the leading Presbyterian clergymen and seven well-known elders of the New School Church. The convention was opposed by the *Christian Observer*, the *New York Observer*, and the *Detroit Observer* because they believed it was contrary to the Constitution of the Presbyterian Church and would introduce agitating questions into the General Assembly. The critics were answered by the *Watchman of the Valley* with the assurance that the convention had "no sinister aim." A correspondent to the *Watchman of the Valley*, observing that "most strenuous efforts" were being made to prevent the convention, justified the meeting on the ground that every synod in the western free states had declared against fellowship to slaveholding in the church.[49]

When the Presbyterian Anti-Slavery Convention met in Philadelphia, resolutions were passed that any person persisting in the sin of servitude "after due instruction and admonition" ought to be denied fellowship. At the General Assembly meeting, after nine days of debate, that body condemned slavery as "intrinsically an unrighteous and oppressive system," but declined "to determine the degree of moral turpitude." The assembly condemned "divisive and schismatic measures," and the "withholding of fellowship."[50]

The growing opposition to slavery in the Northwest was closely related to the political events of the day. On May 13, 1846, Congress declared war on Mexico. Should slavery be permitted to expand into the territory to be acquired from Mexico? This issue was formally presented to Congress in August 1846 as the Wilmot Proviso. By the end of 1846 all signs pointed to an intensification of the controversy over slavery. The unity of action that the New School Presbyterians and Congregationalists in the West had developed in the conventions from 1841 to 1846 would put the opponents of slavery in a stronger position to deal with the dispute about slavery in the AHMS. The organization of a new antislavery missionary society, the American Missionary Association, in 1846 would give the antislavery advocates still more leverage in their struggle.

In the Northwest, most of the Congregationalists were organized into presbyteries and were represented in the synods of the New School Presbyterian Church. At the local level churches were usually organized as Congregational or Presbyterian according to the majority of the congregation. Local Congregational associations had been organized in the Western Reserve, northern Illinois, parts of Michigan, and Iowa by 1846. In Wisconsin, Presbyterian and Congregational churches had been united into a convention with boundaries that were identical with those of the state. In September 1843, a General Conference of Congregational Churches of Illinois and Iowa was called to meet at Princeton, Illinois, in November of that year.[51] Signers of the call were among the strongest antislavery advocates in the Northwest. Congregationalists in the West had become more denominationally minded because of the slavery question. They felt that they were connected with slavery through the General Assembly and the AHMS. In July 1846, a general Western Congregational Convention met in Michigan City, Indiana, and agreed that the spread of genuine Congregationalism was an effective method to promote emancipation. The leading figure in the movement and chairman of the resolution committee was Jonathan Blanchard. The convention adopted a measure that the AHMS should plant or sustain no churches in slaveholding states that tolerated slavery among the members.[52] Then in the following October a Christian antislavery convention composed primarily of Presbyterians and Congregationalists met in Granville, Illinois. The convention resolved that it was "morally wrong for missionary societies" to receive funds from slaveholding patrons.[53]

In his perceptive and concise study, *Revivalism and Social Reform*, Timothy Smith concluded his chapter on Christian liberty and slavery with the statement, "The conservative temper which preferred to let well enough alone rather than cope with thorny problems became as strong in ecclesiastical assemblies as in the halls of Congress." Smith's conclusion was certainly not true of the western Congregational associations and New School Presbyterian presbyteries in the 1840s and would not be true of the New School Presbyterian General Assembly in the 1850s.[54] The western Congregationalists and Presbyterians worked tirelessly to purify the church. They refused to let well enough alone as the conservatives preferred. Much time was consumed in conventions devoted almost exclusively to dealing with the problem of slavery. The AHMS was pressured to cleanse itself of directors who had a connection with the South, and the New School General Assembly spent more time considering the problem of slavery than it devoted to any other topic. Both the AHMS and the General Assembly were in gradual retreat from conservatism, which would continue to decrease throughout the antebellum period.

Strange Cargo at Montauk Point

*O*n a sunny Monday afternoon in August 1839, the U.S. Navy brig *Washington*, under the command of a young lieutenant by the name of Gedney, moved slowly into Long Island Sound near Montauk Point. Reports of a "suspicious" ship anchored at the point led to rumors that it was a pirate ship. Others related stories of seeing strange black men who spoke a peculiar dialect and wore queer clothing. Several pilot boats had reported seeing a clipper-built schooner of about sixty tons with Negroes on board. Lieutenant Gedney's investigation revealed that the mysterious ship contained a cargo of slaves who had mutinied and taken over the ship. Gedney arrested the occupants and dispatched a party to the shore where part of the crew had gone to secure food. With the full crew of forty-one slaves in custody, the *Washington* brought them to New London, Connecticut. The Negroes were charged with the murder of the captain, the cook, and a crew member and were confined in jail at New Haven to await trial in the September session of the circuit court at Hartford. The full story was revealed after a native African interpreter was found on board the British armed brig *Buzzard* lying in New York Harbor. Professor Hosiah W. Gibbs, of Yale Divinity School, learned the sounds of some of the words spoken by the African natives and went to New York, boarding one ship after another until he found an African sailor from Sierra Leone who recognized the words. With the aid of the interpreter, the captives told their story.[1]

In the spring of 1839, a young chieftian named Cinque and forty-nine of his subjects were kidnapped in Sierra Leone by some of their own countrymen acting as agents of Spanish slave traders. In the custody of a Portuguese slave trader, they were taken to Havana, Cuba, chained wrist to wrist and leg to leg, and confined in quarters with a four-foot-high ceiling. In Havana they were sold for $450 each to two planters—Pedro Ruiz and Jose Montez. This had happened despite the fact that Spain had forbidden the importation of slaves in 1817, effective in 1820. Ruiz and Montez embarked for the port of Guanaja, Cuba, with their slaves on board the schooner *Amistad*. On the fourth day out Cinque and the other captives revolted and killed the captain and the cook. Ruiz and Montez were forced to steer east with Africa as the destination. At night they steered north by west. After two months, this zigzagging course brought them into the Long Island Sound where they dropped anchor on Sunday, August 25.[2]

When this story spread over New England and New York, the abolitionists came to the aid of the slaves. Seth P. Staples, Theodore Sedgwick, Jr., and Roger S. Baldwin were retained as counsel for the Africans, and the court found them to be innocent of murder since their acts had been committed as captives of a slave trader. The defendants were, however, detained in jail to determine if they were free men. The Spanish minister, Calderon, demanded their surrender to Spain. The United States Attorney General, Felix Grundy, declared that the Negroes should be turned over to Spain under the provisions of article nine of the Treaty of 1795. In November the captives were declared to be free by the federal disctrict court. The case was appealed to the Supreme Court of the United States and John Q. Adams won the decision for the blacks before the Supreme Court, which declared them free in March 1841.

The abolitionists organized a group known as the Amistad Committee — composed of Simeon S. Jocelyn, Lewis Tappan, and Joshua Leavitt — to look after the interests of the Africans. It provided the services of Leonard Bacon, Henry G. Ludlow, and Amos Townsend, Jr., of New Haven, to try to secure suitable instruction for the Amistad captives. They were removed to Farmington, Connecticut, where they were cared for and given rudiments of education. Lewis Tappan took eight or ten of the Africans to about fifteen of the principal towns in Massachusetts and Connecticut to raise money to send them back to their native country. The committee offered to send the natives back to Africa in the custody of two missionaries under the auspices of the ABCFM, and the funds the committee had collected would go to the board, provided the board would establish an antislavery mission. After the ABCFM refused the offer, the Amistad Committee converted itself into an antislavery missionary agency, which took the position that it would accept no "unrighteous money." In November 1841, before the blacks were returned to Africa, a farewell meeting was held in New York.[3]

The Union Missionary Society had been organized in Hartford, Connecticut, before the Amistad Committee was formed. On May 5, 1841, James W. C. Pennington, the pastor of the First Colored Congregational Church of Hartford, called a meeting in his church to express to the people of Hartford his feelings of responsibility as a Christian to send the gospel to Africa.[4] This gathering led to a missionary convention in Hartford in August 1841 that organized the Union Missionary Society. Pennington was elected president of the organization and Reverend Amos G. Beman, of a Negro Congregational Church in New Haven, was the corresponding secretary. The chairman of the board of managers was Ichabod Codding, and Josiah Brewer of Wethersfield, Connecticut, was the chairman of the executive committee.[5] The Society pledged itself "to discountenance slavery . . . in collecting its funds, . . . appointing its officers, missionaries and agents."[6] The founders of the Union Missionary Society felt called on to protest against all proslavery connections as a means of cleansing "their skirts entirely from participating in so enormous a sin."[7]

Other antislavery missionary associations came into existence at the same time as the Union Missionary Society,[8] and it was soon obvious to the antislavery Christians that there was a need for a unity of purpose and operations among their small societies and committees. As early as June 1842, at the convention of the AAS, the clergy met separately and resolved that the time had arrived when it was desirable that abolitionist Christians should "select or provide anti-slavery channels" through which their contributions could "flow for the conversion of heathen nations." They recommended that the Union Missionary Society and the Amistad Committee "consider the subject of unity." A committee of five was selected "to act as a missionary committee" for the promotion of the antislavery cause without any alliance with slavery.[9] Following the assimilation of the Amistad Committee into the Union Missionary Society, many of the leading figures in the movement called for a reorganization of the Union Missionary Society.[10] By 1846 the abolitionists had given up all hopes that the ABCFM and the AHMS would take an antislavery position, and there was a growing concern among antislavery advocates about the religious training of the slave. The abolitionists were also determined that their fellow advocates who had been dismissed from churches for antislavery beliefs should not go unsupported. A society that would provide for these new needs was in order.

At the same time steps were being taken to unite abolitionist Christians in a national organization. The invitation for a national convention of Bible Missions to convene in Syracuse on February 18, 1846, stated that "the time has come when those who would sustain missions for the propagation of a pure and free Christianity should institute arrangements for gathering and sustaining churches in heathen lands, from which the sins of caste, polygamy, slaveholding, and the like shall be excluded. To bear such crimes in silence, not to say to . . . practice . . . fellowship therein is enough to paralyze the faith and hope of the church."[11]

The Syracuse meeting adopted an address written by Amos A. Phelps advising Christians that it was time to inquire whether the gospel they were sending out was "not loaded with some fatal disparagement, such as forbids its wide extension." The executive committee of the Union Missionary Society sent a letter to the convention suggesting that a permanent organization be created by the Union Missionary Society or the convention. The new society "should immediately . . . organize a system of Foreign and Home Missions sustaining ministers and churches, who embrace anti-slavery principles in the slave States." Aid should be given to ministers who had been "dismissed on account of their anti-slavery principles. . . . The time has come when the friends of unadulterated gospel ought to rally . . . to rescue Christianity from perversion, and save the missionary cause from ruin," concluded the epistle.[12]

A call was issued for another convention to meet in Albany in September to set up a permanent organization. "All friends of freedom and of missions" who had hitherto cooperated "with the American Board and kindred associations" were asked to meet "to consider principles and plans" that were "to affect the missionary work everywhere — at home as well as abroad."[13] On September 2, fifty-three members signed the register of those present when the convention opened in the State Street Baptist Church. The meeting was presided over by J. H. Payne, a Congregational minister from Illinois. Josiah Brewer, William W. Patton, and others represented the Union Missionary Society. Asa Mahan, president of Oberlin, represented the Western Evangelical Missionary Society, and the West India Missionary Committee had representatives present. The address, drawn up by William Goodell, urged that arrangements be made "for gathering and sustaining Churches . . . from which the sin of caste, polygamy and slaveholding" should be "excluded by the terms of admission, or by disciplinary process . . . To attempt to reform, by fraternization, the corrupt national churches of the East, is, we believe, a fruitless effort inconsistent with the purity of the missionary enterprise, and the integrity of the missionaries themselves," the address stated.[14]

A permanent society called the American Missionary Association (AMA) was organized. Its constitution excluded slaveholders and permitted the withdrawal of support from churches that "departed from the belief of fundamental truths." The constitution also prohibited the association from accepting funds from slaveholders or the employment, as missionaries or agents, of those who held their fellow beings as slaves. The society had been created primarily because of the shortcomings of the ABCFM. Although the new organization found some missionary societies less objectionable in their structure, none were found adequate "to the wants of the time" or fully in harmony with what was conceived to be "the best, the Scriptural methods and instrumentalities of missionary efforts." The association later justified the new movement on the grounds that great reforms on moral subjects occurred only under the influence of religious principles, and because there was "no power out of the church that could sustain slavery an hour" if it were not sustained by the church.[15] The radical religious reformers of the AMA and the moderates and conservatives of the AHMS were in agreement that the church should be the instrument of reforming as well as converting society, but they differed on ways and means. While the conservatives and moderates of the old society proposed to transform the slave society by showing empathy for the slaveholder and winning him over by the law of love, the radical Christians were convinced that change could only be secured by pricking the conscience of the slaveholder by withdrawing fellowship.

The AMA was a nonsectarian benevolent society, but it was essentially made up of Congregationalists. All the existing independent antislavery missionary bodies affiliated with the AMA.[16] It sprang into existence as "a living protest against what was considered the complicity" of the old boards with slavery. There was a close relationship between the personnel who made up the official staff of the antislavery society, the Liberty party, and the AMA. In 1835, when abolitionist literature was first barred from the mail, ten New York citizens signed a public protest against the action, warning that if this encroachment were submitted to, the days of the republic were numbered, and although the abolitionists might be the first, they would not be "the last victims offered at the shrine of arbitrary power." Five of the signers of the protest later became officers of the AMA.[17]

The AMA shared an office with the American and Foreign Anti-Slavery Society, and had several officers in common. Most of the officers and members of the executive committee of the AMA, like those of the American and Foreign Anti-Slavery Society, were drawn from the ranks of the middle class. Arthur and Lewis Tappan were the wealthiest members of the organization. In 1847, Arthur was a member of the executive committee, but he was soon to move to Connecticut and go into semiretirement. Lewis was corresponding secretary of the American and Foreign Anti-Slavery Society and treasurer of the AMA. He was a member of the Tabernacle Presbyterian Church when he started an antislavery society in the church. The session opposed his action and he was eventually tried and ousted from the church after conviction as a disturber of the peace, and for slandering the officers of the church and the pastor. The New School General Assembly reversed the decision of the session, but Tappan never returned to the Tabernacle. Thereafter, he worked with a small group of friends in conducting mixed Sunday school classes and often attended Negro churches and cooperated with their work.[18]

William Jackson was the first president of the AMA. Jackson, who lived at Newton Centre, Massachusetts, had been an active member of the anti-slavery committee for the West India Mission and was known as a man who had never sacrificed principle to obtain popular applause. He had always been a political abolitionist. "Let us who are friends of freedom," Jackson appealed to Garrison, "gird on the whole armor of faith, and go on in the strength of the Lord, and he will fight our battle for us." Jackson was a delegate from Massachusetts to the Liberty party national convention in 1843, and was elected one of the vice presidents of the convention.[19]

The two secretaries of the AMA were George Whipple, as secretary of missions, and Simeon S. Jocelyn, as recording secretary. Whipple was born in Albany, New York, and attended Lane Theological Seminary where he became one of the "Lane Rebels." After leaving Lane, he was ordained a Congregational clergyman, and became a professor at Oberlin College before he went into the service of the AMA. Jocelyn became pastor of the Temple Street Church of New Haven, thus becoming, in 1829, the first white pastor of an all-Negro church. An early member of the New England and American Anti-Slavery Societies, he was firmly convinced that slavery would be abolished through the activities of the church. "We shall prevail," he predicted in 1834, "if we trust in the Lord, and lean not to our own understanding." He served as the recording secretary of the AMA until 1853 when he became home secretary.[20]

The AMA primarily viewed itself as an agency for the foreign field, but it never disclaimed the right to engage in home missions work. From its beginning, the association aided several black churches throughout the East. In June 1847, the AMA voted to aid Oliver Emerson, the Iowa minister who had been first to refuse to take aid from the AHMS in 1844. Although the secretaries pleaded a shortage of funds to all proposals for aid from the West, by the end of the second year of operations the organizations aided five missionaries in the West. The editor of the *American Missionary* pointed out that these men had "relinquished their aid from the AHM Society" because of its "relation to . . . slavery" and had applied to the AMA for assistance. The number of domestic missionaries aided increased until it was necessary to create a home missions department. When the Free Presbyterian Synod of Cincinnati was established in 1847 as an independent antislavery church, the AMA aided ministers of this church.[21]

The executive committee of the association moved cautiously into the field of domestic missions. This was partly due to the lack of funds, but it was also because of a difference of opinion in the AMA. The chief critic of the efforts in the home field was William W. Patton. He objected to spending money in this area because many of the AMA contributors also gave to home missions through other channels and expected the AMA to spend their donations in behalf of foreign missions. He insisted that there was "no generally expressed dissatisfaction with the American Home Mis-[sionary] Soc[iet]y on the part of the abolitionists . . . and a large portion expect to contribute" to that Society. With proper attention in the theological schools to see that none but antislavery seminarians were sent out, Patton felt that the home field would soon be "abolitionized." However, he was not above bringing pressure on the old institution in order to make it a thoroughly antislavery benevolent organization.[22] William W. Patton was the son of the William Patton who had been a member of the executive committee of the AHMS for many years. George Whipple was a staunch defender of the AMA home missionary activity, and he had the support of S. S. Jocelyn. Lewis Tappan, as treasurer of the AMA, counseled a program that was financially conservative so that the society could at all times remain solvent. He, therefore, preferred to go slowly on home missions. Oliver Emerson stood at the other extreme and persistently urged the AMA to take a firm stand in opposition to the AHMS.[23]

But a constant pressure of events moved the AMA into deeper commitment in the domestic field. An important supporter from Connecticut claimed that the western free states were "the most promising missionary field in the world." A staunch advocate of the AMA from Massachusetts advised that many who contributed nothing would contribute liberally to missions in the slave states. Many urged that more should be done in the home department. Churches and clergymen in western and central New York were leaving the Orthodox Congregational associations and New School Presbyterian synods. Many of them desired to associate with the AMA as patrons or mission churches. In September 1847, these dissenting Christians held a convention in Syracuse. Since many of these churches needed aid there was a growing interest in antislavery home missions in this area.[24]

Jonathan Cable, the Northwest agent for the AMA, pointed out that the necessity of relying on support from the old home missions society was the greatest obstacle to the development of a thoroughly antislavery spirit in the Synod of Indiana. "Our cause will never succeed by the efforts of the AHMS," he counseled.[25] But Congregationalists and Free Presbyterians of the Northwest spoke with a weak voice in the AMA because the section was a receiver of charity rather than a contributor. By the middle of 1848 the influence of the Northwest changed radically. In July 1848, the Free Presbyterian Synod of America held a convention and created a Board of Home and Foreign Missions as an auxiliary of the AMA. Two collections were to be made in sustaining churches each year — one for home and one for foreign missions. The new auxiliary received the backing of the officers of the AMA in New York, and supporters in the West predicted there would be many churches leaving the AHMS now that a reliable antislavery alternative was available.[26] While the number of churches that were willing to leave the old domestic society was increasing, the AMA found its operations limited by the refusal of many of the wealthy conservative urban churches in the East to admit the society's agents into their houses and associations to make collections.[27] By 1848, however, the Springfield Missionary Association and the Penobscot County Missionary Association were organized in Massachusetts and Maine as antislavery auxiliaries to the AMA. In 1849, Oliver Emerson rejoiced at the remonstrance that the supporters of the AMA had presented to the ABCFM, but added "I cannot avoid the conviction that this labor would, in the end, have been more efficient had it been employed to remove Slavery from the churches, especially the missionary churches of our own land."[28]

The Amistad episode started a chain of events that led to the establishment of an antislavery missionary society, one that was urged by missionaries and patrons dissatisfied with the failure of the ABCFM and the AHMS to take an antislavery stance. Those who had grievances against the AHMS were not numerous for the first year or two, but developments during the Mexican War and the passage of the Fugitive Slave Law caused the grievances against the AHMS to become more widespread, and the AMA, which had at first concentrated on foreign missions, moved into a period of more active aid to home missions.[29] The Mexican War and the birth of the AMA created a crisis in the AHMS, which reacted by limiting its contacts with the institution of slavery. Although most of the founders of the AMA were members of the American Anti-Slavery Society and the later established American and Foreign Anti-Slavery Society, many of the clergymen who received aid from the AMA were never members of the antislavery societies.

Southern Slavery Threatens
the Harmony of Domestic Missions

*A*t the time the AMA was being organized the AHMS was facing a problem that threatened to disrupt the New School Presbyterian Church as well as the home mission program that the denomination carried on in cooperation with the Congregationalists. In January 1845, John G. Fee, a native of Bracken County, Kentucky, applied to the AHMS for aid in serving as a missionary for the Cabin Creek Presbyterian Church in Lewis County, Kentucky. Fee, who had recently completed his studies at Lane Theological Seminary, was characterized by the secretary of the missions committee as being "a young man of promise, and . . . worthy of confidence."[1] But the secretary did not anticipate the controversy that would center around Fee a little more than a year after he had expressed his confidence in the young missionary. As a boy Fee had worked on the family farm with his father's slaves.[2] By 1845 Fee had become a confirmed abolitionist "who did not fear to tell the truth about slavery, or to speak his mind boldly" on the subject when it touched the question of the church.[3]

The abolitionists north of the Ohio River, in Indiana and Ohio, had long desired the establishment of antislavery churches in Kentucky. In 1825 the agent of the Cincinnati auxiliary agency of the AHMS had pointed out that ministers who opposed slavery were fleeing the state. He urged the AHMS to make extra efforts "to bring . . . and sustain" an efficient ministry in Kentucky to combat the tendency to tolerate slavery south of the river.[4] Before Fee was commissioned as a missionary through the Synod of Kentucky, efforts were made to have Fee commissioned by the Cincinnati AHMS agency to "form churches on non-slaveholding principles" in Kentucky, but the Cincinnati agent informed Fee that a missionary could be sent to Kentucky only if he were in good standing with the Synod of Kentucky.[5]

After serving as a missionary for a year, John Fee applied to the Synod of Kentucky for a renewal. At the same time he served notice on the synod mission committee that he had established a rule that no slaveholders could be admitted to his church. Fee lost half of his support in the Cabin Creek church, and was threatened with violence, but the greatest opposition to his plan came from his fellow clergymen. The Presbytery of Harmony, in which Fee's church was located, contained one slaveholding minister, and the Synod of Kentucky had several who held slaves.[6] The mission committee of the Synod of Kentucky refused to recommend the renewal of Fee's commission. The rejection was based both on expediency and the law of the church. The refusal of fellowship solely on the basis of slaveholding was considered wrong in itself, but it would also cause confusion in the churches of Kentucky, according to the secretary of the mission committee. To have a minister such as Fee forced upon them would be bringing "fire brands" into the churches, and aid from the AHMS on "such a condition" was "undesirable." The decision of the mission committee was sustained by the Synod of Kentucky, and the AHMS was forced to make a decision that the Society would have preferred to avoid.[7]

The first reaction of the AHMS was to mark time and wait for further developments. The junior secretary of the New York society, Charles Hall, asked Fee for private information concerning his attitude toward slavery. "Wherein does slavery throw obstacles in the way of preaching the gospel?" he asked. Fee said he found the system of servitude to be a corruptive influence on the gospel, and it prevented the spread of education among white children. He warned that slavery dried up the fountain of benevolent enterprise because it destroyed the slaveholder's "deep and lasting concern for the . . . welfare of man as man." Charles Hall assured Fee that the secretaries of the AHMS had personally a strong sympathy for him, but the refusal of the Kentucky mission committee posed a problem of bringing into accord the local auxiliaries of the Society. "Meanwhile, during the period of suspense," Hall said, "you may labour on with the understanding that the rate of appropriations as last year will be continued until you hear from us to the contrary."[8]

As weeks extended into months with no assurance of support, and faced with the prospect of choosing between starvation or leaving his field of labor, Fee asked the Society to inform him immediately if his commission would be renewed. "I do not know where I shall get the next months provisions for me and the horse I ride," he revealed. In the meantime the executive committee of the Society decided that the only safe course was to retain Fee unless the Presbytery of Harmony, to which his church was accountable ecclesiastically, excluded him from the ministry. The application was to be sent to the New York office instead of the synod committee. While the Kentucky committee based their rejection on the ground of an "unconstitutional *test of Church membership*," Badger preferred to think of it as a dispute about "conscientious scruples" since no one in fact had ever been rejected from Fee's church as a slaveholder.[9]

The lines were clearly drawn between antislavery and conservative supporters of the AHMS on the Fee case. Would the AHMS support a southern church that barred slaveholders over the objection of the southern church judicatory? The abolitionists across the Ohio River focused their attention on the controversy in Kentucky, and Henry Little warned Badger against a hasty decision on the Fee case without first corresponding widely to determine the consensus. "Our *hottest abolitionists* are on one side of the view and *slave holders* on the other," he warned.[10] An Ohio missionary hastened to bear his testimony in favor of Fee. "All the ministers on this side of the river who are acquainted with him do the same," he added.[11] As the evidence of a strong public opinion in the Northwest against the dismissal of Fee began to manifest itself, the AHMS became more determined than ever not to risk destroying its prestige and support in the North by refusing missionary aid to Fee as long as he had unquestionable standing in his presbytery.[12]

The growing resentment in the South against the position taken by the AHMS on slavery gave rise to an attempt to reopen the issue of slaveholding missionaries, which had been dormant for more than a year. The editor of the *Christian Observer,* Amasa Converse, received a communication for his newspaper in September 1846 claiming that the Society had established a rule that aid would be refused to a missionary who owned a slave even though he was in good standing in his presbytery. Converse asked the AHMS about the accuracy of this correspondence.[13] Hall denied that any such rule existed but admitted that inquiries had been made in individual cases. The missions committees of Virginia, Kentucky, and Missouri, in view of the strong feeling in the North, had decided not to request commissions for slaveholding missionaries.[14] Five days after Converse wrote to the Society, a communication appeared in the *Christian Observer* under the signature of the stated clerk of the Synod of Kentucky, confirming the rumor that the mission committee of Kentucky had refused to recommend the recommissioning of John G. Fee on the ground that he had "constituted *a new test of piety and Church membership to the Presbyterian Constitution.*"[15]

When this communication was copied into the *New York Evangelist,* the controversy became common knowledge among eastern antislavery advocates. The article prompted abolitionist George W. Perkins to ask whether the Society would sustain Fee despite the action of the Synod of Kentucky.[16] The pastor of the Congregational Church in Newton, Massachusetts, asked for information at the request of his church and offered to have his church support Fee if Fee's commission was not renewed. Many in the Newton church were dissatisfied with the AHMS's stand on slavery, and the pastor believed that if the congregation supported Fee it would help unify his church. Hall assured both men that Fee had been recommissioned, but the Society would doubtless lose the support of the South and therefore the loyalty of the North was essential if the AHMS were to prosper.[17]

The *New York Evangelist* disagreed with the position of the Synod of Kentucky. Fee's position was considered both scriptural and constitutional. The editor only hoped Fee would "be enabled to speak the truth in love" and do nothing that would lead to his being driven from a region where every faithful minister was so greatly needed. When it became known that the AHMS had recommissioned Fee, the *New York Evangelist* judged that the decision would "be abundantly sustained by the good sense of the country."[18] The conservative *Christian Observer* disagreed with the *New York Evangelist*. The New School General Assembly of 1840 had made the action of Fee unconstitutional, declared Converse, and this was the latest ruling.[19] He pointed out that the assembly had requested the presbyteries of the Northwest to rescind such resolutions as excluded "slaveholders from their communion."[20] The leaders of the Synod of Kentucky kept in close touch with the *Christian Observer,* and when it became known that Fee's commission had been renewed, the secretary of the synod mission committee asked Badger for an account of what had been done. The Society had reinstated Fee because no charge had been made before the presbytery.[21]

The Kentucky mission committee found the decision of the executive committee in New York to be unsatisfactory. Since Fee made his avowal in connection with a request for aid, the committee insisted that they were "bound, of necessity, to *protest or sanction*" the action of Fee. The course the AHMS had taken, according to the Kentucky committee, was "calculated to fix in the minds" of the people of Kentucky the fear that the AHMS designed "insidiously," through the missionary operations, to introduce and sustain practical abolitionism in Kentucky. The executive committee of the AHMS was asked to reconsider its decision, but after a review the executive committee saw "no other course . . . but to adhere to their former decision." If Fee were brought to trial and suspended from the ministry, "we shall not continue to sustain him," Badger promised. However, he insisted that the question of refusing fellowship to slaveholders was an open question in the Presbyterian Church since many congregations in different parts of the country had taken this stand without censure.[22]

The greatest threat and challenge faced by the AHMS was that posed by Converse. Amasa Converse was born in New Hampshire and went to

Virginia as a missionary in 1825. He stayed in the South to publish the *Southern Religious Telegraph* until 1839.[23] As editor of the *Christian Observer* in Philadelphia, Converse remained as strong an advocate of colonization as he had been in the South. His attitude toward slavery did not change materially, but he became more conservative as he saw the controversy of slavery threatening to disrupt the Union. Converse considered the conservatism of his *Christian Observer* as essential for preserving unity in the Presbyterian Church, and all of his efforts were calculated to create harmony between the North and the South.[24] As a result of his vigorous defense of the South and the conservative position, Converse had more influence in the South than any other Northern New School man. He also exerted a powerful influence among a small but powerful group of New School conservatives in the North.

After Converse heard that the executive committee in New York had retained Fee in the service of the Society, he expressed regret that a missionary who had violated his pledge to sustain the constitution of the Presbyterian Church would be retained. The new rule adopted by Fee was "wholly unauthorized" by the consitution and usage of the church. Badger pointed out to Converse that many of the patrons of the Society had insisted aid be denied to those churches receiving slaveholders. These demands had been rejected on the ground that the AHMS was not an ecclesiastical body and could not prescribe the terms of membership.[25] Converse viewed the new commitment of the secretary as highly satisfactory since the AHMS could not be a vehicle of reform if it were pledged to stand aloof from all parties. The editor of the *Christian Observer*, however, insisted that the Kentucky committee was only doing what the AHMS had always done by appointing missionaries of whom they approved.[26] When a convention of Presbyterian and Congregational churches met at Akron, Ohio, in February 1847 and adopted nonfellowship measures, Converse warned "the church cannot longer afford to tolerate movements which cast reproach upon her character, and subvert the rights guarantied [sic] to many of her members."[27] Converse blamed the development of these divisive tendencies on the *Watchman of the Valley*.[28]

While Converse was appeased to a degree, the secretary of the mission committee of the Synod of Kentucky was determined to see the matter brought to a conclusion.[29] Anticipating action against Fee in the synod, the AHMS urged Fee to send his application early if he expected to ask for a reappointment. "I would suggest the *importance of having this done forthwith*," wrote Hall.[30] Determined to avoid giving the abolitionists an opportunity to make propaganda of the Fee case, the AHMS renewed Fee's commission in June.[31]

When Fee journeyed to Cincinnati in June 1847 to attend the special meeting of the New School General Assembly, he found unexpected assurances of sympathy and cooperation from many sources, including Lyman Beecher, Calvin Stowe, Henry Little, and T. A. Mills, the stated clerk of the Synod of Cincinnati.[32] Henry Little was now convinced that the Society had gained by supporting an antislavery missionary in the South. "It gives us the confidence of the warmest anti-slavery men and prevents them from opposing us," Little reported. Three weeks later, writing from a stronghold of Presbyterian abolitionism in southern Ohio, Little observed that the Cabin Creek affair had done little injury south of the Ohio, while it had helped the Society greatly with the abolitionists. Donations were coming in more freely from the region north of the Ohio River, and many indicated that their change of attitude was due to the stand the Society had taken in Kentucky.[33]

In September 1847, the Synod of Kentucky asked the Prebytery of Harmony to look into the Cabin Creek case. In April of the following year, Fee was censured by the presbytery, which condemned the course pursued and solemnly admonished him to "desist from the Exercise of any such rule in the future." A committee of three was appointed to work with Fee to see if he could be induced to change his course or withdraw from the presbytery.[34]

In July 1848, Fee was reappointed for his fourth year of service, but Hall urged him to become independent of aid as soon as possible. As the Presbytery of Harmony had not yet suspended him, aid was still in order, but once the judicatory had removed him from its connection, the AHMS would experience difficulty in continuing aid to the Cabin Creek church.[35] Although a vice president of the Cincinnati auxiliary of the AMA advised against it,[36] the dilemma ended when Fee returned the commission to the AHMS in September, on the ground that he could no longer retain his connection with a Society that built up proslavery churches. A month later the AMA took steps to supply John Fee with support.[37]

A factor that made the Fee case more divisive in 1846 and 1847 was the cumulative effects of the "Graham Case" in Cincinnati during this period. William Graham, a New School minister of the Presbytery of Cincinnati and a former slaveholder who had liberated all his slaves, denounced abolitionism and defended bondage as a scriptural institution before the synod in 1843. When he published his statements in pamphlet form in the spring of 1844, a member of the Presbyterian Church of Ripley, Ohio, brought a charge against him for using the scripture to defend slavery. The charge was sustained without a dissenting vote in the lower judicatory of Cincinnati. When it was reported in October 1845 that repentance had not been secured from the accused, the synod suspended Graham from the church. Graham defended his position in another pamphlet in which he maintained that his position was supported by the General Assembly.[38]

The Graham case came before the General Assembly of 1846, and the decision of the synod was called "unconstitutional and irregular and therefore null and void." The synod was asked to correct its proceedings, but twenty-nine members of the assembly opposed this resolution.[39] When the Synod of Cincinnati met in October 1846, it refused to reinstate Graham and asked the assembly to reconsider the case.[40] In January 1847, the Presbytery of Hamilton expressed a determination to remain a part of the Synod of Cincinnati only as long as defenders of slavery were denied fellowship. Other western judicatories objected to the decision of the assembly.[41] Graham presented a memorial on his status in the Presbytery and Synod of Cincinnati to the adjourned assembly in 1847, but he was persuaded to withdraw it until the next meeting. When Graham left the synod and took up an Old School pastorate in Pennsylvania, the conflict over this issue died down.[42]

The Fee and Graham cases had clearly drawn the lines between the antislavery and conservative forces of the AHMS. The Southerners supported Graham and believed the denial of fellowship and communion to slaveholders was unconstitutional, unscriptural, and intolerable. They were aided and sustained by conservative Presbyterians in the East. The majority of Presbyterians in the Northwest, reinforced by the antislavery Congregationalists in New England, supported Fee. Northwestern Presbyterians considered Fee's position to be an extension into the slaveholding South of the nonfellowship stand they had taken in 1839. Since both Fee and Graham withdrew from the New School Presbyterian Church before the controversy had run its course, the question was not fully resolved, and the final settlement was delayed until the 1850s.

As the controversy in Kentucky neared its climax, trouble was brewing in Missouri. The problem was partly due to the dual nature of the institutions in that state; both slavery and free institutions were vying for supremacy. Slavery was firmly established in some sections of Missouri, while other areas were committed to freedom. Missouri's position was reflected in the resolutions adopted by the New School Synod of Missouri in 1846. "Living as we do in a slave state," affirmed the synod, "we are yet free to declare to the North and the South, that we desire and pray for the entire removal of slavery from among us, so soon as it can be done with safety and manifest advantage, so much to the master, as to the servants themselves."[43]

Slaveholding among the clergy was not uncommon in the Presbytery of Missouri, and the question of slaveholding missionaries became an issue when a minister became an owner of a slave by inheritance. It was reported in 1846 that four of the eight clergy of the presbytery were slaveholders. The AHMS refused to commission the missionary who had inherited the slave and Artemas Bullard, a St. Louis clergyman and a director of the AHMS, made a much-publicized trip to the East to secure support from the conservative Philadelphia Home Missionary Society and conservative friends in Buffalo to support slaveholding missionaries. Bullard charged the executive committee of the AHMS with sectional prejudice and the relations of the New York office with the Philadelphia auxiliary became strained. In May 1847, the conservatives in the New School Presbyterian General Assembly were able to establish a standing committee on home missions, which set up a church erection committee that competed with the AHMS and drew funds away from it.[44]

The growth of sectionalism in the West after the Michigan City Congregational Convention of 1846, and the rising opposition to the AHMS in the South because of the Society's attitude toward slavery, were important factors in the establishment of the Church Erection Committee. By the end of 1847 Badger had reached a cordial understanding with the Missouri Missionary Society, which agreed to refrain from requesting funds from the AHMS for slaveholding missionaries, but the Society's executive committee refused to concede local control of the missionary funds to the Missouri auxiliary. While tempers flared in Missouri, a controversy concerning servitude in missionary auxiliaries spread to presbyteries in Tennessee, northern Alabama, and Virginia.[45]

The charge of sectional prejudice that had been raised against the AHMS was not easy to put down. In February 1849, the *Home Missionary* attempted to stop the criticism by a presentation of the facts in an article on slavery entitled "The Great Hindrance." The editor, Charles Hall, informed his readers that "two or three times a year some newspaper editorials or correspondents remind the Society that it has but few missionaries in the slave states, while the free states number, in some cases, a hundred each. Why the difference?" To answer his question the editor cited correspondence of anonymous missionaries. "There is *only one thing* that hinders our entire happiness," wrote one of the missionaries, "and that is the curse of *slavery.*" To come out openly and avow hostility to the sacred institution, the missionary would thwart all hopes of doing good. "On this subject," Hall added, "he must wear a lock upon his lips, must smother the impulse of his heart and the convictions of his conscience, or run the risk of being lynched out of the country."[46] The article brought similar responses from many missionaries of the Society who had earlier revealed their feelings to the secretaries.[47] The *Christian Observer,* however, remained unconvinced that the AHMS was free of prejudice against the South, and other conservatives joined the assault against the AHMS.[48]

The majority opinion in the North was generally satisfied with the position of the AHMS. The *Boston Reporter* approvingly revealed that the Society had rejected an offer by an editor who wanted to publish a statement that the AHMS did not have a standing rule that slaveholders would be rejected as missionaries. The proposal had been brought forward as a means of relieving the Society of southern pressure. "They [the Society] are, we believe . . . ready to go farther, and instruct their missionaries to make slave-holding a disciplinable offense in their churches," predicted the *Reporter,* "when convinced that the churches whose almoners they are demand such action."[49] But the antislavery missionary sentiment in the Northwest was not appeased. In March 1849, the *American Missionary,* organ of the AMA, rejoiced to see "The Great Hindrance" article in the *Home Missionary,* but still contended that the AHMS was "either absolutely negatory, or detrimental" to the cause of removing slavery as a hindrance to the gospel. The American and Foreign Anti-Slavery Society admitted in its *Annual Report* that the AHMS had "used bolder language than any of the other professed religious societies not strictly antislavery," but Oliver Emerson was cited to the effect that the Society had brought more slaveholders into the church than all the missionaries of the various denominations to the Indian tribes.[50]

From 1846 to 1849 the AHMS had moved far along the path taken by the advocates of antislavery benevolence. In 1845, the Society had an understanding with southern auxiliaries that they would not recommend missionaries for commissions if they owned slaves for the purpose of personal gain. The southern agencies were of the opinion that a missionary who held slaves as an involuntary slaveholder was under no bar to the charity of the Society. Southerners could not be convinced that divine revelation had doomed their peculiar institution.[51] At first the Society was reluctantly willing to examine the facts in each case. The sectional feeling that had grown out of the events of the Mexican War, and the rise of the AMA forced the AHMS to become more liberal. But by 1850 the Society's position was that no missionary could be retained by the Society, regardless of the case, if he owned slaves. The growing antislavery sentiment in the Northwest was a powerful force pushing the Society toward its new position. The antislavery Congregationalism of rural New England supported the demands of the Northwest. As the Society became aware that a choice had to be made between the Northwest and the South, the former was favored without hesitation.

The New School Presbyterian Church was in a critical dilemma. If it failed to take strong measures against slavery, it would risk losing its more progressive members to the Congregationalists. On the other hand, if it did come out against slavery, it ran the risk of alienating its southern constituency. The controversy was made more critical by the fact that New School Presbyterians were zealous in proving and maintaining the claims to Presbyterian constitutionality as well as their moral purity. The danger was made greater by the existence of the General Assembly where controversies could be aired by a national debating forum.[52]

The Mexican War:
Slavery and the Church

*W*hen President James K. Polk signed legislation on May 13, 1846, declaring war on Mexico, a chain of events was set in motion that ultimately created a more determined opposition to slavery among those congregations in the North who supported the AHMS. The Mexican War allied those strongly committed to pacifism with those opposed to the war on antislavery grounds. As a result of the Mexican War, many moderates who had refrained from taking an antislavery position entered the antislavery movement through the less radical path of pacifism.

The evils of war and slavery were effectively combined by Benjamin Lundy in *The National Enquirer* to convince the North that the Texas revolution was a conspiracy of the "Slave Power" to extend the institution of slavery. With Texas in the Union, the antislavery forces in America expanded the slave power theory to include the idea that slaveholders had instigated the Mexican War so that slavery could be extended to territory that would be taken from Mexico by conquest.[1] The slave power was supposed to be the minority of Southerners who controlled the politics of the South, and through their position in the South controlled the national government. From its origin the American Anti-Slavery Society had given the slave power theory popular currency, and with the coming of the Mexican War the term secured wide acceptance in the religious community of the North. In 1848, Joshua Leavitt, editor of the *Emancipator*, organ of the American and Foreign Anti-Slavery Society, advised his antislavery colleagues that the "incessant use" of the term would "do much to open the eyes and arouse the energies of the people." He urged the opponents of slavery to let it appear that it was "the '*Slave Power*' whose growth we deprecate, whose usurpations we will put down."[2] The question of slavery and the Mexican War became irrevocably connected in the minds of many northern churchmen.

On May 13, the New School Presbyterian *Ohio Observer* reprinted an article from the *New Orleans Delta* recounting the beginning of hostility between the United States and Mexico. The editor of the *Observer* declared that war was "at best a bloody and barbarous business," but it was more to be detested when a nation can "descend to intrigues and corruption . . . to help the abettors of the institution of slavery." George Cheever, editor of the New School *New York Evangelist,* suggested that the war was the beginning of the scourge of God upon the nation for its national sins. The editor of the New School Presbyterian *Watchman of the Valley,* of Cincinnati, was "disgusted" with the war spirit which swept Washington and was convinced that the war was "instigated and waged . . . for the maintenance and perpetuity . . . of slavery."[3]

When some secular newspapers in New York City charged the clergy with entering the political arena because they remonstrated against war, the editor of Chicago's New School Presbyterian *Western Herald* defended the right of the clergy to speak out and insisted that God was the great political as well as ecclesiastical teacher. The *Watchman of the Valley* echoed these sentiments. "Religion and Politics" and "Church and State" were watchwords of Satan that "his political minions" used to try to prevent the pulpit from ever-deprecating war.[4]

Several presbyteries on the eastern seaboard passed resolutions in April 1846 lamenting the growth of the war spirit, and the New School Presbyterian General Assembly passed resolutions recommending that ministers present the subject of peace to their congregations on the first Sabbath of July. After the General Assembly adjourned, the editor of the *Western Herald* pleaded that prayer be rendered incessantly that the spirit of war be rebuked from the earth if consistent with retribution due to the wicked. The editor of the *New York Evangelist* wanted the clergy to do more than pray. Cheever urged the clergy to carry Christianity into politics to check the war spirit. "If it be a duty to pray, it is also a duty to vote," Cheever added.[5]

When the synods of the New School Presbyterian Church met in the autumn of 1846, the opposition to slavery had increased considerably,[6] and the New School clergy matched the Presbyterian journals in opposition to the war. David H. Riddle of the Third Presbyterian Church of Pittsburgh pronounced an "unqualified condemnation" of the Mexican War in the face of a strong war feeling in the community. Riddle, who was a director of the AHMS, classed war and slavery as evils that had no sanction from Christianity. The *Pittsburgh Commercial Journal,* edited by Riddle's brother, an active Presbyterian layman, called on Christians to refrain from making prayers petitioning God to favor the United States in the bloodstained undertaking of carnage. Nathan Beman of Troy, New York, a vice president of the AHMS, was one of the most active Presbyterian clergymen in the

American Peace Society. When *The Book of Peace* was published by George C. Beckwith, a Presbyterian and president of the American Peace Society, Beman was one of the contributors to the anthology. In Troy in 1846 Beman spoke against the war and repeated much of what he had written in *The Book of Peace.*[7]

Albert Barnes, a leading New School man, exerted his influence against the Mexican War. Barnes, a vice president of the AHMS, delivered a Thanksgiving sermon on "The Virtues and Public Service of William Penn" at the time war was threatening with England. The sermon was published and widely circulated during the early months of the Mexican War. Barnes praised Penn for his position on war and slavery. David B. Coe of the Allen Street Presbyterian Church delivered a discourse on war early in 1846 that was published in the *American National Preacher.* Coe, who was to be one of the secretaries of the AHMS in a few years, declared that one of the evils of war was its withering effect on benevolent and missionary enterprises.[8]

Lyman Beecher, president of Lane Theological Seminary, delivered a Thanksgiving sermon in 1846 in which he dwelt on the signs of the times that indicated the day was drawing near when war would be abolished from the earth. Beecher was a vice president of the AHMS. But not all New School Presbyterians denounced the Mexican War. The conservative Joel Parker delivered a sermon on the Mexican War defending the president that was printed in the equally conservative *Christian Observer* of Philadelphia.[9]

The Congregational journals were in harmony with the views of the New School Presbyterian journals on the Mexican War. The independent Congregational *Oberlin Evangelist* "not only despised and deplored" the Mexican War, but "most unqualifiedly" condemned it. A few weeks later, Henry Cowles, the editor, lamented the failure of the united voice of Christianity to rebuke, in thunderous tones, those responsible for the war. When the editor of the *Vermont Chronicle* learned of the war, he petitioned Heaven to avert the dire calamities and "spare our guilty land."[10]

The normally conservative Congregational *Boston Recorder* received a communication from a correspondent urging that fellowship with slaveholders should no longer be tolerated and that citizens should refrain from voting for or supporting the elevation of slaveholders to positions of influence in the councils of the government. Two weeks later, Martin Moore, the editor of the *Recorder,* informed readers that citizens could not support the authorities in the conduct of the war without becoming "partakers" of the guilt and "without doing violence" to conscience. The *Christian Mirror* of Portland, Maine, also expressed opposition to the war. As "barbarous" and "detestable" as was war, the *Congregational Journal* saw "alleviating considerations" coming from "the all pervading and all-controlling providence of God."[11]

The Congregational associations lost little time in protesting against the war. The Worchester North Conference was typical. It called the Mexican War "an unrighteous war . . . for the purpose of extending and perpetuating the system of American slavery." On May 27, 1846, fifteen hundred people gathered in a mass meeting at Oberlin, Ohio, under Congregational and college leadership and denounced the United States government for making war on Mexico in order to plunder the land to extend slavery. Two weeks later the Western Reserve General Congregational Association met in Portage County, Ohio, and adopted resolutions deprecating the existence of war and slavery.[12]

The Congregational clergy, who had denounced the annexation of Texas in large numbers, turned their attack on the Mexican War in 1846. On December 20, 1846, George B. Cheever spoke on war with special reference to the Mexican War before the American Education Society. A series of articles written for religious journals by Rufus W. Clark, a Congregational minister, received the widest circulation of any pronouncements on the war. Clark, who was a life member of the AHMS, denounced war because it was "opposed to the progress of the gospel." He was convinced that the Mexican War was produced by the influence of slavery. Other Congregational clergymen wrote or spoke against the war.[13]

During the last half of 1846 the New School journals continued their barrage against the Mexican War. The *New York Observer*, which had taken the lead in opposing war when conflict with England appeared imminent early in 1846, broke its silence concerning the Mexican War in August. The editor was firmly committed to the conviction that it was the duty of Christian people to raise their voices against further hostilities. He urged petitions from every city in the country as a means of bringing the fighting to an end. In December the *Observer* printed a petition form furnished by the American Peace Society, and implored Christians to send appeals to Congress.[14] Calvinist opposition to the war came from three sources. Many who strongly opposed the war were members of the American Peace Society and were advocates of the peace movement. The anti-slavery Calvinists were primarily driven by their commitment to free soil. The conservatives were often motivated by the fear of war with England. After the threat of conflict with England was removed and only the free soil issue remained, the *New York Observer* and other conservative journals ceased to oppose the government.

When the presbyteries of the New School church met in the winter of 1847, the subject of the Mexican War occupied the attention of many sessions. The Presbytery of Grand River, Ohio, held that ministers were "imperiously bound to preach against war," and the Presbytery of Elyria, Ohio, agreed that it was "the duty" of ministers "to preach on the subject of peace." In April, George B. Cheever addressed the Third Presbytery of New York on the necessity of taking action on the Mexican War. The presbytery assigned Cheever, William Patton, and Edwin F. Hatfield to a committee to draft the presbytery's position on the subject of war. Patton and Hatfield were members of the executive committee of the AHMS. The presbytery adopted the report presented by the committee declaring that all Christians, ministers, and churches were called upon to "use all their influence to arrest the progress" of the war.[15]

After July 1846, the Congregational journals turned from a protest against involvement in an unjust and unnecessary war to an examination of the purpose and probable results of the conflict. The *New England Puritan* became convinced in August that the war was being conducted for the sake of conquest, which should be earnestly protested by Christian patriots. Among other reasons, annexation should be opposed because the extension of slavery would endanger civil and religious institutions. The editor of the *Oberlin Evangelist* cautioned the Christian public that unless people humbled themselves and gave up the warfare and its objective, a tremendous catastrophe would be visited upon the nation. The editor of the *Boston Recorder* suggested that citizens should "vote more in the *fear of God* than in the fear or favor of . . . party," so as to bring to an end "the most needless, and . . . savage war," which was being fought "to strengthen and lengthen slavery's accursed reign." A correspondent to the *Christian Mirror* declared that public opinion was united in the belief that the war had been instigated to enlarge the boundaries of slavery, but if people resisted this master effort, it would be slavery's expiring throe. The suggestion that Christians should take their cause to the ballot box received general approval from the Congregational press. In an editorial entitled "Duty of the Christian in Relation to the War," the editor of the *New England Puritan* called on Christians to "promote repentance and national reformation" by prayer and the exercise of "Political franchise." The editor of the *Vermont Chronicle* also urged political measures because God would "hold every man accountable for the views and feelings which he entertained." He urged that Congress be petitioned as the American Peace Society suggested.[16]

The issue of the church's involvement in politics did not remain in the abstract. On August 8, 1846, President Polk asked for an appropriation of two million dollars to enable him to bring about a speedy peace. When the House of Representatives took up the measure, David Wilmot, a representative from Pennsylvania and a Calvinist layman, proposed an amendment to guarantee that slavery would be prohibited in any territory acquired from Mexico. The Wilmot Proviso passed the House but was defeated in the Senate, and it was necessary to carry the proposal over into the second session of the Twenty-Ninth Congress. As the second session met in December 1846, the editor of the *New York Evangelist* thought it probable that the extension of slavery to the territories wrested from Mexico would come up for discussion. With this issue before Congress, the editor informed his readers that it was in the power of Christians to rule the country by Christian principles and to check the "fetters" that endangered the nation. He expressed surprise at the unanimity and firmness of feeling in the North during the congressional debate on the proviso when another appropriation bill for three million dollars was introduced. The *Evangelist* was opposed to the acquisition of territory that would be open to slavery because it would offer no "gain to the great American people" but would "stimulate the slave markets" of the East. When the House of Representatives initially adopted the appropriation bill with the proviso, the editor reported that the power of the slaveholding interests had been checked by the assertion of the principles and interests of the free labor states, and when the proviso failed to be adopted by the Senate, he named the five senators from the free states who had voted against it so that their baseness could be more easily remembered.[17]

The more conservative *New York Observer* was of the same view as the *Evangelist* concerning the question of the acquisition of territory in which slavery was tolerated. The *Observer* called on the religious press "to give utterance to their sentiments on this momentous question." Two months later, after the appropriation bill passed without the proviso, the editor served notice that the North did not want any more territory that was open to slavery. The conservative *Christian Observer* of Philadelphia steered clear of political questions, but expressed approval of the movement, which was flooding Congress with petitions urging that peace be secured without "any further effusion of blood."[18] The New School Presbyterian press in the West did not discuss the free soil issue during the first half of 1847.

The *Anti-Papist*, a Presbyterian journal in Cincinnati edited by Epaphras Goodman, informed its readers that there was moral power enough to rebuke the "blood-thirsty spirit" if those who opposed war would but speak out. During the period of the Mexican War, the nativist movement declined significantly. The efforts of some Democratic press to rally the support of the Protestant churches to the administration by suggesting that Mexican church property be seized met with condemnation by the Protestant journals. The churches emphasized that war was being made on a weak sister republic. Protestant churches and journals were preoccupied with raising funds for relief of Ireland's famine in 1847 instead of conducting a religious crusade against Mexico. "O that the millions of treasure which it has cost . . . to butcher the Mexicans . . . had been expended to feed the starving masses of Europe," lamented the editor of the *Watchman of the Valley*. The spirit was taken out of the nativist movement by the uniform support of the war by the Catholic press and the united opposition to the war by Protestant journals and clergymen.[19]

Charles B. Boynton, pastor of the Sixth Street Congregational Church of Cincinnati, was a favorite speaker at nativist meetings in the West, but during the Mexican War, Boynton directed his oratory against slavery and the war. In January, 1847, he delivered a lecture before the Library Association of Cincinnati in which he predicted that the United States would ultimately extend its territory to all of the region north of Panama, but he condemned the Mexican War because "institutions propagated by the sword also perish." On July 5, Boynton delivered an address before the Native Americans of Cincinnati. Instead of dwelling on Protestant-Catholic relations, he spoke on the theme that the Mexican War was a southern plot to seize new territory for the expansion of slavery. He beseeched Christians to arouse themselves to create a public sentiment that would "end the war, and the power of slavery forever."[20]

The Congregationalists on the Western Reserve were united in their opposition to war and slavery. Amasa Walker, a professor at Oberlin College, spoke regularly on the subject of peace. On July 4, 1847, Professor John Morgan delivered an oration in Elyria in which he condemned war and slavery and showed the relation between them in the current crisis, and Asa Mahan, president of Oberlin College, attended peace meetings held locally as well as many that met abroad, often speaking at them. Mahan eventually recorded his sentiments on war in his book, *Science of Moral Philosophy*.[21] The Mexican War contributed to a final break in the limited cooperation between the AHMS and independent Congregationalists on the Western Reserve, who formed a closer alliance with the AMA.

Reverend Henry Ward Beecher, pastor of a New School Presbyterian church in Indianapolis, had formerly believed the church should not be concerned with social reforms, but by 1846 Beecher felt the Mexican War had crystallized the sentiment of the pastor and congregation enough that he began to discuss slavery and war from the pulpit.[22] However, Beecher was criticized by conservatives for preaching "Whig political sermons from the pulpit."[23] In the autumn of 1847, Beecher accepted a call to the Plymouth Congregational Church in Brooklyn, New York, where he was to achieve significance and continue his new course without hesitation.[24] One of the most critical sermons delivered against the Mexican War came from a pulpit occupied by Rufus Clark, a Congregational minister in Portsmouth, New Hampshire. Clark asserted that to enter on a bloody and destructive war for the extension of slavery was "to be false to the principles on which our institutions were founded, false to our religion, false to our high mission, and false to our God."[25]

The action of the New School Presbyterian General Assembly in May 1847 increased the number of sermons in New School churches on the subject of war. The Presbytery of Utica had instructed its commissioner to the General Assembly to urge the church to recommend that ministers preach on peace. The commissioner's resolution was adopted and the second Sabbath in July was designated. The *Watchman of the Valley* reported that the day set aside for peace sermons was extensively observed with hundreds of discourses. Although a majority were abstract discussions about war, many dealt specifically with the Mexican War and condemned it in strong language.[26]

The greatest response to the General Assembly's recommendation came from the Ohio Presbyterians. The pastor of the Third Presbyterian Church of Cincinnati spoke on the subject of American independence and alluded to the Mexican War, expressing decided opposition to it. The pastor of the Presbyterian Church in Elyria, Ohio, asserted that the Mexican War was "the most cruel and oppressive, inexcusable, and nefarious" war that the pages of history recorded. If supplies were cut off, he asserted, the butchery, bloodshed, and rapine would have to stop. Samuel C. Aiken, of the First Presbyterian Church of Cleveland, was convinced that the war was being fought to extend slavery. The pastor of the Presbyterian church in Ohio City delivered sermons against the Mexican War on two consecutive Sundays, entering fully and fearlessly into the question of slavery and war and condemning both in severe language.[27]

Horace Bushnell, pastor of a New School Presbyterian church in Cincinnati, undoubtedly had the greatest impact on Christian opinion. Bushnell, who was soon to take charge of a Congregational church in Hartford, Connecticut, delivered the address at the annual meeting of the AHMS in May 1847 on "Barbarism, The First Danger," in which he issued a timely warning concerning slavery and the war.[28] When the New School Presbyterian Synod of Cincinnati met in October 1847, Bushnell addressed the clergy and urged them to follow the principles of the gospel instead of the standard of public sentiment. The synod proceeded to adopt resolutions condemning the Mexican War.[29]

The discourse that attracted the most attention throughout the nation was the sermon preached in Springfield, Illinois, by Albert Hale, an Illinois agent for the AHMS. He asserted that many regarded the Mexican War to be a master stroke of policy on the part of our government "to protect, perpetuate and extend slavery by the acquisition of new territory to be formed into new slave states." The next day the session of the Illinois Constitutional Convention vigorously debated Hale's sermon. A delegate from southern Illinois introduced a resolution to withdraw the invitation that had been extended to Hale to lead devotions the following week. The resolution was tabled, but when Hale appeared, the delegate interrupted the prayer by hissing, clapping his hands, and withdrawing from the hall. As a precaution against insults to other clergymen, subsequent morning devotions were cancelled. On June 17, 1847, Hale and the other AHMS agents, missionaries, and patrons of the northwestern states met in Chicago for the Fourth Presbyterian and Congregational Convention. The question of slavery and war took priority in the meeting. The convention adopted measures on slavery and condemned the Mexican War in strong language. Slavery and war were considered equally hostile to the prosperity of domestic missions.[30]

During the Thanksgiving season, the clergy renewed their denunciation of war. Samuel D. Buchard preached a sermon in New York and enumerated the causes of national solicitude of which the most serious were slavery, the "ulcer upon our body politic," and the "dreadful and terrible evil" that existed in the Mexican War. Nathan Beman was severely censured by the Democratic Party press for speaking against war and slavery. Beman, a director of the AHMS, viewed war as a curse that had for ages scorched and withered nations, but he was convinced that the time would come when it would be removed from the face of the earth.[31]

When the New School Presbyterians met in the autumn sessions of the synods, the subject of the evils of the Mexican War occupied a place on the agenda of several meetings. In October the Synod of New York and New Jersey met and "boldly and fully condemned" the Mexican War by adopting resolutions recommending that all ministers "labor by prayer, preaching, and all other approved means, to bring an end to the war."[32]

The Synod of Cincinnati resolved that it was the duty of Christians to speak out "plainly the words of truth and soberness" on the war, "the greatest of physical and moral evils." The *Watchman of the Valley* reported that "the clear and decided expression of sentiment was adopted without a dissenting voice." The *Cincinnati Enquirer* accused the clergy of trying to preach a crusade against the government. The same resolutions were brought before the Synod of Indiana and adopted after amendments were made to remove the phrase *"an unrighteous war"* in an ecclesiastical document. The Presbyterians in Chicago took the lead in calling a local peace convention in Chicago. The resolutions committee was made up of a Baptist minister and the New School Presbyterians Flavel Bascom and R. W. Patterson, life member and life director, respectively, of the AHMS. The members of the convention were distressed that the nation's resources were being wasted on a war that conflicted with the gospel when those resources could be used to improve the harbors and navigable waters, to develop the country's vast resources, and to diffuse knowledge as well as public morals and religion.[33]

In Troy, New York, the Liberty Street Presbyterian Church withdrew from all ecclesiastical connection on March 5, 1848, because the church considered sectarianism to be the source of war and slavery. War with Mexico also contributed to the separation of the Free Synod of Cincinnati from the New School Presbyterian Church in 1847. John Rankin of the Presbytery of Ripley called a convention to meet at the end of the sessions of the General Assembly. When the General Assembly failed to take radical action to deal with the Mexican War's new potential for expanding slavery in both church and state, the Free Synod of Cincinnati was formed. At the time of the separation, the Free Synod drew up an address that, among other measures, avowed that the Mexican War was being fought "by the slave power" for the purpose of securing a portion of "territory in order to extend and perpetuate the curse of slavery and domestic slave trade."[34]

The Congregational associations showed a hostility to war similar to the Presbyterian judicatories. The New Haven East Congregational Association regarded the Mexican War as peculiarly abhorrent because "it was commenced for the purpose of acquiring or securing more slave territory." The Vermont Congregational Association condemned both slavery and war. The association recommended that the churches make the early termination of hostilities a subject of special prayer, and urged the churches to aid the American Peace Society. The Woburn (Massachusetts) Association of Congregational Ministers, the Rutland Congregational Consociation, and the Crittenden Congregational Consociation, both of Vermont, condemned the Mexican War in strong language.[35]

Many individual Congregational clergymen were inclined to speak against the war in stronger language than the associations. The clergymen ridiculed the arguments that the war was necessary to preserve national honor or that it was an act of divine providence. Burdett Hart of Connecticut pointed out that there was a "higher honor" demanding that a powerful nation treat a weak neighbor with "long suffering and forebearance" rather than with arbitrary high-handedness. To expansionist assertions that the United States was destined to expand its boundary from ocean to ocean, Milton Bramen of Massachusetts countered with a question: "How do they know what the divine decree is with respect to the ultimate extent of the Union?"[36]

In April 1847, the Congregational clergy delivered the traditional Fast Day sermons on subjects of public interest. A considerable number of the sermons dealt with the subject of war. Joseph C. Lovejoy of Cambridgeport, Massachusetts, charged that the object of the war was "to extend slavery over a free territory" that would "make *fifteen or twenty States.*" He urged that public meetings be called in every town throughout the country "to condemn the war and demand a speedy peace" by recalling the army from Mexican territory. The *Hartford Daily Courant* reported that attacks were opened up from the Congregational pulpits upon the iniquities of the administration. Fast Day sermons were delivered in Hartford, Connecticut, by Walter Clark, William W. Patton, and Horace Bushnell. All of the sermons condemned the war as a wicked invasion of Mexico. Clark, Patton, and Bushnell were all directors of the AHMS.[37] William S. Tyler, a life member of the AHMS, stated in a Fast Day sermon in Amherst, Massachusetts, that those who insisted the war was started by an act of Mexico had "uttered a *monstrous lie.*" Tyler denounced the political expediency that he felt had brought on the war.[38]

The Congregational journals, in 1847, showed progressively more determined opposition to the war on the grounds of antislavery. "While Humanity is outraged, our country disgraced, the Laws of Heaven suspended, and Hell put in force, by the conduct and continuance of the Mexican War," the editor of the *Boston Recorder* pledged, "we shall not cease . . . to rouse the public mind to a sense of the awful guilt brought upon this nation." By August 1847, the editor of the *New England Puritan* saw "war and slavery, two of the worst monsters that ever cursed the earth," as partners engaged in a war to extend "the dominions of slaveholders." The *Christian Observatory*, of Boston, agreed that the Mexican War was being fought "for the extension and perpetuation of negro slavery." Although the *Vermont Chronicle* counselled that the evils of war should be dealt with by memorials and petitions to Congress, the *Observatory* believed that the solution was to have every vote cast "under a deep sense of responsibility" to God and country. By October 1847, the *Boston Recorder* could rejoice that "so many religious papers, nearly, if not quite all in the *free* states" had arrayed themselves against the war. In December 1847, the *Congregational Journal* warned that slavery was threatening to break up the Union unless it was permitted to extend its borders. The editor urged the North to limit the boundaries of slavery.[39]

During the last half of 1847 the Presbyterian journals became increasingly concerned about territorial acquisitions from Mexico. The editor of the *Ohio Observer* agreed with the *Boston Recorder* in its statement that the United States should end the war by withdrawing from Mexican soil. The controversy concerning the extension of slavery kept the Wilmot Proviso before Congress, and the editor of the *Evangelist* urged all opponents of territorial annexation to close ranks in support of the proviso. The editor of the conservative *Christian Observer* prided himself on his silence on party questions connected with the war, but weariness with its prolongation caused him to express gratification at the military victories that were won.[40]

From the beginning of the war, journals that supported the Democratic administration had delivered strong rebukes to clergy who denounced the war from the pulpit. The *Boston Post* had taken the lead in New England, and the *Cleveland Plain Dealer* was among the most vocal in condemning clergy in the West. The Whig press, by contrast, defended the clergy who spoke against the war. David Hale, editor of the *New York Journal of Commerce* and an active Congregational layman, defended the clergy and urged Christians to demand that the war be abandoned. It was the *New York Tribune*, however, that took the lead in defending the right of the clergy to speak their sentiments.[41]

There was evidence that the efforts of congregations and religious press and the measures of the religious associations were beginning to have an impact on public opinion by the early months of 1848. A correspondent to the *New York Tribune* was convinced that Henry Ward Beecher's sermon "A politico-moral discourse . . . on the Mexican War" delivered at Providence, Rhode Island, in May had "uncommon effect." He saw significant changes in public opinion taking shape. "Hundreds more of our citizens will now look to the principles involved in their votes at the Presidential election, than four years ago, particularly to its effect on the awful problem of Slavery," he added.[42]

In New York the Presbyterian clergy were accused of entering the election and using their influence to bring about an unexpected turn of events. The *New York Observer* defended the clergy because some political questions were "so intimately related to the moral interests of the country that no time or place" was "too sacred for their discussion." The *Christian Observatory* also supported the right of clergy to speak out on civic questions. "The same authority which requires them . . . to pray, requires them also to discharge all the offices of the Christian patriot," instructed the editor.[43]

When the church associations met in 1848, the new concern about the extension of slavery to the territories was given consideration in the sessions. The presbyteries of Utica and Buffalo requested that ministers keep the subject of the crisis before their people and the presbyteries of Chemung and Angelica, New York, felt the time had arrived to deny fellowship to slaveholders.[44]

The end of the war brought the Presbyterians and Congregationalists fully into accord on the necessity to resist the extension of slavery to the territories. On February 2, 1848, the Mexican commissioners signed the Treaty of Guadalupe Hidalgo and forwarded it to President Polk. Now that the issue of the continuation of the war was removed from the public forum, the New York Evangelist turned its full attention to the extension of slavery. "We have all the hope," the editor said, "of a growing hostility to slavery among the people of the North." When John Calhoun pressed for equal rights for the institutions of the South in the territory, the editor of the New York Observer warned that if Congress permitted "the foot print of the slave" to corrupt territory that was formerly free, "the spirit of revolution" would revisit the land. A week later the editor returned to the subject. "We Solemnly believe that if the Southern proviso is insisted on," he warned again, "the calculating men of the East, and North will begin to figure out the value of the Union." He added, "disunion lurks in this slavery question, and . . . the Southern Senators, in pressing their views, are aiding the abolitionists in the suicidal work of federal dissolution." The New York Evangelist challenged Calhoun's argument by denying that justice to the South required that a legislative mandate be given to "new markets for human flesh among the mines of New Mexico." The Religious Recorder of Syracuse, New York, refrained from commenting on the political issues of the Mexican War but spoke out on the moral questions.[45]

The New England Puritan accepted the political challenge that came as a result of a war that had been "fought to acquire territory for the expansion of slavery." The editor was convinced that the mass of people were tired of a policy of subservience to the South. Martin Moore, editor of the Boston Recorder, asserted that the extension of slavery to a newly acquired territory that had always been free was a moral question that related to political action. "By every lawful and constitutional means we are bound to prevent the extension of slavery," he maintained.[46]

The question of the extension of slavery to the territories became the dominant issue in the presidential election of 1848. Several denominations insisted that it was a moral question that deeply concerned Christianity. Clergymen urged Christians to set aside party loyalty and vote their conscience. Since Zachary Taylor was a slaveholder, and Lewis Cass, the Democratic candidate for President, advocated a settlement of the status of the territory by the people who lived there, many clergy and Christian laymen adhered to the Free Soil party, which stood on the platform of the Wilmot Proviso. Reuben Hitchcock, an active layman in the New School Presbyterian Church, united with the Free Soil movement and delivered political lectures throughout northern Ohio in support of this party. Hitchcock, who was the brother of Peter Hitchcock, Jr., a Presbyterian minister of Columbus, Ohio, had formerly been an active and committed Whig. Samuel Blackwell, a "staunch Presbyterian and a dedicated Whig," spoke against Taylor, calling him "the Robber President."[47]

The masses of the Christian public who had strong antiwar convictions entered the ranks of the antislavery movement because they were now convinced that the aggressive tendencies of slavery knew no bounds. Antislavery men who had no deep-seated feelings concerning war, because of their belief in the manifest destiny of the Christian republic, condemned the war as a plot of the slave power. The peace movement became the door through which many in the religious community entered the ranks of the free soil and antislavery movements. Abolitionism was much more controversial and radical during the 1830s, and many moderates refrained from becoming active in the movement. They participated in the peace movement, however, and as the peace movement was transformed by antislavery political action in 1848, they followed the opponents of the Mexican War into antislavery politics. The Mexican War broadened the support of the antislavery movement considerably by convincing many moderates of the aggressive nature of slavery.

The American Peace Society had been closely identified with the clergy and laymen who directed the AHMS. Laurens P. Hickok, a director of the AHMS and a professor at Auburn Theological Seminary, was one of the earliest writers and speakers on the subject of peace. George C. Beckwith, the corresponding secretary of the American Peace Society, was a member of the Presbytery of Newburyport, Synod of Albany, and a life member of the AHMS. Aaron Foster, his brother-in-law and a Presbyterian minister, sometimes served as an agent of the American Peace Society. After the Mexican War broke out in 1846, Theodore Frelinghuysen, a leader in the Dutch Reformed Church and a vice president of the AHMS, became president of the American Peace Society. He replaced Anson G. Phelps, a Presbyterian layman and a life director of the AHMS. Henry Dwight, of Geneva, New York, president of the AHMS, was also a vice president of the American Peace Society. When the Mexican War got under way, Milton Badger, secretary of the AHMS, requested the American Peace Society to send the missionaries of the AHMS free copies of the principal peace publications. Beckwith complied and solicited funds to cover the expense of the project through Presbyterian and Congregational journals and church associations in New England and the North Atlantic states.[48]

Edward Norris Kirk, pastor of Mount Vernon Church, Boston, was one of the most important links in the common efforts of the American Peace Society and the AHMS. Kirk, a director of the American Peace Society and an influential clergyman in both Presbyterian and Congregational circles, delivered a discourse on "War, An Evidence of Human Depravity," in the Mount Vernon Congregational Church in 1846. He traced all wars to the depraved passions of men. In 1847 Kirk spoke at the anniversary of the American Peace Society. He "came forth with all the thunder of his eloquence against the war and the extension of slavery." He was convinced that the Mexican War originated from three causes: "the predominance of the slave power, the extension of slavery, and a third, for military glory."[49]

Since Christian and benevolent people believed that the objective of the Mexican War was to secure territory for slavery, the American Peace Society and the AHMS joined hands in resisting the twin evils of war and slavery and in preventing the assumed objective from being carried out. This marriage of the Peace Society and the AHMS would be a factor in causing most of the Calvinist peace advocates to shed their commitment to peace when the Civil War began. Once the Mexican territory was acquired, the friends of domestic missions were determined that this virgin missionary field would be free. Free missions were fundamental to the concept of free soil. Free schools and free labor were correlative concepts. Free missions and free religion would help to force a sectional confrontation of enormous proportions. Garrison saw the effects of the war on religious groups that were committed to domestic missions. "I long to see the day when the great issue with the Slave Power . . . will be made by all the free States," he wrote to his wife in July, 1848. "The Free Soil movement inevitably leads to it, and hence I hail it as the beginning of the end."[50]

The clergy's involvement in politics during the Mexican War surpassed its past political experience, and the stage was set for future involvement when slavery became a moral as well as a political question. The morality of slavery was not a question of religious dogma or an issue confined to particular religious groups. The nativist movement, which had reached its peak in 1844, was dissipated by the Mexican War. The annexation of Texas and the Mexican War established slavery as the unnatural monster and beast that threatened a free society and religion. The war checked the Protestant minority that would have welcomed a religious crusade and dealt nativism a serious blow, turning Protestant attention to the fear of the extension of slavery in the territories. The War with Mexico accelerated the growth of antislavery influence in the domestic missionary organizations of all denominations, and firmly established among the northern churches the concept of the slave power, which molded antislavery sentiment in the North into a more general and pervasive anti-southern feeling. It was only when a lull developed in the sectional controversy that the nativist movement would surface during the canvass of state and local elections. Many clergymen who had formerly stood aside entered the political contests on the side of antislavery. "Never again would they stand mute," wrote Richard Sewell, "when presented with threats of slavery expansion." Evangelical leaders had formed a common front and they warned expansionists that if Manifest Destiny was taken up again, slavery must have no part in it.[51]

The Fugitive Slave Law:
Ferment and Agitation
in Church and State

*I*n November 1846, Jonathan Blanchard wrote to the *Western Citizen* that a sermon he had preached "without opprobrium in . . . the West, occasioned a Monday explosion when delivered in an old congregation in Massachusetts." Expressions of opposition to slavery were common correspondence coming into the New York office of the AHMS from missionaries in the Northwest. Thaddeus B. Hurlbut, assistant editor of the *Alton Observer,* urged that the method of dealing with slavery should be that of taking away "the forage of this monster Beast." It was rumored, Hurlbut revealed, that the missionaries of the AHMS were afraid to speak out their convictions and if they should, their reports would be suppressed. He warned the New York office that the issue of slavery was becoming more important in the West. The West, which had long been recognized as more friendly to the cause of abolitionism than the East, continued to be the nucleus of the antislavery feeling in the Presbyterian Church.[1]

Although addressing itself primarily to the problems of the ABCFM, the Synod of Cincinnati, early in 1846, spoke in universal terms when the body declared: "It is of vital importance that the gospel which the missionaries preach, and practice, should give no sanction, directly or indirectly, to the sin of slaveholding."[2] Even though the synod was strongly antislavery in sentiment, it was not sufficiently advanced to satisfy the Presbytery of Ripley. In July, 1846, the Presbytery of Ripley published a statement that it could hold no relation with the General Assembly that "implied fellowship," until all constitutional means had been used "to purge itself from slavery." The presbytery would consult with sister judicatories on the propriety of forming an antislavery Presbyterian Church. The following week it issued a call for a convention to meet in Cincinnati, after the Assembly of 1847, to establish a new denomination.

On October 10, 1846, Judge S. C. Stevens of Indiana issued a call for a meeting of evangelical Christians to convene in Cincinnati concurrently with the Ripley meeting "to devise means of action against slavery." The decision of the assembly in the Graham case and the extension of the New School Presbyterian Church in the South to include the Synod of Mississippi had created a determination in the Presbytery of Ripley to leave the New School Church unless the Assembly of 1847 took a stand against slavery. The convention met and the Free Presbyterian Church was created by the congregations that withdrew from the Synod of Cincinnati.[3]

The demands for action against slavery by the denominations and the benevolent institutions went far beyond the Synod of Cincinnati. In January 1847, Presbyterian and Congregational representatives from Portage, Summit, and Medina (Ohio) counties convened at Akron to decide if a convention should be held on the New School Church and slavery problems. The convention met in February and asked the forthcoming General Assembly to issue a new declaration of its position on slavery. The meeting resolved that the missionary boards with which they were connected "ought to make a declaration of sentiment, disapproving of the admission of slaveholders to the mission churches."[4]

The Presbytery of Grand River, Ohio, began to suffer severely because of withdrawals of churches in 1847. Congregations in Austinburg, Painesville, and Thompson withdrew because they opposed human bondage. Many of the churches that left the Western Reserve associated themselves with the AMA. The presbytery requested the Assembly of 1847 to take "uncompromising action" on the subject, and when this was not done, the presbytery was pressured to withdraw from the assembly and to organize a new body on the principles of a "New England Association." In June 1847, a writer from the Presbytery of Knox, Illinois, complained to the editor of the *Watchman of the Valley* that his presbytery had lost almost half of its members during the past year because of the position of the church on human bondage. The Synod of Western Reserve refused a request to withdraw from the assembly in September 1847.[5]

In May 1847, aware of the upheavals that had taken place in the Northwest, and knowing that greater storms were brewing, the secretaries of the AHMS returned to the subject of slavery in their publication, the *Home Missionary*. Three missionaries were cited to show that slavery was the great hindrance to the gospel. Charles Hall, the Presbyterian editor, felt this should be convincing evidence against the extension of slavery to the national domain or any territory annexed to our country. But the importance of retaining missionaries in the slave states was vindicated. "By whatever steps this gigantic obstacle . . . shall be removed," concluded Hall, the missionaries "feel confident that the ministration of the Gospel must have a large share in the results."⁶ The officers of the AHMS were probably influenced in the publication of the *Home Missionary* article by the fact that the fourth Presbyterian and Congregational Convention of the Northwest was scheduled to meet in Chicago in June 1847. The sentiment on slavery expressed at the convention was more conservative than the viewpoint of the rank and file among the Calvinist Christians of the Northwest. Resolutions were reported and adopted by the convention expressing the belief that the church had "the power so to apply the principles of the gospel to the institution of slavery . . . that it shall soon wither and die."⁷ A resolution in favor of antislavery missions introduced from the floor was rejected.⁸ The mission board exerted much influence on the convention.

Jonathan Blanchard assessed the value of the convention by reminding antislavery Christians that the AHMS had sustained John Fee as an antislavery missionary while refusing to commission a slaveholder. He, however, criticized the Society for maintaining forty-five churches that admitted slaveholders to fellowship.⁹ Antislavery Christians wanted free soil principles to apply in church as well as state.

The political events of 1849 and 1850 caused antislavery Christians to take a less flexible attitude toward slavery in relation to missions. In February 1850, a committee in Cincinnati proposed the organization of a Christian Anti-Slavery Convention to convene in April in that city. A circular was printed and distributed throughout the West announcing the meeting. More than one thousand responses had been received to the call by the middle of March. According to one of the organizers, the consensus was "let us have action." Epaphras Goodman informed the editor of the *Oberlin Evangelist*, Henry Cowles, that "disorganization" was not the objective of the convention. "We would fain avert such a catastrophe by expelling the most dangerous disorganizing element that ever threatened the organic integrity of the Church. . . . If it can not be done, then we must try to secure the Church and let her *organism* go." In an editorial, Cowles agreed with these conclusions. "We have long felt that it is vain for the free North to hope that God in his providence will abolish slavery until his Church shall have done their duty in the case," Cowles responded.¹⁰

While Congress considered the admission of California to the Union and a stronger Fugitive Slave Law, the Christian Anti-Slavery Convention convened in Cincinnati on April 17, 1850.¹¹ The convention was composed of many denominations, but principally of Congregationalists and Free Presbyterians. Many supporters of the AHMS were present. The developments in 1850 brought about a change in Blanchard. He headed a committee of the Central Congregational Association of Illinois that petitioned the Cincinnati convention to start a movement "to divorce American Christianity from American Slavery." The fact that the AHMS had "increased its slaveholding dependencies" despite the antislavery agitation gave impetus to Blanchard's sentiments.[12]

When the convention met, Judge S. C. Stevens was selected to preside over this determined body. A resolution proposed by John Fee was adopted urging "the friends of a pure Christianity" to separate themselves from all slaveholding churches, ecclesiastical bodies, and missionary organizations that were not fully divorced from the sin of slaveholding. George Whipple represented the AMA at the convention. From New York, Lewis Tappan urged him not to be reluctant to speak out boldly. "When such men as Dr. [Leonard] Woods and Professor [Moses] Stuart sign a letter approving of D[aniel] Webster's speech, it is time we all took open and decided ground. I fear we have been too timid." Whipple attempted to show that the ABCFM and AHMS were intimately connected with slavery, and their slow gradual yielding to public sentiment still left them far from being satisfactory to antislavery men. In a discussion of the work of the Christian Anti-Slavery Convention and its criticism of the AHMS, the *Central Christian Herald* of Cincinnati, organ of the New School synods of the West, expressed hope that the AHMS would "speedily withdraw all connection with slaveholding churches."[13]

The convention set the stage for a vigorous Christian antislavery movement that organized the Western Home and Foreign Missionary Association (WHFMA) in June 1850 to aid antislavery churches that had withdrawn from the AHMS. The new society's constitution pledged that it would not support missionaries or churches that supported, countenanced, or tolerated slavery. The WHFMA was considered an auxiliary to the AMA, but the organizers of the new society aimed at making it more than a western agency. It was the desire of the directors of the WHFMA that the control of the western home missionary field would be entirely under their aegis.[14]

An aggressive campaign began to collect funds and organize local societies affiliated with the WHFMA. The *Oberlin Evangelist* was critical of the new organization. It was the belief of Henry Cowles, the editor, and F. D. Parish, an Ohio director of the AMA, that the effort could be better administered through the channels of the AMA. The new society took over support of churches in the Free Synod of Cincinnati that had been aided by the AMA. The Board of Home and Foreign Missions of the Free Presbyterian Church of America, which had been formed in 1848 as an auxiliary to the AMA, was absorbed into the WHFMA.[15]

The Cincinnati-based organization held its first annual meeting in Cleveland in October 1850. The Cleveland assembly agreed that the society should sponsor a publication, and in December 1850 the *Free Missionary* of Cincinnati appeared, edited by Epaphras Goodman and Charles B. Boynton. The publication took as its motto "*No Religious Fellowship* with Scandalous Sins," and stated that its purpose would be to "purge out the deadly foes that nestle" in the bosom of the church.[16]

During the same period an article appeared in the *Home Missionary* revealing the extent of the division. The article, "Men of the Right Stamp," contained an excerpt of a letter from a Missouri missionary and a reply by the editor. This article was to furnish material for the strongest defense of the AHMS in the antislavery Northwest during the critical period that lay ahead in 1851. In the columns of the *Home Missionary*, T. S. Reeve, of St. Joseph, Missouri, was anonymously quoted in reference to a request that a larger portion of missionaries be sent to labor in the bounds of the Presbytery of Lexington, Missouri. "Send . . . men who will let politics alone — let slavery alone — except to bring to bear upon it the express instruction of Paul." In answer the editor replied: "This society seems to be the province of the missionaries as ministers of Christ, amenable to Him and to their respective ecclesiastical bodies, to determine for themselves the occasion and the way in which they will bring the Gospel to bear on this and every other evil."[17]

Knowing that it was in the Northwest that public opinion was more demanding for a new position concerning slavery, Badger sent his Illinois friend, G. S. F. Savage, correspondent for the *Prairie Herald*, two extra copies of the November issue of the Society's journal. "Would the article, if copied into the 'Prairie Herald' be likely to quiet the apprehensions of any in your region, who are told that the American Home Missionary Society is a pro-slavery institution?" he inquired. A correspondent to the *Independent* reported that "the friends of the AHM Society . . . in the Northwest" regarded the remarks in the *Home Missionary* "as indicative of progress in the right direction." The *Ohio Observer* approved of the article in the Society's journal. "The gospel is the only remedy for sin and all its consequent evils," agreed the editor.[18]

But a growing number of clergy in the Northwest now demanded action rather than resolutions. M. N. Miles, of Illinois, was in this category. In March 1851, he delivered a sermon entitled, "The Gospel Versus Sin," in which he maintained that it was a delusion to assume that the gospel had the power to exterminate sin while it was still given a seat in the church. The "Men of the Right Stamp" article did not vindicate the Society but rather "fully established the Truth . . . that the lips of the missionary are sealed in Missouri," he concluded.[19] Thus the opponents of servitude in the West were divided into two groups concerning the institution of slavery. One group felt the scripture was adequate to remove the southern system if given free rein. The other believed that the gospel could have no effect as long as slaveholders were admitted to the southern churches. During 1851 these two groups were to come into direct conflict.

New political events accounted for a rising radicalism in the church with slavery as "the focal point of clerical public discourse."[20] The revival ethos had played a large part in making slavery a critical political issue, and now the introduction and passage of the Fugitive Slave Law caused a ferment in the church as well as the state. The degree to which the Fugitive Slave Law was responsible for the rising antislavery sentiment in the churches of the Northwest is recorded in the proceedings of the churches and the denominational newspapers. The Presbytery of Galena, Illinois, denounced the act for violating "in its spirit and operation, the law of benevolence and mercy laid down in the Bible," and the Synod of Peoria, Illinois, adopted identical measures. When the General Assembly met, the Presbytery of Belvidere, Illinois, sent up a memorial asking the highest judicatory to take action on the Fugitive Slave Law. After the assembly failed to act, the Presbytery of Alton, Illinois, adopted resolutions condemning the law as "contrary to the dictates of humanity, . . . the principles of justice, and . . . the law of God," and the Synod of Illinois bore testimony against the "inhumanity and injustice" of the law. Other Presbyterian judicatories in the Northwest came forward and took a "higher law" stand. Only the Synod of Michigan failed to take action after considering the question of higher law and civil obedience. Some black and some white ministers sustained by the AMA went a step further by actively participating in the work of vigilance committees resisting the Fugitive Slave Law.[21]

Among the Congregational associations of the Northwest, sentiment against the Fugitive Slave Law was equally strong. For example, the Kalamazoo, Michigan, Congregational Association denounced the act as "in direct conflict with the word of God . . . and . . . not, therefore, obligatory upon conscience." The Western Reserve Association went a step further and denounced the efforts of some clergymen to defend the law as "indicative of a deplorable perversion of the ministry of righteousness and the paramount law of God." When the Christian Anti-Slavery Convention met in Chicago in April 1851, it reflected the sentiment of the Calvinist churches of the Northwest when it resolved that "all human constitutions and laws which contravene the Laws of God" were null and void. In the East the judicatories were less disturbed by the civil enactment of 1850.[22]

The sentiments expressed by the church organizations had been crystallized by a thorough airing of the political controversy in the religious press. Before the Fugitive Slave Law was adopted the voice of warning rose from religious journals. While Congress debated the Compromise of 1850 the conservative *New York Observer* instructed: "If the law of the land requires a man to violate the law of God, he must refuse to obey the law of the land; for the law of God is paramount to all other law." The Presbyterian *Central Christian Herald* condemned the Fugitive Slave Law without reservation. After the law was adopted, the liberal Presbyterian *New York Evangelist* served notice that it could "consent to no such infringement upon rights which we have never surrendered." Both the *Central Christian Herald* and the *Independent* recommended passive resistence. As the controversy shifted from the press to the pulpit, the conservative *Christian Observer* of Philadelphia deplored the fact that agitation had entered the church and involved the clergy who were "hardly competent to guide the people on questions of this kind."[23]

The passage of the Fugitive Slave Law called forth a barrage of sermons, especially on Thanksgiving Day. The condemnation of the law came mostly from rural areas and the countryside. When Daniel Webster challenged the statement that there was a higher law than the Constitution, the American Anti-Slavery Society reported that about 150 sermons from the east coast were written in defense of Webster's position. The forces of influence among the board of directors and vice presidents of the AHMS counseled obedience to the law and supported Webster. The most effective and renowned defense of the Massachusetts senator was that penned by Moses Stuart, a professor at Andover and a member of the Massachusetts Missionary Society. "If there is a higher law, it was discovered by the abolitionists who condemn the conduct of Paul," Stuart insisted. These men drew this new theory from "their own passions and prejudices." William Adams of the Fourth Presbytery of New York and a director in the AHMS informed those who opposed the law that "Before you bring His [God's] name to sanction resistance to human laws, you must show us that it is His will that we should do so." A. D. Smith, of the Third Presbytery of New York and a member of the executive committee of the AHMS, in a sermon on Thanksgiving, opposed the law but advocated only a passive resistance. The Congregational clergy in the urban centers of New England also spoke in opposition to the higher law doctrine. For example, in May 1850 William M. Rogers of Boston, in a sermon before the Massachusetts Home Missionary Society, denounced the disunion tendencies as "treason against the nation, and rebellion against God."[24]

The strongest sentiment against the higher law theory came from the business community in the Eastern cities. Their chief organs were the

Journal of Commerce and the *New York Evening Express*. On October 29, 1850, a call to assemble for a "union meeting" on October 30 in Castle Garden, New York, in support of the Union and the laws of the land appeared in many of the leading newspapers. The call was signed by almost all the leading New York merchants. When the Castle Garden meeting convened, the merchants who organized the meeting were charged by the *New York Post* with selling their principles to southern customers. The conservative firm of Cant and Rottenhouse advertised in the *Journal of Commerce* and the *New York Herald* that their attendance at the meeting was not to dispose of their "Northern principles" and entire stock of goods to the South. They had a large supply on hand to sell to customers in the East and West as well.[25]

The conservative press accused the liberal merchants who did not attend the meeting of selling their merchandise in one shop and their principles in another. When it was suggested that the conservative newspapers were trying to use the meeting to destroy the trade of the liberal merchants who had not attended the Castle Garden affair, the *New York Herald* denied this. The *Evening Post* revealed that the plans to call the meeting were drawn up by a group of merchants who met in the counting room of Carleton and Company, a silk firm that sold almost entirely to the South. "They are, of course, the natural enemies of Messrs. Bowen and McNamee, a much more extensive firm, with whom the former, having found themselves unable to compete by fair means, have concluded to try another kind," wrote the editor. Henry C. Bowen was a part owner of the *Independent*, and a life member of the AHMS, as well as a son-in-law of Lewis Tappan. The *Journal of Commerce* implied that all merchants whose names were left off the call refused to sign the role of sponsors. Henry Ward Beecher responded to this attempt to intimidate the nonsigners by calling on all these men and suggesting that they stand firm in their principles. One of those singled out by the union committee for boycott by the South was Bowen, who came to his pastor, Henry Ward Beecher, with the request that a card be drawn up in reply to the antislavery blacklist. With the help of a parishioner, Beecher drew up the notice that appeared in the *New York Daily Tribune*: "Our goods and not our principles are in the market. The attempt to punish us as merchants for the exercise of our liberty as citizens we leave to the judgment of the community."[26]

The southern newspapers joined the efforts to boycott the liberal merchants. A card from Charlotte, North Carolina, appeared in a southern journal announcing that the firm of Chittenden and Bliss of New York should "no longer . . . receive a cent of money from the South." The *Charleston Courier* carried articles concerning the boycott, and the *Mont-*

gomery Daily Journal copied a list of six wholesale firms from the *New York Day Book* that were characterized as abolitionist merchants. The firm of Chittenden and Bliss headed the list. Simon B. Chittenden operated one of the three largest wholesale firms in the Union and had the largest southern trade of any firm. He was on the executive committee of the AHMS and was one of the founders of the Congregational Church of the Pilgrim in New York. Chittenden was instrumental in securing the call of Richard S. Storrs, another member of the executive committee, to the Church of the Pilgrim. Chittenden placed ads in the newspapers denying that he was an abolitionist and declaring the published statements had "no foundation whatever in truth." He pledged to conduct his business "on principles" that would "commend themselves to all men of integrity and honor." Liberals such as Bowen and Chittenden were few in number in the business community. Meetings similar to the Castle Garden affair were held in several other northern commercial centers.[27]

One of the most powerful forces working against the Fugitive Slave Law was the editorial staff of the New York *Independent*, a liberal Congregational newspaper established after the Mexican War. The workhorse of the group was Joshua Leavitt, one of the most influential abolitionists in the country. As an assistant editor his influence was informal and unofficial. He was closely allied with the AMA. Leonard Bacon, the chief corresponding editor, was a moderate antislavery man. The two editors were Joseph P. Thompson and Richard S. Storrs, and both were members of the executive committee of the AHMS. In January 1851, Storrs wrote editorially, "The Law is . . . essentially iniquitous. It directly and radically contradicts God's Law." Thompson published a sermon in November 1850 strongly denouncing the law. He incurred much condemnation and animosity, and was nearly overthrown in his church as a consequence of the stand he publicly took on the Fugitive Slave Law. Writing from Rome in December 1850, Bacon sternly announced: "I yield to it none other than a passive obedience." Back in his church in New Haven on Thanksgiving Day, 1851, he preached that the higher law bound both citizens and legislators with an obligation that could not be dissolved.[28]

The supporters of the AMA were more united than the members of the AHMS in their opposition to the enactment of 1850. Stephen Thurston of Maine spoke out against the action of Congress. William W. Patton, a member of the executive committee of the AMA, delivered a sermon and published it in a pamphlet under the title of *Conscience and Law*. He counseled that "the law must be *broken in its precept*, while quietly submitting to the penalty."[29]

When the AMA met for its anniversary in Rochester, New York, in the autumn of 1850, it resolved that the Compromise of 1850 was "equally at variance with the principles" of the association, the Constitution, and the law of God. The Rochester meeting recommended disobedience to the new law "whatever persecution or penalty" might be suffered. In May 1852 Professor Charles D. Cleveland, David Thurston, and nine others of Calvinist tendencies, mostly supporters of the AMA, drew up "An Address to the Anti-Slavery Christians of the United States" urging them to stand firmly against all aggression by the forces of slavery. In the following year the American and Foreign Anti-Slavery Society circulated the address as a pamphlet throughout the country. At the same time the society distributed a pamphlet entitled *The American Missionary Society and Slavery*.[30]

The clergy beyond the Appalachian Mountains also spoke in strong language against the Fugitive Slave Law. Lucius Smith, of Middlebury, Ohio, insisted that the law "ought to be overthrown. *It must be.*" In Galesburg, Illinois, Flavel Bascom and Jonathan Blanchard spoke before meetings protesting the Fugitive Slave Law, and Wisconsin was also the scene of many meetings dominated by the friends of the antislavery missionary societies. J. W. Loguen and Samuel R. Ward, black members of the AMA, ranged over the North Atlantic states and into the Northwest to convert these states to the ranks of the opposition to the new measure. One of the most active areas of resistance to the new measure was the Western Reserve. The Compromise of 1850 was denounced by E. H. Nevin of the Free Presbyterian Church and by the New School Presbyterian clergyman, Samuel C. Aiken, a director of the AHMS.[31]

The campaign against the Fugitive Slave Law helped bring about a change in the public opinion of the North, especially in the Northwest. The change in northern sentiment led to an increasingly stiff opposition to slavery among the religious and benevolent associations. While few clergymen went as far as to take overt action against slavery, many were moved to denounce the Fugitive Slave Law as a violation of the "higher law." The religious opposition to the law made antislavery expressions respectable in evangelical religious circles. After the Mexican War, a majority of evangelical Calvinist clergy were committed to vigorous resistance to the expansion of slavery by political action. The Compromise of 1850 brought some clergy and Calvinist congregations of the Northwest and rural America to the point of being willing to oppose, passively resist, and sometimes violate laws of the federal government that they considered to be contrary to their religion. In the years after 1850 they worked to make institutional changes in their religious organizations and benevolent societies that reflected their new stance on slavery.[32] The evangelical churches were made up of antislavery and moderate as well as conservative Christians. Only by relying exclusively on the sources of the abolitionist movement and failing to draw on church records can one arrive at the conclusion that the church was proslavery and thus accept the abolitionists' criteria for judging the churches' stance.[33]

The Rise of Radicalism
in the Western Church

*I*n May 1849 Blanchard wrote to a patron in Massachusetts that the West was moving strongly against aid to slaveholding churches in the South. As evidence, he cited the measures of the Wisconsin General Convention and the Association of Congregational Churches in Iowa and Illinois in favor of such action. Blanchard informed Badger in September 1850 that his (Blanchard's) name was being used as a vice president of the WHFMA without his permission. "I would have wished to think my responsibilities all lay another way a spell longer; but the principles of that association are my principles. I believe they are God's principles, and I am resolved to follow . . . where they lead. . . . meantime, I mean to take up a sort of labor with your Society," Blanchard warned. In December of the following year, Blanchard served his final notice on the AHMS. He had let it be known throughout the Northwest that unless action were taken at the next anniversary meeting, there was "no rational ground" for hoping the Society would do anything against slavery except to "utter a deprecation and feeble testimony." In January 1851, Flavel Bascom, pastor of the Congregational Church in Galesburg and formerly an agent of the AHMS, wrote to the New York office that he feared that WHFMA would "cover the West with its agencies and . . . everywhere reap the fields" that the AHMS had "cleared and fenced and tilled for years. I see no way by which your society can avoid collision with the new society" except by "stealing its thunder," he explained.[1]

Early in March Blanchard opened his offensive against the AHMS by soliciting aid of an Iowa missionary in securing signatures to a memorial, among the missionaries in that region, urging the AHMS to free itself of any connection with slavery. Blanchard charged that "the combined influence of all organized bodies together," did less "to make slave-holding popular than the Home Miss[ionary] Society." Circulars were sent to all the missionaries whose names were published in the report of the Society as well as all other ministers connected with the New School Presbyterian

Church and Congregational associations whose names and addresses could be secured. The chief instrument of communication for the campaign against the Society was a newspaper, *The Christian Era*, a Congregational sheet edited at Galesburg, Illinois, by Flavel Bascom. Galesburg, in the opinion of Badger, was the seat of "ultra-anti-slavery or Blanchardism" in the West where "a war of extermination was being waged against the domestic missions organizations."[2]

Three missionaries in Iowa agreed to circulate a petition among their fellow workers, and the public was left with the impression that the mature idea originated in Iowa. When the petition began to circulate in Illinois, it brought a response from agents in that field. Albert Hale, the mission agent of central Illinois, had no sympathy with "the spirit and *manner* of the appeal . . . but with its *object*" he had "the fullest and warmest sympathy." Although his sympathies were with the AHMS, Hale informed his superiors that he endured "with the deepest pain this great error and wrong." The agent in southern Illinois, William Kirby, expressed the opinion that "if the AHMS retained its hold upon the affections and confidence of many of our most active and devoted churches, it will be obliged" to carry out the proposal of the petition.[3]

William Carter, a Congregational clergyman and director, was probably the Society's most loyal supporter in Illinois. In March, Carter sent Badger a copy of the circular that was printed in *The Christian Era*, and suggested that it be answered in the *New York Independent* or the *Prairie Herald* in Chicago. Carter concluded that "the roots of Blanchard's error" were in "laying the sin of American slavery upon every case of slave-holding." Julius A. Reed reported that the petition was circulating in Iowa, and warned the New York secretaries against taking any "special notice of it . . . before the meeting of the Iowa Association." The secretaries learned from Dexter Clary that the missionaries in Wisconsin were not waiting for the outcome of the petition campaign. Many ultras were taking their churches into the antislavery missionary movement and moving on to new churches, which they also persuaded to leave the AHMS. Clary reported that "the tendency" was "to get up a Free Mission *organization*." The Wisconsin agent added, several weeks later, that "*many* not of the Free mission distinction" thought that the Society would "greatly extend its influence for good by taking the ground of *not aiding any* more slaveholding ch[urc]hes." The degree of opposition of missionaries to slavery was revealed in April when three members of the Presbytery of Ottawa, in northern Illinois, acting independently of the petition movement, urged the AHMS to adopt a course of action that would free the Society from any relation with slavery.[4]

The secretaries of the AHMS received the petition from Bascom in June. Bascom informed the Society that a majority of the members of the General Association of Illinois "were in favor of disconnecting . . . home missions from Slavery. Few are ready to dispair of the AHMS and to leave it. But they are making up their minds to leave ere long, if no token of progress in the right direction appears." Another petition bearing thirty-one names was received by the New York secretaries. It included a statement that more names would follow. The memorial was first published in the *North Western Gazetteer* on February 27 as an appeal to the Society from the friends, patrons, and missionaries of the organization in the West. The editor of the *American Missionary* rejoiced because the petition came "from a right source" and was "eminently kind towards the body" it memorialized, but the American and Foreign Anti-Slavery Society pointed out that the AHMS petition movement originated with the Society's own missionaries.[5]

The AHMS did not acknowledge or take any public notice of the petition, which urged the executive committee to commission no new churches that contained slaveholders. Long before the petition was received, the Society had decided to follow rather than lead the churches on the question of fellowship. "They want to use us as a cat's paw to pull their chestnuts out of the fire," Badger protested. Although Hale had not always agreed with the opinions of Blanchard on the question of slavery, he considered it a great injustice to class the president of Knox College with men whose principles and acts he held in "detestation." Knowing that the meeting of the Illinois General Association would give rise to an organized effort by the antislavery clergy to urge measures against the position taken by the AHMS, Badger urged William Carter, a fellow Congregationalist, to attend the sessions of the association and set the affairs right. "Blanchardism can never have the respect and confidence of good men" by using the tactics they were resorting to against the churches, Badger predicted optimistically.[6]

As if in preparation for the struggle that would come up in the western Congregational associations, the *Home Missionary* centered onto a discussion of the evils of the day. "Evils, sanctioned by time and defended by law, lie in the way of the world's conversion," declared the editor. Hall pleaded for tolerance among friends of home missions who agreed with the desired ends. Andrew Benton, agent of the WHFMA, considered the "views" presented in the *Home Missionary* as "right," but he did not expect the AHMS to go beyond a verbal expression of opposition to slavery.[7]

The officers of the AHMS expected a large secession from the ranks of the churches when the Illinois General Association met in Galesburg in May following the meeting of the Central Association at the same site.

The Central Association voted to recommend that the Society's operations "be confined to communities and ch[urche]s where a minister may call upon the people to 'break every yoke and let the oppressed go free' without being mobbed." Carter led the defense of the AHMS in the Illinois General Association. He was aided by Julius A. Reed, who still "sometimes doubted if the secretaries were doing all their duty," but William Kirby offered little support for the Society that employed him and took the stand that he would "neither defend nor justify" the AHMS before the association in the sessions of 1851. Blanchard served notice in both the district and state associations that "*his conscience compelled* him to leave" the old Society and "throw his means and influence into another channel." He introduced a measure that carried in the district association of Illinois, to the effect that the churches should be left free to choose between the old home mission board and "Free Missions," but it was beaten down. Although both Bascom and Blanchard withdrew support from the AHMS, they insisted their object was "not to kill" the Society "but to give it a sweat."[8]

When the General Assembly of Michigan met early in 1851, it declared "unabated interest" in the old boards, and in the General Association of Iowa a resolution was introduced expressing regret that the AHMS used its funds to aid slaveholding churches, and earnestly entreated the executive committee to discontinue this aid. The measure was postponed due to the lateness of the session. "I am persuaded that nearly, if not quite all, the ministers in our State feel that it is time for such action," John C. Holbrook, an Iowa minister, wrote to the *Independent*.[9]

The Christian Anti-Slavery Convention call was issued February 14, 1851, inviting "all evangelical Christians who desired to divorce the church from slavery" to convene in Chicago on July 3. It was signed by Whipple, Tappan, and Goodell of the AMA and Fee, Blanchard, and some of the other officers of the WHFMA. On May 27 and June 5 a call appeared in the *Prairie Herald* and the *New York Independent*, announcing a missionary convention scheduled to meet in Chicago on June 19. The committee signing the announcement included the most important conservative and liberal supporters, officers, and friends of the AHMS and the ABCFM. Known antislavery clergy were conspiciously absent from the list of sponsors.[10]

Blanchard perceived that the organization of this new convention was more than a coincidence, as did Samuel G. Wright, pastor of the Toulon, Illinois, Congregational Church, who felt the scheduling of the June 19 meeting "looked like an effort to keep from the convention" those who were "active in getting up the convention on the 3rd of July." The editor of the *Prairie Herald* denied that there was any motive in the selection of June 19 except to secure a date that would not conflict with the meetings of the presbyteries and associations. The missionary meeting was proposed and organized by I. M. Weed, northwestern agent of the ABCFM, and Robert Patterson, Presbyterian clergyman of Chicago. The date was proposed by Swan L. Pomroy, secretary of the ABCFM (Foreign Board), who knew very little about the schedules of the other northwestern meetings. "The particular object of the meeting is to increase the Missionary zeal of the Northwest," Weed explained to one of the organizers.[11]

The Missionary Convention met in Chicago on June 19 and the Christian Anti-Slavery Convention met in the First Presbyterian Church of Chicago two weeks later. The Missionary Convention resolved that the diffusion of the gospel through the South was "an instrumentality wisely adopted to melt off those chains" that would otherwise be removed only by "convulsion and blood." The report on home missions at the Christian Anti-Slavery Convention was made by Blanchard. He denied that the clergy who were supported by the AHMS preached the whole gospel in the South. The convention resolved that "silence by a missionary body once connected with slavery" implicated that body in the sin and guilt of the system. The convention recommended that all Christians who desired "to propagate a pure Christianity" seek channels for their contributions that had no connections with slavery. In July 1851, after the Chicago Missionary Convention adjourned, the *Prairie Herald* stated editorially that it was willing to "leave Slavery and all other evils at the South, to the ministers and churches there." The editorial, however, warned, "We will accept no apologies, such as, that 'slavery is too strong for the Gospel'." J. A. Wight, the new editor of the *Prairie Herald*, wrote to Badger that the editorial was the best he could do. "The Society's relation to slavery must be met and I can see no way through it but that taken in that article.[12] Wight correctly gauged the sentiment of the supporters of the AHMS in the Northwest.

The Missionary Convention of June 19 stirred up considerable public discussion. For example, the *Western Citizen* described the Chicago Missionary Convention as a "conservative" and "anti-progressive" meeting in which the moving spirit was "to defend the missionary societies, not to urge them on." In comparing the two Chicago conventions the *New York Independent* concluded that "in the feeling of opposition to slavery and the conviction that this evil must be rooted out of the churches and discountenanced by all missionary associations, there was *no difference* between them." The AHMS had no representatives from the East who could speak for the New York office and a large number of missionaries wrote to the domestic missionary headquarters expressing regret that at least one of the secretaries was not in attendance. "The AHMS suffered considerably because there was no head," wrote Calvin Clark, the Michigan agent. Clary and Kent echoed the same sentiment.[13]

Badger was extremely irritated that the western brethren "put the cause in such a fix." Although he admitted the general invitation in the newspaper had carried an informal invitation to the Society, that Kent had urged him to attend, and that Pomroy had spoken to him about the convention at the request of I. M. Weed, northwest agent of the ABCFM, Badger complained that "not one word" had been written to the home secretaries. He insisted that the Society should have received a formal invitation, yet he explained that the convention had occurred in a season when four state auxiliaries were holding anniversaries that the secretaries had to attend.[14] In the absence of an officer representing home missions, the strongest defense of the Society was the *Home Missionary* article "Men of the Right Stamp." But this was not enough to calm the rumbles of discontent in the West.

The conventions in June and July and the agitation that followed led R. M. Pearson and G. F. Savage, both moderates, to meet with Kent and Clary at the parsonage at Beloit, Wisconsin, "under an old Oak," and review the action of the Chicago Missionary Convention. All of them except Kent were "disappointed in the action of the Body, as having come short of that progress which they had hoped it would reach." They thought the resolutions adopted "did not meet the views of the convention," and that another should have been included asking the Society "to announce that they would not hereafter commission men to churches that tolerate slaveholders." It was concluded at the Beloit meeting that the sentiments of the Northwest were for refusing aid to churches that tolerated slavery, and each man present agreed to express his feelings in his own way to the New York secretaries. Badger was very angry that the western agents and two missionaries in the pay of the Society had the effrontery to join together and propose that AHMS adopt a new policy that they were aware had been rejected by the executive committee when requested by the abolitionists.[15]

During the same period John C. Holbrook aggressively attacked slavery in the churches. He was the leader of Congregational sectarianism in the ranks of western churchmen just as Patterson of Chicago represented a similar wing in the ranks of Presbyterianism. It was Holbrook's objective to use slavery as an excuse for the separation of the Congregationalists from the Presbyterians, by the creation of a new Congregational home missionary organization that would draw all of the Congregationalists and Presbyterians of New England origin away from the AHMS, and secure the return of many Congregationalists from the AMA. The growth of denominationalism, along with the slavery dispute, was part of a two-pronged controversy that was to become widespread in the West. Thus, says Frederick Kuhns, the slavery controversy was "inextricably bound up with the church extension policies of these two denominations."[16]

The AHMS became uneasy about the effects of the slavery problem on this growing spirit of sectarianism. The officers of the AHMS particularly saw a danger in the increasing opposition in the ranks of western Congregationalism that was led by Holbrook. J. S. Clark, secretary of the Massachusetts Home Missionary Society, privately cautioned Holbrook against adding more fuel to the flames of controversy, but the Iowa clergyman insisted that some kind of action should be taken to dissolve the partnership with the Presbyterians in home missions. Clark felt that the two denominations in the West were acting like two peevish children who needed their ears boxed. His solution to the problem was for the Congregationalists to maintain a studied silence and to let the AHMS handle the Presbyterians when they got out of line. Badger believed that Holbrook's drive to break up the partnership in home missions by raising the slavery issue was simply playing into the hands of ultra-Presbyterianism. He bitterly resented the activities of the Iowa minister who he characterized as a bishop who looked at things "from the top of his little watch tower" and imagined that he was "editor-in-chief of all religious press."[17]

The increased tensions concerning slavery and home missions were sparked by the political events of the early 1850s. In March 1852, Myron Trace, Western Reserve agent, wrote to the New York office that the "Free Soil Movement" had been much in his way during the last two years. "It has virtually excluded me from some churches, and very much diminished our receipts from others," he complained. The political excitement growing out of the Compromise of 1850 drew the religious institutions of the nation deeper into the sectional controversy, and during the autumn of 1851 and the early months of 1852 there was a general exodus from the AHMS. The passage of the Fugitive Slave Law, coupled with the convention during the summer of 1851, caused many of the Congregationalists and not a small number of Presbyterians to desert the old mission boards. Sentiment turned strongly against the old boards among the clergy of the Fox River Union Association. This association was one of the most aggressive antislavery Congregational organizations in Illinois. In September, one of the members of the committee on missions of the Fox River Union wrote to Kent that three of the Society's missionaries were departing from its service. William Beardsley, the Fox River Union missionary at large, had been one of the three missionaries who had written the home missions society in April, calling for action. In July, he informed the AMA that he would not renew his commission with the AHMS and in August he secured aid from the AMA.[18]

Other Congregational associations were affected by the changing sentiments brought about as a result of the passage of the Fugitive Slave Law and the failure of the Chicago Missionary Convention to take positive action. The Rock River Congregational Association expressed "confidence in the integrity and aim of the AHM Society," but confessed to "a strong desire" to see it "both in name and fact, entirely separate from the system of slavery." In the Central Congregational Association, the influential clergymen Blanchard, Bascom, and Miles had withdrawn from the AHMS after the petition failed to secure a change of policy in the spring of 1851. In December 1852, the Central Association adopted a resolution that it was "the duty of every Christian who believes in the moral antagonism between slavery and the gospel to refuse all aid, and all cooperation with that society when satisfied that he had done his duty in the way of remonstrance." The clerk of the Central Association warned Badger, "Something must be done or the Northwest will leave you." But Badger maintained the position that the Society was not an ecclesiastical body and must follow the churches, not precede them in policy.[19]

During the months following the Christian Anti-Slavery Convention in Chicago, the AHMS was bombarded with requests for information on its relation to slavery, and for action concerning the institution. With Charles Hall suffering from a serious illness and the Society therefore short of secretarial aid, Badger resorted to the use of standard answers copied by clerks and sent out to answer the numerous requests coming from the Northwest. Churches dropped ministers who were certified by the AHMS in preference for others supported by the AMA, but the results were the same, whether dissatisfaction arose from the pastor or congregation — a steady stream of churches left the old board to find aid through the channels of the free missions movement.[20]

As dissatisfaction with the Society increased, many friends of domestic missions in the West believed that another missionary convention was the only way to restore the confidence of the West. In September 1851, Kent had proposed that a missionary convention be held in the Northwest in the spring of 1852, as the friends of the AHMS "were desirous that the Society should take a step in advance," perhaps to adopt a new rule to the effect that "no church shall be aided that contains and receives slaveholders." A. L. Chapin also suggested a convention, but David B. Coe, the new secretary, discouraged such a step because the Northwest would use it to "precipitate a response" that the Society wished to prevent.[21] Coe was a Congregationalist.

By the end of the first quarter of 1852 a crisis was facing the AHMS. On the one hand sectarianism was growing in the West and threatened to disrupt the Plan of Union that was the basis of the AHMS. On the other hand the West was becoming more radical on the issue of slavery in the churches. Many Congregational churches found the AMA more desirable as a domestic missionary agency because it was controlled by Congregationalists and was also antislavery. Many New School Presbyterian churches in the West were also withdrawing from the New School General Assembly to unite with the Free Presbyterian Church, and affiliating with the WHFMA. The sentiment in the West for another Presbyterian and Congregational missionary convention was viewed as a threat in the East by both the AHMS and the eastern Congregational associations, who feared the western associations would use such a convention to become independent Congregational associations and would transfer their loyalty to the AMA. The idea of a general Congregational convention in an eastern city was advanced as a measure to check radicalism in the West.[22]

10

The Albany Convention and Free Missions

*I*n September 1851, the Illinois General Association appointed Jonathan Blanchard as a visiting delegate to the New York General Association of Congregational Churches. When the subject of home missions came up in the New York meeting, Blanchard insisted experience had shown that attempts to reform the South by sending ministers from the North were a waste of time as the South threw out all that it "could not saturate to its own specific gravity." Blanchard cited Julius A. Reed, AHMS agent from Iowa, as the authority for his statement that "four out of five of all the men sent by the Home Missionary Society into the Slave States became the advocates of Slavery." The chairman of the New York association questioned whether Blanchard was speaking to the point before the assembly, but Joseph P. Thompson of the *Independent* and a member of the executive committee of the AHMS moved that Blanchard be heard out. Blanchard did not want the Society to drop the slaveholding churches it currently had on its roster, but he wished for "something prospective, some looking toward the end." He insisted that he did not desire to have the gospel withdrawn from the South, but he thought it wrong for the Society to increase the slaveholding churches three times, and their nonslaveholding churches by one-fifth. Badger was present at the sessions of the New York General Association. He denied that the number of slaveholding churches under his charge was increasing. Badger showed by the statistical reports of the Society that the number of churches sustained in the slave states had been greatly reduced. He repeated his standard answer, which he had stated so often, that it was the Society's task "to send . . . men and means, and leave all ecclesiastical questions to the churches."[1]

Blanchard proposed a general Congregational convention similar to the one he had suggested before the Christian Anti-Slavery Convention of Chicago in 1851. The New York General Association selected a committee composed of Joseph P. Thompson, Henry W. Beecher, and D. C. Lansing — moderate antislavery men. They called for Congregationalists to meet in Albany, New York, in October 1852 to discuss the relations of the AHMS to slaveholding churches and the danger to the domestic missions that was growing out of the rising denominational spirit in the West. For a short time many in the West feared the question of slavery and home missions would be pushed into the background. Blanchard, who originated the idea of the call, assured the western Congregationalists and the antislavery advocates that the call was worded in such a way that slavery would be the "leading and engrossing topic."[2]

Western Congregational clergymen urged that a large delegation from the West attend the Albany convention as a means of getting the Congregational "position right." Holbrook proposed "a North-Western Convention" be held prior to the Albany convention to plan the strategy of uniting the West. He journeyed to the East before the convention to lay the groundwork for a church building fund and to solicit support for a new independent Congregational home missionary society that would take an antislavery position. He warned his western associates that they "must be careful to keep clear of Blanchardism and keep him in the background.[3]

The feeling in New England was not too enthusiastic about the convention, but since it was taking place, the leadership of this section decided they should be there in force. Massachusetts, for example, appointed twenty-one delegates. Leonard Bacon warned the editor of the *New England Puritan*, Parsons Cooke, that any attempt to suppress a free discussion of slavery by the East would lead to a separation of northwestern Congregationalism from the East. The East, however, should not accept the "violent antislaveryism" of the Northwest.[4]

Oliver Emerson informed his antislavery patrons in the East that the Congregationalists in the West were enthusiastic about the Albany convention because they "wished to act by themselves in order to be free from the responsibility of sustaining the slaveholding churches. The free Northwest . . . will soon speak with a united voice, and in tones loud enough to be heard among slaveholding professors at the South and the venders of Cotton-theology at the East," he predicted. Whether the western Congregationalists would secede from eastern orthodoxy appeared to rest with the Albany convention. Henry Cowles, of the *Oberlin Evangelist*, maintained that the Albany convention "must and ought" to discuss the relations of churches and mission boards to slavery. "All in vain is the effort to stave off this discussion. Dogmatism cannot overbear it; conservatism cannot compromise it; the alarm cry of schism cannot frighten honest men back from their earnest thinking and solemn protests," he wrote editorially.[5]

The conservative Presbyterians, like the conservative Congregationalists, were suspicious and uneasy about the Albany convention. The editor of the *Christian Observer* hoped that the Congregationalists attending the Albany convention would not interfere with the AHMS. "It is well known that . . . the Rev. Mr. Holbrook of Iowa and the *Independent* and other reformers, are endeavoring to divorce the churches from each other," Converse wrote. He understood that one of the secretaries of the AHMS was in favor of a separation of the Presbyterians and the Congregationalists.[6]

A month before the Albany convention the ABCFM held its anniversary in Troy, New York. During the Troy meeting, a hurried convention of Congregationalists was held between sessions of the foreign missions meeting. Joel Hawes, Absalom Peters, Leonard Bacon, and William T. Dwight were active in the Congregational consultation. Dwight became president of the convention and Peters was a former secretary and vice president of the AHMS. Hawes and Bacon were also vice presidents of the Society. Except for Bacon, these men were distressed about the Albany convention. "They seemed to think that some irresponsible parties had stolen the march on them" Bacon observed. Hawes had invited Nathan Beman, a Presbyterian clergyman of Troy, New York, to attend the meeting and address the gathering. Beman regretted that the Albany convention had been called, but since it was to be, they should "attend and display a masterly inactivity." J. A. Reed got the floor and said if a masterly inactivity were followed it would separate the two denominations.[7]

When the Albany convention met, 463 delegates were present, over 300 of them from New England. It represented the first general convention of Congregationalists since the Cambridge Synod in the mid-seventeenth century. Hawes's opening address set the stage for a conservative convention. He deprecated the introduction of anything that should lead to a separation from their Presbyterian brethren in their action at the West. A committee on home missions was selected, composed of fifteen members, nine of whom were strong antislavery men. On the second day after the committee had drawn up its report, Blanchard, who was on the committee, wrote to his wife: "We are for once in the majority in committee." Absalom Peters, the chairman, "struggled long . . . with most admirable tact, but he could get only *five* out of fourteen to go with him" on a conservative position, he reported. Blanchard's most effective ally on the committee was Henry Ward Beecher, who had been instrumental in aiding Blanchard in securing the call for the convention. The majority report considered it the duty of missionary societies to grant no aid to churches that admitted slaveholders who held servants for personal gain. Only Blanchard and Beecher spoke in defense of the report. Peters presented a minority report recommending that the Society give aid only to churches that permitted the gospel to be preached in its purity. William Patton, Richard S. Storrs, Jr., and Bacon — all officers of the AHMS — spoke in favor of the minority report. Lewis Tappan moved that both proposals be sent back to the committee for reconsideration and the committee then returned a stronger version of the minority report that was adopted unanimously. The convention urged the AHMS to aid only ministers who "so preach the gospel, and inculcate the principles and application of Gospel discipline that . . . it should have its full effect . . . in bringing to pass the speedy abolition of that stupendous wrong." The essential change in the amended minority report was the omission of two phrases which referred to preaching the gospel "with a wise discretion in their ministry . . . so it shall have its full effect in mitigating the oppression of slavery." The removal of these two phrases, in the view of antislavery Congregationalists, was a withdrawal of a tacit recognition of the permanence of slavery. The antislavery advocates were satisfied with the convention's position as they considered that it took higher grounds than the minority report presented by Peters.[8]

The abolitionists approved of the Albany resolutions to a degree that was not contemplated even by an informed observer. George W. Perkins, who was on the home missions committee at Albany, sent an article to the *American Missionary* concerning the measures adopted by the convention. "The friends of Free Missions have received great encouragement from the recent action," he wrote anonymously. "If they had met for the express purpose of commending the *American Missionary* to the confidence and support of the churches, they could not have more effectually done it," he added. When the secretaries of the AMA did not express enthusiasm for the article, Perkins informed them that it need not be published. "I must still think the resolution . . . contains the substance of the principle we have been contending for."[9] The article by Perkins appeared in the last issue of the *American Missionary* for 1852.

Oliver Emerson received the news from Albany with "surprise and delight." He observed that the resolution declared that "*slavery* — not its adjuncts, but *slavery* — is a 'stupendous wrong'." When the Congregational associations met, not a single group dissented from the position taken at Albany. The general associations of New York, Vermont, New Hampshire, and the Piscataguis Conference of Maine approved of the action of the convention.[10]

Presbyterians generally refrained from expressing public opinion on a question that was primarily denominational. The *Christian Observer*, however, objected to the stand taken at Albany by printing a critical letter in the space ordinarily reserved for editorials. Robert Patterson, the leading conservative Presbyterian in the West, criticized the Albany convention in the columns of the *New York Evangelist* in two letters to the editor, and Holbrook answered the charge in the pages of the *New England Puritan*.[11]

By the end of December 1852, the antislavery forces were making great efforts to convince the public that the AHMS was no longer in harmony with the sentiments of the Congregationalists. They claimed that the Society would make no statement of its attitude in regard to the position taken at Albany. Blanchard was sowing seeds of doubt in Illinois. In February 1853 Blanchard wrote to the *American Missionary* that if the AHMS ceased to aid churches that did not discriminate in admitting slaveholders, he was sure all slaveholding in the church would cease. If the Society did not inform the public that they would change their practice of aiding churches that were open indiscriminately to slaveholders, explained Blanchard, the dissatisfaction in the West would increase. The editor of the *American Missionary* saw no signs from the AHMS that it had changed its policy. The *Independent* approved the action of the Albany convention, and rejected the position of Blanchard by saying that "discipline in slavery should be for a specific offense not just slavery," and Charles Boynton, editor of the *Christian Press* in Cincinnati, organ of the Western Home and Foreign Missionary Association, made an attack on the AHMS that was so violent that even Blanchard "disapproved of the spirit and letter" of the article.[12]

In January 1853, Dexter Clary, agent for Wisconsin, informed Badger that he "rejoiced in the action at Albany" because it was "making progress and thus opening the way for the society to advance also." The Wisconsin agent concluded by advising Badger that should the impression be made that no progress is to be expected as a result of the convention, "the last error will be worse than the first."[13] The secretaries of the AHMS did not respond, and Clary remained in the dark, as he had been in 1851.

In December 1852 Holbrook and Samuel Wright urged the Society to publish a statement that it would act in accord with the policy set forth at Albany. As a sincere friend of the Society, Holbrook asked that an article that would strengthen the position of the friends of the old board and silence its enemies be inserted in the *Home Missionary*. Badger left his correspondents free to publish any information they had, but stated it as his view that it would not be best. Since the measures at Albany were not in conflict with the policy of the Society, and were not intended to be at the time they were adopted, Badger saw no reason "for a public manifesto." He made it clear, however, that the Society did not interpret the Albany action as identical with the antislavery majority report that was defeated. "The two denominations for which we act are now substantially agreed that it is not for us to interfere with the discipline of the churches, but to provide them with such preaching as will awaken and enlighten the moral sense, and inculcate the principles and application of discipline," Badger informed his correspondents. The New School General Assembly had adopted a report in 1850 resolving "that the holding of our fellow-men in the condition of slavery, except in those cases where it is unavoidable . . . is an offence in the proper import of that term, as used in the Books of Discipline . . . and should be regarded and treated in the same manner as other offences." The assembly, however, considered the sessions and presbyteries as the proper judicatory for trial of these offenses.[14]

Badger had revealed to Holbrook that the Society was collecting information concerning the status of the missionary service in the slave states that would be made available as an exposition to satisfy the friends and patrons of the Society. An article was in preparation that would set forth the position of the AHMS on slavery. Before Holbrook received a response from Badger, he wrote in the columns of the *Independent* that he had the very best reason to believe that the Society would "conform to the expressed view" of the Albany convention, especially since the Presbyterian General Assembly at Detroit in 1850 had adopted a resolution that would "fully sustain the society in carrying out the views of the convention." Two weeks later the *Independent* removed all doubts as to where the editors stood by declaring that they were "still . . . the steadfast friends" of the old boards.[15]

Hall's article in the *Home Missionary* appeared in the March 1853 issue. The Society "claimed it as the right and duty of the missionaries so to bring the gospel to bear on this subject that the moral sense of their people shall be awakened and enlightened, and they may be led to free themselves from its guilt," wrote Hall, the editor. He claimed the Society stood on the same ground as the great body of the New School Presbyterian and Congregational churches. Although this commitment was not as strong as the Albany measures, it could be interpreted as saying the same thing. The effects of the statement, however, were weakened. It was prefaced with the understanding "that missionaries who live" where slavery existed were "bound, in the exercise of a due discretion as to time and method, to make their ministry tend, in the most effectual manner, to the removal of this giant evil." The Society "does not . . . make the exclusion of slaveholders from communion a condition of missionary aid, and thus interfere with the right of the churches to define their own terms of membership," he admitted.[16] Although this position went so far that it offended many northern conservatives, it also alienated the antislavery advocates.

On the twenty-first of February, before the *Home Missionary* went into general circulation, Badger sent copies to Holbrook and Wright. "Our friends . . . will now see that we do not propose to be a whit behind the Albany Resolutions, in our sympathies and principles or our action but that, on some points, we are in advance of it," he informed them. Samuel G. Wright, who was negotiating with the free missions movement for an appointment as an agent, was satisfied with the *Home Missionary* article after he was assured it did not have a hidden interpretation. Wright also was interested in securing the appointment as the AHMS agent for central Illinois, which had been vacated by the death of William Kirby. He asked Badger if the AHMS would recommission a man under such circumstances if the executive committee was satisfied that he was preaching such a doctrine. When Badger informed him that a defender of slavery as a Bible institution would not be recommissioned under such circumstances, Wright requested that he be permitted to publish in the *Christian Era* the fact that the AHMS would no longer commission proslavery missionaries. But the Illinois missionary was told that the Society preferred to retain the power "to choose for itself the time and occasion for coming before the public with its position." Wright concluded his controversy with the AHMS by withdrawing from the Society as he had threatened and becoming an agent in the free missions movement. He was under the influence of Blanchard and was working closely with him to push the AHMS to become an antislavery missionary institution by using the threats and the growth of the free missions movement to effect this change.[17]

At the same time the antislavery missionaries and patrons in the West were pressuring the AHMS toward an antislavery position, a group in the Northwest already committed to free missions was trying to undermine the position of the AHMS by urging the *Independent* to open its columns to criticism of the old boards. The *Independent*, which was operated by two members of the executive committee and a vice president of the AHMS, had defended the Society's position and had given a somewhat conservative eastern interpretation to the Albany measures. James B. Walker, who was not a strong advocate of free missions, condemned the *Independent* for being willing to fellowship slavery. The *Independent* replied: "In our judgement it is in everyway better — more candid, more manly, and more in accordance with scriptural principles of church order to separate from the N. S. Presbyterian Church because it is Presbyterian than to do so under the plea that its General Assembly had shown an unchristian reluctance to testify against the wickedness of slavery." Walker planned to submit a series of articles to the *Independent* that would tend to undermine the remaining support the old boards had among the friends of the slave. He submitted his articles through Whipple, secretary of the AMA, who sent them to Thompson, editor of the *Independent*. The *Independent* agreed to admit discussion of the old boards and slavery after several weeks of negotiation. Although the AHMS claimed it had taken the same position as the Albany resolutions, it was Walker's view that the Society's missionaries did not conform to the Albany measures. Walker criticized the General Assembly for declaring slavery an offense and then referring it to presbyteries which had contended that slavery was not a disciplinable offense.[18]

Holbrook began the publication of the *Congregational Herald*, which replaced the defunct *Prairie Herald*, in April 1853. The new press was organized to meet the demands of the Congregationalists who were dissatisfied with the Prairie Herald as a result of its views on slavery after the Chicago Missionary Convention of 1851, and because of its alleged domination by Presbyterians. Robert Patterson started the *Chicago Evangelist* to supply the needs of the Presbyterians who had subscribed to the *Prairie Herald*, but it did not survive. Holbrook hoped to win over subscribers who supported the new board as well as those who supported the old boards, and opened the columns to the friends of both the old and new boards. The free missions men had been invited to purchase an interest in the *Congregational Herald* and to be represented on the editorial staff, but they declined because Holbrook would not break with the old boards. Holbrook found that his position made him vulnerable to criticism and attacks from both sides, but he found support for his antislavery position in the ranks of the AHMS. Asa Turner, an antislavery director of the AHMS from Iowa, wrote to Holbrook that the AHMS "must take a stand against slavery." It was only "a question of time" until slaveholding churches would be refused aid. Holbrook agreed that missionary churches "should exclude selfish and voluntary slaveholders from their communion," but he felt the reform should come from within the Society. On the other hand, M. N. Miles, of Metamora, Illinois, a former missionary of the old board and currently a free mission man, charged the editor with defending evil.[19]

Elsewhere in the West the ranks of the Congregational associations were in ferment as a result of the Albany convention. Michigan was swept by so many conflicting currents of feeling and opinion concerning home missions in relation to slavery that at the suggestion of Harvey D. Kitchel, a director of the AHMS, the General Association of Michigan appointed a committee to report on the position of the AHMS toward slavery. Kitchel, who was a president of the Fugitive Home Society, was chairman of the committee. He was an old hand at reconciling the divergent views on slavery in the church. In 1840 he had authored a pamphlet, *An Appeal for Discussion and Action on the Anti-Slavery Question*, that remained the most convincing argument that the church and the clergy had been put in a false position on slavery by the public mind. As chairman of the special committee, Kitchel wrote to the AMA for any evidence they had to back the charges being made by supporters of free missions. He requested information from Badger that would aid the committee in vindicating the AHMS. Kitchel did not intend to make a neutral investigation. The material from the Society was sent to the Michigan committee, and Badger assured Kitchel that the Society had "made progress" and expected "to continue to do it."[20]

When the Michigan General Association met at the end of May, the most effective defense of the AHMS yet made was presented to the meeting. The members of the association were doubly implicated in any wrong of the Society since they were both patrons and beneficiaries, the report informed the members. After reviewing the measures adopted by the Society, the report concluded that "a more pointed rebuke of slavery, a more emphatic testimony . . . could not well be devised." The report agreed with the article in the *Home Missionary* of March 1853 that no other equal number of persons were doing more against slavery than the Society's missionaries in the South. The report was unanimously adopted without discussion. Walker, who was present, refrained from expressing an opinion because "nine-tenths of the ministers" were the old Society's beneficiaries and because the report called slavery everything evil. Goodman, looking toward the next Michigan association meeting, felt that the Michigan men were as strongly antislavery as those in Illinois, but for want of a leader like Blanchard, they were led by other commanding spirits in a different direction relative to free missions. Despite the unanimity of the meeting many left the association sessions feeling less than satisfied. Professor E. M. Barlett of Olivet College and Francis E. Lord, Congregational clergymen of Olivet, Michigan, planned a general convention of evangelical Christians to be held at Ann Arbor. They corresponded with Whipple, Boynton, Walker, and Blanchard, and secured hearty approval and promises of aid. The convention, however, did not materialize, partly due to the weakness of the free missions movement in Michigan, and partly because of the death of Lord during the following month from cholera.[21]

In June 1853, the General Association of Iowa adopted resolutions urging the AHMS to withhold aid "from churches admitting voluntary slaveholders to their communion." Julius Reed "stood alone in opposition to the resolutions." He opposed the resolutions because they proposed action by dealing with the churches instead of missionaries. The Albany convention had rejected similar measures in favor of action dealing with the missionaries rather than the churches, explained Reed. He reminded the association that they were virtually pledged to give the plan of the convention a fair trial.[22]

Since the *Home Missionary* article of March was primarily a response to the demands of the Congregationalists to know where the Society stood in relation to the Albany resolutions, the Presbyterian judicatories, to a considerable degree, did not take notice of the American Home Missionary statement. The Society had stated that it was in harmony with the assembly action of 1850, and had emphasized that the statement did not put the AHMS on new grounds. Although the great majority of the Presbyterian organizations remained silent, several expressed approval of the statement of the Society's position. The Presbytery of Franklin, Ohio, affirmed its confidence in the old domestic board. The Synod of Michigan took up the resolutions of the General Association of Michigan of 1853 and adopted these measures as its own.[23]

In the East among the Congregationalists, the *Home Missionary* article found very few complaints that it did not go far enough. Besides the support from Bacon in the columns of the *Independent*, the secretaries of the Society received the endorsement of William T. Dwight of Maine, Joel Hawes, and Thomas S. Williams, directors of the AHMS. Noah Porter of Connecticut preached two sermons on church communion that made reference to the article. His sermons were published and distributed widely. Porter's sermon of February 27, 1853, was intended to show that the missionary societies should not deny aid to slaveholding churches. In his second sermon, "On Excommunion," Porter turned to the action of the Albany convention. He revealed that the AHMS had "expressly and fully indorsed" the Albany resolutions in a forthcoming issue of the Society journal, and since the AHMS had accepted the Albany resolutions, it had taken a position that all fair men in the North could approve. "I must say, with all my heart, *Go on and prosper,*" declared Porter. The *Home Missionary* article was approved by Benjamin F. Stone, agent for New Hampshire, who said, "It will be satisfactory to all reasonable antislavery men." Most Congregational journals also approved of the article. Even Gerrit Smith informed the officers of the AMA that the March article in the *Home Missionary* disposed him somewhat to make a donation to the AHMS. Lewis Tappan urged him to wait until after he saw the article that Tappan had prepared for the April number of the *American Missionary*. But Gerrit Smith approved of the March article sufficiently to move him to send the AHMS a donation after many years of refusing aid in its support. He informed Tappan that he demanded "anti-slavery perfection" of the AMA, but in the case of the other Society, Smith hailed "with joy every inch of its rising out of the pro-slavery mire." When the April number of the *American Missionary* came out, it charged that "the Society had not fled from slavery," and the annual conference of the AMA expressed "unfeigned sorrow" that the AHMS was "deeply implicated in upholding slavery."[24]

Since so many antislavery men felt that the AHMS had complied with the position taken by the Congregationalists at Albany, the American and Foreign Anti-Slavery Society was moved to issue a pamphlet "to disabuse them" of what it considered was a "premature belief" that the Society would act in harmony with the objectives adopted at Albany. The pamphlet bore the title of *The American Home Missionary Society and Slavery.* The publication stated that the position taken by the AHMS would "fail to satisfy the intelligent friends of Free Missions." It concluded that "no change had been effected," and none was promised. It was charged that "only a partial gospel" was preached in the South. The American and Foreign Anti-Slavery Society's answer to the *Home Missionary* article was: *"Action Speaks Louder Than Words."* The missionary journal was quoted to the effect that the AHMS "does not . . . make the exclusion of slaveholders from communion a condition of missionary aid. There's the rub. That is the ground of dissatisfaction."[25] The American and Foreign Anti-Slavery Society was, in effect, serving notice that it would be satisfied with nothing short of an abolitionized church. The AHMS was far from being an instrument of the abolitionists, but the developments since 1852 had committed the Society to a progressive movement that would ultimately remove slavery from the domestic missions it served.

One of the reasons for calling the Albany convention had been to check the growing tendency of the western churches to break with the orthodox eastern churches in their cooperation with conservative benevolence. Following the Christian Anti-Slavery Convention in Chicago in 1851, there was an acceleration of the growth of free mission societies in the West. The Albany convention did not slow the pace of the movement to free missions. The free mission movement, encouraged by the AMA and free associations, became auxiliary to this antislavery missionary organization in New York. Western movement, however, was not only alienated from the East because of the lack of antislavery enthusiasm in the urban centers, but also due to a desire for western self-determinism and a jealous aspiration for independence from the East.[26]

The Albany convention was significant because it gave national form to Congregationalism. It confirmed that the denomination was the same in the West as in the East by resolving that insinuations and charges of heresy in doctrine and disorderly practices made against Congregationalists of the West were discountenanced. The convention provided a fund for church erection in the West and closer ties between the East and West were urged. All of this appeared to make the slavery resolutions stronger and sealed the fate of AHMS.[27]

As the decade of the 1850s advanced, the free missions movement developed enough unity and power to permit them to compete on more favorable terms with the older conservative missionary organizations. In 1852 the western Congregationalists had forced the eastern leaders of the denomination to take higher antislavery ground, which was used to pressure the AHMS into an advanced position. The Congregational clergymen on the executive committee of the AHMS, as editors of the Congregational *Independent*, took the lead in establishing a stronger position that they hoped would reconcile the differences between the Congregationalists of the East and West without destroying the delicate alliance with the Presbyterians in church missions. The resolutions of the Albany convention and the position taken by the AHMS in March 1853 did not bring the slavery controversy in domestic missions to an end. It brought the differences concerning slavery and independent church erection activities of the Presbyterians and Congregationalists to the point that separation in the work of the Plan of Union was inevitable. For many of the Congregationalists in the West, the movement of the AHMS toward an antislavery position was a case of too little too late. The western Presbyterians who had identified with the Free Presbyterian Synod were in agreement with the Congregationalists who were moving toward independent associations. The Free Presbyterians' antislavery sentiments were stronger than their desire for denominational unity. Liberal New School Presbyterians could follow the lead of independent Congregationalists and Free Presbyterians. The AHMS was forced to take advanced action. Presbyterians and Congregationalists accelerated their movement into free missions. By 1856, the free missionary movement had Congregational auxiliaries or agents of the AMA in all of the western states. The antislavery missionary organizations were now in a position to contest effectively the supremacy of the AHMS in the domestic mission field. To many conservative Congregationalists and Presbyterians in the East, the AHMS had committed itself to becoming an agency to change the institutions of the South. Denying that this was the proper mission of the Society, the conservatives began to discuss the formation of a new agency to send the gospel to the South.

The Southern Aid Society

*T*he changes in the Presbyterian Church and the activities of the AHMS to quietly bring an end to the aid given slaveholding churches met with firm resistance among conservatives in the North and open rebellion on the part of southern churches. On July 4, 1853, a convention of southern New School Presbyterians met at Murfreesboro, Tennessee, to consider the General Assembly measures and the relations of the southern presbyteries to the national judicatory. The convention advised southern congregations to reject the request for information and called on conservatives in the North and West to unite with the South in order to preserve the integrity of the church. It recommended that the southern synods set up a missions board, with a corresponding secretary and an agent, that would have the flexibility to permit the acceptance of aid from the AHMS, the General Assembly's church extension committee, or any other agency that met the needs of the southern church.[1]

In discussing the Murfreesboro convention, the New York *Journal of Commerce* surmised that one of the purposes of the convention might be to consider the policy of the AHMS in refusing to aid missionaries in the South. A northern correspondent agreed with the suggestion of the *Journal* and concurred with the editor's charge that the refusal to aid missionaries who owned slaves was unreasonable. The correspondent felt that there had been enough abuse of the South and everything southern, perpetuated by men who found it easier to abuse slaveholders than to lift a finger to remove slavery by well-directed Christianity in the South. A southern minister explained that his presbytery had been so crippled and cramped by the rule of the AHMS that the members had decided to do what they could on their own and let the rest go undone.[2]

In late July, a group of conservative laymen and clergy met in New York City and proposed that a society be set up to assist churches in the South that would rise above the narrow prejudice and miserable fanaticism of the day. They concluded the AHMS was becoming inoperative and inefficient in the South, and a new society was needed. The editor of the *Christian Observer* agreed with the conclusions of the meeting. He cited a case in Virginia in which the AHMS dismissed a missionary who married a woman who had inherited three slaves. The *Home Missionary* article of March 1853 seemed to verify that this was not an isolated incident. The editor revealed that when a missionary became, either voluntarily or involuntarily, the owner of a human being, he was "dropped from the list of its agents."[3]

A Presbyterian minister from Mississippi maintained that the position announced by the Albany convention was the real position of the Society. Apparently in answer to the *New York Evangelist's* claim that the cause of the scarcity of missionaries in the South was not due to slavery but to the lack of personnel, the Mississippi clergyman denied that the shortage was from a lack of "adequate donations" but insisted rather that it was the result of "abolitionism." A minister from Virginia wrote to the editor of the *Journal of Commerce* that a southern aid society was badly needed in the South because the people were so widely scattered as a result of the peculiar circumstances of plantation life, and another correspondent stated that without aid from other regions the ministers were compelled to augment their scanty means from the farm and the schoolroom, and much time and strength were lost from the proper work of their office.[4]

The convention to organize the Southern Aid Society was held in New York, September 28 and 29, 1853. Conferees agreed that it was expedient and necessary to establish a society to bring gospel truth to the southern states, and a committee was selected to draw up an address at a meeting in October. The address of the convention stated that the Southern Aid Society was organized to take over where the AHMS "paused or faltered." The new society was established because the course the AHMS marked out for itself did not permit it to aid missionaries in the South who under any circumstances were slaveholders, and the impression was generally held in the South that the AHMS was closely allied with abolitionism. "Our object is not to enter at all into the absorbing question of slavery and antislavery. . . . We do not propose to enter into any conflict with other missionary organizations," declared the address. But the promoters of the Southern Aid Society promised a new approach in the way they would deal with the South. "Reproach, calumny, and all sorts of injustice have been tried upon the South for a quarter of a century, without any good results; the Southern Aid Society will try the opposite policy of kindness, sympathy, and co-operation in every good word and work," they promised. The executive committee was to be composed of at least one representative from the Dutch Reformed, New School Presbyterian, Old School Presbyterian, and Congregational denominations.[5]

The new society was eagerly welcomed by the conservative religious press, but the more liberal sheets expressed reservations. The *New York Evangelist* did not view the new organization with much gratification. "The prime qualification for its favor will be slaveholding, and its influence, so far as it goes, will be to multiply the number of ministers and churches holding that relation," the editor predicted. "I cordially endorse your efforts," wrote Amasa Converse, the editor of the *Christian Observer*, in a letter to Joseph Stiles, the secretary of the Southern Aid Society. "We owe it to the North and South and to the Savior," he continued, "to do something in this work which has been so sadly overlooked." Henry Cowles, editor of the *Oberlin Evangelist*, organ of the independent Congregationalists, said he bade the Southern Aid Society Godspeed if they preached the whole gospel to the South. But if they aimed especially, not to say chiefly, to assure their southern brethren that they would stand in full repute as unblemished Christians, despite their holding men as property, "then we say—Let Our Hands Be Off!" he added.[6]

The Southern Aid Society was well received in the South. No fewer than eighteen southern clergymen, almost all New School Presbyterians, attended the organizational meeting. Since the division of the Old and New School Presbyterian churches in 1837, no aid had been granted to new churches in the lower tier of southern states. When an attempt was made to secure aid for churches in Alabama in 1847, the AHMS rejected the request due to the ties of the ministers to slavery. In 1851, the Synod of Mississippi set up its own missionary society as a result of the failure of the AHMS to grant aid, and because of the unwillingness of the churches to receive aid through the national society under its recognized terms. In 1853, the Domestic Missionary Society of Virginia took its mature form and the Synod of Mississippi, after expressing disapproval of the action of the assembly of 1853, "hailed with gratification" the creation of the Southern Aid Society as a "demonstration of fraternal feeling."[7]

The New School denomination in the South was ready for new developments, either in the form of a church extension board in the Presbyterian Church or a new voluntary organization that would let slavery alone. The Presbytery of Hanover, Virginia, served notice on the North that it would not respond to the queries from the assembly for information about slavery. The Presbytery of Winchester, Virginia, sent a circular letter to all northern New School presbyteries, warning that the southern church must have some reasonable assurance that the crusade against her would cease, or the church would be broken up.[8]

The New School congregations in Tennessee did not limit themselves to threats in 1853. After the Murfreesboro convention, the Synod of Tennessee resolved that her presbyteries would hold themselves ready to respond to wider fields of domestic missions than they filled with the AHMS. The synod, however, disclaimed any desire to disturb the cooperation with the AHMS. When the Presbytery of Richland held its next meeting, it followed the suggestion of the synod by authorizing its domestic missions agent to correspond with the general agent of the Southern Aid Society and secure whatever means could be obtained from that source to enable the feeble churches to sustain the gospel.[9] Thus the groundwork was completed at the local level for the establishment of a conservative national society.

Outside the South, the rise of the Southern Aid Society served as an excuse among liberals, especially in the West, for a complete break of the AHMS with the South. It was claimed that there was now an organization to take care of that region and that the executive committee of the AHMS should turn its attention to other areas. In New England, except among the conservatives, the existence of the Southern Aid Society placed the AHMS in a more favorable position. For example, in the summer of 1854, the Southern Aid Society's general agent was permitted to present his case before the General Association of Connecticut.[10]

The Southern Aid Society's address declared that most of its members were supporters of the AHMS, and that some of them were among its largest contributors. The organizers of the Southern Aid Society informed the public that they still expected to help the old Society, and the *Presbyterian Magazine* observed that the Southern Aid Society was under the influence of the New School Presbyterians, "judging from its officers." Of fifty clergymen in attendance at the organizational meeting of the Southern Aid Society, thirty-two were from the North, including twenty New School pastors, five Congregationalists, three Old School Presbyterians, and two Dutch Reformed clergymen. The conservative officers of the AHMS were opposed to the new developments at Albany and the statement of policy of the AHMS in the March number of the *Home Missionary*, as well as the collection of information on slavery from the missionaries in the South. Fourteen of the AHMS officers were present at the opening meeting of the Southern Aid Society, and eleven became officers of the new society. Two others, Charles Butler and Joseph Corning, both members of the executive committee of the AHMS, became life members of the Southern Aid Society. All sixteen were from the East. Three of them had led the debate against the General Assembly measures of 1853. Henry A. Rowland and Ansel D. Eddy had introduced resolutions to postpone the report requesting information from the South in order to substitute milder measures.[11]

Henry A. Rowland, who took the lead on the conservative side of the debate in the New School Assembly in 1853, was pastor of the Presbyterian church in Honesdale, Pennsylvania. In the assembly of 1846, Rowland had informed his colleagues that slavery was recognized in the Bible in the same way that the parental government was recognized. After the assembly of 1853 adopted measures requesting information on slavery from the southern churches, Rowland published a pamphlet on the subject denying that the assembly had any constitutional authority to take such action. He assured his readers that the northern churches were no more responsible for the continuance of slavery than they were for that of the despotism of the Russian czar. It was his opinion that fellowship with one in great error did not imply sanction of that error.[12]

Ansel D. Eddy began his ministry in the South as Rowland had, later going to New York and then serving twenty years as pastor of the Park Presbyterian Church in Newark, New Jersey. When he left this church, he was replaced by Rowland. In the assembly of 1853, Eddy took the lead in calling for "repose from . . . agitation." Eddy was a strong advocate of the American Colonization Society and attended the annual meetings in the 1840s and 1850s. After the political fortunes of Stephen A. Douglas were shaken in northern Illinois by the Kansas-Nebraska Act, Eddy was persuaded by Douglas to come to Chicago to take over a New School congregation. Douglas contributed liberally to Eddy's support, and the pastor defended the senator's position so firmly that those who were of antislavery sympathies represented him as a proslavery Douglas man.[13]

Samuel Cox, the third leader of the conservative triumvirate in the assembly of 1853, had started his career as an antislavery advocate and turned conservative in the late 1830s. In the assembly of 1853, he represented himself as being the friend of the black man, but held it as a conviction that ecclesiastical bodies had nothing to do "with the laws of Caesar. . . . Christ so taught" that this was the case, Cox explained. When he was invited to take a seat on the board of directors of the Southern Aid Society, he accepted and added: "We go for our whole country." If the AHMS could not occupy the whole country, Cox was in favor of having a new institution occupy the neglected field. Like most of the colleagues in the new organization, Cox was a life member of the American Colonization Society.[14]

Christopher R. Robert, who headed the mercantile firm of Robert and Williams, was the recording secretary of the AHMS and later its treasurer after Joseph Corning retired from that office. Robert was the only member of the Society's executive committee to become an officer of the Southern Aid Society. He served as a ruling elder of the Laight Street Presbyterian Church, and for nearly thirty years was superintendent of one of the largest Sunday schools in New York City. Before organizing his firm in New York, Robert operated a business in New Orleans. He was known for his benevolence, such as the endowment of an Old Testament chair at Auburn Theological Seminary, aid to needy seminary students, and the establishment of the Lookout Mountain Educational Institution. Robert was also a large contributor to the American Colonization Society.[15]

Aristarchus Champion, an officer in the Southern Aid Society as well as a vice president of the American Colonization Society, was a merchant and land speculator in Rochester, New York. In 1856, he became president of the AHMS. It was his custom to give a thousand dollars yearly to the benevolent organizations that he helped sustain. In 1854, when the American Tract Society came under attack because of slavery, he gave fifteen hundred dollars to purchase life memberships in the Tract Society for the missionaries in the AHMS. In 1854, he left the Presbyterian Church to take up membership in a new Congregational church.[16]

Many offices of the Southern Aid Society were held by Christians who, while not officers of the AHMS, were important patrons of the organization. James Boorman, a life member of the AHMS and an active Presbyterian layman, was president of the Southern Aid Society. He was a member of the firm of Boorman, Johnson, and Company, tobacco and iron merchants. For many years Boorman had been a vice president in the American Colonization Society. The treasurer of the Southern Aid Society was Gerard Hallock, the editor of the *Journal of Commerce*. Hallock was born in Massachusetts and remained an active Congregational layman throughout his life. The South Congregational Church in New Haven was built with money supplied by him. He was probably the most important individual involved in bringing the new society into existence. The general agent of the Southern Aid Society was Joseph C. Stiles, a New School clergyman who was born in Georgia and served churches in Kentucky and Virginia. Stiles was a former slaveholder. When Hallock had the South Congregational Church constructed in New Haven in 1852, Stiles was brought to serve as its pastor. When the war broke out, Stiles also became a supporter of the Confederacy.[17]

In 1854, the executive committee of the new organization considered it the duty of the church, threatened with disruption, to endeavor to heal and bind together the union of the states. The Southern Aid Society was declared to be sectional in its operation, but national in its spirit. At the first annual meeting in 1854, Oscar Newton, Presbyterian clergyman of Mississippi, addressed the society and informed the audience that the political influence of the organization would be most beneficial. With attention focused on the political turmoil caused by the Kansas-Nebraska

Act, the members agreed that "no violence or political animosity, no abhorrence of the institutions of slavery, no imaginable combination of powerful objections, could possibly exonerate" them from the obligation to send the gospel to southern territories, had they never constituted a part of the nation; "therefore, the fact that the Southern states are . . . an integral portion of our common country does not absolve us from this solemn duty."[18]

During the Southern Aid Society's annual meeting in 1854, Leonard Woods, professor at Andover Theological Seminary and a vice president of the society, addressed the members and said he had longed to persuade the North to cherish a spirit of Christian kindness toward the South. He had, many years ago, projected such a society, and therefore he hailed the formation with great interest and delight. The principal goal of the annual meeting in 1854 was to strengthen the financial base. In an effort to broaden its source of funds during the following year, the Southern Aid Society pointed out in an address to the public that it was not motivated by prejudices, sectional or sectarian, but simply by the desire to secure a more equitable distribution of the immense home missionary power throughout all sections of the country.[19]

A Boston branch of the Southern Aid Society was organized in 1854, and sent out a circular letter announcing that it would make a call for funds in New England. In 1856, an anniversary meeting was held in Boston. Joel Parker, a leading conservative Presbyterian clergyman, addressed the friends of the society. "Under God this Society has already done something to save the Union! When the salvation of the union can be promoted at the same time with the salvation of souls," he said, "what intelligent patriot can refuse to help forward a mission thus doubly blest?" Nehemiah Adams, a Congregational clergyman of Boston, rejoiced that the Southern Aid Society had softened sectional animosities. He looked upon it as "the olive-branch brought by the dove, telling of the subsidence of the flood." The *New York Tribune* commented on Adam's speech. "We look upon the Doctor as the dove that brought it," said the editor.[20]

The Southern Aid Society sent out an "appeal" in 1857 stating that the South welcomed the preaching of the entire word of God to bond and free. The *Congregationalist* of Boston agreed that no missionary of the society had been molested, but he claimed that there were hundreds of important passages in the Bible of which the organizations's missionaries could not make an honest exposition and faithful application to the obvious spiritual needs of the people without danger of martyrdom, or expulsion from the South. The *Christian Intelligencer* of New York, organ of the Dutch Reformed Church, insisted, however, that the Aid Society was doing a good work. The *Christian Observer* maintained its faith in the Southern Aid

Society and added, "It is not only 'a good work' which the Society is doing—it is a great work."[21]

John Todd, a Congregational clergyman of Pittsfield, Massachusetts, and a director of the Boston branch of the Southern Aid Society, spoke at the Boston auxiliary meeting in May 1857. It was as asburd, he said, to withhold the gospel from the South because of slavery as it would be to stop the sale of manufactured goods to the South. George W. Bethune, a Dutch Reformed clergyman, spoke next and informed the audience that it was the duty of Christians to aid the South regardless of how much they hated slavery. He regarded the gospel as the only remedy for the evils of slavery just as it was the remedy of evils that were characteristic of the North. Bethune predicted that more and more the Southern Aid Society would carry along with it the reasonable and Christian people of the North. In reply to a statement made in the meeting that it was infidelity to refuse the gospel to the South because they were sinners, the editor of the *New York Tribune* observed that the gospel could be preached only to those who were willing to hear it.[22]

The national Southern Aid Society also held its anniversary in Boston in October 1857, and Todd was again the principal speaker. In 1820 he had gone to Charleston, South Carolina, for his health and had been befriended and treated kindly by the people of the region. Todd emphasized that the gospel provided the only mode of destroying evil and should be preached to all men. Talking, wrangling, and voting had not solved the problem of slavery, said Todd. The society report for 1857 pointed out that missionaries who went to the South to preach the sinfulness of the relation of master and slave and thus by their doctrine worked directly to destroy the foundations of society would surely meet a prompt and indignant rejection. But those who followed Jesus and his apostles and contented themselves with proclaiming the scriptural duties of the master and the servant were promised a warm reception. "Standing between the North and the South—passing down the missionary contributions of one, and bearing back the grateful acknowledgements of the other—like its Master, the Southern Aid Society is a Peace Maker," stated the report of the secretary of the society, Joseph Stiles. He reported that the Synod of Mississippi had hailed the Southern Aid Society with gratitude and pride because it revealed that there were those who, although widely separated from them in sectional position, deeply sympathized with them in a common work.[23] This was the sentiment that prevailed at the meeting during this critical year when the New School Presbyterian Church was split over the issue of slavery, and the AHMS broke off its ties with the voluntary slaveholders of the South.

Thus the Southern Aid Society strove to occupy a position that was national in its stance at a time when all institutions around it were becoming sectional. It was directed in this course, no doubt, by mixed motives. No other benevolent society could match the Southern Aid Society membership in wealth and economic leadership. Of the twenty-nine northern laymen who served as officers, at least seventeen could be included among the elite of commerce, banking, and industry. Many of these had long-standing business ties with the South. Many were active political figures, including three ex-governors, and most of those who had held public office were lawyers by training and usually by practice. A large majority of the laymen were Whigs, but Democrats were also represented. There were, therefore, ties that dated back to the rise of the second-party system.

The twenty-six northern clerical representatives among the officers of the Southern Aid Society were also made up of the elite in ecclesiastical circles. They were ministers to the wealthiest urban churches and the officers of numerous other conservative benevolent societies. Twenty-three of the twenty-six were doctors of divinity. The remaining three were youthful members of the calling. They moved in the most conservative circles of society.

Individuals and officers of the Southern Aid Society had many personal and social ties with the South. Whig and Democratic party connections were maintained with southern party leaders. Merchants, industrialists, and bankers did extensive business in the South. In the period after the War of 1812, many merchants had operated businesses at Charleston, New Orleans, Savannah, and other southern cities. Early in their careers, many of the clergy had served as missionaries or pastors in the more aristocratic sections of the South. Twelve northern officers had lived in the South, seven had been born there, and five had relatives living in the lower South. The Southern Aid Society was probably not speaking of a few isolated letters and comments of thanks when it recorded in the report of 1857 that "many a Northern family has been laid under lasting obligation by the attention of the Society's agents to their wretched and friendless relatives in the far South."[24]

The Southern Aid Society was made up of men who, with a few exceptions, had followed a lifelong tradition of conservatism. The close ties between the conservative American Colonization Society and the Southern Aid Society can be seen by the fact that fifteen of the officers of the Southern Aid Society were also officers of the American Colonization Society, and thirty-six sustained the Colonization Society to the extent that they were life directors, life members, or officers. The close connection between the two societies can be confirmed by the presence, at the organizational meeting of the Southern Aid Society, of R. R. Gurley and William McLain, general agent and secretary of the American Colonization Society. James C. Dunn, who was the official printer of the American Colonization Society during the 1830s, became one of the directors of the Boston branch of the Southern Aid Society.[25]

After the Southern Aid Society was firmly established, the increased friction between the northern and southern judicatories of the New School Presbyterian Church caused the home missionary committees of the synods of the upper South to become much more independent in their dealings with the AHMS. The committees expressed a willingness to work with the AHMS provided the Society's rules on slavery were not enforced on them too severely, and if part of the funds collected could go to Presbyterian church extension.[26] The executive committee could not yield on the last point any more than it could compromise on the first. The Congregational associations were firmly opposed to the Presbyterian church extension program. They suspected that Presbyterian funds would go into a church building program and that Congregational benevolence would be used to supply a ministry to the Presbyterian churches. Unlike the slavery question, on church extension the moderates and many conservative Congregationalists were united with their radical colleagues.

As political and sectional hostility mounted, the synods of Tennessee and Missouri fell under the control of the opponents of the AHMS, and the missionary committees in each moved toward independence. The secretaries of the AHMS challenged the policy of dividing their domestic missions funds between the AHMS and the church extension committee by cutting off additional aid until they agreed to commit all of their funds to the treasury of the AHMS. In the Synod of West Tennessee, where slavery existed on a large scale, the domestic missionary committee appeared less independent. The synod appealed to the AHMS for aid. The domestic missions secretary wrote that the committee could not believe that "simply because the 'field already ripe for the harvest'" lies in the North the "region of domestic servitude which called for aid would not be heard." Apparently the call was not heard. In the lower South the New School leaders were making efforts to pull the presbyteries of eastern Tennessee and southwestern Virginia away from the AHMS. Through the columns of the *Presbyterian Witness*, Oscar Newton of Jackson, Mississippi, urged Presbyterians to leave the AHMS in preference for the Southern Aid Society. Frederick Ross, a powerful figure among New School Presbyterians of the upper Tennessee Valley, exerted his influence through private correspondence. Voluntary agents of the Southern Aid Society were competing for funds that had normally gone to AHMS agents in Kentucky, Missouri, Tennessee, and Virginia. Many of the destitute areas looked upon the Southern Aid Society as a means of supplementing the funds secured from the AHMS, but Badger and Coe, the secretaries, objected to this arrangement in the name of the AHMS executive committee.[27]

At the national level the AHMS moved more cautiously against the Southern Aid Society. When the Southern Aid Society was organized in 1853, eleven of its officers were also officers of the AHMS, twenty-one others were life directors, and five were life members. Since so many of the AHMS officers and supporters were deeply committed to the Southern Aid Society, the secretaries hesitated to oppose it openly. In January 1854, however, Badger privately warned an AHMS agent to advise against unqualified endorsement of the Southern Aid Society. But the AHMS saw fit to maintain a studied silence and to withhold public statements concerning it. A clash of the two viewpoints in the ranks of the AHMS seemed imminent, but the march of events prevented the Southern Aid Society from becoming an effective competitor in domestic missions. The existence of the Southern Aid Society served as an excuse for the moderates in the AHMS to stand with the radicals in demanding that the executive committee of the AHMS deny aid to southern churches that were involved in the system of human bondage.[28] The slaveholding churches now had their peculiar domestic missionary society. Under the pressure created by the election of 1856, the executive committee of the AHMS adopted a new rule on December 22, 1856, denying aid to churches with slaveholding members unless it could be proven that the relationship was sustained for the benefit of the servant, which was highly improbable. With the acceleration of events, before falling leaves announced the coming of another winter, the AHMS had withdrawn all aid from the slaveholding states, and all southern Presbyterian congregations had seceded from the New School General Assembly.[29] The creation of the Southern Aid Society and the withdrawal of the prosouthern or proslavery faction from the AHMS gave the antislavery forces more power in the Society. With the quickening pace of political developments, the coming of the Civil War made the dispute over home missionary aid a pointless question, but the sectional dispute concerning domestic missions contributed to the cleavage in society and made a political division more difficult to prevent.

Kansas, Domestic Missions, and the Election of 1856

*I*n the spring of 1854 developments in the United States Congress thrust the sectional controversy before the public with so much emotional force that the march of events kept the nation in constant turmoil until the country was torn asunder by the violence of armed conflict. On January 4, 1854, Stephen A. Douglas introduced a bill to organize the whole domain between the Rockies and the western boundary of Missouri, Iowa, and Minnesota as the territory of Nebraska. Although the region was free soil under the Missouri Compromise of 1820, he proposed that the status of slavery in the territory should be determined by the principle of popular sovereignty—letting the people in the territory determine the destiny of slavery there. The region was divided into the territories of Nebraska and Kansas, and the bill which came to be known as the Kansas-Nebraska Act was adopted by Congress on May 30, 1854.

As the bill moved through Congress, a storm of protest swept through the North. The core of the opposition was centered in the religious community. On February 6, the citizens of Fall River, Massachusetts, held a public meeting to oppose the passage of the Nebraska Bill. Eli Thurston, a Congregational clergyman and an AMA director, joined with another minister to draw up resolutions denouncing the measures before Congress. Ten days later, for example, a meeting was held in Faneuil Hall in Boston, attended by the clergy and others from all parts of Massachusetts. Joshua Leavitt was one of the principal speakers. During the same week the pastors of the churches in New Haven, Connecticut, requested that Leonard Bacon speak to them on the Nebraska Bill at a joint meeting. It was Bacon's opinion that any clergyman who remained silent in this crisis, or did not protest against the Nebraska Bill, was guilty of a crime before God. One week later Horace Bushnell and a Baptist minister were the principal speakers at an anti-Nebraska meeting in Hartford. Thomas S. Williams, a conservative Congregational layman and a vice president of the AHMS, presided over the meeting. On February 23, a second meeting was called by the opponents of the Nebraska Bill to meet in Faneuil Hall. When George W. Blagden, one of the most conservative Congregational clergymen, spoke in terms that were interpreted by many as an attempt to prove that slavery was sanctioned by the Bible, the gallery responded with disapproval. Meetings multiplied throughout New England.[1]

In the Middle Atlantic states and the Northwest the same spirit of opposition swept over the land. Eliphalet Nott, a vice president of the AHMS and president of Union College, seemed to crystallize the thinking of many clergymen when he informed Thurlow Weed in January that the time might be at hand when "those who think together may act together." Joseph Bittinger, of the Presbytery of Cleveland, declared: "Right and wrong admit no compromise. Every compromise in the domain of ethics is treason or dereliction," he warned. Thomas Skinner, of the Fourth Presbytery of New York City and a director of the AHMS, presided over a group that met to protest the bill at Lockport, New York, and William Fuller of the Presbytery of St. Joseph, Michigan, introduced anti-Nebraska resolutions at a similar meeting in Michigan. The clergy also played roles and took the lead in meetings in Milwaukee, Elmira, and Auburn, New York.[2]

The uprising of the religious community was not entirely spontaneous. Before the Nebraska Bill had been put in its final form, an alarm was sent out in the form of an "Appeal of the Independent Democrats in Congress to the People of the United States." The appeal called on the moral forces of the nation to repudiate the action taken by Douglas. "We implore Christians and Christian ministers to interpose. Their divine religion requires them to behold in every man a brother, and to labor for the advancement and regeneration of the human race." Dated January 19, 1854, the appeal was signed by Joshua R. Giddings, Salmon P. Chase, and Edward Wade of Ohio; Gerrit Smith of New York; and Charles Sumner and Alexander DeWitt of Massachusetts. It found a highly receptive audience among the religious forces of the nation. The *Journal of Commerce* reported that 3,263 anti-Nebraska sermons were preached in New England and New York during the six weeks following the introduction of the bill in Congress in response to the appeal.[3]

The remonstrance had been the brainchild of a small group of Congregationalists. Harriet Beecher Stowe suggested the appeal and paid for its circulation. Chase, Sumner, and their colleagues sent a copy of the appeal along with a petition to every Congregationalist, Presbyterian, Methodist, and Baptist minister in the northern states. The clergy who composed the inner circle of the group that aimed at mobilizing public opinion against the Nebraska Bill were the leading Congregationalists of New England and New York. Lyman, Edward, and Henry Ward Beecher, Leonard

Bacon, Calvin E. Stowe, Henry Dexter, and Joel Hawes were the prime movers. Edward Beecher had toured the East and conversed with the leading ministers to effect a plan. They agreed to immediately concentrate all possible force against the Nebraska Bill by sermons and public meetings. Dr. Hawes suggested that a massive petition campaign be organized to secure the signature of every minister of every denomination to a remonstrance against the Nebraska Bill. At a meeting of the Congregational ministers in Boston, Henry M. Dexter, one of the editors of the Boston *Congregationalist*, brought the proposal before members of the association who ratified the proposal. The central committee that sent out the petition was selected so that Congregationalists, Baptists, Methodists, and Unitarians would be represented. In the words of Calvin Stowe, the clergy proclaimed "war to the knife" against the aggressions of slavery. Throughout the East smaller spontaneous independent petition movements mushroomed against the bill among an aroused people. In New York, George B. Cheever of the Church of the Puritan prepared a petition for signature by the clergy of New York City. In Worcester, Massachusetts, a petition was sent to Edward Everett signed by 150 clergymen from the county.[4]

The petition, which was sent out from Boston, was signed by some 3,050 New England clergymen and contained the names of most of the clerical leaders of the area except the Roman Catholics. The *Puritan Recorder* observed that "the list included the signature of nearly all the Presidents of . . . New England colleges, professors of Theological Seminaries, and other clerical persons." It included at least fourteen officers on the board of directors of the AHMS and at least four of the conservative New England supporters of the Southern Aid Society. The *New York Evangelist* reported: "Nothing that has yet been done to arrest the consummation of this gigantic fraud so affectually reached the fears, and excited the ire of the conspirators" as the petition with "two hundred feet of names."[5]

In New York, 151 clergymen signed a remonstrance to Congress. This petition included the conservative supporters of the Southern Aid Society as well as the moderates in the ranks of the AHMS. The effects that the Kansas-Nebraska Bill was to have on the AHMS can be seen by the fact that every minister on the executive committee of the Society signed the New York petition. Forty-five clergymen of Rochester, New York, signed a memorial to Congress, and fifty-seven from Pittsburgh followed suit. In Chicago, twenty-five men of the cloth met and petitioned Douglas, and they followed this up by enlarging the memorial to include five hundred and four names in Illinois and the adjoining states before it was sent to Washington with the request that Sumner see that it was read in the Senate and impressed upon that august body. The clergy of Michigan followed the example of their co-workers elsewhere and circulated a petition to protest the Nebraska Bill. The New York petition was presented to the clergy of the Western Reserve through the columns of the *Ohio Observer* of March 15, 1854, and the presbyteries of Portage, Pataskala, Trumbull, and Alton petitioned their senators and representatives in Congress and asked that they oppose the Nebraska Bill.[6]

On the floor of the Senate, Douglas denounced the clergymen for interfering in politics and Everett apologized for the action of the clergymen. A storm of resentment against conventional politics was aroused in New England. The New England petition itself and many other documents reached the Senate too late to influence the action of that body. When the Kansas-Nebraska Bill passed over the objections of the clergy, a committee was appointed by the Boston Congregational Association to meet with others to consider the expediency of calling a convention of New England clergymen to discuss the question of future action against the new law. Many urged a convention of two thousand clergy to protest against the bill as well as "against the assaults of Douglas and Company." After consultation it was decided that it was inexpedient to call a convention at that time.[7]

Although Douglas bore the brunt of the clerical and antislavery pressure and denunciation, the New England clergy made a determined effort to influence congressional lawmakers who represented New England. As early as January 4, John Greenleaf Whittier urged Robert Winthrop to support "a broad, generous northern movement" not confined to the limits of party to avert the "great and terrible evil" confronting the nation. On February 14, Leonard Bacon wrote a public letter to Isaac Toucey, senator from Connecticut, after learning from the newspapers that Toucey presided over a caucus that favored the passage of the Kansas-Nebraska Bill. Bacon warned Toucey that he could not vote for the bill "without committing a crime which ought to make you infamous."[8]

The counterattack from Democratic politicians only strengthened the clerical movement. In March the *New York Times* found "all the most influential clergymen" in New York City opposing the Nebraska Bill, and the *New York Evangelist* was pleased that the clergy had shown "no favor to this traitorous aggression on the rights of humanity." A Chicago minister, traveling in the East, wrote to the *Chicago Daily Tribune* that "the deep indignation of the religious community" was everywhere directed against Douglas and slavery.[9]

The religious press matched the clergy with a stern condemnation of the Nebraska Bill. The *Free Presbyterian* of Albany, New York, the *New York Evangelist,* and the *Christian Press* of Cincinnati condemned the nullification of the Missouri Compromise as morally unacceptable. After the bill passed, the *Congregational Herald* trusted that "every friend of religious liberty and humanity" would solemnly resolve that the matter would never rest again until the law was "repealed and the territory . . . restored to freedom." The *Iowa Republican* reported that a friend who had access to more than fifty religious papers of various denominations in the North had not found a single religious journal supporting the Nebraska Bill.[10]

The most significant difference between the protest of the religious community in 1850 and that of 1854 was the growth of the protest movement in urban centers and among conservatives in 1854. In a protest meeting at the Tabernacle on February 18, Henry Ward Beecher spoke of the united opposition to the Douglas measure. "I find myself hand to hand with the men who for years have denounced me as a fanatic . . . and even the Castle Garden men stand by us," he declared. In February, Henry Dexter observed that the clerical petition program had the cordial support of Dr. George Blagden, and "many of his stamp in this city [Boston], and when that is the case we can have but little doubt about the country clergy." Blagden was among the most conservative members of the Southern Aid Society. In the pages of the *New Englander*, Bacon warned those who were responsible for the legislation that when there were questions of natural justice or governmental action that directly counteracted the legitimate influence of religion, "the clergy in these free States were accustomed to make themselves heard."[11]

On the printed page and on the platform, the substance of the ideas of most clerical writers and speakers was that expediency must be replaced by principle in the minds of the electorate; and when right and wrong was a question of politics, the clergymen should enter the political arena. Everywhere, the clergy urged that party politics should be done away with in the North, and that the electorate should unite on common northern principles without regard for party. At protest meetings held in New Haven on March 8 and 10, Nathaniel W. Taylor of the Yale Divinity School and Leonard Bacon spoke with determined opposition to the Nebraska Bill. On the same spot where Bacon had urged the people to sustain the Compromise of 1850, he now warned that the North would "never submit" to the Nebraska Bill. "Let the North unite . . . lay aside past differences of Whig and Democrat" and sustain freedom.[12]

After losing the contest against popular sovereignty in the halls of Congress, the free soil advocates determined to challenge the proslavery forces on the soil of Kansas. In May 1854 a group met in Boston and organized the Boston Emigrant Aid Company, later chartered as the Massachusetts

Emigrant Aid Society and the New England Emigrant Aid Society. The stated purpose of the society was to settle Kansas with people from free states in order to prevent Kansas from becoming a slave state. The *New York Evangelist* predicted that "a *cordon sanitaire* of free settlers" would bind the southern frontier of Kansas and act as an eternal barrier to the inroads of slavery.[13]

The first colonizers went out from Boston on July 17, 1854. A month later, a group from Massachusetts joined a band from New York City and others from Albany to set out for Kansas. During the month of August, James H. Fairchild, president of Oberlin College, and professors James A. Thome, Timothy B. Hudson, Henry E. Peck, and others of the religious community organized the Oberlin Kansas Emigrant movement. A Cincinnati Kansas League was organized, and the American Reformed Tract and Book Society sent out Charles Boynton, a Congregational clergyman, to accompany them in order to survey the needs of antislavery tracts in Kansas; and early in 1855 Philo Carpenter and Epaphras Goodman, officers of the Illinois Home Missionary Association, met with others in the Plymouth Church in Chicago to organize an Emigrant Aid Society.[14] Throughout the North the men who were active in domestic missions in the Congregational and Presbyterian churches were the leaders in the Kansas Aid Societies.

In March 1856, in response to Jefferson Buford's advertisement in Alabama for men capable of bearing arms, a meeting was held in New Haven to equip with Sharpe's rifles the men leaving for Kansas, under the leadership of C. B. Lines. Henry Ward Beecher, who attended the meeting, promised that he would supply twenty-five rifles from Brooklyn if that number were supplied by the New Haven meeting. Before the end of the month he redeemed his pledge and advised those connected with the project that there were times "when self-defense" was "a religious duty."[15]

When the ecclesiastical bodies met in 1854, there was a general expression of opposition to the recent legislation. The General Association of Ohio, the General Association of Michigan, and the Minnesota Congregational Association called the legislation a crime against liberty and humanity that should be resisted at the ballot box. Almost all other Congregational associations in the Northwest took similar action. The General Association of Massachusetts considered the Kansas-Nebraska Act "opposed to the manifest will of God," and the General Association of Maine called on their members to resist the efforts of the slave power "in all proper ways." Other New Engand associations adopted similar measures. Several associations urged the AHMS to take stronger measures against slavery or to send missionaries to Kansas, and the Presbyterian judicatories spoke with a firmness that matched the determination of the Congregationalists.[16]

The officers and agents of the Emigrant Aid Society kept in close touch with the Congregational associations and whenever possible tried to have a representative present at the conferences. At the meeting of the executive committee of the Emigrant Aid Company on June 9, 1855, "the expediency and practicability of financially interesting the three thousand ministers who signed the protest to Congress, in the plan and operation of the Emigrant Aid Company," was discussed and a circular was prepared and sent to the clergy in order to solicit their aid. General S. C. Pomeroy, general agent of the organization, was invited to speak before the Essex South Conference of Congregational Churches of Massachusetts on June 12. He showed the connection between the Emigrant Aid Company and the extension of religious influence in the territory. The plan to have shares purchased in the names of the three thousand clergymen who signed the protest to Washington was proposed, and the Essex Conference adopted the plan as practicable. Several individuals pledged their Sunday schools and churches to buy shares in the names of their pastors. The conference agreed to provide shares of stock for all its members. The Worcester, Massachusetts, association also undertook to make up a fund to buy shares for its members.[17]

Sunday schools and public education played a significant role in the struggle against slavery in the territories. The friends of free soil were convinced that education would not thrive where slavery existed, and Christian education was considered the most effective tool to reform society. Both sectarian schools and public education were part of a pervasive Protestant crusade to keep the western territories free. Horace Mann believed the schools, when fully developed, would wield mighty energies against the giant vices of "intemperance, avarice, war, slavery" and other evils. Schools and churches were partners in the quest to create the Kingdom of God in America, and slavery was the great barrier to the millennium. The circular that was sent out by the Emigrant Aid Company was titled, "Education, Temperance, Freedom, Religion in Kansas." It was signed by a committee of the leading clergymen in Massachusetts and Connecticut. The evangelists in the West were equally alert in viewing education, freedom, and religion with a broad perspective.[18]

By the middle of summer, $1,557.78 had been contributed in the clergy's name and more followed later. On September 13, 1855, the executive committee of the Emigrant Aid Company decided more should be done to enlist support of the clergy, and by the end of September a new circular had been issued. Although most of the conservative clergy's names were conspicuously absent from the list of stockholders, the roster included such names as Leonard Bacon; Joseph S. Clark, the secretary of the Massachusetts Missionary Society; R. S. Storrs, Sr.; Joel Hawes; S. W. S. Dutton of New Haven; Jeremiah Day; Calvin Stowe; and Charles Walker, all officers in the AHMS.[19]

The advantage of identifying domestic missions with the Kansas struggle was recognized by Joseph Clark, who informed Badger that the most effective argument for "zeal in the H[ome] Missions" was the movement to colonize Kansas "with a free population as a preventive of slavery there." He revealed that the friends of domestic missions and the AHMS who were "cool and considerate would be . . . glad now to see more in the H[ome] Miss[ionar]y touching the Anti-Slavery power of H[ome] Missions." When the American and Foreign Anti-Slavery Society met in May 1854, the abolitionists found it "a matter of astonishment that so many should support societies that receive slaveholders into mission churches, and thus present the melancholy spectacle of protesting against the extension of the unchristian system in the State while they countenance its existence in the Church."[20]

When the General Association of Congregational Churches met at Fall River, Massachusetts, during June, Badger conversed with some of the members of the association on the subject of sending missionaries to Kansas. It was agreed that Kansas should receive the prime attention of the Society. The AHMS often sent out missionaries with emigrant groups that left the East, and transmitted the early payments of the missionary's salary through the company's general agent. The Kansas-Nebraska Act gave the AMA a new respectability. In the autumn of 1854 the association was permitted to hold a missionary meeting in Seth Sweetser's church in Worcester. Horace James and Horace Bushnell were among the four or five ministers who occupied the pulpit. The friends of the AMA and the free missions movement found the doors of the eastern churches open where formerly there had been no invitations. Charles Boynton, who was touring through the East on a speaking engagement, "met no repulses, and with much positive encouragement." Although he found many still cautious, Boynton was encouraged to observe that a man did not lose caste by being antislavery. Epaphras Goodman of Chicago was also speaking in the East and found the people interested in western missions in the days following the passage of the Kansas-Nebraska Act. "The infamous Nebraska plot . . . is rousing" the indignation, and "melting away" the proslavery sympathies of the supporters of the old missionary boards, reported a minister in New Hampshire. The agent of the AMA in Maine concluded that the Kansas-Nebraska Act had helped antislavery missions, and it was his opinion that the supporters of the old boards had now taken the front lines in the battle against the slave power.[21]

Like the AHMS, the AMA maintained a working relationship with the Emigrant Aid Company. J. P. Williston, the brother of Samuel Williston, was an officer in both organizations. Williston was one of the strongest advocates of the antislavery movement among the men of wealth in Massachusetts. He was one of the chief sustainers of antislavery newspapers and other abolitionist causes. The harmony of the two organizations can be seen by their willingness to work together. In September 1854, Eli Thayer expressed thanks to S. S. Jocelyn for the interest that the AMA had shown in the Emigrant Aid Company. He expressed a desire to work with the AMA to make Kansas not only a free state, but also an example of moral and religious leadership. Lewis Tappan and other officers of the AMA showed a similar interest in a cooperation of the two societies. In June 1855 Lewis Tappan accompanied Samuel Pomeroy to an Emigrant Aid meeting in Springfield, Massachusetts, as one of the main speakers in a program to interest the public in the efforts to win Kansas.[22]

The AMA used the events in Kansas to broaden its domestic missions program and its source of funds. Its chief means of informing the public of its Kansas efforts was by means of its journal. In June 1854, the *American Missionary* carried an article on the need for missionaries in Kansas. The editor informed the friends of the AMA that the association was in correspondence with parties engaged in aiding emigration. The June article also invited "true men" who were inclined to the Kansas field to correspond with the secretaries. Many volunteers came forward for missionary service in Kansas as a result of the article. By June 1856, the AMA had seven missionaries serving in Kansas, all of whom were "thoroughly Anti-Slavery" and were "laboring most devotedly . . . to make Kansas a Free State."[23]

Although the political developments of 1854 galvanized the entire country north of the Ohio River with the urgency of need for political action, one of the most striking results of the Kansas-Nebraska Act was the complete transformation it created in the attitude of the East toward slavery. In Maine, for example, religious conferences and individual clergymen condemned the extension of slavery. When the Maine legislature met after the election of 1855, the editor of the *Portland Advertiser* observed that the Republican movement had resulted in a decrease in the number of lawyers and an increase of clergymen in the legislature. The Compromise of 1820 had been made over the opposition of the South in Congress, but the religious leaders now looked upon the Kansas-Nebraska Act as a measure that broke a sacred and time-honored pledge that stood almost as fundamental as the Constitution. The prime motive for the fierce opposition to slavery in a region that most agreed was unsuitable for slavery and would be primarily free soil by default was largely due to the awareness of the political importance of the new West. The new antislavery spirit was partially based on fear of the extension of political power of the South as well as her institutions. "A Conservative," thought by many to be Nathaniel Taylor, affirmed in an article in the *New Englander* that slavery in Kansas was not the greatest danger. He agreed with an editor of a southern journal that the true aim was "to establish the principle of federal non-intervention in regard to Slavery."[24] It was recognized by many that the party that controlled the West would also command the destiny of the nation. The religious forces could shape the character of these virgin lands providing the political environment was not unduly adverse. It was believed that Illinois and Missouri offered opposite examples of what the combined forces of religion and the organic laws could do in their relations to society in shaping the nature of a state.

The importance of the Mississippi Valley was understood by many even in the 1830s. "You are well aware of the fact that this western country is soon to be a mighty giant that shall yield not only the destinies of our own country but of the world. 'Tis yet a babe. Why not take it in the feebleness of its infancy and give a right direction to its powers, that when it grows up to its full stature we may bless God that it has such an influence?" a western man urged Theodore D. Weld. That the theme was an old subject by 1844 is evident by Calvin Stowe's address before the AHMS concerning the West—"of its inevitable political influence, of the unspeakable interest of this its forming crisis, you have heard enough," Stowe reminded his audience. Horace Bushnell saw the West as the battleground of freedom and slavery. "Religion is the only prop on which we can lean with a confidence: And Home Missions are the vehicle of religion," he informed the supporters of the AHMS in 1847.[25]

In 1849 Albert Barnes characterized the West as a region where "every wind of opinion" has been "let loose," and was "struggling for mastery." In 1850 the Western Home and Foreign Missionary Association resolved that since "the political power of the nation may soon be wielded by the inhabitants of the West the churches should redouble their efforts to create, under God, a moral and religious sentiment by which this power may be directed to the maintenance of righteousness and freedom." E. L. Cleveland of New Haven spoke before the AHMS in 1853 and anticipated the coming storm: "The elements are gathering, the forces are mustering along those watercourses and over those broad prairies, which are to determine the future legislation, the general course, and final destiny of the whole country. We have long foreseen that the controlling influences which are to mold not only American government, but American . . . morals and religion, are in due time to be found West of the Alleghenies," he prophesied. At the height of the struggle for Kansas, A. W. Brooks, a Presbyterian clergyman of Chicago, had grave words of warning for the friends of freedom: "Give to slavery the territories of the West and she is crowned sovereign of the American nation, to hold the sceptre until God's eternal providence shall blot us from the record of the nations; or until rotten with our moral and social corruption, we shall become the bane and disgust of the world." But the battle in Kansas was not lost to slavery. "What a heroic struggle was that when the Christian souls of Kansas stood almost alone against the concentrated force of our national government in its perversion, and won the battle for liberty and human right!" recalled Chapin in later years.[26]

The challenge of the extension of slavery in the territories, however, was a dual assault. The rush to settle Kansas was matched by a march on the ballot boxes to cleanse the national government. Since 1840 the Liberty party had single-mindedly advocated a moral commitment to antislavery politics. It consistently urged the religious community to cast its votes in accord with moral principles rather than political expediency. But the Liberty party failed to influence a large segment of the religious community partly due to the tendency of the party to function as a superchurch. After the Mexican War the ranks of those who favored political action as a solution to the slavery problem were swelled far beyond the narrow limits of those who were formerly identified with political abolitionism. The change was due to a large degree to the departure of the religious leaders from their position of keeping religion and politics completely separate. The Mexican War reversed the traditions that had developed in the nineteenth century and initiated a return to a political involvement that was characteristic of the church during the revolutionary period. The churches' opposition to slavery and the war was galvanized to shape the new political involvement because of the belief that slavery was taking on an aggressive stance in the territories. Political abolitionism took on a new appearance after the passage of the Compromise of 1850. New faces appeared in the antislavery political conventions, and clergy and college professors became more active in the movement. A free soil convention met in Medina, Ohio, and Professor T. B. Hudson of Oberlin advocated independent political action by all citizens who opposed the new law, regardless of past political connections.[27]

The passage of the Kansas-Nebraska Act, however, broke the calm that had existed after the dispute over the Compromise of 1850 receded into the background. The controversy over Kansas put the attack on slavery on the plane of a religious crusade. The act of 1854 brought about a union of the rural and urban religious communities on the slavery question that the Compromise of 1850 failed to achieve. The rise of the Republican party was due to the transformation that took place among moderate antislavery men as a result of the repeal of the Missouri Compromise.

The union of the new coalition was consummated in the mass meetings held after the passage of the Kansas-Nebraska Act. To a great extent those who directed domestic missions presided over the new political union. In the "Tabernacle" speech of February 18, 1854, in New York, Henry Ward Beecher spoke with a considerable degree of accuracy when he told the audience that all shades of antislavery men were working together. Even the conservative Presbyterian clergyman Eliphalet Nott wrote to a friend that it would be better "to be out of the union than in it if slavery was to be indefinitely extended."[28]

The extent of the cooperation among northerners was made more obvious by the Citizens' Protest Meeting held in a New York park on May 13. Conservative William E. Dodge, an officer of the Southern Aid Society, was secretary of a meeting called to protest against the Kansas-Nebraska Act, which had already passed the Senate. Benjamin F. Butler, an officer of the AHMS, had been forced by illness to cancel his appointment to speak in the "Tabernacle" during February, and at the anti-Nebraska meeting in Albany during March. Now fully recovered, he attended the protest meeting in New York. Butler urged the people of the free states to organize and elect lawmakers who would restore section eight of the Missouri Compromise.[29]

The clergy were ready and determined to unite. To the continued clamor that the clergy remain silent on politics, Eden B. Foster of the Congregational church in Lowell, Massachusetts, answered in a sermon that the congressmen who spoke and voted for the extension of slavery would be retired from office. "Our Duties as citizens are not ended at the polls. . . . We can influence our rulers by encouragement, by counsel, by warning, by petition, by protest, by all manner of moral influence to deter them from crime," instructed Rev. Joseph P. Thompson. Richard S. Storrs, Jr., another Congregational minister, gave a lecture on slavery before the New York Anti-Slavery Society and instructed the audience that every citizen was under obligation to vote only for those pledged to oppose the extension of slavery.[30] Thompson and Storrs were members of the executive committee of the AHMS.

The sectional conflict in Kansas welded the free soil coalition of 1854 into a permanent political union. The unique feature of the new Republican party was the conspicuous part played by clergy, lay leaders, and the religious press. During 1854 and 1855 state organizations took form in many northern states, and in January 1856 a call was issued for a preliminary national Republican convention to meet in Pittsburgh in February 22, 1856. The call was issued by Lawrence Brainard, a leading Congregational layman and president of the American Missionary Association. Josiah Brewer, a Congregational minister and a member of the board of managers of the AMA, who had signed the New England clerical petition, served on the committee to nominate permanent officers. John G. Fee, a Calvinist clergyman from Kentucky, was made a member of the national executive committee. The Illinois abolitionists and evangelical clergymen, Ichabod Codding and Owen Lovejoy, delivered significant addresses before the Pittsburgh convention. A considerable number of the delegates were active in the great national benevolent organizations and very few were professional politicians.[31]

When the National Republican Committee issued a call in March 1856 for a nominating convention, the friends of benevolence and the church were conspicuous among the twenty-two signers of the call. The Republican National Convention met in Philadelphia in June, and a Presbyterian clergyman, Albert Barnes, "one of the earliest and most logical and solid champions of the cause of Freedom," offered the opening prayer. Many names that were associated with benevolent and religious movements of the nation were also prominent as members of the convention and as electors on the party ticket.[32]

After John C. Frémont was nominated by the Republican party, the New School Presbyterians accelerated their opposition to the Democrats, a stand that lasted throughout the canvass for the election of 1856. Robert Aikman, a Presbyterian minister of Elizabeth, New Jersey, wrote a letter to the *Jersey Tribune* in which he contended that it was "the duty of the Presbyterians to resist the indefinite extension of slavery, and in the present campaign . . . to array themselves on the side of freedom." The same attitude prevailed in New York among the New School clergy. It was the violence connected with the Kansas controversy that brought many into open political activity. As late as the meeting of the General Assembly of 1853, Edwin F. Hatfield, pastor of a New School church in New York City and a member of the executive committee of the AHMS, had urged that "God had taken the subject of slavery into his own hands, and there was no need of agitation." On the Saturday after Charles Sumner was attacked in the Senate, Hatfield attended a protest meeting in Brooklyn and spoke to several thousand Republicans. He urged them to do their duty and trust in God by electing men to office "who would be true to Freedom and their country." Although most of the New School clergy had become involved in some degree early in the campaign, it was not until the week before the election that the more cautious considered the political question facing the electorate. On the Sunday before the election, Asa D. Smith, a member of the executive committee of the AHMS who was said to have preached a higher law doctrine "when courage was required," joined his colleagues in New York City by delivering a sermon on the relations of religion to the political question posed by the election of 1856.[33]

It was in the Northwest that the Presbyterian Church became most completely involved in the Republican movement. For example, O. H. Newton, a pastor of the Second Presbyterian Church, Delaware, Ohio, called upon all Christians to act in accordance with the great principle of right. "I believe God calls upon us to throw beneath our feet that *slave power* which has so long controlled our nation," he informed his congregation. In Warren, Ohio, William G. Clark preached several sermons on slavery as a political institution and in August he dealt more specifically with the "outrages" being committed by the Democrats in Kansas. Anson Smith of Columbus, Ohio, went so far as to campaign for the Republican party and accept nomination as a candidate for school commissioner, and D. Howe Allen, president of Lane Theological Seminary in Cincinnati, made a series of speeches for the Frémont party. The Presbyterians in the other northwestern states became similarly involved.[34]

The Congregationalists more than matched the Presbyterians as political activists. Henry Ward Beecher was one of the most influential individuals in popularizing the Republican party. He threw himself into the political contest in 1856 with the vigor of a political war-horse breathing the excitement of a victory near at hand. The local Frémont headquarters was in the business office of one of Beecher's parishioners. Beecher preached, spoke, and wrote constantly and vehemently. He worked throughout the state of New York, speaking two or three times a week for three hours at a time, to open-air audiences of eight to ten thousand. He made so many speeches that he became so hoarse he could hardly talk by October. Two weeks after Frémont was nominated, while campaigning in New Hampshire, Beecher observed that the people everywhere were "aroused to the great question of the times." It seemed to him that the North had at last "determined to fulfill her mission and restore to the land the principles which she first planted." In September he made another tour of New England and New York state, taking the position throughout the campaign that the surest road to peace was to elect Frémont. Beecher attacked slavery by defending the "inalienable rights" of man, and the idea that "every man" belonged to himself. He appealed to both the Bible and the principles of American government. As the campaign became more intense, Beecher secured the services of Richard S. Storrs, Jr. to take over his pastoral duties completely so that he could devote full time to the political contest.[35]

Beecher's activity differed from that of other clergymen largely in degree rather than in substance. Joseph P. Thompson, Jr., George B. Cheever, and Leonard Bacon were among the most active Congregational clergymen in exerting an influence on the election. Throughout New England the sentiments of Congregational clergymen were the same.

Congregational ministers in the West were particularly inclined to leave the pulpit and mount the political platform in order to be more fully involved in the Republican movement. For example, in June Charles G. Finney, president of Oberlin College, announced from the pulpit that the professors and clergymen of Oberlin College would hold a political prayer meeting each morning for one week before the Philadelphia Republican National Convention. The subject of the meetings was to be Kansas and the success of the Republican party. A. L. Chapin spoke in Kenosha, Wisconsin, before a Frémont Club in September 1856, and J. M. Sturtevant, president of Illinois College, later recalled, "If I had formerly been remiss in the duties of a citizen, I did what I could to atone for it" in the canvass of 1856. John P. Holbrook of Chicago was so active in the campaign that his church was called the "abolition Opera House" by the opponents of the Republican party.[36]

In the Northwest it was the missionaries of the domestic missionary societies who became the most effective agents of the Republican party. A Presbyterian missionary in Wisconsin saw the "contest for the presidency" as a "great struggle between freedom and slavery," and a Presbyterian missionary in Morrow County, Ohio, preached regularly against the aggressions of slavery and urged the people to vote as the Lord would approve. The missionaries in the service of the AHMS in Wisconsin and Michigan viewed the election with a similar perspective.[37]

The missionaries of the AMA were even more active and determined in their support of the Republican party than the missionaries of the AHMS. For instance, a missionary of the AMA in Indiana took to the campaign trail for the Republican party and made a series of political addresses that kept him occupied from June to November. Another missionary in Ohio labored industriously "to resist the encroachment of the *Slave Power*" by purchasing campaign literature from the Republican committee and distributing it to promote the cause. The leaders of the free mission movement and the AMA largely came into the fold of the Republican party as the rank and file had done. Lawrence Brainard, president of the AMA, urged the association leaders to "put on the whole armour and fight manfully the battle of God and Humanity." William W. Patton, an association officer of Hartford, held a series of meetings to promote "correct civic sentiments," and George W. Perkins, also an officer in the AMA, was active in support of the Republicans. He wrote one of the most effective pamphlets circulated during the campaign. Almost all of the old Liberty party Christians came out for the Republican party. Even Gerrit Smith announced that he would support Frémont after being urged to take that course by William Goodell.[38]

During the campaign several missionaries from Kansas toured the Northwest and the East, bringing firsthand experiences of the situation in Kansas as evidence of the conditions that existed there. Their accounts seemed to furnish proof of the need for replacing the Democrat administration with Republicans, and eastern clergymen who had visited Kansas used information gained there for political lectures.[39]

Among the laymen who were deeply involved in domestic missions, previous political affiliation was an important factor in Republican affinity. Many of them had formerly been Whigs, and when the party of Clay and Webster began to die out, they transferred their allegiance to the Republican party. This was not only because they were seeking a new political home, but also because the moderate antislavery commitment of northern Whigs was somewhat similar to the Republican stand. The sacking of Lawrence, Kansas, and the assault on Charles Sumner that occurred late in May 1856 swept many into the mainstream of Republican opinion who had previously been only lukewarm. Indignation meetings, which were dominated by clergymen, multiplied throughout the northern states.[40]

The opinions expressed by the clergy were largely individual sentiments. Denominational associations, however, spoke with a collective voice from the church. The Beloit, Wisconsin, Congregational and Presbyterian Convention met in September 1856 and resolved that when a great moral question like that of human liberty was depending on the ballot box it was "the duty of the Christian ministry to act with their fellow citizens in every honorable effort to advance righteousness." The Chicago Congregational Association was "deeply solicitous for the success of right principles" and in the current political crisis they were "still more anxious" to see American Christianity "purged from all complicity with the system of Slavery," and the General Association of Maine instructed its members to "vote for rulers who gave the fairest promise of standing right on the question of *Freedom to all.*" Similar action was taken by almost all other Congregational associations and many Presbyterian synods and presbyteries.[41]

The support of the clergy, the associations, and the synods for the Republican party was matched by the enthusiasm generated by the religious journals. The Republican nominating convention had hardly adjourned before the *Independent* took its stand for Frémont. Even the most conservative Congregational press firmly supported the Republican party. The *Vermont Chronicle* was the only Congregational journal that "retained its speciality" as "a religious journal." The *Congregational Herald* supported the Republican party and complained of the efforts to keep morals out of politics. "Every vote for the 'Democratic' or American parties is a testimonial before God and man, that he who gives it is in favor of the Kansas outrage," declared the editor of the conservative Boston *Congregationalist.* Most Presbyterian press also strongly supported the Republican party. A more conservative position was taken by eastern Presbyterian newspapers. The Old School *New York Observer* urged that prayer for the country was the "chief service of Christian Patriotism," and the New School *Christian Observer* charged that the ministers who entered the political arena were perverting their office, character, and influence. The Old School *Presbyterian,* of Philadelphia, professd to "a stubborn neutrality" and condemned the churchmen who joined the hue and cry as partisans, and fomented discord.[42]

Almost all of the secular press had something to say about the activities of the clergy in supporting the Republican party. The Democratic press opposed the partisanship, and the Republican sheets lauded the clergy for their patriotism and civic consciousness as well as for their determination to fight against sin and evil. The *Journal of Commerce* expressed the hope that public opinion would disapprove of the political activities of the Congregational clergy. The editor trusted that "such a prostitution" of the most sacred places in the land would not long continue. The *Chicago Times* used language that was equally strong. "There does not exist a more degraded *band of professional liars* than can be found wearing the garb of clergymen in the northern part of the state of Illinois," charged the editor. "Those old blue bellied Presbyterians that hung the witches and banished the Quakers, are determined," scorned the editor of the *Cleveland Plain Dealer,* "to convert the people of this region into a race of psalm singers, using the degenerate dregs of the old puritans remaining here to drive the Democracy out."[43]

The anti-Nebraska Christians did not respond favorably to political nativism. The Chase forces were willing to see the Democrats win the Ohio governor's race in 1855 rather than tolerate Know-Nothing control of the Republican party. Throughout the West, where the Republican party quickly took root, the Know-Nothing party failed to prosper. Austin Blair, an antislavery Congregational layman who was in the forefront of the Republican organizers in Michigan, saw the Know-Nothing party as "a gigantic secret society based upon political and religious bigotry." Blair was typical of the antislavery wing of the Republicans in the West. During the 1830s there had been an avalanche of nativistic propaganda and the AHMS had profited by the fact that anti-Catholic propaganda had broadened its appeal, but the nativist campaign had tapered off in the 1840s until revived by the vacuum created by the death of the Whig party.[44]

In his monumental study of the origins of the Republican party, William Gienapp contends that realignment of political parties in the 1850s began due to the rise of ethnocultural issues that disrupted the second party system and dealt a death-blow to the Whig party. Know-Nothing lodges suddenly grew by leaps and bounds, and in 1854 and 1855 the Know-Nothing or American party carried elections in several states.[45] Nativism could never have served as the basis of a successful party, however, and the Know-Nothings proved to be only a fleeting and transient phenomenon. Ethnocultural issues prospered more in 1854 and 1855 than they had in other mid-term elections during the existence of the second party system, but as the federal elections approached and national questions fully emerged, the slavery problem dwarfed ethnocultural issues.[46]

Before 1856 many free-soilers lent their support to the American party,[47] but conscientious and faithful free-soilers deplored the Know-Nothing fad as a red herring that diverted attention from the slavery problem, the true and vital question of the age.[48] Some free-soilers and liberal Democrats hoped to take over the new American party and convert it to their own purpose.[49]

Antislavery Christian laymen cautioned their political friends against trifling with the Know-Nothings. A devout antislavery man warned, "In 1856, if not before, every antislavery Know-Nothing will be compelled to *violate his conscience or his oath*." Many of the leaders of the American Missionary Association urged antislavery missionaries to stay clear of secret societies. Gamaliel Bailey, editor of the *National Era*, was a persistent foe of the Know-Nothing party in the 1850s. John G. Fee commended him in a public letter in the *National Era* for his stand against the "secret caucus" and "midnight walks" of the Know-Nothing party. "You, as an editor," he wrote, "have faithfully rebuked a movement which is manifestly the enemy of freedom." Fee reminded readers of the *National Era* that foreigners had helped the United States acquire its independence, and the benevolent and Christian spirit of the nation ought to reach out and help "poor foreigners" who "seek freedom from oppression" and refuge from "famine and pestilence" in their native land. Fee condemned the false patriotism of the American party and reminded his readers of a word that set forth a better sentiment; the word philanthropy does not stop "at narrow precincts, but grasps a *world* in its embrace." Fee formed churches in Kentucky that opposed secret societies, as well as caste and slavery.

They were fully committed to promoting these causes by political action. Fee informed his associates, "Our Lord said: 'I ever spake openly in the temple and in secret have I said nothing.' If I follow Christ, I cannot go into a secret lodge." Rev. Jonathan Blanchard bitterly opposed the Know-Nothings despite the argument that they might give help to the antislavery cause, and Lewis Tappan declared that secret societies were "Profane and Blasphemous."[50] Despite all the concern about the Know-Nothing craze, the most significant and main ethnocultural issue in the campaigns was the anti-black racism injected by the Democrats who portrayed the "black Republicans" as favoring black equality—social as well as political.[51]

One searches in vain in the New School Presbyterian synod and presbytery records, from the pastoral letter and addresses to the minutes of the ecclesiastical meetings of 1854 and 1855, for consideration of ethnocultural issues. The same is generally true of the Congregational associations. Both the New School Presbyterians and the Congregational Churches were preoccupied with concerns about the strained relations betwen the East and the West. From 1850 until the Civil War, the New School Presbyterians were totally engrossed in the slavery problem. With the Southern Aid Society on the right and the American Missionary Association on the left, the Congregational associations as well as the New School Presbyterian judicatories were completely absorbed with internal problems created by the slavery question.[52]

In 1856 Republican campaign rhetoric and the platform focused on sectional questions, not ethnocultural issues, and although the Democratic press made efforts to identify the clergy and the church with Know-Nothingism, the nativist party failed to secure any significant support from the clergy. For example, Joshua Leavitt expressed his firm opposition to Know-Nothingism in an article in the *New Englander*. Forced to choose between nativism and antislavery, most New England evangelists chose antislavery. As a result, in the former stronghold of Know-Nothingism, the American party lost out completely to the Republican party. The Know-Nothings forgot the issues of their formative period and confined their campaign to pleading for the preservation of the union, warning that the election of either of the other two candidates would lead to civil war because they were sectional aspirants. Despite its platform, the Know-Nothing party represented opposition to "antislavery more than it represented nativism." John Hammond asserted that the party did not have the support of voters in revivalist areas. His study refutes the argument that nativism and abolitionism or reform revivalism had the same roots. Dale Baum reaffirms that Republicans did not run particularly well in areas where the antiforeign, anti-Catholic Know-Nothing party received disproportionately high levels of support in the 1850s. Eric Foner was correct in arguing that Republicanism was incompatible with the exclusivism that was central to nativism. The fact that the Know-Nothing party sometimes added opposition to the extension of slavery in its platform was calculated to broaden the appeal in hopes of enticing opponents of slavery to join the movement. Opposition to extension of slavery by the Know-Nothing party in 1855 represented opportunism rather than genuine and deeply felt opposition to slavery. Baum has convincingly shown that the short-lived bargain between the Know-Nothings and Republicans in Massachusetts was engineered by unprincipled schemers who drastically underestimated the vote-getting power of the moral issue of slavery. The fate of political nativism was sealed in the 1850s by the growing fear of southern intentions in Kansas and by being overshadowed by the larger issue of sectionalism. The American party found most of its support in the upper South where the union issue had its strongest appeal. Clergymen who had been avowed nativists during the early 1840s had deserted the cause in order to join the sectional struggle against slavery in Kansas in 1856. The strongest advocates of the nativist movement, such as the Beechers—Lyman, Henry Ward, and Edward—E. N. Kirk, Edwin Hall, and Absalom Peters, were firm supporters of the Republican cause in 1855 and 1856.[53]

The prominent clergy who publically supported Buchanan could be numbered on the fingers of one hand—Nathan Lord, Samuel Cox, Joseph C. Lovejoy, David Fosdick, and Joel Parker—three of whom were orthodox Calvinists. A. D. Eddy was the only Presbyterian in the West for whom a record is available that revealed he supported the Democrats. He had only recently arrived from the East.[54] One looks in vain for evangelical clergy of standing or active laymen who spoke for the Know-Nothing party in 1856.

The Kansas-Nebraska Act increased the commitment of the churches to an antislavery stance and the clergy viewed political action as the most appropriate and expedient means of checking the expansion of slavery. In 1855 many political prophets predicted that the Republican party would die out before the election of 1856, but violence in Kansas kept the new party before the public. It was not ethnocultural issues that gave rise to the Republican party, but fear of slavery expansion. The controversy over the extension of slavery into the territories was still considered the critical moral question in 1856.[55]

As the campaign progressed and antislavery sentiment rallied more and more people to the Republican banner, the Democrats made more determined efforts to identify the Republican party with abolitionism. A circular was sent out to the clergy under the franking privileges of Senator

William Bigler of Pennsylvania, a former Democratic governor of the state, which charged that Frémont's campaign for the presidency was under the influence of abolitionist fanaticism, which assailed all true religion and jeopardized the Union. The document, "An Open Letter to the Friends of Religion, Morality, and the American Union," was apparently sent to most clergymen. Rather than follow Bigler's lead in trying to win the clergy away from the Republicans, Lewis Cass condemned them for their activities. "If more charity and less virulence were exhibited, more of the gospel of Jesus Christ and less of Sharpe's rifles issued from the arsenals of some of the churches . . . , the good old days of peace and fraternal regard would soon return to cheer the land," he wrote. A more severe position was taken by William J. Flagg, a Democrat of Cincinnati, who urged the leaders of the party to deal effectively with the political priests who were speaking against them from ten thousand pulpits. They were "the worst of all infidels" because they had no faith in the efficacy of the gospel," he declared.[56]

The Calvinist clergymen who opposed the political activities of their colleagues were almost always identified with the conservative Old School faction of the church. Although all Calvinists were deeply committed to Christian benevolence and the redemption of society, the conservatives were distrustful of any efforts to reform society outside the confines of the church's institution. On one hand, some believed that the state should be a Christian institution guided by Christian principles. On the other hand, there were many who championed the idea that the civil magistrate was shaped and guided by natural law without regard for the scripture or ordinance of the church. Others felt that the task of the church was to bring personal salvation, and reform of social evils would follow.[57]

Another factor shaped the attitude of the people concerning the political contest of 1856. In western New York and the Northwest in areas where the Plan of Union operated, many migrating settlers had carried with them, as they moved west, the tradition of multiestablishment — government support of more than one church. Although the institutional structure of the multiestablishment did not take root, the tradition encouraged mutual involvement of both church and state in the whole life of society. The areas of the Northwest that were colonized by settlers with a Virginia heritage followed Jefferson and Madison's complete separation as set forth in the Virginia Act for Establishing Religious Freedom.[58]

The tendency of Calvinists to communalize the sin of slaveholding was a significant force drawing many into political involvement.[59] The belief in collective guilt inspired much of the controversy concerning slavery in the New School Presbyterian General Assembly, synods, and presbyteries as well as in the missionary conventions. By 1856 this sense of collective sin prompted its advocates to unite in political action to oppose the expansion of the South's peculiar institution. When war broke out in 1861, most of the presbyteries of the Northwest saw God's retribution arrayed against the nation.

Much of the involvement of the clergy in the political contest did not come because they sought out a political role. Since the 1830s many revival churches had held a Monday night prayer meeting for the slaves. As slavery was the principal issue in the election contest of 1856, the clergymen who followed this tradition suddenly found themselves enlisted in the political struggle without seeking involvement. The separation of the clergymen between those who became politically involved and those who remained neutral followed a rural-urban division as much as a conservative-liberal classification. Many rural clergy were also prominent in the attacks on the Democratic administration because of the graft and patronage scandals and because of the temperance issue. Some settlers defended the position of the Democrats because they resented the moral smugness of the North. Northern virtue, it was rightly felt, was due more to geography than to sanctity.

The antislavery clergymen had been the main supporters of the antislavery societies during the 1830s. After the passage of the Kansas-Nebraska Act, these men were prone to accept the abolitionists' identification of the enemy of the nation and Christian society as the "Slave Power." The indigenous nature of the slave power was considered a serious threat, especially among those who were convinced of the millennial destiny of the nation under the special providence of God. It was considered to be a great moral truth that the toleration of sin leads to corruption and that aggression grows by submission. Thus the "Slave Power" became one of the chief themes of sermons and judicatory resolutions, and the faithful were called on to meet the threat of the "Slave Power" conspiracy.[60]

Many Calvinists were also driven by their commitment to stewardship over God's domain. A relatively small group of Presbyterians and Congregationalists were the directors and managers of the numerous benevolent societies that existed in antebellum America. They believed that God chose not to intervene directly to make sinners walk in righteous paths, but rather that he appointed guardians of the nation's conscience to reform the sinners. Since slavery was the great national sin, it was the great moral work that they were called on to perform.[61]

To many clergymen the nation's failure to stem the aggressions of the "Slave Power" indicated that a moral bankruptcy existed in public life. The jeremiad sermons were necessary to purify public life and to check the moral erosion that threatened American institutions. Some saw the amorality of political parties, which condoned bargains with the slavery forces and permitted political corruption, as a greater threat than that which came from the southern institution. The purification sermons would not only bring morality to politics but would also serve notice that there could be no compromise with evil. The image of the South in reference to the gospel was a significant factor in determining the stance of the individual clergyman during the election of 1856. Many were convinced that the gospel was corrupted and the clergyman became an apostate when in contact with slavery. The Democratic party still carried the election despite the extensive groundswell that took place throughout much of the North. The Democratic appeal to fear had carried the day—fear of change, fear of secession, and fear of abolition.[62] But the results of the election witnessed the creation of a new party that had grown within the two years to a close contender for control of government. That the Republican party was able to carry all of New England, New York, and all of the Northwest except Illinois and Indiana as due in a large part to the influence of the church. The dire prediction that a Democratic victory would result in a spread of slavery to Kansas and the territories did not come true. The churches contributed to the ultimate crisis of 1861 by injecting a highly charged and dogmatic stance into the sphere of political dealings where compromise is necessary. They could not avoid doing this, however, without nullifying their purpose for existing.

The controversy that arose as a result of the Kansas-Nebraska Act had great implications for the church. As a result of the attack made on the institution of slavery in the last decade of the antebellum period, the churches plowed the ground from which the social gospel would spring. By the time of the Civil War the convictions had become commonplace that society must be regenerated through the power of a sanctified gospel and that all the evils resulting from greed, alcohol, and slavery could be done away with only by a transformation of the whole social order.[63]

The political and moral conflict growing out of the Kansas-Nebraska Act and the election of 1856 resulted in the merging of the political and ecclesiastical movements. After the rise of the abolition movement, antislavery Christians condemned slavery and called for its eventual end, but did not develop a program of action or a direct strategy for its abolition. They denounced slavery as a moral evil but few related antislavery opinion to one's personal standing with God. Piety was divorced from morality and there was little tendency to stress the connection between a Christian's personal relationship to God and his duty as a citizen. As a result of the Kansas-Nebraska Act, the antislavery clergy brought a change by convincing their followers that there was a direct connection between piety and public duty.[64]

During the canvass of the election of 1856, the clergy had insisted that the secular community deal with slavery as a moral problem, and after the election was over the churches were inclined to take a stronger stand against slavery in their religious institutions. The strong sectional position that was taken by the New School Presbyterian clergy and journals during the election campaign of 1856 added fuel to the passions that had been stirred up by the New School General Assembly action in May at Schenectady where the church ruled that the assembly had the constitutional power to remove slaveholders. This action was viewed gravely by the South because the General Asembly that met in Buffalo in 1853 had requested that the southern judicatories send information concerning the status of slavery in their churches. During the same year the AHMS had requested that the mission churches provide the society's executive committee with similar facts. As the political struggle became more bitter, the resentment growing out of the assembly action of 1853 and 1856 caused the New School congregations in the South to be pushed into a stronger defense of slavery. Antislavery Presbyterians were convinced that the Democratic party's victory in 1856 foreshadowed the doom of the free church, free speech, free labor, and common schools in Kansas, if not in the entire Missouri and Mississippi valleys. This attitude caused the western judicatories to return with renewed vigor to the slavery controversy in the General Assembly, and to demand that the church be immediately cleansed of any relation to the southern institution. Within six months after the election of 1856 the AHMS separated from the slaveholding churches, and the southern synods withdrew from the New School assembly because of the controversy concerning slavery.[65]

Domestic Missions
and Divisions in the Church

*T*he Kansas-Nebraska Act and its aftermath created a determination
to free their churches from any connection with slavery among many
Calvinist Christians in the Northwest. A Presbyterian minister serving
the AHMS in Licking County, Ohio, found the "wicked prejudice" against
the old domestic home missions board to be "the most painful thing" to
confront him in his work.[1] Other clergy and churches in the North experi-
enced similar problems of the relation of the AHMS to slavery.[2] The dissension was often so widespread that it involved entire associations and
presbyteries. J. H. Newton, agent for the AHMS in the Western Reserve,
complained of the failure to secure adequate collections in the churches
of his field. "Many of the churches have been torn into fragments" by
the controversy over the connection of the churches with slavery. "What
the end will be is difficult to divine," he said.[3] At the Ohio Congregational
Conference in June 1856, Thomas Wicks, secretary of the Marietta, Ohio,
agency, found it necessary to defend the AHMS when it was charged with
discrimination against Congregational churches on the Western Reserve.
The reason so few were aided, he explained, was because "a large portion . . . had withdrawn their sympathies and support from the AHMS,"
and given their contributions to other socieities after denouncing the AHMS
on account "of its complicity with Slavery." The effects of the political
response to the Kansas-Nebraska Act in Illinois was similar to the reaction
in Ohio, and in Wisconsin by 1855 the opposition to slavery had grown
so strong and the sympathy with the "free missions" movement had increased so much that the supporters of the AHMS found it necessary
to open their churches and pulpits to the agents of the AMA as a means
of staving off division in the church. The Wisconsin agent of the old
board spent much time and energy in attempting to answer the complaints
of churches in the state against the Society because of its connection with
slavery. He, however, had so little sympathy with the position of the
AHMS on the "vexed" question that he made no attempt to answer the

charges of the agent of the other society who spoke in the Beloit Congregational Church. Clary remained silent because he felt he could not deny the main thesis that the AHMS aided churches to whose fellowship members were admitted who held and treated their fellow men as property.[4]

When Flavel Bascom spoke before the Presbyterian and Congregational Convention of Wisconsin in 1856, he accused the old board of being in favor of the extension of slavery to the territories. This was because they were building up slaveholding churches in the South, he reasoned. The AMA, on the other hand, took the position of the Wilmot Proviso in church and state. Aratus Kent informed Badger that the supporters of the AHMS "greatly disapproved" of what was said but "were not prepared to contradict" it.[5] Clary could go no further than to state the facts, which were stale stories in any meeting in Wisconsin in 1856. While opposed to secession from the AHMS, the facts were that the Wisconsin AHMS agent and directors sympathized with the policy of the antislavery domestic missions organization. A great majority of the friends of the old board sympathized with Clary in his desire to see the Society instruct missionaries to bar voluntary slaveholders from the missionary churches they organized. In urging the adoption of such a rule, Clary reminded the AHMS officers that Daniel Noyes, one of the secretaries, while touring the West in June 1855 had agreed that "public sentiment" of the friends of the Society in the West required that some such policy be followed toward the southern institution.[6]

In Iowa, after the adoption of the Kansas-Nebraska Act, Asa Turner, a director of the AHMS, became a life member of the AMA The latter organization had been making efforts to persuade Oliver Emerson to become its agent in Iowa. Although Emerson was on the point of rejecting the bid, he accepted it on the insistence of Turner, who felt that "few if any" of the churches in Iowa would refuse to listen to the plans of the AMA if stated by Emerson. It was Turner's belief that most of the churches "would put a portion at least of their missionary collections" into the treasury of the AMA. J. A. Reed, the AHMS agent for Iowa, urged Emerson to take the agency as the best means of preventing an "alienation and division" on the "subject of slavery." Emerson took the agency, but the association agreed to send another to act as a representative in part of the field.[7] Because of the proximity of Iowa to the conflict in Kansas, public opinion had undergone much change.

Before the passage of the Fugitive Slave Law, Congregationalists in the West had been members of the Presbyterian synods, but after 1851 they set up their own associations. The attack on the AHMS in the West was to a great extent spearheaded by these associations. While western Presbyterians were by no means silent on slavery, they largely channeled their complaints and grievances to the General Assembly. During the 1840s no western Presbyterian judicatory complained directly to the Society, but in the 1850s they began to show concern about the stance of the AHMS as well as that of the General Assembly.[8]

The influence of the events of the times on the AHMS was revealed by a more radical choice of a speaker at the anniversary meeting for 1856. The Society chose, among others, the radical Congregational clergyman, Horace James, of Worcester, Massachusetts, and left the subject to his "own selection." It was James's object to "embolden timid ones to speak more freely," and to "encourage faint-hearted men" to be fearless and self-sacrificing in the declaration of the Gospel," rather than to divert the audience with "clap trap." He considered it an opportunity "to act . . . upon public opinion respecting the great Evils" of the land, and "their appropriate remedy."[9]

The changing sentiment of the AHMS was also reflected in its publications. The *Home Missionary* for January 1856 carried an article on "Religious Liberty in America" that was commended by the *Congregationalist* for its "aptness to the existing state of opinion" on the subject. The *Home Missionary* for May declared that servitude was the greatest obstacle to the gospel in the land because the institution of slavery infused "a subtle demoralization throughout the community." In the annual report of the Society published during the same month, the editor maintained that the effort to extend slavery to Kansas was "pernicious to the cause of religion and good morals."[10]

When an article appeared in the *Home Missionary* condemning the "Slave Power" as exercising an arbitrary censorship over the press, and often prescribing expositions for the pulpit, a minister in Virginia challenged the correctness of the statement and defended the southern clergymen. Daniel Noyes, the editor, explained that he had not intended to refer to missionaries, but defended his position. "This is true not only of many Southern but even of many Northern pulpits," he added. As proof, Noyes cited the example of the clergyman at Baptist University, South Carolina, who was prevented from returning to the state because he failed to attend a meeting called to express sympathy for Preston Brooks, who attacked Charles Sumner in the Senate.[11]

The stronger antislavery position of the AHMS received a favorable reception from some of the western Congregational associations. The General Association of Iowa rejoiced in the position of the Society in regard to slavery, as indicated in the May 1856 number of the *Home Missionary*, and the Ohio General Association noticed "with unalloyed pleasure the clear and decided witness" the Society had recently borne in its publications against American slavery "as constituting one of the greatest obstacles to the spread of the gospel." The association voted approval of the AHMS's refusal to commission slaveholders and the denial of aid to all churches in which missionaries were "not to be allowed to bear their testimony."[12]

Despite the strong statements published in the *Home Missionary*, many judicatories and church conferences expressed a lack of confidence in the AHMS. The Congregational Association of Western Pennsylvania resolved that it could not place confidence in the AHMS nor give the organization their support because the Society sustained churches that received slaveholders as members. The conflict following the Kansas-Nebraska Act and the campaign of the presidential election of 1856 had made many religious bodies more conscious of the problem of slavery in American society. The Illinois General Association restated its earlier position declaring slaveholding to be an immorality and the defense of the institution to be a doctrinal heresy, either of which disqualified a member for church fellowship. The General Association of New York was silent on any obligation of the churches to the AHMS, but commended the AMA "to the prayers and contributions of the churches as deserving especial attention from the extraordinary exigencies of the country and the cause of Christ." The Elgin, Illinois, association went even further in its cooperation with antislavery missions. The association instructed its committee on missions "to secure a competent missionary to labor within its field under a commission from the Illinois Home Missionary Association," which cooperated with the AMA.[13]

The western critics of the AHMS succeeded in maneuvering the Society into a most progressive position concerning slavery. When the agent for western Wisconsin and Minnesota asked for specific information on the position of the AHMS in reference to slavery so that he could answer complaints that were occurring with more regular frequency, David Coe repeated the old argument by pleading that the Society was not an ecclesiastical organization and could not make terms of fellowship barring slavery from the churches. But Coe advanced a step beyond the stand that the Society had taken in public print. He informed the western agent that the executive committee meant "to sustain none but fearless, faithful antislavery men" who were "instructed and exhorted to deal with slavery, as well as all other sin."[14]

By June 1856, the General Association of Iowa decided that the time had fully arrived when the AHMS "should no longer grant aid to any church" that allowed "the practice of slaveholding by its members." The measures were adopted as an alternative to separation from the New School

Presbyterians in the home missions work. The clerk explained that due to "the recent enormities of slavery" in Kansas the association was of the opinion that the system of bondage should no longer have "a place in the house of God." In November the Iowa resolution was referred to a special subcommittee of the executive board for consideration. Badger assured the Iowa clerk that "in due time he trusted that a communication could be sent to Iowa that would be satisfactory to all friends of the cause."[15]

On January 29, 1857, the *Congregational Herald* announced that the executive committee of the AHMS had adopted a rule that financial aid would not be granted "to churches containing slaveholding members," unless it could be proven that the relation was sustained for the benefit of the servant. The *Herald* published a letter from one of the members of the executive committee of the Society. In reference to the new rule the writer of the letter was purported to have said, "We are to be the judges and not the churches or presbytery." William W. Patton was on the editorial staff of the *Herald* and his father, William Patton, was still on the executive committee of the AHMS. It was said that the information on the new rule and the letter to the *Herald* had come from the elder Patton.[16]

The Society had responded to the new developments that had taken place in the church under the impact of the struggle in Kansas and due to the heat of the election of 1856. In 1855 the Consociation of Congregational Churches of Rhode Island voted to refrain from appointing a delegate to ecclesiastical bodies that tolerated slaveholding. The General Association of New York suspended correspondence with the New School Presbyterian General Assembly for a year.[17] The Presbyterians and Congregationalists were in strong disagreement about independent church extension work. As the territorial question drew the lines more clearly throughout the nation, the sectional difference within the Presbyterian church became more marked. Since the New School church had an abolitionist reputation, with the growth of southern nationalism the New School members in the South found it necessary to come forward with a stronger defense of the institutions of their section.

At the Buffalo meeting of the General Assembly of 1853, Robert McLain, of Mississippi, informed the church that slaves were held by as many southern Presbyterians as could afford them.[18] In 1856, William E. Hollet, of the Presbytery of South Lexington, Mississippi, admitted on the floor of the assembly that he held slaves by choice and principle, and Alexander Newton, of Jackson, Mississippi, addressed a series of letters to the *Christian Observer*. "As were our fathers," he wrote, "so are we slaveholders from principle. Slaveholding is not a sin any more than monarchy, oligarchy, and aristocracy are sins." The most outspoken defender of the

South, however, was Frederick A. Ross. When the request for information from the southern church was proposed in 1853, Ross made a counter-proposal asking for information from northern churches on "the number of members who seek to make money by selling . . . negro clothing, hand-cuffs, and cowhides" in the South.[19] At the Schenectady meeting of the General Assembly of 1856, Ross challenged the measures adopted by the assembly in 1850 as meaning nothing.

> They are a fine specimen of Northern skill in platform making. . . . A plank for the North, a broad board for the South. . . . It is a gum-elastic conscience stretching now to a charity covering all the multitude of our Southern sins, con-tracted now, giving us hardly a fig leaf righteousness.[20]

Late in 1856 Ross wrote a series of letters to Andrew Blackburn of the Knoxville, Tennessee, *Presbyterian Witness*. Ross maintained that the North was racked with infidelity and the discussion of servitude would "result in the triumph of the true Southern interpretation of the Bible. The sin *per se* doctrine will be utterly demolished," he confidently predicted. His letters were widely reprinted. Ross approved of the position of New-ton and wrote a series of letters to the *Christain Observer* in answer to Albert Barnes's recent book, *The Church and Slavery*. Barnes had insisted that the subject of servitude should be "agitated and discussed" in the church. "The churches should detach themselves from all connexion with slavery," Barnes had advocated. In reply, Ross defended slavery as a Bible institution.[21]

The rise of southern nationalism among the southern churchmen was matched by similar expressions by the judicatories of the section. The New School Synod of Mississippi in 1856 found agitation in the church to be crip-pling its efforts and influence, and voted to form a committee to correspond with other southern judicatories for the purpose of forming a southern as-sembly. The Presbytery of Hanover, Virginia, also decided to separate "if agitation should be continued." The Presbytery of Shiloh, Tennessee, re-solved that it was "an unquestionable fact" that the public mind in the South regarded the relation between master and servant to be "sanctioned by the word of God."[22] As the political struggle became more bitter, the New School men and churches in the South were pushed into a stronger defense of slavery that was not demanded of the Old School Presbyterians.

As a result of the feeling that slavery was expanding and the belief that the defense of servitude was growing, the western church moved to a posi-tion of demanding discipline. The Presbytery of Portage asked the Synod of Western Reserve to withdraw and become independent if no decisive measures were taken in 1857.[23] The synod agreed to petition the assembly, and memorialized the highest judicatory to send down a requisition to the Synod of Mississippi to enjoin upon the Presbytery of Lexington, South, to take steps to discipline W. E. Holley, one of its members. The ground for the charge was the statement made by Holley on the floor of the assembly in 1856. All of the presbyteries were asked to take similar action.[24] After the death of Holley early in 1857, the Presbytery of Lexington, South, adopted resolutions to the effect that all its members were open to the same charge that the Western Reserve had made against him. Other judicatories made similar charges against Holley; Robert McClain of Newton, Mississippi; Alexander Newton of Clinton, Mississippi; and Frederick Ross of Richland, Tennessee.[25]

When the Assembly of 1856 resolved that it had the power to remove slavery from the church, the southern delegates addressed a letter to the New School Presbyterians residing in the slaveholding states and assured them that the action of the highest judicatory did not make slavery *prima facie* evidence of sin. If the assembly should conclude that "the relation of master and servant, in any case, is an offense," said the southern commissioners, "we shall unitedly dissolve our connection with that body." The presbyteries of Illinois and Springfield and the Synod of Illinois asked for a statement that would counteract the circular letter. These judicatories also requested that the churches be enjoined to consider slavery *prima facie* evidence of unfitness for membership in the church. The Synod of Cincinnati united with other Presbyterian judicatories in calling for discipline for southern churches and asked for the adoption of a Declaration and Testimony to answer "the erroneous impressions" spread abroad. The *Central Christian Herald* urged the northern Presbyterians to support the Cincinnati resolutions and memorials were sent up from other judicatories in the West appealing to the assembly to take stronger measures. The Presbyterian churches in the East, being more conservative than those in the West, were less inclined to be affected by the new growth of antislavery sentiment, and the Fourth Presbytery of New York went so far as to protest against the antislavery position and testimony.[26]

The developments in the Presbyterian Church were a factor in the AHMS assuming a new position in 1856. It was claimed that the action of the executive committee was only following the ecclesiastical grounds taken by the Presbyterian Church in 1850 and 1853. The secretaries of the Society explained that increased opposition to the Society in the South, the activity of the Southern Aid Society, and the inquiries of the Society concerning the status of mission churches had reduced the number of churches in the South looking for aid to a very nominal figure. Many southern ministers had come forward to sustain slavery as a scriptural institution, and some publicly boasted of being slaveholders themselves "on principle and from choice," so that it became more difficult to determine on what principle slaves were held by southern church members. Thus, the rule was adopted stating that the fact that a church contained slaveholders was *prima facie* evidence against it and the burden of proof was on the church. Badger claimed that there were few missionaries left in the South since "men faithful and true 'had felt obliged' to shake the dust 'off their feet', in accordance with the Resol[ution] of the Albany Convention, and seek some other field of labor."[27]

But the Society met almost united opposition from the Presbyterian press. The new rule was prematurely published in the *Congregational Herald*, and the silence of the official organ of the AHMS until May 1857 tended to delay the full effects of the new development until after the Society had published its statement concerning the new rule. In February, the *American Presbyterian* considered it "scarcely credible" that Presbyterian members of the executive committee would acquiesce in a rule constituting a power for the executive committee over church members that would be above that of the church, the presbytery, the synod, or the General Assembly. The *Christian Observer* found the new rule to be "subversive" to the constitution of the Society and charged that the executive committee had been "goaded forward" by the western Congregational associations. The *New York Evangelist* complained that the rule tended to "irritate and divide," and the *Genessee Evangelist* charged that the new rule was an assumption of ecclesiastical power by a mere missionary agent. The strongest stand was taken by the editor of the *New York Observer*, who warned the AHMS that the churches would not "bow the knee to the Baal of abolitionism." By the end of March the *New York Evangelist* was outdoing the more conservative journals by protesting "against the whole thing from beginning to end." It was "a gross assumption of power never conceded to them," added the editor. "Who would have anticipated that the *New York Evangelist*, once a pioneer in the antislavery cause . . . would have arrayed itself against a rule so imperatively required by the spirit of the Gospel," retorted the *Congregational Herald*. The *Presbyterian Witness* of Knoxville, Tennessee, spoke for New School Presbyterians in the South. It served notice on the Presbyterian Church that the union of Congregationalists and Presbyterians in the support of home missions must end or the assembly "must consent to be ruled" by the Society. Among the Presbyterian journals, the *Central Christian Herald* of Cincinnati stood alone. "If the AHMS rule is . . . in strict accordance with the spirit of the resolutions of the General Assembly at Detroit in 1850, we do not see how our church can, with any propriety, object to the action of the society," said the editor. The *Congregational Herald* was supported by the editor of the *Oberlin Evangelist*, who defended the right of the Society to express an opinion on the morality of slavery and act upon it. The *American Missionary*, however, had no faith in the ability of the AHMS to meet antislavery standards. The editor served notice that antislavery Christians would not relax their efforts until the AHMS was "free from all complicity with the great sin."[28]

Shortly after the Society's rule was made public, the secretaries began to receive correspondence from the eastern seaboard opposing the action of the executive committee. In western and central New York, councils were divided. The influence of Samuel Cox was exerted against the Society in public protests "against the innovation" in the benevolent institution of which he was one of the oldest supporters. The strong voice of William Wisner spoke out against the home mission rule. "Satisfy abolitionists: You might as well attempt to fill up the Dark Abyss of the Bottomless Pitt, as to satisfy abolitionists," Wisner had warned earlier. This influential Ithaca clergyman was expected to carry western New York with him. The *Genessee Evangelist* saw western New York rising in a united opposition to the new rule. "As far as we have had an opportunity to judge, there is one prevailing sentiment on the subject in this section, among the ministers and the laity," reported the editor. John A. Murray, agent for the Geneva, New York, area, warned the home office that something should be published to show the reason for the adoption of the recent ruling. The course of central New York was also still doubtful. Theodore Spencer, agent of Utica, New York, was not sure that the action was desirable.[29]

The Philadelphia auxiliary of the AHMS opposed the action of the executive committee. Robert Adair, corresponding secretary of the Philadelphia branch, wrote to Asa D. Smith: "In this city and vicinity there is but one mind among the ministers and laymen on this subject. All regard it as the introduction of a new policy. . . . One that conflicts with the Constitution of the Presbyterian Church." The Philadelphia branch circulated a petition against the decison, gathering signatures from as far as western New York. The Philadelphia Home Missionary Society published a "Protest" against the action of the parent Society that claimed the AHMS was violating its own constitutional object to send the gospel to destitute regions "within the United States." The "basis and character" of the Society had been changed "into a sectional and partisan institution," added the *Christian Observer*.[30]

In answering the charges of the opponents of the new rule, Asa D. Smith bore the burden of defense for his colleagues on the executive committee of the AHMS. Since the attacks came from Presbyterians, the best strategy for the Congregationalists on the executive committee was to remain silent. The committee faced the public with the claim that they were unanimous in the decision to adopt the new rule. Asa Smith assured his fellow Presbyterians in the editorial columns of the *New York Evangelist* that the new rule was not a Congregational plot. "It is the management of our own funds, not the changing, or annulling, or any way affecting ecclesiastical standing of any one," explained Smith. Smith's letters were combined with other correspondence, printed in pamphlet form, and distributed widely. He took the position that the decision of the executive committee was necessary because "the Kansas Outrage and the late decision of the Supreme Court" had aroused a spirit in the North and West that forced a choice.[31]

The May number of the *Home Missionary* was the Society's official defense of its new position. The article was aimed at those who had not yet formed an opinion concerning the controversy and was "designed to meet the opposition from the conservative side." An attempt was made to show that the Society had followed a tradition of progress in harmony with the changing times, and had taken the middle ground concerning the rule adopted in 1856. Shortly after the article appeared in the *Home Missionary*, the secretaries made efforts to have it printed in all of the Presbyterian and Congregational journals, reprinted in pamphlet form, and circulated throughout the land along with Asa Smith's *Home Missions and Slavery*.[32]

Early in April, Theodore Spencer, the Utica agent of the AHMS, received through the mail copies of an anonymous pamphlet entitled *The Position of the Southern Church in Relation to Slavery*. Spencer guessed immediately that the secretaries and executive committee were "at the bottom" of the movement. The Utica agent considered the pamphlet "a most capital hit. Its publication just now, and circulation over the country, is striking the nail exactly on the head." The pamphlet contained material that revealed the extreme position of some of the more radical proslavery southern Christians. The Utica agent reported that many were now of the opinion that southern Presbyterians should withdraw from the General Assembly. In case of refusal, the prevailing opinion was that they should be driven off. Spencer asked for more of the pamphlets to circulate. Badger denied that the *Home Missionary* men proper had anything to do with the pamphlet, but admitted that the anonymous author was, indeed, Asa Smith. Smith reasoned that the best means of strengthening the position of the AHMS and securing support for its new rule was to expose the true position of the more outspoken forces in the southern church. He explained that he was distributing Ross's letter to the *Christian Observer* in answer to Barnes's *The Church and Slavery* because the *Observer* did not have a large circulation in the North. Smith stated that the "eminent" Frederick Ross might be fittingly "styled a 'representative man'" in the South.[33] The circulation of the anonymous pamphlet did much to turn the tide against the conservatives, and to shift the debate to the question of what should be done about the AHMS and to the question of what the General Assembly should do about the South.

After Asa Smith took up the defense of the Society, other Presbyterians came to its aid by giving Smith moral support in his efforts. A few faithful patrons of the AHMS in the North Atlantic states registered their support of the Society. When Smith published his article in the *New York Evangelist*, Chief Justice Joseph Hornblower of New Jersey, a Presbyterian vice president of the Society, expressed cordial approval of the position taken. Laurens P. Hickok, the moderator of the Assembly of 1856 and a well-known seminary professor, stood by the executive committee. An anonymous pastor of a large and influential eastern Presbyterian church confided to the editor of the *Congregational Herald* that he rejoiced in the stand taken by the executive committee. "I am ready to sustain Dr. Smith . . . in the ground he has taken," he informed the editor.[34] But eastern supporters of the Society's new position remained few in number, and their support was generally in the form of private agreement or anonymous backing.

When the judicatories of the New School Presbyterian Church met in 1857, the eastern seaboard presented a united front against the Society. Only in the Third Presbytery of New York was there a strong defense of the Society. The debate in the presbytery took up the larger portion of three days. This was because the presbytery's membership included D. B. Coe, A. D. Smith, C. R. Roberts, and Edwin Hatfield, all members of the executive committee of the AHMS. Hatfield took the lead in supporting the Society. Thomas Skinner, George L. Prentiss, John J. Owen, Alfred E. Campbell, and Roswell Hitchcock opposed the Society. Skinner, Prentiss, and Owen were officers in the Southern Aid Society. The whole question was eventually postponed without a decision by the presbytery. Joseph Stiles, who had been absent from the last three sessions of the presbytery due to his duties as the agent of the Southern Aid Society, rejoiced at the moderation of the judicatory in declining to commend the AHMS. He followed his approval of the presbytery's action with a devastating attack on the AHMS as a tool of the abolitionists.[35]

In the Fourth Presbytery of New York, futile efforts were made to censure the Society but the effort aroused very little discussion and less support. The Presbytery of Newark and the Fourth Presbytery of Philadelphia considered the rule to have struck a perilous blow at the independence of all mission churches. The Presbytery of Montrose, Pennsylvania, continued to cherish uncompromising hostility to the system of American slavery, but could give no sanction to the AHMS.[36]

In western and central New York the judicatories were more divided in their opinions. In April 1856, the presbyteries of Genesee, Champlain, Cortland, Otsego, Utica, and the board of missions of the Presbytery of Rochester approved the measures adopted by the AHMS. All except the last two, however, took action after the southern presbyteries had taken steps to withdraw from the General Assembly. Theodore Spencer, the AHMS agent of central New York, was very active in the meetings of these judicatories in urging that the Society be sustained.[37]

In the Northwest, sentiment was united in support of the new rule. Professor D. Howe Allen of Lane Theological Seminary expressed approval, and all the western agents were greatly relieved to hear of the new position that the Society had taken. The circular reprinted from the *Home Missionary* was sent to the agents in quantity, and the *Home Missions and Slavery* pamphlet was made available to them. When the presbyteries of the Northwest met in the spring of 1857, the AHMS found a staunch ally. In most cases, approval of the action of the Society by the presbyteries was unanimous or without a recorded vote. Only two western judicatories took a stand against the new regulation. The Detroit presbytery, under the influence of Duffield, petitioned the assembly to denounce the attempt of a voluntary society to establish ecclesiastical control over the Presbyterian Church. Duffield had long considered the Congregationalists "political intriguers," but the principal cause for his conservative opposition to the AHMS resolutions and the action of the New School General Assembly was his deep commitment to premillennialism. The Presbytery of Dubuque, Iowa, unanimously condemned the action of the AHMS. There had been strong sectarian feelings between this presbytery and the Congregationalists of the region. The new rule had been adopted in response to the memorial of these Congregationalists.[38]

Public opinion in New England was everywhere in favor of the Society's new rule. The New England home mission secretaries and agents all spoke favorably of the action of the executive committee. Benjamin P. Stone, New Hampshire home missionary secretary, viewed the new rule as "one link in the chain of events that will ultimately bring about a separation of the great antagonistic principles in the land — freedom from Slavery, Congregational voluntarism from Presbyterian ecclesiasticism." The Maine Missionary Society approved the executive committee measure, and the General Association of Maine concurred in this action when it convened.

The Massachusetts General Association gave its "hearty approval" to the Society "without debate and without dissent" except from "a small number of Southern Aiders." The General Associations of Connecticut and New Hampshire, and the district associations approved the action of the Society. The Congregational associations in the West expressed similar unanimity, but often used stronger language.[39]

The AMA supporters were divided on the attitude they should now take toward the AHMS. J. P. Williston, one of the members of the executive board of the AMA, expressed approval of the AHMS's position, and sent a donation as proof of his sincerity. Oliver Emerson admitted to his colleagues in Iowa that he no longer opposed the AHMS and would modify his course of action, and E. D. Seward concluded that the AMA no longer needed a home department. But after the *American Missionary* article of May 1857 was published, many of the AMA supporters concluded that the old board acted under the influence of outside pressure that should be maintained. By 1861, however, Oliver Emerson had once again been added to the roll of the AHMS. During the same year, Flavel Bascom became reconciled with the old board and encouraged the agent of the Illinois Missionary Association to become the representative of the AHMS for northern Illinois. The Illinois agent accepted the appointment with the AHMS after consulting with Jocelyn.[40]

The supporters of the Southern Aid Society were among the most severe critics of the AHMS's new measures. A minister from Tennessee took advantage of the situation to make visitations in the churches of Kentucky to collect funds for the Southern Aid Society. It was reported that he told "the people of the horrible abolition monster called the AHMS," which had taken recent action against slavery.[41] At the Southern Aid Society anniversary in 1857, J. Duché Mitchell, of the Domestic Missionary Society of Richmond, Virginia, accused the AHMS of violating "its own constitution by withdrawing . . . aid from the South."[42] Some of the supporters of the Southern Aid Society had broken with the majority of their congregation who supported the AHMS even before the new ruling. Early in 1856, George D. Phelps left the Church of the Puritan in New York because of the political abolitionism of the pastor, George B. Cheever.

The most effective attack that was made on the Society's new rule was made by Joseph C. Stiles, agent of the Southern Aid Society, in *Modern Reform Examined.* The focus of his attack was that the new rule was the "legitimate off-spring of the abolition spirit."[43] But its force was checked by AHMS publications. In the week before the AHMS anniversary meeting in May 1857, the executive committee released its thirty-first annual report. Included in the report that was prepared for distribution at the opening of the meeting was an article on the new rule adopted from the *Home Missionary* for May of that year. It was again emphasized that the Society had long been making inquiries concerning slavery. The executive committee would use its judgment as to the merits of the slaveholding churches in the distribution of its funds. By ignoring the existence of the Southern Aid Society, the alternative that the executive committee appeared to be proposing was to have the decision made by the moderate AHMS or by the abolitionist AMA. When the meeting moved to take up the business before the session, Joseph Clark, secretary of the Missionary Society of Massachusetts, proposed that the report of the executive committee of the AHMS be accepted. The report included the new rule of the executive committee. Although there were many opponents of the new measure on the floor, no opposition was offered to its adoption.[44]

The General Assembly of the New School Presbyterian Church met in Cleveland during the week following the anniversary meeting of the AHMS in New York. The issue of slavery and the position of the AHMS were in the forefront of questions that were expected to be discussed before the Assembly. In April, the *Genesee Presbyterian* had anticipated that the General Assembly would be "nearly united" on the issue of the new rule. "The committee will retrace its steps, and retreat from its present position, or we shall be forced to withdraw our co-operation."[45] The *American Presbyterian* was not so optimistic. It saw the action of the executive committee as throwing "an apple of discord in the Assembly." To the *American Presbyterian* the objective of the designers of the new measure was to break up the Presbyterian Church. The *Christian Observer* surmised: "No churches within our bounds . . . will ever give the N[ew] Y[ork] committee an opportunity to inquire into motives of their members in continuing to hold the relation which they sustain to their servants."[46]

Frederick A. Ross and Robert McLain were on hand to defend themselves before the assembly. Ross restated his position: "The relation of master and slave is sanctioned by the Bible; . . . The evils in the system are the same evils of oppression we see in the relation of husband and wife, and all other forms of government."[47] The public position of the southern church in the spring of 1857 effectively directed the attention of the assembly away from the AHMS and toward the pronouncements of the southern judicatories and clergymen. The memorials of the presbyteries condemning the AHMS and asking for censure of the Society were passed over and the western judicatories' petitions to discipline the South for sustaining a connection with slavery were considered.[48]

When the committee report was presented to the assembly, the western antislavery forces tried without success to substitute stronger measures denying fellowship to advocates of the doctrine that slavery was a Bible institution, and calling on the Presbytery of Lexington, South, "to review and rectify their position." Another substitute resolution "earnestly condemned the position" of the Presbytery of Lexington, South, and called on the Mississippi presbytery to "review and correct their position." When this measure was adopted by the assembly, a group of southern delegates protested against the measures as being a "virtual exscinding of the South."[49]

While still in Cleveland, the southern delegation met and drew up an "address" to the church. The southern commissioners announced that they were withdrawing from the General Assembly because of the unconstitutional measures adopted at the Cleveland meeting. This address fastened the blame for the troubles in the church on the western judicatories by declaring,

> In consequence of the political agitation of the subject and the pressure brought to bear upon them by Congregational Churches holding most ultra abolition sentiments, many of our western presbyteries have become more urgent in demanding progressive action of the Assembly. . . . They have desired the Assembly to express its views of the sin of slaveholding so clearly, that they can be made the basis of discipline by the courts of the Church.

An eastern "Conservative" correspondent to the *New York Observer* judged that the southern schism was necessary to establish peace in the church because "Ohio would never let the subject rest." The southern address called for a meeting of all Presbyterians opposed to the agitation of the sectional controversy to meet in Washington (later changed to Richmond) to organize a new General Assembly. When the southern Presbyterians met in Richmond, they withdrew from the New School General Assembly, and adopted measures declaring slavery to be an institution of the state that did not properly belong "to the Church judicatories as a subject for discussion and inquiry." A meeting was called for April 1858 to organize the United Synod of the Presbyterian Church.[50]

With the secession of the southern Presbyterians, the AHMS rapidly withdrew from all churches containing slaveholders. The withdrawal was accelerated because the AHMS added the requirement that all churches receiving aid had to belong to judicatories that sustained the Society. By 1860 the secretaries could announce that there was not a single church sustained by their funds that contained slaveholders.[51] The Society had not anticipated the speed with which the transition would take place. Early in 1857 the secretaries had begun to take up the case of each church involved with the southern institution to determine which should be retained in the missionary organization.[52] The information contemplated under the rule "has been cheerfully furnished, in many instances, before and since the Resolution was adopted" announced the secretaries in their publication in May 1857. When the secretaries did not secure enough information, they pursued the question further by asking for additional facts. If a church session refused to comply with the request for information on the ground that the Society had no authority to inquire into ecclesiastical matters, the Society withdrew its aid. In one case in which a church refused to furnish a reply on ecclesiastical grounds, the executive committee renewed the commission on the basis of a sincere reply from the missionary even though the church contained three slaveholders.[53] Badger informed the missionary that he had the confidence and sympathy of the New York office. "There has been a very unjust impression and a very unnecessary alarm in certain quarters in regard to its action on the subject of slavery," Badger assured him.[54] But many missionaries voluntarily left the South, and many missionaries native to the South withdrew from the service. In May 1857, the largest southern auxiliary, the Missouri Home Missionary Society, announced that it could not accept the new rule, and officially withdrew in 1859.[55] Meanwhile, missionaries in Kentucky, Tennessee, and Virginia were cut off when their judicatories ceased to cooperate with the AHMS after they withdrew from the Presbyterian Church.

In 1858 the New School Presbyterian Church created a Permanent Committee on Home Missions. The Presbyterian committee had taken over denominational domestic work so completely by May 1860 that the executive committee of the AHMS reported that Presbyterian contributions had fallen off 40 percent in the past five years. The Permanent Committee on Home Missions announced that Presbyterian congregations were free to contribute to any domestic missionary organization, but it requested that churches that were not supported by the AHMS take up collections for the Presbyterian committee. When some commissioners requested that the Presbyterian committee deny aid to churches containing slaveholders, it refused because there was no defensible principle by which the committee could make discrimination on moral grounds.[56] After the Presbyterian Committee on Home Missions made the request for funds from churches not aided by the AHMS, the executive committee of the AHMS broke off all relations with the Presbyterian Church, thus ending a partnership that had existed since 1826.

The Die Is Cast:
The Election of 1860

*W*e are enemies as much as if we were hostile States. I believe that the northern people hate the South worse than ever the English people hated France; and I can tell my brethren . . . that there is no love lost upon the part of the South," Alfred Iverson, the senator from Georgia, frankly informed his northern colleagues in the United States Senate one month after the election of Lincoln.[1] This was the state of affairs in the nation as seen from the perspective of a southern senator in December 1860. The election of Lincoln had set the stage for the last episode of the panorama of a divided nation. After the Compromise of 1850, the last threads of union had been broken one by one. The election of 1860 took place in an atmosphere in which opinions, North and South, were far more crystallized than during the campaign of 1856. Events had taken place that made both sections more determined to maintain their positions.

In 1857 and 1858 the North was swept by waves of religious revivals that affected urban churches no less than their rural counterparts. The religious awakening led to deeper national soul-searching and made antislavery sentiments more acceptable. As a result a sectional candidate was more acceptable in the North in 1860. The antislavery measures taken by northern churches as a result of the moral reawakening caused the South to take a more defensive stance. The Dred Scott decision delivered on March 6, 1857, by the United States Supreme Court burst like a bombshell over a nation that had already been turned into two hostile camps by the struggle over Kansas. "The most important decision ever made by the Supreme Court of the United States was announced yesterday," declared the *New York Times*. "The supreme tribunal of the land decided that . . . Congress has no power to prohibit slavery from any portion of the federal territory, nor to authorize the inhabitants thereof to do so," explained the *Times*.[2] By this decision slavery had been given freedom in the public domain.

The response of the religious community was prompt and determined.

"If our union really stands on that basis . . . the union may go into a thousand million fragments and the sooner the better I say," wrote a Congregationalist from Massachusetts to A. L. Chapin.[3] "No decision . . . has been so momentous and wide reaching in its influence; and none has been received by the people, with such feelings of amazement and indignation," observed Levi Field, pastor of a Congregational church in Massachusetts.[4] The impact of the events filled the ranks of the advocates of "higher law." "Democracy and slavery: — what a brotherhood! . . . away . . . with this last and most loathesome phase of political hypocracy," thundered Nathan Beman against what appeared to him to be an unholy alliance between the government and slavery.[5]

The Dred Scott decision played its part in shaping the spirit that led to the division of the New School Presbyterian Church less than three months after its pronouncement. But the rights that the Supreme Court granted to slavery in the territories were largely theoretical rights rather than practical guarantees. In Kansas, the lawless southern settlers had been driven out and lawless northern colonists were in the saddle. In October 1857, the free-soilers got control of the Kansas Territorial Legislature by a large majority. The tide in Kansas had turned in favor of the free state advocates and without the Dred Scott decision and the John Brown raid on Harpers Ferry conditions could have receded from the emotional peak as they had in 1851.

John Brown's raid on Harpers Ferry in October 1859 accelerated the breakup and division of the national program of domestic missions in the Calvinist churches and contributed to the separation of the federal union in 1861. Since slavery was considered a sin or evil by a large majority of northern clergy, and violence against society was likewise sinful, many clergy and religious journals discussed the John Brown raid.[6] A large number of the clergy condemned the violence but praised Brown's motives and principles.[7] After Brown was hung he became a martyr to many in the North who considered slavery sinful. J. B. Bittinger, a New School Presbyterian and corresponding editor of the *Central Christian Herald*, wrote that Brown was drawn into the affair because "the Spirit of God" was "abroad in men's hearts." The raid "magnetized the feelings of the whole country."[8] In an article appearing in the *Anglo-African*, James W. C. Pennington, a black Presbyterian minister, praised the purpose of Brown's raid and urged all to pray for Brown, and Henry H. Garnet, another black Presbyterian clergyman, told an audience at Shiloh Presbyterian Church in New York that the hanging of Brown would bring forth divine retribution. Joshua Giddings, who was a commissioner to the New School Assembly in the 1840s, wrote to a friend shortly after the raid that Brown "deserved the character of a hero." The old abolition Calvinist, Beriah Green, called Brown a "Servant of God" and "a true Hero — a genuine Son of Humanity."⁹

Some Congregationalists praised Brown in reverent terms. Jacob Manning, pastor of the Old South Congregational Church, spoke in Tremont Temple, Boston, and asserted that Brown had been "the instrument of Providence. . . . God has used this man." Later, at a meeting to raise funds for Brown's family, Manning compared Brown with Crispus Attucks, "the black man who died for the white race,"¹⁰ and H. M. Dexter, editor of the *Boston Congregationalist* and pastor of the Pine Street Congregational Church, wrote to a prayer meeting for Brown that while he did not justify Brown's raid, he thought it would be glorified in the future as resulting in good for "the cause of freedom."¹¹ Henry W. Beecher also saw the significance of the martyrdom of Brown. In a sermon in Plymouth in October, he pleaded: "Let no one pray that Brown be spared. Let Virginia make him a martyr." Some of the most radical sermons were made by George B. Cheever. In a sermon in his Church of the Puritan, for example, he insisted that Brown "was as properly engaged in seeking the deliverance of the enslaved . . . as Commodore Decatur [was] in seeking to break up the piracy of the Algerines."¹² Sermons of this type were reported in the South as typical in the North and powerfully influenced the attitude of southern church and political leaders.

Many Congregational laymen thought in the same terms as the clergy. Timothy Howe, a Wisconsin Congregational layman and later a congressman from Wisconsin, wrote that he was sure that, in the courts of Virginia, Brown "stood not a ghost of a chance for acquittal." But in "'Heaven's Chancery' it may appear that Brown struck . . . not selfishly but benevolently, not for his own good but the good of his fellows."¹³ Theodore Tilton, who later became editor of the *New York Independent*, informed an audience in Philadelphia that Brown had set a "Christian example of unwavering heroism." An Ohio layman saw retribution in store for the South and wrote to his congressman that though the South may stave off the evil day for a time, "it is only that the storm may burst with greater force."¹⁴

The AMA took a radical position on the raid. While not justifying the raid, the *American Missionary* expressed hope that the uprising would further "the cause of emancipation." Samuel Adair, an agent of the AMA in Kansas, was Brown's brother-in-law. John G. Fee told a New York audience that the country "needed more John Browns, not with guns but spiritual weapons." The conservative press reported that Fee had only said that the country needed more Browns.¹⁵ The reaction in the South was furious and violent.

The AHMS took a more moderate stance. Richard Storrs, Asa Smith, and Joseph Thompson, members of the executive committee of the AHMS, preached Thanksgiving sermons in which they did not mention Brown at a time when almost all sermons gave considerable attention to the raid. In a similar sermon Leonard Bacon rebuked the "unchristian spirit" of sympathizers with the insurgents, and followed up his sermon with a letter to Governor Henry Wise in which he claimed that Brown had been mentally ill for some time.[16]

The émeute dealt a blow to the nonviolent effort to end slavery. Since 1856 Elihu Burritt had worked on a plan to end slavery by compensating slaveholders with a fund derived from sale of public lands. President Eliphalet Nott, of Union College, and Mark Hopkins, president of Williams College, were active supporters of the program. Nott was a vice president and Hopkins a director of the AHMS. The rise in sectional tensions as a result of the raid caused the program to be abandoned. The Brown uprising destroyed all hope of AHMS mission work in the South and led to the final break between the New School Presbyterian Church and the AHMS. It brought the gains the AMA missions had made in the South to a halt and all of its missionaries and supporters were driven from the region. J. Scott Davis and John Fee fled from Kentucky and Daniel Worth escaped from North Carolina.[17]

In the southern states the effect of John Brown's raid was to transform the election of 1860 into a referendum on whether the Union should be continued. Following the Harpers Ferry raid, the South started a campaign to cleanse itself of all northern contamination.[18] "Though the Southern mind is divided on every other subject, social, moral and political, on slavery it is a unit," warned the *North Carolina Presbyterian*.[19]

The controversy concerning the part the clergy should play in political contests and elections never completely subsided after the campaign of 1856. Most antislavery Christians remained as uncompromising in speaking on the moral question of slavery after 1856 as before, but they resisted efforts to attract the Know-Nothing supporters. When the *New York Tribune* suggested that the Republicans bargain with the Know-Nothings, F. D. Parrish, the Ohio vice president of the AMA, urged Republican leaders to "stand firm" on their principles against a bargain with the Know-Nothings or the party "would loose [sic] the hold it now has upon the moral sense of the nation." When the suggestion surfaced later that the American vote be courted, Carl Schurz warned a Republican rally that if the party tried to catch a few Know-Nothings, it would "throw away the support of two hundred thousand of the most unselfish and faithful Republicans." Journals that took a conservative stance and the Democratic press continued to condemn clergymen who delivered political sermons.

In an editorial in the *Christian Observer,* Converse disagreed with those who claimed that politics and religion could not be separated. "If it be proper for the minister of the gospel to enlighten his people on these subjects, it may also be proper to bring the influence of his pulpit instruction to judgement at the ballot box," he added.[20] As the controversy continued, the *Cincinnati Gazette* expressed its views on the subject. "A man who has any religion will carry it into all relations of life, and a man who has none, will be pretty sure not to exhibit any in his politics." As the discussion began to apply more specifically to the election of 1860, the *Boston Congregationalist* advised the Christian community that if they would bring their Christianity to bear upon their politics, they must adopt as their fundamental rule "to side with no political interest for which they *cannot* pray."[21]

Nathan Lord challenged the thinking of those who believed that a moral reform could be achieved by the church and the clergy. He set forth his beliefs in a letter to a friend in Virginia. The letter was later printed in many newspapers throughout the country. "Whether we have democracy, anarchy or despotism, we shall not be rid of slavery till the day of the Lord. . . . Without a miracle, I see not but that slaves will yet be called for in New England, and by New England men — slaves having attributes, if not the name, of slaves, and possibly in worse condition than we now complain of in reference to the south," he predicted.[22] Lord, however, found few in the North who would agree with his position.

The northern Christians who controlled the benevolent organizations were committed to a reform of society. When the Republican convention opened in Chicago in May, the influence of the friends of benevolence and the church was present in the councils of the convention. The first session was opened with a prayer by Zephaniah Humphrey, pastor of the First Presbyterian Church of Chicago. Humphrey's prayer revealed that the anti-slavery spirit of the Republican party was still very much alive. "We ask that Thou wilt deliver us from all the evil to which we are exposed, and that Thou wilt make us to shake off, and put away all those evils which we are too apt to cherish. . . . Show us the way of rescuing the oppressed from the house of bondage, and make this country truly free," beseeched the Chicago clergyman. But the convention did not have as much of an atmosphere of a religious crusade as that of 1856. The leaders of religion and benevolence were not such familiar figures as they had been four years earlier, and the professional politician was observed on every hand. William Jessup, elder of the Presbyterian church in Montrose, Pennsylvania, was chairman of the committee on platform and resolutions. On the second day of the convention, he presented the platform and successfully defended it.[23] The platform committed the party on many economic issues far removed from slavery, but the original antislavery character of the party was preserved by its firm opposition to the extension of slavery in the territories.

Gerrit Smith saw the Republican party as a conservative force holding back true political abolitionism. He lamented the decline of a truly radical antislavery spirit and urged the clergy and the church to take an active part in the campaign.[24] An abolitionist from Maine disagreed with Smith's view of the Republican party. Abolitionists, he said, would support the Republican party because of its platform.[25] But all of the abolitionists in Maine did not agree with him. The elderly vice president of the AMA, Reverend David Thurston, wrote in his journal: "I would not vote for either of the four candidates for the presidency. Not for Lincoln of Illinois, though doubtless the best of the four, because he is not in favor of abolishing slavery in the District of Columbia, nor the internal slave trade, and is in favor of the fugitive slave act."[26]

Many of the radical antislavery advocates participated in the campaign by fulfilling various speaking engagements. Edgar Ketchum, an active member of the Congregational Church of the Puritan in New York and soon to become treasurer of the AMA, was a zealous Republican during the presidential campaign. His services were acknowledged in 1861 when Lincoln appointed him collector of Internal Revenue for the eighth district in New York. The old renegade abolitionist clergyman, Ichabod Codding, who had done more to lay the antislavery political foundations in Illinois and Wisconsin than anyone else, campaigned extensively for the Republicans in Iowa, Illinois, and Wisconsin as he had in 1856. The conservative Republicans tried to push Codding to the side and bar him from participating in the campaign, but popular demand forced the conservatives to yield. Although Codding freely admitted that the Republican party was not entirely what he desired, he threw himself into the contest and identified himself with the objectives of the party. In his speeches he maintained that the issues were clear-cut and distinct between the parties. In July, Codding told an Illinois audience that the campaign was "the 'conflict of ages' between Liberty and Despotism, Freedom and Slavery."[27]

In Wisconsin, E. D. Holton, president of the Wisconsin Missionary Society and former Liberty party member, traveled within the state as a Republican speaker, and the Michigan Republicans showed their antislavery leaning by nominating James Birney, son of the abolitionist James G. Birney, for lieutenant governor. Some Garrisonian abolitionists, however, admitted that they favored the Democrats. They saw the possibility of progress toward disunion as a result of a Democratic victory.[28] Both the Democrats and Republicans accused each other of having the support of the abolitionists, and the journals of each party refused to accept the honor.

The urgency of the struggle over Kansas in the summer and autumn of 1856 was gone in 1860, but after the nomination of Lincoln, the controversy concerning the political activities of the clergy was renewed. The clergy's dire predictions of the consequences that would follow the election of Buchanan had not materialized. Instead of becoming a slave state, Kansas was securely in the hands of the free soil forces. The *Albany Atlas and Argus* saw the religious crusade of 1856 as being largely absent in the campaign of 1860. As the editor understood it, "Clergymen feel no impulse of duty to become political missionaries." What appeared to be an absence of a deep-seated religious conviction in the days preceding the election of 1860 was largely a lack of political controversy and disagreement within the ranks of the religious community. Political harmony had increased so much in many areas that during the campaign of 1860 there was "very little excitement" because people were "too much of one mind," as Republicans.[29] But the clergy did not remain silent. To the majority of the leaders of the church and benevolence, a great moral issue was at stake. N. S. Dickinson, pastor of a Congregational church in Massachusetts, instructed his congregation in September that "prayer accompanied by no effort for good" was a mockery. "If you pray that oppression may cease, that the oppressed may go free, then vote for men who will bring about such results. . . . Be consistent," he added. "Vote as you pray. Remember the eye of God is upon you as much at the ballot-box as in your closet."[30] William N. Cleveland, a Long Island pastor, spoke to his congregation shortly after the election on the issues of the day. "This may be with some a political question only, but . . . with the vast mass of conscientious and Christian men at the North, it is virtually a religious question. I am persuaded that the voice of the people, so emphatic and decisive at the ballot-box lately, has been prompted by moral feeling."[31]

The Calvinist journals took the lead in urging Christians to take an active part in the election. "Arouse the conscience of the nation against the iniquity of slavery, and there will be a moral power in political action which will never rest until the Federal government is divorced" from slavery, vowed the editor of the *Independent*. The *Boston Congregationalist* urged every Christian to "carry religion into politics as a performance of duty," and the editor of the *Congregational Herald* admonished all to pray God would incline all citizens "to exercise aright their high prerogative at the ballot-box."[32] The *American Presbyterian* observed that there were sermons on every subject involving the questions of the day, including free soil, popular sovereignty, and the power of the Supreme Court. As the date of the election drew near, the *American Presbyterian* considered religion and politics, and found them to be not so very far apart in principles and effects. "Let the character of our politics be elevated, as we believe is beginning to be the fact. Let their objects be understood to be, not partisan but public — not expediency but principle," said the editor.[33] The *Independent* instructed its readers that it was the imperative duty of every Christian to labor in the election and guard the ballot box "with holy jealousy."[34] Since Protestant congregations were more united in opinion in 1860 than they had been in 1856, the sermons concerning the political campaign did not come into the press for a public airing as often as formerly. However, in one case in Michigan when a pastor preached a sermon on the sins of the age in which he mentioned slavery as a crime against humanity, a minority of the congregation who sympathized with the Democrats walked out of the church. Since the officers in charge of the school house where the congregation met opposed the sermon and sympathized with the minority, the door was locked and barred against the minister and a placard notified the public that there could be "no more Black Republican preaching" in the building. The clergyman was, however, determined to maintain his course of action even if he had to speak out in the open spaces.[35]

In Illinois the clergy remained actively interested in politics. The *Chicago Press and Tribune* reported that clergy and missionaries in southern Illinois were under continuous harrassment because they were Republicans, and a Sabbath school was burned in Mount Vernon, Illinois, because it contained abolitionist books. During May, the Reverend C. C. Phillips, of Rock County, Illinois, delivered an address in which he charged that the "democratic party was pledged, by its platform, to defend and protect slavery" wherever the stars and stripes floated. After the National Republican Convention adjourned, he was the principal speaker at a meeting that convened in Rock County to ratify the action of the national convention. During the same month a Republican clergyman in an adjoining county attacked the Democratic party as being guilty of "total depravity." As the campaign became more heated, in Cairo, Illinois, a Democratic stronghold, a clerical speaker for the Republican party was forced to retreat from the speaker's platform under a barrage of rotten eggs. Similar attacks were made on ministers who were speaking for the Republican party in Jefferson and Washington counties, Illinois.[36] This type of response to clerical participation in political activity was largely limited to regions where the Democratic party was strongly entrenched.

The agents of the missionary organizations were in the field again as they had been in 1856. In many parts of the Northwest, however, there was so much unanimity of sentiment that the expression of political opinions from the pulpit did not have the elements of controversy that had existed in 1856. The political influence of the pulpit, therefore, attracted less attention in the press. A missionary working in the bounds of the Presbytery of Franklin, Ohio, informed his superiors that he endeavored according to instructions from "the secretaries and from the Great Head of the Churches" to make the preaching of the gospel "enlighten the understanding and quicken the conscience, that error and sin, in every form . . . may be exposed, rebuked, and by the blessing of God, abandoned." But he met with some opposition from his own church members, especially when he touched upon the sin of slavery and of upholding, countenancing, and extending it.[37] A Congregational minister, serving the AHMS in Ohio, reported that his church was obnoxious to the Democratic party, which worked to prevent "an attendance" in his church "in so far as they can."[38]

In Indiana the missionaries of the AMA were most active in the campaign. A missionary in Adams County, Indiana, complained that the "pro-slavery professors of religion" and the "pro-slavery politicians" were doing all they could to "cripple" his efforts and "destroy" his influence. By September, he reported that the issues in the election were narrowing down "to the naked question of proslavery or antislavery."[39] Another missionary in the service of the AMA traveled to many localities in both Indiana and Illinois to lecture on the issues and speak on the contrast between Christianity and slavery. He often received extended petitions from citizens asking him to lecture in their community.[40] The *Johnson County Enquirer* reported at the height of the campaign: "Our brother the missionary . . . is here. He will give unto such as have money, very small books, wherein it is written all about the poor African and our brother Abraham, the rail splitter."[41]

In Michigan the clergy, supported by the AHMS, had more to report. A Congregational missionary wrote that the Democrats poured out "the vials of their indignation" upon his congregation and himself because they were Republicans. The political leaders of the Democratic group combined and mustered their entire force to thwart the clergyman's efforts "to influence and mold society." The Democrats objected because the pastor prayed for the overthrow of slavery, and they called him "the D — — Black Republican Minister."[42] A clergyman serving the AHMS in a Congregational church in Calhoun, Michigan, urged his congregation "to act and vote as Christians . . . under a sense of responsibility to God."[43] The missionaries in Illinois, Iowa, and Wisconsin were equally active.[44]

The most influential leaders in the Congregational and New School Presbyterian churches in the Northwest, who were officers in the AHMS and the AMA, identified themselves with the Republican party cause. Jonathan Blanchard had supported the Republican party in 1856, and in 1858 he had delivered a two-hour oration in support of Lincoln. He condemned the Democratic program as morally wrong and destined to lead to political ruin. In an address in January 1860, before the Literary and Library Association in Galesburg, Illinois, Blanchard advised his listeners to act "from principle instead of time-serving expediency" on public questions. The true mark of success, he said, was the approval of God.[45] Years later when J. M. Sturtevant, a director of the AHMS, recalled the campaign of 1860, he remembered the period as one in which "the political excitement moved the community to its very depths. . . . The hopes of many for the speedy triumph of righteousness, alternating with inexpressible horror at the thought of its defeat . . . mingling in our own streets and around our own firesides rapidly formed and intensified individual and national character," reminisced the former president of Illinois College. Lincoln was peculiarly qualified to meet the spirit of the times. As Sturtevant, Lincoln's intimate friend, stated, "His appeal was to the moral convictions of his hearers." Many laymen also wrote and spoke in the campaign in religious terms. John Wentworth, a member of the Second Presbyterian Church of Chicago, wrote in his *Chicago Democrat* that John Brown was an apostle of freedom like John the Baptist, crying in the wilderness of slavery and preparing the way for Lincoln who "will break every yoke and let the oppressed go free."[46]

As the campaign progressed, many leaders of churches and benevolent societies in the East filled the ranks of those making the campaign circuit for the Republicans. William Jessup, a vice president of the AHMS and the Southern Aid Society, was one of the most active. After completing his service to the party as chairman of the platform committee, he took to the campaign trail as a speaker. He met with the supporters of John Bell, the presidential candidate of the Constitutional Union party, in Newark, New Jersey, in July and attempted to win them over to the Republican ranks. In September, he again toured parts of New Jersey and spoke at Elizabethtown and other population centers. As election day drew near, Jessup crossed over into New Jersey for the third series of engagements and gave addresses at Jersey City and other locations in this strong Democratic state.[47]

When the New Jersey Republican state convention met at Trenton, New Jersey, in August, the aged Joseph C. Hornblower, who was a vice president of the AHMS and other benevolent societies, was present. He was given the honor of heading the list of New Jersey Republican electors by the state convention. During September when Hornblower attended a political meeting in Newark, the band struck up "Hail to the Chief" as former Chief Justice Hornblower entered the hall. The audience greeted him with a standing ovation and much applause even though he was not scheduled to address the rally. At the New Jersey convention, which nominated the Republican party's choice for governor, Hornblower was on hand and made an extended speech despite his advanced years. Although eighty-four years old, he journeyed to Hartford, Connecticut, to attend a political meeting. Ex-Governor William Pennington of New Jersey introduced him as one whose blood still ran warm for the cause of liberty. "He would say, God bless the wide-awake cause," said Pennington of the elderly statesman who sat on the platform with the speakers of the evening.[48]

Late in September the Republican Central Campaign Club called a meeting at Cooper's Union at which Simon D. Chittenden, one of the members of the executive committee of the AHMS, was one of the principal speakers. Although Chittenden was one of the largest wholesale dry goods dealers in the country, he urged the people to vote for Lincoln because Lincoln was honest and the Democratic rule was corrupt. Chittenden was one of the few dry goods dealers to back the Republicans. The *New York Daily Express* denounced Chittenden as being an abolitionist of fifteen years standing even though he had given fifty dollars to a campaign collection that the *Express* had sponsored ten years previously for the Whig party. At the end of September a committee of fifteen, composed mostly of dry goods merchants and thus called by their opponents the "Dry Goods Committee," met for the purpose of a fusion between the Democrats and Constitutionalists. When it appeared that the fusion movement might succeed, Theodore Tilton, one of Henry Ward Beecher's parshioners and part owner of the *Independent*, denounced the movement as the "dry goods fusion" and insisted that the Republican party was the only group that could be identified with the principles held by the Founding Fathers. Chittenden delivered another speech in New York City on the day before the election. He again predicted "death and destruction to all commercial interests" of New York if the contest went before the House of Representatives. "I tell you, gentlemen, I have determined I should not act under the influence of fear," Chittenden informed the audience with determination. At the same meeting William Dodge presented a paper signed by many of his colleagues that expressed the idea that the election of Lincoln was the only means of preventing the transference of the contest for the presidency to the halls of Congress where it would be certain to renew, in an intensified form, the disgraceful scenes of the previous winter and thus subject the government "to more fearful peril" than any it had hitherto encountered. If the election were thrown into the House of Representatives, the paper predicted that it would "destroy confidence, paralyze business, and depreciate the value of property." Dodge, an AHMS director, had become so much identified with the Republican campaign that he was called on by a banker in New Jersey to help one of the New Jersey congressional districts finance its campaign.[49]

By 1860, in the eyes of the conservatives, George Cheever was probably the most hated clergyman in the nation. He had become progressively more caustic and uncharitable toward the slaveholder and those who sympathized with him. In an address in July 1860 Cheever endorsed Lincoln as being sound on the slavery question. "The question was soon to be, not the extension of slavery where it did not exist, but of its *entire abolition* where it did," promised Cheever in his sermon. He became one of the most active members of the Church Anti-Slavery Society, and his church became the unofficial headquarters of the society. Yet public opinion had moved along with him to the extent that he was elected as a regent of the University of New York in 1859. Many radical Christian abolitionists finally came to the point of supporting Lincoln because, as one said, it would be one step closer to placing "the hand of Freedom on the jugular . . . of the slave oligarchy."[50]

Although Henry Ward Beecher was not as active in the campaign as he had been in 1856, he delivered many addresses and sermons, both from the pulpit and the public platform. Early in 1860, when it was rumored that he was no longer a sound antislavery man, he defended his faithfulness in the columns of the *Independent*. He claimed that he had "given up nothing, changed nothing, except as a bud changes to a blossom and fruit. . . . We never were more invincibly determined to make no terms with it, but to carry on legitimate war to the . . . destruction of it," Beecher insisted. Shortly after Lincoln was nominated, Beecher called on the people to perform their duty as voters. "No man who is the tithe of a man must think that he had a right to withdraw himself from the proper performance of that duty which belongs to him as a citizen. . . . You can no more shirk your duty as a citizen and be without guilt before God . . . than you can shirk your duty as a Christian and be without guilt before God," he charged his congregation. The *New York Daybook* and other Democratic papers styled him the "political parson." As the election day drew near Beecher stepped up his political activities. Near the end of October, he spoke in a Methodist church in Newark, New Jersey, on "Young America." "Our institutions do not turn on the idea of the right to govern, but on the right of manhood, which is inherent in every breast of every color." On the Sunday before the election, Beecher made one of his most effective speeches. The creed of a Christian, he said, should be "God and his fellow-men, piety and patriotism, country and religion, one and inseparable," while the Devil's creed was "religion is religion and politics is politics." Beecher climaxed his election activities by taking his aged father, Lyman, who had cast his first vote for Washington, to the polls so that he could register his last vote for Lincoln. On the Sunday after the election he told his congregation that they must have courage to meet the consequences of victory. "There were always croakers, and timidity is infectious, but we must make courage infectious," he advised.[51]

In the West the clergy responded to the results of the election much as the clergy of the East. On Thanksgiving Day in Cincinnati, Charles B. Boynton, pastor of the Vine Street Congregational Church and sometime editor of the *Christian Press*, saw the struggle then in progress as not essentially between sections or parties, but between "two antagonistic forms of national life . . . striving for mastery." Boynton was thankful for the steady growth of religious sentiment and believed that in the future the church and the party of freedom would move together. To J. M. Sturtevant, the question before the nation was simple. "Shall the government which our fathers founded to secure the blessings of liberty, be administered hereafter for the furtherance of that holy purpose, or for the extension and nurturing of slavery?" Sturtevant saw religion as the most potent weapon wielded in behalf of liberty.[52]

As signs of secession began to become visible in the South, Joseph P. Thompson, one of the members of the executive committee of the AHMS, served notice on his congregation that he was utterly opposed to compromise. "If . . . you ask me to sanction Slavery by some political compromise, you ask me to surrender that great natural charter of liberty which God has given me. . . . I cannot be a party to reducing any man to Slavery," Thompson warned. When the president proclaimed a national day of fasting, Thompson cautioned against compromise as he perceived that some business men were ready to make peace "upon any terms."[53]

David Thurston, like many radical abolitionists, was for letting the South depart in peace. "Let the deluded insane Southerners go," he wrote to a friend. The majority of the clergy, however, were for standing firm. Religiously committed Americans tended mystically to resign themselves to the will of an avenging God, for they considered that bloodshed was His punishment for the terrible sin of slavery. Occasionally they assured the nation that no crisis existed. In November, a reporter in New York inquired of an uptown pastor if he were going to allude to "the crisis" in his sermon. "Crisis?" said the preacher, "I know not of any crisis; that was passed last Tuesday; I tried to do my duty beforehand, and so thoroughly is this church indoctrinated with antislavery sentiment, that I do not believe you will find two members of it who did not vote for Mr. Lincoln. Indeed, I do not know of one," he added. The *Independent* agreed, and informed its readers that the wickedness of slavery should continue to be laid before the public so that the tone of public life would not only be kept up, but elevated.[54]

In January 1861, an Anti-Slavery Church Convention met in New York and resolved that whatever the government's power over slavery in time of peace, it had "in the present exigency, by the act of rebellion or insurrection, the right to suppress rebellion and to abolish slavery, the cause of it." Many viewed this spirit as the chief cause of the conflict. It was the "political parsons of New England," concluded an angry conservative, and their principles who taught that "civil war and the resort to Sharpe's rifles were in accordance with the fundamental doctrines of Christianity." They put on the "Sword of the Lord and Gideon" and preached to the people that God had "called them especially to the work of liberating the slaves."[55]

But not all clergy stood firm against compromise and advocated progress in the antislavery cause. A small minority felt that all possible means should be used to give assurance that fugitive slaves would be returned and slavery in the South was secure. Many conservatives who were closer to the South immediately recognized the full significance of the election of Lincoln. "A momentous event—one of the most so in my time," wrote George Prentiss in his diary on the day after the election. As the dark clouds of civil war began to take shape on the horizon, one month after the election, Prentiss looked out of his study at the fierce snowstorm that signaled the beginning of winter, and recorded his impressions in his diary: "A dull gloomy week in the natural and political world."[56] Nehemiah Adams, of the Essex Street Congregational Church in Boston, as was expected, took a conservative position. He condemned the abuses of slavery, but he argued that slavery was a divine institution, recognized as such in the Bible. He claimed there would be no peace or quietness in the land until the community came to recognize and treat it as such. In the urban centers of the East the conservatives began to influence public opinion. Early in December, an abolitionist meeting and memorial assembly for John Brown was broken up in Boston by a public that suddenly returned to its old hostility toward the abolitionists.[57]

After the election the religious press remained consistent with the stand they had taken before the election. The day after the election the editor of the *Christian Observer* called for prayer beseeching God to "still the tempest of human passion" so that "the Union, the Liberties, and the Rights of every State in the Confederacy" could be preserved. The *Congrega-*

tionalist viewed the whole controversy as an "irrepressible" contest "between light and darkness, civilization and barbarism." The whole interest in the success of the Republican party "lay in the moral question at issue," explained the editor. The *Independent* thanked God that the rule of slavery that threatened to corrupt and debase Christianity had been checked.[58]

The Presbyterian journals were less optimistic that the crisis was over. By mid-November, the *Christian Observer* expressed hopes that both sections would exert their influence to maintain "to the letter and spirit, the principles of compromise embodied in the Constitution" by the Founding Fathers. The *New York Observer*, however, did not think the political compromise of the past could continue. The editor found "that many of the most exemplary Christian gentlemen" of the South believed that the time had come for secession.[59]

By January 1861, the conservative clergy in the urban centers of the East had begun to organize to restore harmony to the nation. Thirty-two influential conservative clergymen from New York and Philadelphia addressed a circular letter to the South on January 1, 1861. The circular assured the South that the North did not support extremist views and that the region had been greatly misrepresented in the press and elsewhere. The signers appealed to southern clergy to exercise a moderating influence on their section. Thirteen of this group were Old School Presbyterians. Two of the signers were New School Presbyterians and two were Dutch Reformed clergymen, and all four of these were officers in the Southern Aid Society. A convention of Presbyterian ministers and elders of Pittsburgh and the surrounding area addressed an appeal to the whole country, and a group of clergymen in Chicago made a similar appeal. A convention of educators, primarily from Union Theological Seminary, Virginia, sent out an address to the North and South in response to the New York circular letter, and secured signatures from Virginia and the Wilmington, North Carolina, area. The address called on the people of that section to avoid needless embitterment or complications of the crisis. It asked the North to remove the cause for separation by guaranteeing full rights for the South in the common territory. No collective response came from the deep South, but many individual letters received from this area denied that the New York circular letter expressed the true sentiments of the free states.[60]

Most conservative clergymen of the North supported Lincoln's administration after war was declared. Shortly after Fort Sumter was captured, the Presbyterian ministers of the Pittsburgh area met and pledged "unalterable and unconditional allegience" to the federal government. They called the developments in the Confederate states "treasonable" and classified as enemies of the country those who afforded "aid, comfort or countenance" to the new government. The *Southern Presbyterian* of May 11 expressed surprise that the "leading ministers of the Old South at the North — especially Dr. [Gardiner] Spring, and the Clergy of Pittsburgh," had gone over "to the support of Lincoln's war policy."[61]

The church became the strongest backer of Lincoln's position. Slavery had become a political issue and was exposed to all the exaggerated emotional feelings that colored political questions. Since slavery was also a moral issue, the church had become deeply involved. As the perceptive foreign clerical observer, Count Agenor de Gasparin, correctly analyzed the situation, the war came as the result of the "uprising of the great people" faced with a moral dilemma that allowed no compromises.[62] The controversy between the North and the South was largely a contest for political power that had reached a point where compromises were not possible because it had become a moral issue. The Fugitive Slave Law took on an importance entirely out of all proportion to the number of slaves that actually escaped or were aided in remaining free. The political rivalry over slavery in the territories developed after the issue had run its course in the territories and was no longer a practical problem.

Although war had come as a result of a multitude of causes woven into a complex pattern, the final events were clouded with political controversy on a moral issue. The possibility of avoiding war as a solution to the slavery question faded away when slavery became the overriding political issue. The division of the churches and their subsequent behavior reinforced sectionalism and accelerated the political controversy that led eventually to political rupture and civil war.[63]

The election of 1860 showed that a majority of Americans were now in favor of halting the expansion of slavery. A significant factor in the new state of mind was the tendency of northern evangelical Calvinists toward humanitarian rather than scriptural religion, which brought a firm endorsement of Republican philosophy. The growing antislavery sentiment in the church was strongly felt in political affairs. The evangelists believed the millennial period was being ushered in by the promotion of revivalism, social reform, and the growing sense of social responsibility that brought new reliance upon human measures to hasten the divine mission of the nation.[64]

The long agitation over slavery that had been carried on in the church prepared evangelists to take a definite stand when the Civil War came. Church people considered the war primarily a moral and religious struggle. They believed God would have a grievance against the nation until every fetter was broken and the slave was free. Failure to respond to indications of providence would bring God's judgment and retribution upon the nation. Attention must remain focused on the moral question of right and wrong. The great national sin must be purged in preparation for the millennial reign of God on earth. Evangelicals believed a special burden rested on them to act morally and to purify the republic by resisting compromise.[65]

The election of 1860 and the coming of the Civil War brought changes in the church. Conservatism all but disappeared under the wave of patriotism as the church rallied behind the government. By fostering the sentiment that made war acceptable, the evangelists brought about their own decline. After 1861 the clergy became less important than politicians, generals, editors, and businessmen in shaping events and influencing public opinion. The churches emphasized denominational loyalty at the expense of interdenominational and national interests. The Plan of Union of 1801 was terminated and benevolent societies became denominational organizations.[66]

Early in the nineteenth century the church had been more concerned about spreading the gospel, not offending the South, and increasing membership rolls than they were in doing what they felt was morally correct. They winked at slavery while it was increasing its strength in the lower Mississippi Valley. In this sense there was a neglect of duty in the church that was as grievous as that on the part of statesmen who suppressed the discussion of slavery in the halls of Congress. After the Mexican War the evangelists were swept along by the antislavery movement toward war as a means of obtaining their objective because they were incapable of finding a peaceful solution to the problem of the expansion of slavery. The Civil War indicated a failure in leadership on the part of the clergy just as much as on the part of statesmen and politicians. The coming of the war was helped along by evangelists who held that they were right and that God was on their side. The action of abolitionists in criticizing the northern church was less effective in purifying the moral outlook of the northern church than it was in strengthening the proslavery stance of the southern church. Changes came in the northern church because of what northern churchmen considered excesses of the South and because of the growing influence of radical Christians within the church that awakened the Christian conscience.[67]

The church could no longer compromise with sin and evil; no deals could be made with Satan. The religious community was often more concerned with safeguarding its moral position and listening to its newfound conscience than with finding a solution that would avoid resorting to war. Until the slavery question moved into the realms of a strictly political issue after the Mexican War, the church saw evidence that progress was being made. But faced with the choice of voting slavery "up or down," the question took on the nature of a moral absolute when slavery threatened to expand into the territories. There was no option between principles and expediency in this context, and the tendency was to slavishly follow principle even though a departure from principle might have moved society closer to the final objective. If the war had not intervened, enough antislavery sentiment might have been created in the churches to bring about a peaceful end to slavery, but ironically the seeds of failure were inherent in the inability of antislavery Christians to envision a working compromise that would have permitted a partial victory over the sin of slavery.[68] From the viewpoint of our day, it is not for us to condemn the refusal of many to compromise on questions of morals — or even to attempt to evaluate whether this was right or wrong. The lesson for contemporary society seems to be that, after weighing the extent of harm to society involved on each side of the question and the extent to which practices confirm or contradict the ethical standard of our civilization, questions of a moral nature on which society does not agree would best remain, if possible, outside the realm of politics.[69]

Abbreviations Used in Notes

AAPP	Amos A. Phelps Papers, Boston Public Library
ACSP	American Colonization Society Papers, Library of Congress
AHMSC	American Home Missionary Society Correspondence, Amistad Research Library
ALCC	Aaron L. Chapin Correspondence, Beloit College
AMAC	American Missionary Association Correspondence, Amistad Research Library
ARAAS	Annual Reports, American Anti-Slavery Society
ARACS	Annual Reports, American Colonization Society
ARAHMS	Annual Reports, American Home Missionary Society
ARAMA	Annual Reports, American Missionary Association
ARMAS	Annual Reports, Massachusetts Anti-Slavery Society
ARNEAS	Annual Reports, New England Anti-Slavery Society
ARVAS	Annual Reports, Vermont Anti-Slavery Society
ASSUP	American Sunday School Union Papers, Presbyterian History Society
BFP	Breckinridge Family Papers, Library of Congress
CCJP	Charles Colcock Jones Papers, Tulane University
CGFP	Charles G. Finney Papers, Oberlin College
CSP	Charles Sumner Papers, Houghton Library, Harvard University
DCP	Dexter Clary Papers, Carroll College
EWP	Elizur Wright Papers, Library of Congress
GBCP	George B. Cheever Papers, Worcester Antiquarian Society
GDD	George Duffield's Diary, Detroit Public Library
GSP	Gerrit Smith Papers, Syracuse University
JARC	J. A. Reed Correspondence, Grinnell College
JBFP	Jonathan Blanchard Family Papers, Wheaton College
JGFC	John G. Fee Correspondence, Berea College
JHCP	John H. Cocke Papers, Library of Congress
LBP	Leonard Bacon Papers, Yale University
LTP	Lyman Trumbull Papers, Library of Congress

MGAPC	Minutes of the General Assembly of the Presbyterian Church (New School)
MTS	McCormick Theological Seminary
PHS	Presbyterian Historical Society
SM	Slavery Manuscripts, New York Historical Society Library
SPCP	Salmon P. Chase Papers, Pennsylvania Historical Society
SPL	Stephen Peet Letters, Beloit College
SWC	Samuel Williston Correspondence, Williston Academy
UM	University of Michigan
WHS	Wisconsin Historical Society
WLGP	William Lloyd Garrison Papers, Boston Public Library
WSPC	William S. Plumer Correspondence, Presbyterian Historical Society

Notes

INTRODUCTION

1. Merton L. Dillon, "The Failure of American Abolitionists," *Journal of Southern History* 25 (May 1959):162–63; Harry V. Jaffa, *Equality and Liberty* (New York: Oxford University Press, 1965), 118–19; Ronald D. Rietveld, "The Moral Issue of Slavery in American Politics, 1854–1860" (Ph.D. diss., University of Illinois, 1967), 5; J. F. Maclear, "The Republic and the Millennium," in *The Religion of the Republic*, ed. Elwayn A. Smith (Philadelphia: Fortress Press, 1971), 188–89; Linda J. Evans, "Abolitionism in the Illinois Churches, 1830–1865" (Ph.D. diss., Northwestern University, 1981), 125–27.

2. John R. McKivigan, *The War Against Proslavery Religion: Abolitionism and the Northern Churches, 1830–1865* (Ithaca: Cornell University Press, 1984), 70, 77, 203–20.

3. Ira V. Brown, "Watchers for the Second Coming: The Millenarian Tradition in America," *Mississippi Valley Historical Review* 39 (August 1951):447–48; Evans, "Abolitionism in the Illinois Churches," 79, 133–34; Whitney R. Cross, *The Burned-over District: The Social and Intellectual History of Enthusiastic Religion in Western New York, 1800–1850* (New York: Harper and Row, 1965), 222, 261.

4. Charles L. Sanford, *The Quest for Paradise in Europe and the American Moral Imagination* (Urbana: University of Illinois Press, 1961; reprint, New York: AMA, 1979), 93; *Home Missionary* 18 (1845):93; *New York Recorder* cited by *Home Missionary* 19 (1846): 117.

5. Richard Mosier, *Making of the American Mind* (New York: Columbia University Press, 1947), 41.

6. *Congressional Globe*, 28th Cong., 2d sess., 19 February 1845, 14, Appendix, 413–15; *Congressional Globe*, 28th Cong., 2d sess., 22 January 1845, 14, Appendix, 346–47.

7. J. L. Tracy to Theodore Weld, 24 November 1831 in *Letters of Theodore Dwight Weld, Angelina Grimké Weld and Sarah Grimké, 1822–1844*, ed. Gilbert Barnes and Dwight Dumond (1934; reprint, Gloucester, Mass.: Peter Smith, 1965), 57; Robert P. Ludlum, "Joshua R. Giddings, Radical," *Mississippi Valley Historical Review* 23 (June 1936):57–58.

8. Evans, "Abolitionism in the Illinois Churches," 433.

9. Lester H. Cook, "Anti-Slavery Sentiment in the Culture of Chicago, 1844–1858" (Ph.D. diss., University of Chicago, 1952), 104.

10. Rietveld, "The Moral Issue of Slavery in American Politics," 1–2; D. F. Fehrenbacker, "The Republican Decision at Chicago," in *Politics and the Crisis of 1860*, ed. N. A. Graebner (Urbana: University of Illinois Press, 1961), 36. Eric Foner, *Free Soil, Free Labor, Free Men: The Ideology of the Republican Party Before the Civil War* (New York: Oxford University Press, 1970).

11. Stephen E. Maizlish, *The Triumph of Sectionalism: The Transformation of Ohio Politics, 1844–1856* (Kent, Ohio: Kent State University Press, 1983); Dale Baum, *The Civil War*

Party System: The Case of Massachusetts, 1848-1876 (Chapel Hill: University of North Carolina Press, 1984).

12. John Bodo, *The Protestant Clergy and Public Issues, 1812-1848* (Princeton: Princeton University Press, 1954); Charles Cole, Jr., *The Social Ideas of the Northern Evangelists, 1826-1860* (New York: Columbia University Press, 1954); H. Shelton Smith, *In His Image, but . . . Racism in Southern Religion, 1780-1910* (Durham, N.C.: Duke University Press, 1972).

13. C. C. Goen, *Broken Churches, Broken Nation: Denominational Schisms and the Coming of the Civil War* (Macon, Ga.: Mercer University Press, 1985), 1-2, 13.

14. McKivigan, *The War Against Proslavery Religion*, 15.

CHAPTER 1

1. Joseph S. Clark, *A Historical Sketch of the Congregational Churches in Massachusetts from 1620 to 1850* (Boston: Congregational Board of Publications, 1858), 29; Lois Kimball Mathews Rosenberry, *The Expansion of New England* (1909; reprint, New York: Russell and Russell, 1962), 267; see: Stephen A. Marini, *Radical Sects of Revolutionary New England* (Cambridge: Harvard University Press, 1982).

2. David D. Hall, *The Faithful Shepherd: A History of the New England Ministry in the Seventeenth Century* (Chapel Hill: University of North Carolina Press, 1972), 132, 190; Donald Scott, *From Office to Profession: The New England Ministry, 1750-1850* (Philadelphia: University of Pennsylvania Press, 1978), chap. 4.

3. John A. Andrew III, *Rebuilding the Christian Commonwealth* (Lexington: University Press of Kentucky, 1976), 41-42.

4. James D. Essig, *The Bonds of Wickedness: American Evangelicals Against Slavery, 1770-1808* (Philadelphia: Temple University Press, 1982), 103-4. The New Light clergy advanced the doctrine of sanctification by faith instead of election and supported revivals to promote faith.

5. Joseph Conforti, "The New Divinity and the Edwardian Evangelical Tradition." Paper read at the Organization of American Historians Convention, April 1983, 9; Clifford S. Griffin, "Religious Benevolence as Social Control," *Mississippi Historical Review* 44 (December 1957):444.

6. Fred J. Hood, *Reformed America: The Middle and Southern States, 1783-1837* (University: University of Alabama Press, 1980), 27-28, 172, 174.

7. Hood, *Reformed America*, 27-28, 172; Paul E. Johnson, *A Shopkeeper's Millennium: Society and Revivals in Rochester, New York, 1815-1837* (New York: Hill and Wang, 1978), 141; Lois W. Banner, "Religious Benevolence as Social Control: A Critique of an Interpretation," *Journal of American History* 55 (June 1973):41; Winthrop D. Jordan, *White Over Black: American Attitudes Toward the Negro, 1550-1812* (Baltimore: Penguin Books, 1969), 364-65; M. J. Heale, "Humanitarianism in the Early Republic: The Moral Reformers of New York," *Journal of American Studies* 2 (October 1968):173; John R. Bodo, Charles C. Cole, Jr., Clifford S. Griffin.

8. Oliver Wendell Elsbree, *The Rise of the Missionary Spirit* (Williamsport, Pa.: Williamsport Printing Co., 1928), 56; Randolph Anthony Roth, "Whence This Strange Fire? Religious and Reform Movements in the Connecticut River Valley of Vermont, 1791-1843" (Ph.D. diss., Yale University, 1981), 131; Bernard Weisberger, *They Gathered at the River: The Story of the Great Revivalists and Their Impact upon Religion in America* (Boston: Little, Brown and Co., 1958), 3-4; Glenn C. Altschuler and Jan M. Saltzgaber, *Revivalism, So-*

cial Conscience, and Community, in the Burned-Over District: The Trial of Rhoda Bemeent (Ithaca: Cornell University Press, 1983), 38.

9. Essig, *The Bonds of Wickedness*, 128, 133–34; Donald G. Matthews, "The Second Great Awakening as an Organizing Process, 1780–1830: An Hypothesis," *American Quarterly* 21 (Spring 1869):42.

10. Elsbree, *The Rise of the Missionary Spirit*, 56.

11. Hood, *Reformed America*, 181–82, citing *Evangelical Guardian* 2 (November 1818): 316–19.

12. Earl R. MacCormac, "The Development of Presbyterian Missionary Organizations, 1790–1870," *Journal of Presbyterian History* 43 (September 1965):152; Colin B. Goody-koontz, *Home Missions on the American Frontier* (New York: Octagon Books, 1971), 96, 112; Andrew, *Rebuilding the Christian Commonwealth*, 95.

13. William G. McLoughlin, *New England Dissent, 1630–1833*, 2 vols. (Cambridge: Harvard University Press, 1971), 2:810–11; Andrew, *Rebuilding the Christian Commonwealth*, 66–67.

14. Minutes of the General Assembly, 1801, in *Minutes of the General Assembly of the Presbyterian Church U. S. A., 1789–1820*, 212.

15. The judicatories of the Presbyterian Church are: the session, which is the court corresponding to the congregation; the Presbytery, which includes all of the churches in a contiguous geographic region; the synod, which often corresponds to the boundaries of the states; and the General Assembly, which is the highest judicatory or national authority of the church.

16. Earl MacCormac, "The Transition from Voluntary Missionary Society to the Church as a Missionary Organization" (Ph.D. diss., Yale University, 1960), 46, 48; Richard D. Birdsall, "The Second Great Awakening and the New England Social Order," *Church History* 39 (September 1970):355, 359; Essig, *The Bonds of Wickedness*, 103; Emory Elliot, "The Dove and the Serpent: The Clergy in the American Revolution," *American Quarterly* 31 (Summer 1979):200.

17. Lois W. Banner, "The Protestant Crusade: Religious Missions, Benevolence and Reform in the United States, 1790–1840" (Ph.D. diss., Columbia University, 1970), 208; Charles Cole, *Social Ideas of the Northern Evangelists, 1826–1860* (New York: Octagon, 1966), 196. Banner dissents from the social control thesis advanced by Griffin, Conforti, and others.

18. Cushing Strout, *The New Heavens and New Earth: Political Religion in America* (New York: Harper and Row, 1974), 156.

19. David B. Davis, "The Emergence of Immediatism in British and American Antislavery Thought," *Mississippi Valley Historical Review* 49 (September 1962):209–30; Essig, *The Bonds of Wickedness*, 161; Ronald G. Walters, *The Antislavery Appeal: American Abolitionism After 1830* (Baltimore: Johns Hopkins University Press, 1976), 39.

20. "Records of the Synod of Indiana," *Journal of the Presbyterian Historical Society* 5 (December 1926):267–70.

21. Gilbert H. Barnes, *The Anti-Slavery Impulse* (New York: D. Appleton Century, 1933), 11; J. Stanley Mattson, "Charles Grandison Finney and the Emerging Tradition of 'New Measure Revivalism'" (Ph.D. diss., University of North Carolina, 1970), 246–48; Benjamin P. Thomas, *Theodore Weld: Crusader for Freedom* (New Brunswick, N.J.: Rutgers University Press, 1950), 100–117; Robert H. Abzug, "Theodore Dwight Weld: A Biography" (Ph.D. diss., University of California, Berkeley, 1977), 145–80.

22. Bertram Wyatt-Brown, "Conscience and Career: Young Abolitionists and Missionaries," in *Anti-Slavery, Religion and Reform: Essays in Memory of Roger Anstey*, ed. Christine Bolt and Seymour Drescher (Hamden, Conn.: Dawson and Sons, 1980), 185, 187;

William G. McLoughlin, "Evangelical Childrearing in the Age of Jackson: Francis Wayland's Views on What and How to Subdue the Willfulness of Children," *Journal of Social History* 9 (Fall 1975):22; Milton Sernett, *Abolition's Axe: Beriah Green, Oneida Institute, and the Freedom Struggle* (Syracuse, N.Y.: Syracuse University Press, 1986), 4–5; Ronald Walters, "The Erotic South: Civilization and Sexuality in American Abolitionism," *American Quarterly* 25 (Winter 1973):200.

23. Banner, "The Protestant Crusade," 371–72.

24. Lyman Beecher, *Autobiography*, ed. Charles Beecher, 2 vols. (New York: Harper and Bros., 1864), 2:189; Scott, *From Office to Profession*, 85–86; Lawrence Sesick, *The Lane Rebels: Evangelicalism and Antislavery in Antebellum America* (London: Scarecrow Press, 1980), 145–6; Lawrence J. Friedman, *Gregarious Saints: Self and Community in American Abolition, 1830–1870* (Cambridge: Cambridge University Press, 1982), 19; Scott, *From Office to Profession*, 85.

25. Charles G. Finney to Theodore Dwight Weld, 21 July 1836, in *Letters of Weld and Grimké*, ed. Barnes and Dumond, 1:319.

26. Walters, *The Antislavery Appeal*, 53.

27. Altschuler and Saltzgaber, *Revivalism, Social Conscience, and Community, in the Burned-Over District*, 18.

CHAPTER 2

1. These include eighteen clergymen and four laymen. See: ARACS, 13:51; 14:34–35; 16:23; 25:20, 25; 29:42; 32:51–53; 33:11–12; 24:29; *African Repository* 1 (September 1825): 224; 3 (June 1827):128.

2. Calvin Montague Clark, *American Slavery and Maine Congregationalists* (Bangor, Maine: Calvin Clark, 1940), 36; *Liberator*, 14 December 1833.

3. William Lloyd Garrison,*Thoughts on African Colonization* (New York: Arno Press, 1969), 21; Lydia Maria Child, *An Appeal in Favor of That Class of Americans Called Africans* (New York: Allen and Ticknor, 1836), 127–28.

4. Ralph V. Harlow, *Gerrit Smith, Philanthropist and Reformer* (New York: Henry Holt, 1939), 113–20; ARAHMS (1843), 6; ARACS (1831), 14:34; Benjamin P. Thomas, *Theodore Weld, Crusader for Freedom* (New Brunswick, N.J.: Rutgers University Press, 1950), 33; James G. Birney to Clement C. Clay, December (n.d.) 1832 1:46–48; Birney to Ralph G. Gurley, 27 December 1832, 1:48–50; 24 January 1833, 1:50–53; 24 September 1833, 1:88–90; Dwight L. Dumond, ed., *Letters of James Gillespie Birney, 1831–1857,* 2 vols. (New York: D. Appleton, 1938); see: Betty Fladeland, *James Gillespie Birney, Slaveholder to Abolitionist* (New York: Cornell University Press, 1955), 70–71, 80–89; ARACS (1831), 14:34; Lewis Tappan, *The Life of Lewis Tappan* (Hartford, Conn.: E. Hunt, 1850), 134; Arthur Tappan to Absalom Peters, 24 October 1830; Peters to Tappan, 2 November 1833, Letter Book, vol. G, AHMSC; Absalom Peters to Lewis Tappan, 29 January 1834, Letter Book, vol. G., AHMSC; Arthur Tappan to Absalom Peters, 9 May 1840, AHMSC; see: ARAHMS (1839), 13:5; 1840 (n.d.), 14:5.

5. *New York Observer*, 12 October 1833; ARAHMS (1834), 8:84; ARACS (1842), 25: 20; *Liberator*, 19 October 1833; E. N. Kirk to R. R. Gurley, 23 March 1830, ACSP; *New York Observer*, 5 October 1833.

6. *New York Daily Times*, 19 August 1879; *New York Daily Tribune*, 19 August 1879; Theodore D. Bacon, *Leonard Bacon, A Statesman in the Church* (New Haven, Conn.: Yale University Press, 1931), 194, 196–98; Eugene Fortlette Southall, "Arthur Tappan and

the Anti-Slavery Movement," *Journal of Negro History* 15 (April 1930):173; *Niles Weekly Register,* 1 October 1831, 41:88; Clark, *American Slavery and Maine Congregationalists,* 23, 43.

7. Frederick Clayton Waite, *A History of Western Reserve College and Academy at Hudson, Ohio, From 1826 to 1882* (Cleveland: Western Reserve University Press, 1943), 95–103, 121, 158.

8. Beriah Green to S. S. Jocelyn, 5 November 1832, printed in the *Abolitionist: or Record of the New England Anti-Slavery Society* 1 (Boston, February 1833):29.

9. Green to Jocelyn, 5 November 1832, in the *Abolitionist* 1:29; Waite, *A History of Western Reserve College,* 97; James B. Walker, *Experiences of Pioneer Life in the Early Settlements and Cities of the West* (Chicago: Sumner and Co., 1881), 171–72; Waite, *A History of Western Reserve College,* 102–3; ARAHMS (1838), 12:5; Sernett, *Abolition's Axe,* 24–29.

10. D. W. Lathrop to Absalom Peters, 10 August 1835, 26 September, 17 October 1834, AHMSC.

11. Absalom Peters to D. W. Lathrop, 1 September 1835, Letter Book, 1835–1836, vol. I, AHMSC; Absalom Peters to D. W. Lathrop, 1 August 1834, Letter Book, vol. H.; Lathrop to Peters, 26 February 1836, AHMSC; ARAHMS (1836), 10:70.

12. Sherman Weld Tracy, *The Tracy Genealogy Being Some of the Descendants of Stephen Tracy of Plymouth Colony, 1623* (Rutland, Vt.: Tittle Publishing Co., 1936), 65–66; *African Repository* 1 (October 1825):253.

13. ARACS (1854), 37:17; P. J. Staudenraus, *The African Colonization Movement, 1816–1865* (New York: Columbia University Press, 1961), 98.

14. *Liberator,* 19 October 1833, 22 August 1835; *The Friend of Man* (Utica, N.Y.), 14 July 1836; Louis R. Mehlinger, "The Attitude of the Free Negro Toward African Colonization," *Journal of Negro History* 1 (July 1916):249; *The Friend of Man,* 1 June 1841.

15. *Boston Recorder,* 6 February 1835; *New York Observer,* 19 March 1857.

16. *American Missionary* 18 (May 1874):110; *New York Daily Times,* 28 March 1874; *Boston Weekly Transcript,* 31 March 1874; *Anti-Slavery Reporter* 2 (April 1864):106; *Proceedings of the New England Anti-Slavery Convention . . . of May, 1834* (Boston: Garrison and Knapp, 1834), 15–16, 45–48; Amos A. Phelps, *Lectures on Slavery and Its Remedy* (Boston: New England Anti-Slavery Society, 1834), v–vii; *African Repository* 10 (November 1834): 279–83; *Cincinnati Journal,* 27 June 1834.

17. *Liberator,* 11 August 1837; Stephen S. Foster, *The Brotherhood of Thieves or a True Picture of the American Church and Clergy* (Boston: American Anti-Slavery Society, n.d.), 42; Parker Pillsbury, *The Church as It Is — or the Forlorn Hope of Slavery* (Concord, N.H.: Republican Press Association, 1885), 2d ed., 82; *Oberlin Evangelist,* vol. 8, 13 August, 22 September, 5 November 1851; *New York Express,* 31 July 1851; William Goodell, *Slavery and Anti-Slavery* (New York: W. Harned, 1852); see: James G. Birney, *The American Churches, the Bulwarks of American Slavery* (Concord, N.H.: Parker Pillsbury, 1885).

18. Samuel Reeve to Absalom Peters, 7 February 1834, AHMSC.

19. Peter B. Battle to Absalom Peters, 13 February 1834; Corbin Kidder to Absalom Peters, 27 February 1834, AHMSC; *New York Evangelist,* 9 July 1834; Birney, *American Churches,* 8, 9.

20. *African Repository* 6 (July 1831):155; 7 (February 1832):367; 9 (September 1833):199; 10 (March 1834):8–17; 10 (August 1834): 162–68; P. J. Staudenraus, *The African Colonization Movement,* 68; Early Lee Fox, *The American Colonization Society, 1817–1840* (Baltimore: Johns Hopkins University Press, 1919), 94–100, 125–26, 136–38; R. R. Gurley to J. H. Cocke, 26 July 1831, JHCP.

21. William Lloyd Garrison, *Thoughts on African Colonization,* 143.

22. *Liberator,* 30 July 1831, 23 June 1837, 3; Garrison, *Thoughts on African Coloniza-tion,* 12–24; Zion's Herald, 8:123.

23. *First Annual Report of the Board of Managers of the Boston Prison Discipline So-ciety* (Boston: Boston Prison Discipline Society, 1826), 35–38.

24. Garrison, *Thoughts on African Colonization,* 13; Lewis Perry, *Radical Abolition-ism: Anarchy and the Government of God in Antislavery Thought* (Ithaca: Cornell Univer-sity Press, 1973), 49–50; Cortlandt Van Rensalear to the Board of Managers of the American Colonization Society, 20 March 1833, ACSP.

25. Staudenraus, *The African Colonization Movement,* 134–35; Thomas H. Gallaudett to R. R. Gurley, 26 July 1831; R. R. Gurley to John H. Cocke, 14 September 1831, JHCP.

26. Thomas H. Gallaudett to John H. Cocke, 18 July 1834, JHCP; *Journal of Freedom,* 17 May, 27 August 1834.

27. Charles Tappan to John H. Cocke, 2 September 1834; John Tappan to John H. Cocke, 24 October 1834, JHCP; E. A. Andrews to Leonard Bacon, 30 May 1834, LBP; Henry T. Tuckerman to R. R. Gurley, 1 October 1832; S. M. Worcester to Secretary, 5 November 1834; R. H. Rose to R. R. Gurley, 11 November 1834, ACSP.

28. E. A. Andrews to Leonard Bacon, 30 May 1834; L. P. Hickok to Leonard Bacon, 23 June 1834, LBP.

29. ARACS (1833), 16:xviii–xxii; Leonard Bacon to R. R. Gurley, 19 March 1833; R. R. Gurley to Leonard Bacon, 3 April 1833; S. M. Worcester to Leonard Bacon, 19 February 1834, LBP; Moses Kimball to Leonard Bacon, 28 January 1835, LBP; Theodore D. Bacon, *Leonard Bacon: A Statesman in the Church,* 235; Robert J. Breckinridge to Sophinisba Breck-inridge, 2 August 1834; Robert Breckinridge to Charles Hodge, 31 July 1834, BFP; *Journal of Freedom,* 27 March 1835; Ebenezer Watson to R. R. Gurley, 20 April 1833, ACSP; *Aboli-tionist* 1 (March 1833):43–44.

30. *The Spirit of the Pilgrims* 6 (July 1833):281; *Cincinnati Journal,* 27 June 1834; *Afri-can Repository* 10 (November 1834):281; Beecher, *Autobiography of Lyman Beecher,* 2:259–60; Elizur Wright, Jr. to A. A. Phelps, 20 August 1834, EWP.

31. *Boston Recorder,* 26 December 1834; T. H. Gallaudett to General John Hartwell Cocke, 18 July 1834; R. R. Gurley to John Cocke, 14 September 1834, with enclosure from Gallaudett to R. R. Gurley, 21 July 1831; Cortlandt Van Rensalear to John Cocke, 25 Novem-ber 1834; John Tappan to John Cocke, 24 October 1834, JHCP; Martin Boyd Coyner, "John Hartwell Cocke of Bremo" (Ph.D. diss., University of Virginia, 1962); Charles C. Jones to Mary Jones, 3 February 1830; C. C. Jones to Mary Jones, 18 May 1830, CCJP; Charles C. Jones, *Second Annual Report of the Missionary to the Negroes in Liberty County, Georgia* (Charleston, S.C.: Observer Office Press, 1834), 19; Charles C. Jones to William S. Plumer, 28 June 1834, WSPC.

32. *Boston Recorder,* 26 December 1834; *Journal of Freedom,* 9 January 1835.

33. *Boston Recorder,* 26 December 1834; "Circular" (Boston), 5 January 1835, American Union for the Relief and Improvement of the Colored Race, LBP; *New England Spectator* (Boston), 3, 10 January 1835. For the abolitionists' explanation of how the exclusion of the im-mediatists was affected in the convention, see correspondence from "H. B. B." in the *Liber-ator,* 31 January 1835, and from "F" in the 7 February 1835 issue; R. R. Gurley to Leonard Bacon, 3 January 1835, LBP.

34. *Boston Recorder,* 16 January 1835; *Liberator,* 31 January 1835. For other considera-tions of the Union see Bertram Wyatt-Brown, *Lewis Tappan and the Evangelical War Against Slavery* (Cleveland: Case Western Reserve Press, 1969) and James R. Stirn, "Urgent Gradual-ism: The Case of the American Union for the Relief and Improvement of the Colored Race," *Civil War History* 25 (December 1979):309–28. Stirn presents a narrow view of the Union

and fails to place the organization in its proper setting. He does not see the full implications of the Union as a missionary organization that was aimed primarily at the slave. He neglected to examine the reaction of the South to the Union.

35. *Liberator,* 24 January 1835; George Thompson's Journal, no. 3, printed in *Glasgow Chronicle* office, 14 January 1835, WLGP; Correspondent to *Christian Mirror,* 16 January 1835, cited by *Journal of Freedom,* 29 January 1835; A. A. Phelps to Wife, 16 January 1835, AAPP.

36. *Liberator,* 24 January 1835.

37. *Liberator,* 17 January 1835.

38. Cortlandt Van Rensalear to John H. Cocke, 27 November 1834, JHCP; R. R. Gurley to Leonard Bacon, 3 January 1835, LBP; Leonard Bacon to Gerrit Smith, 23 January 1835, GSP; *New England Spectator,* 14 January 1835; *Boston Recorder,* 9 January, 9, 30 October 1835; Gerrit Smith to Leonard Bacon, 6 February 1835; Gerrit Smith to Jacob Abbot, 22 April 1835, GSP; Gerrit Smith to R. R. Gurley, 24 November 1835, ACSP.

39. Lewis Tappan to Theodore Weld, 29 September 1834, SM, New York Historical Society Library; Earl J. Thompson, Jr., "Lyman Beecher's Long Road to Conservative Abolitionism," *Church History* 42 (March 1973):102; Staudenraus, *The African Colonization Movement,* 231; Wyatt-Brown, *Lewis Tappan,* 127–128; Leonard Bacon to Sarah H. Wisner, 26 January 1835; B. B. Edwards to Leonard Bacon, 31 January 1835, LBP; George W. Benson to Samuel J. May, 27 January 1835, WLGP.

40. Arthur Tappan to A. A. Phelps, 17 January 1835, AAPP.

41. *Boston Recorder,* 23 January 1835; Elizur Wright, Jr. to A. A. Phelps, 5, 22 January 1835, EWP; Elizur Wright, Jr. to Theodore Weld, 9 January 1835, *Letters of Weld and Grimké,* 1:196.

42. *Liberator,* 31 January 1835.

43. George W. Benson to Samuel J. May, 27 January 1835; Henry E. Benson to George E. Benson, 2, 25 February 1835; William L. Garrison to Helen Garrison, 16 March 1835, WLGP; Wendell Phillips Garrison and Francis Jackson Garrison, *William Lloyd Garrison, 1805–1876* (New York: Century, 1885), 1:473; Elizur Wright, Jr. to Beriah Green, 7, 19 March 1835; Elizur Wright, Jr. to A. A. Phelps, 9 February 1835, EWP; Elizur Wright, Jr. to Theodore Weld, 16 March 1835, *Letters of Weld and Grimké,* 1:210.

44. ARVAS (1835), 1:iv; ARNEAS (1846), 4:8; ARAAS (1836), 2:44; Daniel Noyes to Leonard Bacon, 5 February 1835, LBP.

45. E. A. Andrews to Leonard Bacon, 26 January 1835; Leonard Bacon to Sarah H. Wisner, 26 January 1835; Moses Kimball to Leonard Bacon, 28 January 1835; G. W. Blagden to Leonard Bacon, 30 January 1835; B. B. Edwards to Leonard Bacon, 31 January 1835; Daniel Noyes to Leonard Bacon, 5 February 1835; Leonard Bacon to Wife, 14 February 1835; R. R. Gurley to Leonard Bacon, 3 January 1835; Elliott Cresson to Leonard Bacon, 12 February 1835; E. A. Andrews to Leonard Bacon, 28 February, 28 March 1835, LBP; Leonard Bacon to Gerrit Smith, 23 January 1835, GSP; *Exposition of the Object and Plans of the American Union for the Relief and Improvement of the Colored Race* (Boston: Light and Horton, 1835), 4, 7–10, 17; *Liberator,* 28 March 1835; *Boston Recorder,* 28 March 1835. For a complete summary of the "Exposition" see: Werner T. Wickstrom, "The American Colonization Society and Liberia: An Historical Study in Religious Motivation and Achievement, 1817–1867" (Ph.D. diss., Hartford Seminary Foundation, 1958), 274–76; *African Repository* 11 (April 1835):137–44.

46. Daniel Noyes to Leonard Bacon, 5 February 1835, LBP.

47. *New England Spectator* cited by the *Liberator,* 4 April 1835; *Boston Recorder,* 26 June 1835; *Report of the Proceedings and Views of the Taunton Union for the Relief and Improve-*

ment of the Colored Race, May, 1835 (Taunton, Mass.: Bradford and Amsbury, 1835), 10; Boston Recorder, 31 July, 2 October 1835; Christian Mirror, 10, 17 September 1835; New York Observer cited by Cincinnati Journal, 23 October 1835; Liberator, 10 October 1835; Proceedings of the Convention Which Formed the Maine Union in Behalf of the Colored Race (Portland, Maine: Merrill and Byram, 1835), 4–5.

48. Boston Recorder, 20 February 1835.

49. Charles C. Jones, The Religious Instruction of the Negroes in the United States (Savannah, Ga.: Thomas Purse, 1842), 78–79; Minutes of the Synod of Kentucky, 5:50–52, Louisville Presbyterian Theological Seminary; Boston Recorder, 26 December 1834; Address of the Synod of Kentucky on Slavery in 1835 (Pittsburgh: United Presbyterian Board of Publications, 1862), 19–20; Cincinnati Journal, 14 July 1835; James G. Birney to Lewis Tappan, 19 March 1835, Letters of James Gillespie Birney, 1:186; Western Luminary cited by Boston Recorder, 7 August 1835; Emancipator (September 1835), no. 2.

50. Boston Recorder, 13 November 1835.

51. Lexington Luminary, 26 August 1835, cited by Boston Recorder, 11 September 1835; Cincinnati Journal cited by The Ohio Observer, 26 November 1835.

52. Cincinnati Journal, 10 December 1835, cited by Boston Recorder, 8 January 1836.

53. Robert Davidson, History of the Presbyterian Church of the State of Kentucky (New York: Robert Carter, 1847), 340–41.

54. Jones, The Religious Instruction of Negroes in the United States, 79; W. P. Harrison, The Gospel Among the Slaves: A Short Account of Missionary Operations Among the African Slaves of the Southern States (Nashville: Publishing House of the Methodist Episcopal Church, South, 1893), 80.

55. New England Spectator, 3 June 1835; Boston Recorder, 29 May 1835.

56. Liberator, 20 February 1836.

57. Boston Recorder, 3 June 1836; Liberator, 18 June 1836; Report of the Executive Committee of the American Union at the Annual Meeting of the Society, May 25, 1936 (Boston: Perkins and Marvin, 1836), 10.

58. Jones, The Religious Instruction of the Negroes, 72–74; Eduard N. Loring, "Charles C. Jones: Missionary to Plantation Slaves, 1831–1847" (Ph.D. diss., Vanderbilt University, 1976), 320–27; Minutes of the Synod of South Carolina and Georgia (1833), 24, 34, Presbyterian Foundation; Henry A. White, Southern Presbyterian Leaders (New York: Neale Publishing Co., 1911), 295; Ira Berlin, "Slaves Who Were Free: The Free Negro in the Upper South, 1776–1861" (Ph.D. diss., University of Wisconsin, 1970), 407; North Carolina Recorder (Raleigh), 28 January 1835; Stephen Taylor to Secretaries, 26 June 1833, AHMSC; R. H. Rose to R. R. Gurley, 11 November 1834; Corlandt Van Rensalear to Board of Managers, 20 March 1833, ACSP; Ethan Allen Andrews, Slavery and Domestic Slave Trade in the United States (Boston: Light and Stearns, 1836), 191, 200; Southern Religious Telegraph cited by the Ohio Observer, 19 February 1835; Journal of Freedom, 17 September 1834; Appleton's Cyclopaedia of American Biography, 6:252.

59. Absalom Peters to J. W. Douglass, 1 April 1834, Letter Book, vol. G., AHMSC; J. W. Douglass to Absalom Peters, 17 April 1834, AHMSC.

60. Samuel Reeve to Absalom Peters, 7 February 1834, AHMSC.

61. James G. Hamner to Secretary, 25 July 1833, AHMSC.

62. D. A. Campbell to Absalom Peters, 15 September 1834; N. H. Harding to Secretary, 11 February, 1 November 1835; 11 January 1836, AHMSC.

63. New York Observer cited by Boston Recorder, 1 May 1835.

64. William Plumer to John H. Cocke, 27 May 1834, JHCP.

65. Andrews, Slavery and the Domestic Slave Trade, 191–92.

66. Martin Boyd Coyner, "John H. Cocke," 350-51; John H. Cocke to Benjamin H. Rice, 19 September 1832, AHMSC.

67. *Boston Recorder*, 6 March 1835; *Colored American* (New York), 25 March 1837.

68. Leonard Woods to Editor, *Boston Recorder* cited by *Religious Intelligencer* (New Haven, Conn.), 15 February 1835, 616; Ralph Emerson to Samuel Osgood in *Boston Recorder*, 3 August 1838.

69. Henry H. Simms, *Emotion at High Tide: Abolition as a Controversial Factor, 1830-1845* (Baltimore: Moore and Co., 1960), 81, 85-86, 106-7; W. Sherman Savage, *The Controversy Over the Distribution of Abolition Literature, 1830-1860* (Washington, D.C.: Association for the Study of Negro Life and History, 1938), 27-31.

70. *Niles Weekly Register*, 19 September 1835, 49:40; William E. Hatcher, *Life of J. B. Jeter, D. D.* (Baltimore: H. M. Wharton, 1887), 190; Mary Burnham Putnam, *The Baptists and Slavery, 1840-1845* (Ann Arbor, Mich.: George Wahr, 1913), 15.

71. Diary of George A. B. Walker, 17 September 1837, Georgia Department of Archives and History.

72. *Niles Weekly Register*, 21 November 1835, 49:194.

73. John Dickson to Fred W. Porter, 30 April 1834, ASSUP; Edwin Adams Davis, ed., *Life in the Florida Parishes of Louisiana, 1836-1846: As Reflected in the Diary of Bennet H. Barrow* (New York: Oxford University Press, 1943), 45; C. C. Jones, *The Religious Instruction of Negroes in the United States*, 236.

74. Russell B. Nye, *Fettered Freedom: Civil Liberties and the Slavery Controversy, 1830-1860* (East Lansing, Mich.: Michigan State University Press, 1963), 171; *Liberator*, 10 October 1835, 20 February 1836; Louis Filler, *The Crusade Against Slavery, 1830-1860* (New York: Harper and Row, 1960), 132.

75. *The Friend of Man* (Utica, N.Y.), 1 June 1841.

76. *Report of the Executive Committee of the American Union at the Annual Meeting of the Society, May 25, 1836*, 33.

77. Robert Cholerton Senior, "New England Congregationalists and the Anti-Slavery Movement" (Ph.D. diss., Yale University, 1954), 87; W. P. Garrison and F. J. Garrison, *William Lloyd Garrison*, 1:475; Dwyn Mecklin Mounger, "Bondage and Benevolence: An Evangelical Calvinist Approaches Slavery — Samuel Hanson Cox" (Ph.D. diss., Union Theological Seminary of New York, 1975), 52; Staudenraus, *African Colonization*, 231; Wyatt-Brown, *Lewis Tappan and the Evangelical War Against Slavery*, 89-90, 99-100, 138-42.

78. ARMAS (1840), 8:6. For a full treatment of evangelicalism and the Negro in antebellum America, see: Milton Sernett, *Black Religion and American Evangelicalism: White Protestants, Plantation Missions, and the Flowering of Negro Christianity, 1787-1865* (Metuchen, N.J.: Scarecrow Press, 1975).

79. Donald G. Mathews, "Charles Colcock Jones and the Southern Evangelical Crusade to Form a Biracial Community," *Journal of Southern History* 41 (August 1975):319; David T. Bailey, *Shadow on the Church: Southwestern Evangelical Religion and the Issue of Slavery, 1783-1860* (Ithaca: Cornell University Press, 1985), 223-24, 226-28; Fredricka Bremer, *The Homes of the New World*, 2 vols. (New York: n.p., 1835), 1:237; Donald G. Mathews, *Religion in the Old South* (Chicago: University of Chicago Press, 1977), 174.

CHAPTER 3

1. Samuel S. Hill, ed., *Encyclopedia of Religion in the South* (Macon, Ga.: Mercer University Press, 1984), 570-72; Hood, *Reformed America*, 169-71; C. Bruce Staiger, "Aboli-

tionism and the Presbyterian Schism of 1837–1838," *Mississippi Historical Review* 36 (December 1949):391–414; Victor B. Howard, "The Anti-Slavery Movement in the Presbyterian Church, 1835–1861" (Ph.D. diss., Ohio State University, 1961), 42–88.

2. *National Anti-Slavery Standard*, 11 June 1840; Dwight L. Dumond, *Anti-Slavery Origins of the Civil War in the United States* (Ann Arbor: University of Michigan Press, 1959), 47.

3. Edmund Fuller, *Prudence Crandall: An Incident in Nineteenth Century Connecticut* (Middletown, Conn.: Wesleyan University Press, 1971), 33–34; Earl Ofari, *"Let Your Motto Be Resistance": The Life and Thought of Henry Highland Garnet* (Boston: Beacon Press, 1972), 6–7.

4. *New York Observer*, 29 August 1835; *Liberator*, 12 September 1835; *Raleigh Register and North Carolina Gazette*, 15, 22 September 1835; *Liberator*, 19 September 1835; Dumond, *Anti-Slavery Origins of the Civil War*, 55–56; Theodore D. Weld to Angelina G. Weld, 15 January 1842, *Letters of Weld and Grimké*, 2:894; Birney, *American Churches*, 37, 41; ARACS (1847), 30:34; Edward Beecher, *Narrative of Riots of Alton in Connection With the Death of Reverend Elijah P. Lovejoy* (Alton, Ill.: G. Holton Co., 1838), 150.

5. James G. Birney to Gerrit Smith, 13 September 1835, *Birney Letters*, 1:343; Albert Barnes, "The Supremacy of the Law," *The American National Preacher* 12 (August 1838):115, 125; Theodore Dwight Weld to James G. Birney, 22 January 1842, *Birney Letters*, 2:663.

6. Sernett, *Abolition's Axe*, 109; Beriah Green to Gerrit Smith, 19 October 1838, GSP; Goodell, *Slavery and Anti-Slavery*, 468–69; Henry Wilson, *Rise and Fall of the Slave Power*, 3 vols. (Boston: James R. Osgood and Co., 1877), 1:407–8.

7. *Emancipator*, 8 August 1839; *The Friend of Man*, 21 August 1839; James G. Birney to Myron Holley, Joshua Leavitt, and Elizur Wright, Jr., 11 May 1840, *Birney Letters*, 1:566–67; *Liberator*, 3 December 1841; Clark, *American Slavery and Maine Congregationalists*, 101–4; Dumond, *Anti-Slavery Origins of the Civil War*, 34, 94–95, 100; *New York Daily Tribune*, 17 January 1873; David W. Bartlett, *Modern Agitators or Pen Portraits of Living American Reformers* (Auburn, N.Y.: Miller, Orton and Mulligan, 1855), 162.

8. *Western Citizen*, 30 November 1843, 12, 19 January 1847.

9. ARAHMS (1833), 4:4; (1859), 30:123; *Dictionary of American Biography*, 3:356; 7:17.

10. *New York Daily Times*, 11 March 1882; *National Cyclopaedia of American Biography*, 2:414; Joel Schor, *Henry Highland Garnet* (Westport, Conn.: Greenwood Press, 1977), 56; Charles H. Wesley, "The Participation of Negroes in Anti-Slavery Political Parties," *Journal of Negro History* 29 (January 1944):43; W. B. Brewer, "Henry Highland Garnet," *Journal of Negro History* 13 (January 1928):36–52; Howard H. Bell, "National Negro Conventions of the Middle 1840s; Moral Suasion vs. Political Action" and "Expressions of Negro Militancy in the North, 1840–1860," *Journal of Negro History* 42 (October 1957):237–60, 45 (January 1960):12; *Emancipator*, 12 October 1843; *Liberator*, 8 September 1843; *Western Citizen*, 31 August 1843.

11. Benjamin Quarles, "Ministers Without Portfolio," *Journal of Negro History* 39 (January 1954):34. Samuel R. Ward to J. A. Murray, 18 August, 10 November 1843; 1 February 1844; Geneva Congregational Church to Secretary, October (n.d.) 1843; Milton Badger to J. A. Murray, 22 December 1843, Letter Book vol. Q, AHMSC.

12. Earl Ofari, "Let Your Motto Be Resistance," 24; the fugitive slave, Henry Bibb, campaigned for the Liberty party in Michigan. See: Benjamin Quarles, *Black Abolitionists* (New York: Oxford University Press, 1969), 185; ARAHMS (May 1944), 18:28; Committee, Liberty Street Presbyterian Church to Secretaries, 18 May 1843; Milton Badger to Henry H. Garnet, 24 November 1843, Letter Book vol. Q; Garnet to Secretaries, 13 May 1844; Charles

Hall to J. H. Noble, 6 June 1844, Letter Book, vol. R, AHMSC; H. H. Garnet to Charles Hall, 28 June 1844; Charles Hall to H. H. Garnet, 1 July 1844, Letter Book, vol. R, AHMSC.

13. John A. Murray to Milton Badger, 28 March 1844; Badger to Murray, 24 April 1844, Letter Book, vol. Q, AHMSC; *Western Citizen*, 12 October 1843.

14. Charles Doolittle to Charles Hall, 9 October 1844, AHMSC.

15. C. G. Clark to Secretary, 15 October 1844, AHMSC.

16. Lewis Tappan to John Scoble, 19 October 1843, in *A Side-Light on Anglo-American Relations, 1839-1858*, ed. Annie H. Abel and Frank J. Klingberg (Lancaster, Pa.: Lancaster Press, 1927), 149, 186; Lewis Tappan to Secretaries, 18 July 1844; Badger to Tappan, 29 July 1844, Letter Book vol. R, AHMSC; ARAHMS (May 1844), 17:95.

17. Thomas Lafon to Lewis Tappan, 2 March 1842, *Western Citizen*, 13 January 1843; Lewis Tappan to A. A. Phelps, 4 January, 30 September 1844, AAPP; Thomas Lafon, *The Great Obstruction to the Conversion of Souls at Home and Abroad* (New York: Union Missionary Society, 1843), 10, 16, 20-21; Lewis Tappan to John Scoble, 31 July 1844, in *A Side-Light on Anglo-American Relations*, ed. Abel and Klingberg, 188; *National Anti-Slavery Standard*, 29 June 1843.

18. Gerrit Smith to Abijah Crane, 26 August 1844, AHMSC.

19. Lewis Tappan to John Scoble, 31 July 1844, in *A Side-Light on Anglo-American Relations*, ed. Abel and Klingberg, 187.

20. Matthew Spinka, *A History of Illinois Congregational and Christian Churches* (Chicago: Conference of Illinois Congregationalists, 1944), 152; Illinois Association of Congregational Ministers, 1834-58 (Chicago Theological Seminary MSS) 1, unpaged.

21. *Western Citizen*, 26 July, 5 August 1842.

22. *The Liberty Tree* (Chicago), 1 February 1844, 3:31-32.

23. G. W. Elliott to Milton Badger, 15 August 1845; M. N. Miles to Secretaries, 5 January 1845, AHMSC.

24. *Western Citizen*, 20 July 1843.

25. *Weekly Herald and Philanthropist*, 24 June 1844.

26. Stephen Peet to Milton Badger, 9 May 1844, SPL; *Western Citizen*, 20 April 1843.

27. M. A. Boardman, ed., *Historical Sketch of the Grand Avenue Congregational Church of Milwaukee* (Milwaukee: Publication Committee, 1907), 5; Records of the Congregational Church and Society, First Church, Beloit, Wisconsin, 1:8, 23 (Beloit College Library MSS); District Convention of the Congregational Church of Beloit (1842-61), 84 (Wisconsin Historical Society MSS); Stephen Peet to A. L. Chapin, 16 February 1846, ALCC.

28. W. W. Wight, *Semi-Centennial Retrospect, 1844-1894, of the Old White Church* (Milwaukee: Publication Committee, 1894), 7; Family Diary of Lucinda Holton and Edward D. Holton, 1845-83 (Wisconsin Historical Society MSS), 28; A. L. Chapin to Stephen Peet, Milwaukee, 24 August 1846, SPL.

29. Family Diary of Lucinda Holton and Edward D. Holton, 19; *Western Citizen*, 9 February 1847.

30. Family Diary of Lucinda Holton and Edward D. Holton, 24; District Convention of Congregational and Presbyterian Churches of Beloit (1842-61), 128, 134; William W. Woolen, *Biographical and Historical Sketches of Early Indiana* (Indianapolis: Hammond and Co., 1883), 355.

31. John L. Thomas, "Romantic Reform in America, 1815-1865," *American Quarterly* 17 (1965):659-60, 679-80; C. C. Goen, *Broken Churches, Broken Nation*, 156, 160, 184. Gerald Sorin has shown that at least 68 percent of the New York abolitionists were ministers, deacons, elders, and other involved lay leaders. See: Gerald Sorin, *The New York Abolitionists* (Westport, Conn.: Greenwood Publishing Corp., 1971), 64, 112-13; John L. Hammond,

The Politics of Benevolence (Norwood, N.J.: Ablex Publishing Corp., 1979), 69-70. John R. McKivigan found that the Congregationalists and Presbyterians made up nearly half of the three hundred officers of the American Anti-Slavery Society from 1833-40. See: McKivigan, *The War Against Proslavery Religion*, 38.

CHAPTER 4

1. Ernest Trice Thompson, *Presbyterians in the South, 1607-1861*, 2 vols. (Richmond, Va.: John Knox Press, 1963), 1:408.

2. A. C. Dickerson to Secretaries, 1 October 1843, AHMSC.

3. *Watchman of the Valley*, 23 June 1842; Milton Badger to Charles Hall, 15 June 1842, AHMSC.

4. Thornton A. Mills to Milton Badger, 3 March 1842, AHMSC.

5. Milton Badger to Henry Little, 25 November 1843, Letter Book vol. Q; Henry Little to Milton Badger, 9 December 1843, AHMSC.

6. Milton Badger to E. R. Fairchild, 27 May 1844, Letter Book, vol. R; E. R. Fairchild to Milton Badger, 28 May 1844; Badger to I. W. K. Handy, 5 July 1844, Letter Book, vol. R; A. W. Campbell to Secretaries, 31 January 1843, 13 August 1844, AHMSC.

7. Milton Badger to A. W. Campbell, 5 October 1844, Letter Book, vol. R; A. C. Dickerson to Milton Badger, 20 November 1844; Badger to A. C. Dickerson, 2 January 1845, Letter Book, vol. R, AHMSC.

8. *Christian Observer*, 12 June 1846.

9. Cited by *Signal of Liberty*, 23 March 1842.

10. *Signal of Liberty*, 6 April 1842.

11. *Annual Report*, American Board of Commissioners of Foreign Missions (1842), 46; John Bailey Adger, *My Life and Times, 1810-1899* (Richmond, Va.: Presbyterian Committee of Publications, 1899), 136-37, 140-42.

12. *Watchman of the Valley*, 6 July 1843.

13. Adger, *My Life and Times*, 140.

14. Putman, *The Baptists and Slavery*, 55.

15. John Black to Secretaries, 1 February 1845, AHMSC.

16. A. C. Dickerson to Milton Badger, 12 November 1845, AHMSC.

17. Samuel Reeve to Milton Badger, 10 June 1845; Badger to Jacob Mitchell, 27 June 1845; Badger to Samuel Reeve, 15 July 1845, Letter Book, vol. S, AHMSC.

18. Oliver Emerson to Secretaries, 30 March 1843; 29 March, 24 June 1844, AHMSC; Oliver Emerson to J. A. Reed, 11 March 1844, JARC.

19. Milton Badger to Oliver Emerson, 19 July 1844, Letter Book, vol. R, AHMSC.

20. Oliver Emerson to Milton Badger, 16 August 1844, AHMSC; Oliver Emerson to Editor, 16 June 1846, *Union Missionary* (New York) 3 (August 1846):18.

21. *American Missionary*, New Series 1 (January 1857):12-14.

22. George W. Perkins to Secretaries, 1 July 1843, AHMSC.

23. George W. Perkins to Secretary, September 1843, AHMSC.

24. Milton Badger to George W. Perkins, 1, 13 October 1843, Letter Book, vol. Q, AHMSC.

25. *Liberator*, 1 December 1843.

26. George W. Perkins to Secretary, 1, 31 May, 10 June 1845, AHMSC.

27. ARAHMS (May 1844), 18:95; George W. Perkins to Secretary, 27 June 1845, AHMSC.

28. Milton Badger to George W. Perkins, 3, 4 July 1845, Letter Book, vol. S, AHMSC;

George W. Perkins to Secretaries, 28 July, 13 August 1845; Badger to Perkins, 11 August, 8 September 1845, Letter Book, vol. S; A. E. Lawrence to Perkins, 15 August 1845, Letter Book, vol. S, AHMSC.

29. *New York Observer*, 6 June 1840.

30. Howard, "The Anti-Slavery Movement in the Presbyterian Church," 90–95.

31. *The Friend of Man*, 13 July 1841.

32. Thornton A. Mills to Milton Badger, 3 March 1842, AHMSC; *Watchman of the Valley*, 16, 23 June, 7 July 1842; *Philanthropist*, 29 June 1842; Milton Badger to Charles Hall, 15 June 1842, AHMSC.

33. *Western Citizen*, 16 March 1843.

34. *Watchman of the Valley*, 10, 24 November 1842.

35. *New York Observer*, 20 April 1844; *Minutes of the Presbyterian and Congregational Convention Held at Cleveland, Ohio, June 20, 1844* (Cleveland: T. H. Smead, 1844), 2; *Oberlin Evangelist*, 3 June 1844; *Minutes of the Presbyterian and Congregational Convention Held at Cleveland, Ohio, June 20, 1844*, 16; Milton Badger to Charles Hall, 10 June 1845, Letter Book, vol. S, AHMSC.

36. *Watchman of the Valley*, 8 May 1845.

37. *Watchman of the Valley*, 22 May 1845.

38. Cephas Washburne to Secretary, 24 January 1845, AHMSC.

39. Charles Hall to Milton Badger, 3 June 1845, AHMSC.

40. Milton Badger to Charles Hall, 10 June 1845, Letter Book, vol. S; Charles Hall to Milton Badger, 11 June 1845, AHMSC.

41. *New York Observer*, 5 July 1845.

42. *Watchman of the Valley*, 3 July 1845.

43. Charles Hall to Milton Badger, 20 June 1845, AHMSC.

44. *New York Observer*, 5 July 1845; *Signal of Liberty* (Michigan), 30 June 1845; *Watchman of the Valley*, 3, 31 July 1845; Richard S. Taylor, "Seeking the Kingdom: A Study in the Career of Jonathan Blanchard, 1811–1892" (Ph.D. diss., Northern Illinois University, 1977), 298; Charles Hall to Milton Badger, 21 June 1845, AHMSC.

45. George W. Perkins to Secretary, 31 May 1845; Milton Badger to Charles Hall, 10 June 1845, Letter Book, vol. S, AHMSC; Lafon, *The Great Obstruction to the Conversion of Souls at Home and Abroad*, 17.

46. *New York Evangelist*, 3 May 1883; Frederick A. Ross, *The Story of Rotherwood From the Autobiography of Rev. Frederick A. Ross, D. D.* (Knoxville, Ky.: Bean, Warters and Co., 1923), 7–8, 19; Sprague, *Annals of the American Pulpit*, vol. 4, *The Presbyterians*, 748–49; ARAHMS (1841), 4–5; (1842), 4–5; (1843), 4–5; (1844), 4–5; (1845), 4–5; J. E. Todd, *John Todd, The Story of His Life Told Mainly By Himself* (New York: Harper and Bros., 1876), 88–90; ARAHMS (1846), 4–5; *National Cyclopaedia of American Biography*, 24:214; ARAHMS (1847), 4–5.

47. Elias Wells to Milton Badger, 15 September 1845, AHMSC.

48. Records of the Synod of Indiana (1826–45), 1:356–58 (Presbyterian Historical Society MSS).

49. *Watchman of the Valley*, 7 August, 13, 19 November 1845; *Anti-Slavery Bugle*, 20 February 1846; *Watchman of the Valley*, 5 March 1846, citing *Christian Observer*; *New York Observer*, 7 March 1846, citing *Detroit Observer*; *Watchman of the Valley*, 5 March 1846, 8, 18 December 1845, 12 February 1846.

50. *New York Observer*, 30 May 1846; MGAPC (New School, 1846), 28–31.

51. *Western Citizen*, 5 October 1843.

52. *Minutes of the Western Congregational Convention Held in Michigan City, Indiana, July 30–August 3, 1846* (New York: John P. Prell, 1878), 11, 23.

53. *Western Citizen*, 3 November 1846; *Western Herald*, 3, 11 November 1846; Robert T. Handy, *Christian America: Protestant Hopes and Historical Realities* (New York: Oxford University Press, 1971), viii.

54. Timothy L. Smith, *Revivalism and Social Reform* (New York: Harper and Row, 1957), 202–3; Howard, "The Anti-Slavery Movement in the Presbyterian Church," 41–42, 98–99; J. Earl Thompson, Jr., "Lyman Beecher's Long Road to Conservative Abolitionism," *Church History* 42 (1973):107–8; *Watchman of the Valley*, 20 February 1845, 1 January 1846.

CHAPTER 5

1. Lewis Tappan, *History of the American Missionary Association* (New York: American Missionary Association, 1855), 3; Fred L. Brownlee, *New Day Ascending* (Boston: Pilgrim Press, 1946), 2; *Encyclopedia Americana*, 1:576; John W. Barber, *History of the Amistad Captives: Being a Circumstantial Account of the Capture of the Spanish Schooner Amistad* (New York: Hitchcock and Stafford, n.d.), 3; Augustus Field Beard, *A Crusade of Brotherhood: A History of the American Missionary Association* (Boston: Pilgrim Press, 1909), 24.

2. Barber, *History of the Amistad Captives*, 23–25; Brownlee, *New Day Ascending*, 2; Lewis Tappan, *Life of Arthur Tappan* (Hartford, Conn.: E. Hunt, 1850), 318.

3. Beard, *A Crusade of Brotherhood*, 29–30; Tappan, *History of the American Missionary Association*, 8–9; Tappan, *Life of Arthur Tappan*, 318.

4. Tappan, *History of the American Missionary Association*, 10.

5. *Union Missionary Herald* 1 (January 1842):6; Tappan, *Life of Arthur Tappan*, 318–19; Tappan, *History of the American Missionary Association*, 10–12.

6. Tappan, *History of the American Missionary Association*, 11.

7. *Union Missionary Herald* 1 (January 1842):1.

8. In 1837, five Congregational clergymen left for Jamaica to work among the slaves who had recently been freed by Great Britain. They organized the "Committee for the West India Missions." See: Tappan, *History of the American Missionary Association*, 11–15; ARAMA (1847), 1:5; Tappan, *Life of Arthur Tappan*, 319; Beard, *A Crusade of Brotherhood*, 30–32. In 1843, the Western Reserve Congregational Association organized the Western Evangelical Society to carry on missionary work among the Indians. ARAMA (September 1847), 1:5.

9. *American and Foreign Anti-Slavery Reporter*, Extra (May 1843), 8.

10. Tappan, *Life of Arthur Tappan*, 319; Lewis Tappan to A. A. Phelps, 7 November 1844, 16 February 1846, AAPP.

11. Beard, *A Crusade of Brotherhood*, 31.

12. Tappan, *History of the American Missionary Association*, 19.

13. *American and Foreign Anti-Slavery Reporter* (August 1846), 28.

14. Register, nos. 78517, 78518 (1846), AMAC; *New York Tribune*, 7 September 1846; *National Press and Cincinnati Weekly*, 16 September 1846; *Christian Investigator* (September 1846), 359; Tappan, *History of the American Missionary Association*, 20; *Proceedings of the Second Convention for Bible Missions, Held in Albany, September 2, and 3rd., 1846* (New York: J. H. Tobitt, 1846), 7, 11.

15. Constitution, nos. 78519, 78522 (1846), AMAC; *Proceedings of the Second Convention for Bible Missions*, 4, 13; ARAMA (1848), 6.

16. *History of the American Missionary Association* (New York: S. W. Green, 1874), 3–4.

17. Tappan, *Life of Arthur Tappan*, 247, 322.

18. *New York Times*, 23 June 1873; *New York Tribune*, 23 June 1873; *American Missionary* 9 (September 1865), 203; *American and Foreign Anti-Slavery Reporter* (May 1843), 8–9; Joseph P. Thompson, *Memoir of David Hale*, 63–64; Lewis Tappan to A. A. Phelps, 9, 10, 15 January 1839, AAPP; L. Brown to Charles Finney, 2 February 1831; Lewis Tappan to Finney, 2 February 1831, CGFP; David Hale, *Facts and Reasonings on Church Government, Report of a Discussion Held at a Meeting of the Broadway Tabernacle* (New York, 1839); Lewis Tappan, *A Letter to a Teacher Among the Freedmen* (New York: n.p., 1867), 1; *Emancipator*, 6, 13 October, 15 December 1836.

19. Tappan, *History of the American Missionary Association*, 15; *Daily Advertiser*, 3 March 1855; see: William Bushnell, *Sermon Preached at the Funeral of Hon. William Jackson* (Boston: S. Chism, 1855), 11–12; *Liberator*, 22 September 1843; *Western Citizen*, 5 October 1843.

20. *New York Times*, 8 October 1876; *Congregational Year Book* (1880), 22; *New York Daily Times*, 19 August 1879; *Proceedings of the New England Anti-Slavery Convention* (Boston: Garrison and Knapp, 1834), 15; *New York Daily Tribune*, 19 August 1879.

21. Oliver Emerson to Secretary, 28 June 1847, AMAC; S. Fowler to Lewis Tappan, 1 October 1847; Oliver Emerson to Secretary, 27 October 1847, AMAC; George Whipple to Lewis Tappan, 1 November 1847, AMAC; *American Missionary* Old Series 1 (November 1848), 7; Jonathan Cable to George Whipple, 27 October 1847, AMAC.

22. W. W. Patton to George Whipple, 3 July 1848; W. W. Patton to Milton Badger, 18 August 1846, AMAC.

23. Oliver Emerson to George Whipple, 8 August, 27 October, 21 December 1847, AMAC.

24. James T. Dickinson to George Whipple, 8 February 1848; Samuel H. Peckham to Lewis Tappan, 27 January 1848; Jonathan Cable to George Whipple, 5 August 1848; Ovid Miner to George Whipple, 15 October 1847, AMAC.

25. Jonathan Cable to George Whipple, 29 November 1847, 1 May 1848, AMAC.

26. W. G. Kephart to Lewis Tappan, 21 July 1848; Kephart to Editors of the *American Missionary*, 27 July 1848; Jonathan Cable to George Whipple, 27 June 1848, AMAC.

27. Jonathan Garland to Lewis Tappan, 1 November 1847; James Allen to George Whipple, 1 February 1849; James Allen to Lewis Tappan, 25 December 1849; G. L. Hovey to George Whipple, 27 November 1847; S. E. Peckham to George Whipple, 14 February 1848, AMAC.

28. James Allen to Secretaries, 22 January 1848; *American Missionary* O.S. 2 (March 1848), 39; (May 1854), 51; (February 1849), 34; George White to AMA, 7 January 1848, AMAC.

29. The AMA aided the nondenominational Union Churches in Western New York that had broken with the AHMS because of slavery in the late 1830s. See: McKivigan, *The War Against Proslavery Religion*, 115.

CHAPTER 6

1. A. C. Dickerson to Secretary, 26 January 1845, AHMSC.

2. John G. Fee to Charles Hall, 15 May 1846, AHMSC.

3. *The True American* (Lexington, Ky.) cited by *Western Citizen*, 29 April 1846.

4. Henry Little to Secretary, 21 July 1825, in William W. Sweet, *Religion on the American Frontier*, in vol. 2, *The Presbyterians, 1783–1840* (New York: Harper and Bros., 1936), 280.

5. Henry Little to Milton Badger, 14 July 1846, AHMSC.

6. John G. Fee to Milton Badger, 1 April 1846; A. C. Dickerson to Secretary, 8 May 1846, AHMSC.

7. A. C. Dickerson to Secretary, 8 May, 25 November 1846, AHMSC; *Christian Observer*, 6 November 1846.

8. John G. Fee to Charles Hall, 15 May 1846; Charles Hall to John Fee, 1 June 1846, Letter Book, vol. T, AHMSC.

9. Charles Hall to John Fee, 1 June, 6 July 1846, Letter Book, vol. T; John G. Fee to Charles Hall, 1 July 1846; A. C. Dickerson to Milton Badger, 25 July 1846; Badger to Dickerson, 6 November 1846, Letter Book, vol. T, AHMSC.

10. Henry Little to Milton Badger, 14 July 1846, AHMSC.

11. Joseph Chester to Secretary, 13 July 1846, AHMSC.

12. Charles Hall to Henry Little, 1 August 1846, Letter Book, vol. T, AHMSC.

13. Amasa Converse to Charles Hall, 19 September 1846, AHMSC. The correspondence probably came from A. C. Dickerson who wrote to Converse about this time and sent the *Christian Observer* an article on the Kentucky mission committee.

14. Charles Hall to Amasa Converse, 20 September 1846, Letter Book, vol. T, AHMSC.

15. *Christian Observer*, 25 September 1846.

16. *New York Evangelist*, 1 October 1846; George W. Perkins to Secretary, 6 October 1846, AHMSC. John Fee had also written to A. A. Phelps about his troubles and to a friend in Pennsylvania who placed the story in the *Union Missionary*. John Fee to Badger and Hall, 30 September 1846, AHMSC.

17. William S. Leavitt to Charles Hall, 8 October 1846; Milton Badger to G. W. Perkins, 21 October 1846, Letter Book, vol. T; Milton Badger to W. S. Leavitt, 21 October 1846, Letter Book, vol. T, AHMSC.

18. *New York Evangelist*, 22 October 1846.

19. *Christian Observer*, 6 November 1846; Autobiography of Rev. Amasa Converse, 1795–1872 (Presbyterian Foundation, Montreat, N.C. MSS, TS), 27.

20. MGAPC (New School, 1840), 24; *New York Observer*, 6 June 1840.

21. A. C. Dickerson to Milton Badger, 11 November 1846; Milton Badger to A. C. Dickerson, 6 November 1846, Letter Book, vol. T, AHMSC.

22. A. C. Dickerson to Milton Badger, 25 November, 3 December 1846; Milton Badger to A. C. Dickerson, 19 February 1847, Letter Book, vol. T, AHMSC.

23. Autobiography of Rev. Amasa Converse, 1, 12, 16, 17–18, 19, 21, 24; *Southern Religious Telegraph*, 27 January 1832, 15 February 1833.

24. Amasa Converse to Artemas Bullard, 19 July 1847, Artemas Bullard Papers (PHS); *Christian Observer*, 30 November 1846.

25. Amasa Converse to Milton Badger, 17 December 1846; Milton Badger to Amasa Converse, 21 December 1846, Letter Book, vol. T, AHMSC.

26. Amasa Converse to Milton Badger, 28 January 1847, AHMSC.

27. *The Ohio Observer*, 10, 24 February, 31 March 1847; *Christian Observer*, 12 March 1847.

28. Cited by *Watchman of the Valley*, 10 June 1847.

29. A. C. Dickerson to Milton Badger, 10 March 1847, AHMSC.

30. Charles Hall to John G. Fee, 22 March 1847, Letter Book, vol. T, AHMSC.

31. John Fee to Lewis Tappan, 10 June 1847, AMAC; Milton Badger to John Fee, 15 June 1847, Letter Book, vol. U, AHMSC.

32. John Fee to Milton Badger, 1 July 1847, AHMSC.

33. Henry Little to Milton Badger, 1, 21 August 1847, AHMSC.

34. John Fee to Milton Badger, 28 September 1847; John Fee to Milton Badger and Charles Hall, 27 June 1848, AHMSC.

35. Charles Hall to John Fee, 11 July 1848, Letter Book, vol. V, AHMSC.

36. *New York Independent*, 30 January 1851.

37. John G. Fee to Milton Badger, 13 September 1848, AHMSC; John G. Fee to George Whipple, 10 October 1848, AMAC.

38. N. L. Rice, *A Debate on Slavery Held in the City of Cincinnati . . . 1845 Upon the Question: Is Slaveholding in Itself Sinful?* (New York: William H. Moore, 1846), 252; William Graham, *The Contrast of the Bible and Abolitionism: An Exegetical Argument* (Cincinnati, Ohio: Atlas Office, 1844). Both the Presbytery and the Synod of Cincinnati had adopted nonfellowship resolutions. See: Records of the Presbytery of Cincinnati (1835–43), 1:360–66 (Cincinnati Historical Society); Synod of Cincinnati: *The Ohio Observer*, 22 October 1840; *Watchman of the Valley*, 7 November, 12 December 1840; 30 October 1845. William Graham, *The Cause and Manner of the Trial and Suspension of the Rev. William Graham by the New School Synod of Cincinnati* (Privately Printed, n.d.), 3–8.

39. The vote against it was divided as follows: eleven from western New York and Pennsylvania, and eighteen from the Northwest, not including Cincinnati, which did not vote on the matter. MGAPC (1846) 31–33; *New York Observer*, 13 June 1846.

40. *New York Observer*, 31 October, 7 November 1846; *Cincinnati Observer*, 8 October 1840; Taylor, "Seeking the Kingdom," 279–80.

41. Thornton Mills to Robert Bishop, 2 December 1846 (Robert Bishop Papers, Miami University, Oxford, Ohio MSS); Records of the Presbytery of Hamilton (1847–68), 11–13 (Presbyterian Historical Society); *Watchman of the Valley*, 14 January 1847; Presbyteries of Ripley and Knox: *Watchman of the Valley*, 9, 16 July 1846, 3 June 1847; Presbytery of Ottawa: Nahum Gould, "History of the Ottawa Presbytery" (S. McCormick Theological Seminary, n.d.), 133–35; *Western Citizen*, 27 October 1846; *Western Herald*, 21 October, 4 November 1846; 5 May 1847; Records of the Synod of Peoria, 1:41–42; Records of the Synod of Illinois (1831–57), 1:304; Records of the Presbytery of Alton (1836–50), 134–35 (MTS MSS).

42. MGAPC (New School, 1847), 142; Records of the Presbytery of Chillicothe (1846–60), 4:39–40 (Wooster College, Wooster, Ohio); R. C. Galbraith, *The History of the Chillicothe Presbytery, From Its Organization in 1799 to 1889* (Cincinnati, Ohio: Scioto Gazette Book and Job Office, 1889), 180–81.

43. *Christian Observer*, 6 November 1846.

44. Charles Hall to Franklin Davis, 29 January 1847, Letter Book, vol. T; Davis to Hall, 25 February 1847, Letter Book, vol. T; Hall to Timothy Hill, 12 February 1847, Letter Book, vol. T; Hill to Hall, 1 March 1847, AHMSC; James Townsend to Milton Badger, 9 March 1847, AHMSC; Artemas Bullard to Milton Badger, 3 April 1845, Artemas Bullard Papers (PHS); Artemas Bullard to Milton Badger, 24 June, 4 August, 14 October 1847; E. R. Fairchild to Badger, 4 August 1847; Badger to Fairchild, 6 August 1847, Letter Book, vol. U; Badger to Bullard, 2, 23 November 1847, AHMSC.

45. MGAPC (1847), 143, 152; Artemas Bullard to Milton Badger, 23 November 1847, AHMSC; Milton Badger to J. B. Townsend, 18 October 1847, AHMSC; C. P. Wing to Milton Badger, 7 June, 17 September, 18, 28 October 1847; Charles Hall to C. P. Wing, 4 October 1847, Letter Book, vol. U; Samuel Reeve to Hall, 24 January, 7 November 1850; Badger to Reeve, 6 March 1850, Letter Book, vol. W, AHMSC.

46. *Home Missionary* 21 (February 1849):233.

47. Hillery Patrick to Milton Badger, 1 April 1849; John Stuart to Secretary, 26 February 1849, AHMSC.

48. *Christian Observer*, 28 April 1849, cited by *Independent*, 3 May 1849, 14 June 1849;

Samuel Reeve to Secretary, 29 October, 4 December 1849; Charles Hall to Reeve, 28 November 1849, Letter Book, vol. W; J. B. Townsend to Milton Badger (n.d.) 1849, AHMSC; C. S. Adams to A. L. Chapin, 19 February 1850, ALCC.

49. *Boston Reporter* cited by *Herald of the Prairies,* 4 April 1849.

50. *American Missionary* O.S. 3 (March 1849), 44; *Annual Report,* American and Foreign Anti-Slavery Society (1849), cited by the *American Missionary* O.S. 3 (July 1849), 79.

51. Howard, "The Anti-Slavery Movement in the Presbyterian Church," 225–33; George M. Marsden, *The Evangelical Mind and the New School Presbyterian Experience* (New Haven, Conn.: Yale University Press, 1970), 102.

52. Marsden, *The Evangelical Mind,* 86.

CHAPTER 7

1. Merton L. Dillon, *Benjamin Lundy and the Struggle for Negro Freedom* (Urbana: University of Illinois Press, 1966), 235; Henry H. Sims, *Emotion at High Tide,* 180–82.

2. Joshua Leavitt to S. P. Chase, 7 July 1848, SPCP. The "Slave Power" did not exist. In 1861 Jefferson Davis was the only member of the executive branch of the Confederacy who began adult life as an aristocrat.

3. *The Ohio Observer,* 13 May 1846, 2, 3; *New York Evangelist,* 14 May 1846; *Watchman of the Valley* cited by *Religious Telescope* (Circleville, Ohio) 27 May 1846; *Watchman of the Valley,* 28 May 1846.

4. *Western Herald* and *Watchman of the Valley* cited by *Western Citizen* (Chicago), 20 May 1846.

5. Minutes of the Presbytery of Rockaway (April 1846), 345 (PHS MSS); MGAPC (New School, 1846), 19–20, 23–24, 26; *Western Herald,* 3 June 1846; *New York Evangelist* cited by the *Hampshire Gazette* (Northampton, Mass.), 3 November 1846; *New York Evangelist* cited by the *New York Tribune,* 27 April 1846; *New York Evangelist,* 28 May, 4 June 1846.

6. For example see: Minutes of the Synod of Michigan (1846), 278 (New School, PHS).

7. *Spirit of Liberty* (Pittsburgh) cited by *Emancipator,* 5 August 1846; *Pittsburgh Commercial Journal* cited by *The Milan* (Ohio) *Tribune,* 17 June 1846; George Beckwith, *The Book of Peace: A Collection of Essays on War and Peace* (Boston: George Beckwith, 1845), 174. George C. Beckwith was a member of the Presbytery of Newburyport, Synod of Albany. See: MGAPC (New School, 1846), 57.

8. E. Bradford Davis, "Albert Barnes, 1798–1870: An Exponent of New School Presbyterianism" (Doctor of Theology diss., Princeton Theological Seminary, 1961), 386–87; *Herald of Freedom* (Wilmington, Ohio), 7 January 1853; *Religious Telescope* (Circleville, Ohio), 25 March 1846; Albert Barnes, *Thanksgiving Sermon: The Virtues and Public Service of William Penn* (Philadelphia: W. Sloanaker, 1845), 17; David B. Coe, "War as a Means of Settling National Disputes," *American National Preacher* 20 (March 1846):66.

9. *Liberty Hall and the Cincinnati Gazette,* 3 December 1846; *Daily Cincinnati Gazette,* 28 November 1846; *Union Missionary* cited by *Pennsylvania Freeman* (Philadelphia), 13 August 1846.

10. *Oberlin Evangelist,* 27 May 1847; *Oberlin Evangelist* cited by *The Ohio Observer,* 24 June 1846 (should have been dated 1 July 1846); *The Vermont Chronicle,* 20 May, 17 June 1846.

11. *Boston Recorder,* 4, 18 June 1846; *Christian Mirror* (Maine), 21, 28 May, 17 December 1846; *Congregational Journal* (New Hampshire), 25 June 1846. For a study of the anti-

slavery movement in the Congregational churches see: Robert C. Senior, "New England Congregationalists, and the Anti-Slavery Movement, 1830–1860" (Ph.D. diss., Yale University 1954), 346–48.

12. The General Association of Connecticut: *Boston Recorder,* 25 June 1846; The Worcester, North Conference of Congregational Churches: *Boston Recorder,* 18 June 1846; *Oberlin Evangelist,* 10 June 1846; *Cleveland True Democrat* cited by the *Liberator,* 3 July 1846; Robert S. Fletcher, *A History of Oberlin College* (Oberlin, Ohio: Oberlin College, 1943), 1:278; *Oberlin Evangelist,* 8 July 1846; *Ashtabula* (Ohio) *Sentinel,* 27 July 1846.

13. *New York Daily Tribune,* 25 December 1846; *The Herald of Freedom,* 9 April 1852; *Watchman of the Valley,* 16 July 1846; *Boston Recorder,* 23, 30 July, 3 December 1846; *Congregational Journal,* 30 July, 6, 13, 20 August 1846; Clayton S. Ellsworth, "The American Churches and the Mexican War," *American Historical Review* 45 (January 1940):315.

14. *New York Observer,* 1 August, 12 December 1846.

15. Records of the Presbytery of Utica (1847), 233 (PHS MSS); Records of the Presbytery of Grand River, Ohio (1847), 281 (PHS MSS); Records of the Presbytery of Elyria (1847), 119 (PHS MSS); *New York Daily Tribune,* 9 April 1847; Minutes of the Third Presbytery of New York (1847), 283, 286 (PHS MSS); Records of the Presbytery of Genesee (1847), 28, 35 (PHS MSS).

16. *New England Puritan* (Boston), 5 August 1846; *Oberlin Evangelist* cited by *Christian Contributor* (Utica, N.Y.), 2 September 1846; *Boston Recorder,* 3 September, 29 October 1846; "Amicus," *Christian Mirror* cited by *The Ohio Observer,* 2 December 1846; *New England Puritan,* 17 December 1846; *The Vermont Chronicle,* 9 December 1846.

17. *New York Evangelist,* 10 December 1846; 21 January, 4 February 1847; *Emancipator,* 6, 13 January 1847; Ellsworth, "The American Churches and the Mexican War," 315; *New York Evangelist,* 14 January, 4 March 1847. For a study of the churches and the events preceding the Compromise of 1850, see: L. Wesley Norton, "The Religious Press and the Compromise of 1850: A Study of the Relationship of the Methodist, Baptist, and Presbyterian Press to the Slavery Controversy, 1846–1851" (Ph.D. diss., University of Illinois, 1959), 128–30.

18. *New York Observer,* 16 January, 13 March 1847; *Christian Observer,* 29 January 1847.

19. *The Anti-Papist* changed its name in 1847 to the *Cincinnati Protestant and True Catholic,* 3 July, 9 October, 13 November 1847; Ray Allen Billington, *The Protestant Crusade, 1800–1860* (New York: Macmillan Company, 1938), 238; *Watchman of the Valley,* 4 March 1847.

20. Charles B. Boynton, *Our Country, The Herald of a New Era: A Lecture Delivered Before the Young Men's Mercantile Library Association of Cincinnati, January 19, 1847* (Cincinnati: E. Shepard, 1847), 5; Charles B. Boynton, *Oration Delivered on the Fifth of July, 1847, Before the Native-Americans of Cincinnati* (Cincinnati: Target and Gardner, 1847), 5, 6; *Cincinnati Protestant and True Catholic,* 7 July 1847.

21. *Daily True Democrat,* 21 August 1847; Frederick B. Barnes to "Barns Riverro," Oberlin, Ohio, 4 July 1847, autographed collection of MSS, Oberlin College; Barbara Brown Zikmund, "Asa Mahan and Oberlin Perfectionism" (Ph.D. diss., Duke University, 1969), 305–6; Robert S. Fletcher, *History of Oberlin College* 1:140, 271–72.

22. Donald David Housley, "The Independent: A Study of Religious and Social Opinion, 1848–1870" (Ph.D. diss., Pennsylvania State University, 1971), 150; Paxton Hibben, *Henry Ward Beecher: An American Portrait* (New York: Press of the Readers Club of New York, 1942), 91–93; Clifford H. Clark, Jr., "Henry Ward Beecher: Revivalist and Antislavery Leader, 1813–1867" (Ph.D. diss., Harvard University, 1967), 97–100; Jane Shaffer Elsmere, *Henry Ward Beecher: The Indiana Years, 1837–1847* (Indianapolis: Indiana Historical Society, 1973), 265.

23. Susan Man McCulloch to Hugh McCulloch, 16 June 1846, Hugh McCulloch Papers, Lilly Library, Indiana University; Samuel Merrill to David Merrill, 31 May 1846, Samuel Merrill Papers, Indiana Historical Society Library; *Indiana State Sentinel* (Indianapolis), 25 July 1846, 3 April 1847.

24. Henry Ward Beecher, *A Discourse Delivered at the Plymouth Church, Brooklyn, New York, Upon Thanksgiving Day, November 25, 1847* (New York: Cody and Burgess, 1848), 26.

25. *Anti-Slavery Bugle* (Salem, Ohio), 29 October 1847; *Pennsylvania Freeman* (Philadelphia), 30 September 1847; *Advocate of Peace* 1 (Boston, August 1847):88.

26. MGAPC (1847), 145; *New York Evangelist*, 10 June 1847; *Watchman of the Valley*, 3 September 1847.

27. *National Press and Cincinnati Weekly Herald*, 14 July 1847; *The Ohio Observer*, 29 September 1847; *Elyria Courier*, 3 August 1847; *Cleveland Herald*, 7 July 1847; *Cleveland Daily Plain Dealer*, 9 July 1847; *Daily True Democrat*, 7 August 1847.

28. *The Ohio Observer* 27 October 1847; Horace Bushnell, "Barbarism, the First Danger," *American National Preacher* 21 (1847):210.

29. *Cincinnati Weekly Atlas*, 28 October 1847.

30. *Herald of the Prairies*, 13 October 1847; *Watchman of the Valley*, 3 September 1847; *Sangamo Journal* (Springfield, Ill.), 22 July 1847; *Western Citizen*, 13 July 1847; *Watchman of the Valley*, 15 July 1847; *New York Evangelist*, 8 July 1847.

31. For examples see: *Boston Recorder*, 23 July 1846; *New York Observer* cited by *Liberator*, 30 April 1847; *The Ohio Observer*, 19 May 1847; Samuel D. Buchard, *Causes of National Solicitude: A Sermon Preached at the Thirteenth Street Presbyterian Church, New York, on Thanksgiving Day, November 25, 1847* (New York: S. W. Benedict, 1848), 15, 20; *The Albany Patriot*, 29 December 1847; *Daily True Democrat*, 2 April 1847.

32. *New York Tribune*, 23 October 1847; *Minutes of the Synod of New York and New Jersey*, October 1847 (New York: Leavitt, Trow and Company, 1847), 13.

33. *Watchman of the Valley*, 28 October 1847; *Cincinnati Enquirer* cited by *Cincinnati Weekly Atlas*, 11 November 1847; *Watchman of the Valley*, 9 December 1847; *New York Observer*, 18 December 1847; *Herald of the Prairie*, 29 December 1847.

34. *Cincinnati Morning Herald*, 25 March 1848; *Pennsylvania Freeman*, 6 April 1848; *Free Presbyterian* (Yellow Springs, Ohio), 4 March 1857; Larry Gene Willey, "The Reverend John Rankin: Early Ohio Anti-Slavery Leader" (Ph.D. diss., University of Iowa, 1976), 250–52; *Cincinnati Morning Herald*, 13 December 1847; *The National Era*, 30 December 1847.

35. *Watchman of the Valley*, 15 July 1847; *Christian Reflector* (Boston), 1, 8 July 1847; *The Vermont Chronicle*, 7 July 1847; for the New Haven East Association resolutions see: *New York Journal of Commerce*, 23 June 1847.

36. Burdett Hart, *The Mexican War* (New Haven: Peck and Stafford, 1847), 7; Milton Palmer Braman, *The Mexican War: A Discourse Delivered on the Annual Fast Day, 1847* (Danvers, Mass.: Danvers Courier Office, 1847), 10; see: Richard Tolman, *Evil Tendencies of the Present Crisis: A Discourse Delivered July 4, 1847* (Danvers, Mass.: Danvers Courier Office, 1847); *Emancipator*, 17 February 1847.

37. Supplement to the *New York Daily Tribune*, 10 April 1847; *Hartford Daily Courant*, 13 April 1847; *Emancipator*, 21 April 1847.

38. *Hampshire Gazette* (Northampton, Mass.), 12 April 1847; *The New Englander* (January 1847), 5:140.

39. *Boston Recorder*, 21 January 1847; *New England Puritan* (Boston), 27 February, 15 August 1847; *The Christian Observatory* 1 (Boston, December 1847):534, 546; *The Vermont Chronicle*, 24 November 1847; *Boston Recorder*, 21 October 1847; *Congregational Journal*, 30 December 1847.

40. *Boston Recorder* cited by *The Ohio Observer,* 8 December 1847; *New York Evangelist,* 2, 16 December 1847; *The Christian Observer* cited by *Pennsylvania Freeman,* 16 September 1847; *Christian Observer,* 3 December 1847.

41. *Boston Post* cited by *Cincinnati Morning Herald,* 9 July 1846; *New York Journal of Commerce* cited by the *Elyria Courier,* 13 July 1847.

42. *New York Tribune,* 3 May 1847.

43. *New York Observer,* 15 January 1848; *The Christian Observatory* 2 (February 1848): 68; 2 (March 1848):100.

44. Records of the Presbytery of Utica (New School, 1848), 1:266 (PHS MSS); *New York Observer,* 12, 19 February 1848; Records of the Presbytery of Chemung (New School, 1848), 431 (PHS MSS); Minutes of the Presbytery of Angelica (New School, 1848), 130 (PHS MSS).

45. *New York Evangelist,* 16 March 1848; *New York Observer,* 17, 24 June 1848; *New York Evangelist,* 5 October 1848; Charles J. De Witt, "Crusading for Peace in Syracuse During the War With Mexico," *New York History* 14 (April 1933):108, citing *Religious Recorder,* 28 May 1846; *The Ohio Observer,* 5 July 1848, citing the *Religious Recorder.*

46. *New England Puritan,* 11 March 1848; *Boston Recorder,* 6 October 1848.

47. *The Free Soil Banner* (Hamilton, Ohio), 4 November 1848; Peter Hitchcock, Sr., to Peter Hitchcock, Jr., 19 September 1848, Peter Hitchcock Family Papers, Western Reserve Historical Society; *The True Democrat* (Cleveland), 18 August, 19 October 1848; Elinor Rice Hays, *Those Extraordinary Blackwells: The Story of a Journey to a Better World* (New York: Harcourt, Brace and World, 1967), 51, 76, citing Samuel Blackwell's diaries.

48. Laurens P. Hickok, *The Sources of Military Delusion, and the Practicability of Their Removal* (Hartford: n.p., 1833); MGAPC (New School, 1846), 57; ARAHMS (1848), 22:124, 130; *The Vermont Chronicle,* 30 December 1846; Edson Leone Whitney, *The American Peace Society: A Centennial History* (Washington, D. C.: The American Peace Society, 1928), 66, 78; *Boston Recorder,* 25 June, 2 July 1846; *New York Evangelist,* 17 June 1847.

49. *Boston Recorder,* 12 February 1846; *New York Evangelist,* 3 June 1847; *Emancipator,* 2 June 1847; *Advocate of Peace* 6 (August 1847): 92; Edward Norris Kirk, *The Church Essential to the Republic: A Sermon in Behalf of the American Home Missionary Society* (New York: Leavitt, Trow and Company, 1848), 18.

50. William Lloyd Garrison to Helen, 26 July 1848, WLGP.

51. John Tracy Ellis, *American Catholicism* (Chicago: University of Chicago Press, 1969), 67–68; Ted C. Hinckly, "American Anti-Catholicism During the Mexican War," *Pacific Historical Review* 31 (May 1962):136–37. The Free Soil movement that originated during the Mexican War was called forth by the moral revolt against slavery. The origin of the Republican party can best be understood in the context of this movement. The Republican party did not have its origin in nativism or ethnic politics as set forth by Michael F. Holt, *Forging A Majority: The Formation of the Republican Party in Pittsburgh, 1848–1860* (New Haven, Conn.: Yale University Press, 1969), and Ronald P. Formisana, *The Birth of Mass Political Parties: Michigan 1827–1861* (Princeton, N.J.: Princeton University Press, 1971). For studies on the moral attack on slavery as the central core of the Republican party see: Eric Foner, *Free Soil, Free Labor, Free Men: The Ideology of the Republican Party Before the Civil War* (New York: Oxford University Press, 1970); Don E. Fehrenbacker, *Prelude to Greatness: Lincoln in the 1850s* (Stanford, Calif.: Stanford University Press, 1962); Harry V. Jaffa, *Crisis of the House Divided: An Interpretation of the Lincoln-Douglas Debates* (Seattle: University of Washington Press, 1973); Richard H. Sewell, *Ballots for Freedom: Antislavery Politics in the United States, 1837–1860* (New York: Oxford University Press, 1976), 169; Frederick Merk, *Manifest Destiny and Mission in American History* (New York: Knopf, 1963), 174–75;

Victor B. Howard, "The Doves of 1847: The Religious Response in Ohio to the Mexican War," *The Old Northwest* 5 (Fall 1979):258–61.

CHAPTER 8

1. *Western Citizen*, 8 December 1846; H. R. Howe to Secretaries, 1 April 1846; Flavel Bascom to Secretary, 15 February 1847; Edwin D. Seward to Milton Badger, 7 June 1847; Alexander Montgomery to Milton Badger, 3 July 1847; T. B. Hurlbut to Milton Badger, 29 July 1846, AHMSC; Theodore D. Weld to Lewis Tappan, 5 April 1836, *Letters of Weld and Grimké*, 1:278; James G. Birney to Charles Hammond, 14 November 1835; Charles Stuart to Birney, February 1836, *Birney Letters*, 1:271, 361; Alice D. Adams, *The Neglected Period of Anti-Slavery in America, 1808–1831* (Boston: Ginn and Co., 1908), 99–100.

2. *Liberator*, 20 February 1846.

3. *Watchman of the Valley*, 9, 16 July, 12, 19, 26, 31 November, 11 December 1846; 21 January, 5 August, 28 October 1847; the Free Presbyterian Synod eventually grew to include seven presbyteries, sixty-five congregations scattered from Pennsylvania to Iowa. See: Andrew E. Murray, *Presbyterians and the Negro—A History* (Philadelphia: Presbyterian Historical Society, 1966), 120.

4. *The Ohio Observer*, 10, 24 February 1847.

5. Records of the Presbytery of Grand River, Ohio (1836–49), 2:20, 46, 273, 278–79, 280, 291 (Western Reserve Historical Society); *Watchman of the Valley*, 3 June 1847; Records of the Synod of Western Reserve (1846–67), 1:33, 37 (PHS).

6. *Home Missionary* 20 (May 1847):1, 3.

7. *Watchman of the Valley*, 15 July 1847.

8. *Western Citizen*, 13 July 1847.

9. *Watchman of the Valley*, 24 June 1847; Jonathan Blanchard to Samuel Williston, 7 May 1849, SWC.

10. *Western Citizen*, 17 October 1848; *Herald of the Prairie*, 25 October 1848; *The Ohio Observer*, 13 February 1850; see: Broadside, 18 February 1850, Charles B. Boynton, no. 104769; Johnathan Cable to George Whipple, 13 March 1850; Invitation, 22 March 1850, AMAC; *Oberlin Evangelist* 7 (February 1850):36.

11. *Minutes of the Christian Anti-Slavery Convention, 1850* (Cincinnati: Franklin Book and Job Rooms, 1850), 70.

12. *Tenth Annual Report of the American and Foreign Anti-Slavery Society, 1850*, 49–50; Herman R. Muelder, *Fighters for Freedom: The History of Anti-Slavery Activities of Men and Women Associated With Knox College* (New York: Columbia University Press, 1959), 279; *Minutes of the Christian Anti-Slavery Convention, 1850*, 48.

13. *Minutes of the Christian Anti-Slavery Convention, 1850*, 19; Lewis Tappan to George Whipple, 13 April 1850, AMAC; *Central Christian Herald*, 25 April 1850.

14. *Oberlin Evangelist* 7 (July 1850):109–10; ARAMA (1850), 4:39. *American Missionary* O.S. 5 (December 1850), 12; Andrew Benton to George Whipple, 19 June, 11 July 1850; C. B. Boynton to George Whipple, 18 June 1850, 7 January 1851; Epaphras Goodman to George Whipple, 6 February 1851, AMAC.

15. Aratus Kent to Milton Badger, 14 August 1850, AHMSC; *Oberlin Evangelist* 7 (July 1850):110; F. D. Parish to George Whipple, 21 September 1850; Andrew Benton to Whipple, 19 June 1850, AMAC; ARAMA (1850), 4:39; *Central Christian Herald*, 25 April 1850; Free Synod of the Presbyterian Church of Cincinnati to Executive Committee of the AMA, 28 May 1849, AMAC.

16. ARAMA (1851), 5:49; *Oberlin Evangelist* 7 (December 1850):206.

17. *Home Missionary* O.S. 4 (November 1850):159–60.

18. Milton Badger to G. S. F. Savage, 12 November 1850, Letter Book, vol. X, AHMSC; G. F. M. to Editor, Galena, Illinois, 26 December 1850; *Independent*, 20 January 1851; *The Ohio Observer*, 9 March 1853.

19. "The Gospel Versus Sin," by M. N. Miles in *Western Citizen*, 18 March 1851.

20. Scott, *From Office to Profession*, 152.

21. Hammond, *The Politics of Benevolence*, 106; Records of the Presbytery of Galena (1841–63), 132–33; Records of the Synod of Peoria (1843–59), 1:100 (MTS MSS); Records of the Presbytery of Belvidere (1847–63), 31 (MTS MSS); Records of the Presbytery of Alton (1850–63), 2:39 (MTS MSS); Records of the Synod of Illinois (1831–55), 1:388 (MTS MSS); Ralph A. Keller, "Northern Protestant Churches and the Fugitive Slave Law of 1850" (Ph.D. diss., University of Wisconsin, 1969), 176–77, 214; Records of the Synod of Ohio (1849–69), 2:56 (Wooster College MSS); Records of the Synod of Wabash (1851–69), 38 (PHS MSS); Records of the Presbytery of Elyria (1842–63), 237 (University of Chicago MSS); Presbytery of Franklin: A. C. Crist, *The History of Marion Presbytery, Its Churches, Elders, Ministers, Missionary Societies, etc.* (n.p. 1908), 45; Records of the Synod of Michigan (1842–53), 2:12 (UM MSS). In upstate New York the presbyteries of North River, Cortland, Utica, and Catskill denounced the law, but in somewhat milder terms than was characteristic of the Northwest. See: *Daily Springfield Republican*, 8 March 1851; *New York Observer*, 2 October 1851; *Independent*, 4 March 1852, 23 June 1853; Keller, "Northern Protestant Churches and the Fugitive Slave Law," 332–33; Clara Merritt DeBoer, "The Role of the Afro-Americans in the Origin and Work of the American Missionary Association: 1839–1877" (Ph.D. diss., Rutgers University, 1973), 200–4.

22. *Detroit Daily Free Press*, 28 November 1850, citing the *Peninsular Freeman*; *Oberlin Evangelist* 8 (July 1851):111; Minutes of the Christian Anti-Slavery Convention (Chicago: Western Citizen, 1851), 19–20; Taylor, "Seeking the Kingdom," 375; *New York Observer*, 26 October 1850; *Daily Union*, 11 December 1850; *Independent*, 26 June, 10 July 1851; Clark, *American Slavery and Maine Congregationalists*, 159–60; *Christian Mirror*, 6 February 1851, 22 June 1852.

23. *New York Observer*, 13 April 1850; *Central Christian Herald*, 21 March 1850; *New York Evangelist*, 17 October 1850; *Central Christian Herald*, 7 November 1850; *Independent*, 24 October 1850; *Christian Observer*, 16 November 1850.

24. Charles K. Whipple, *Relations of Anti-Slavery to Religion* (New York: American Anti-Slavery Society, n.d.), 6; Moses Stuart, *Conscience and the Constitution, With Remarks on the Recent Speech of the Hon. Daniel Webster . . . on the Subject of Slavery* (Boston: Crocker and Brewster, 1850), 61, 64; *New York Evening Express*, 11, 26 November 1850; *New York Herald*, 11 November 1850; William Adams, *Christianity and Civil Government* (New York: Charles Scribner, 1851), 33–35; Asa D. Smith, *Obedience to Human Law: A Discourse Delivered in the Brainard Presbyterian Church* (New York: Leavitt and Company, 1851), 29; William M. Rogers, *Sermon Preached Before the Massachusetts Home Missionary Society, May 28, 1850* (Boston: James French, 1850), 11.

25. Philip Foner, *Business and Slavery* (Chapel Hill: University of North Carolina Press, 1941); *New York Herald*, 29, 30 October 1850.

26. *New York Evening Post*, 30 October, 2 November 1850; *New York Herald*, 12 November 1850; *New York Journal of Commerce*, 12 November 1850; *New York Journal of Commerce*, 1, 2 November 1850; N. L. Thompson, *History of the Plymouth Church* (New York: G. W. Carleton, 1873), 78; William C. Beecher and Samuel Scoville, *A Biography of Rev. Henry Ward Beecher* (London: Sampson Low, Marston, Searle and Rivington, 1888), 247;

National Cyclopaedia of American Biography, 1:205–6; *New York Daily Tribune*, 28 October 1850.

27. *New York Daily Tribune*, 6 December 1850; *Montgomery* (Ala.) *Daily Journal*, 31 October, 18 November 1850; *New York Times*, 15 April 1889; *New York Herald*, 6 December 1850; *Hartford Daily Courant*, 27 December 1850; *National Era*, 10 July 1851.

28. *Daily Free Democrat*, 26 November 1850; J. P. Thompson, *The Fugitive Slave Law, Tried by the Old and New Testaments* (New York: William Harned, 1850), 34; John E. Todd, *Memoriam: Rev. Joseph P. Thompson* (n.p., n.d.), 13; *Independent*, 9 January, 13 February 1851; 1 January 1852; 23 January 1873; 29 December 1881.

29. Calvin Montague Clark, *American Slavery and Maine Congregationalists*, 159, citing *Christian Mirror*, 28 November 1850; William W. Patton, *Conscience and Law or a Discussion of Our Comparative Responsibility to Human and Divine Government* (New York: Mark H. Newman and Co., 1850), 27, 33.

30. *New York Daily Tribune*, 3 October 1850; ARAMA (1850), 4:11; Lewis Tappan, *Life of Arthur Tappan*, 330–31; *Annual Report*, American and Foreign Anti-Slavery Society (1835), 13:5.

31. Lucius Smith, *The Higher Law, of Christ and His Law Supreme* (Ravenna, Ohio: Star Print, 1852), 24; *Knoxville* (Ill.) *Journal*, 12 November 1850; *Daily Free Democrat*, 12 October, 27 December 1850; 6 March, 2 June 1851; *Frederick Douglass' Paper*, 21 August 1851; *New York Herald*, 28 November 1850; *Daily True Democrat*, 28 October, 5, 12, 30 November 1850; *Cleveland Plain Dealer*, 12, 28, 29 October 1850; *Cincinnati Enquirer*, 16 October 1850.

32. Conrad J. Engelder, "The Churches and Slavery. A Study of the Attitude Toward Slavery of the Major Protestant Denominations" (Ph.D. Diss., University of Michigan, 1964), 225–26; McKivigan, *The War Against Proslavery Religion*, 154; L. Wesley Norton, "The Religious Press and the Compromise of 1850: A Study of the Relationship of the Methodist, Baptist, and Presbyterian Press to the Slavery Controversy, 1846–51" (Ph.D. diss., University of Illinois, 1959), 282–83.

33. McKivigan, *The War Against Proslavery Religion*, 15, 129.

CHAPTER 9

1. Jonathan Blanchard to Samuel Williston, 7 May 1849, SWC; Johathan Blanchard to Milton Badger, 18 September 1850, AHMSC; Jonathan Blanchard to Milton Badger and Charles Hall, 16 December 1850; Flavel Bascom to Secretaries, 9 January 1851, AHMSC.

2. Oliver Emerson to George Whipple, 15 April 1851, AMAC; S. D. Helms to J. C. Holbrook, 6 March 1851, AHMSC; Milton Badger to Edwin Hall, 5 May 1851, Letter Book, vol. Y, AHMSC.

3. *The Christian Era*, 24 February 1851. Oliver Emerson claimed one missionary, not three. See: Oliver Emerson to George Whipple, 15 April 1851, AMAC; Albert Hale to Milton Badger, 13 March 1851; William Kirby to Milton Badger, 4 April 1851, AHMSC.

4. William Carter to Milton Badger, 25 March 1851; Julius A. Reed to Milton Badger, 7 May 1851; Dexter Clary to Milton Badger, 24 February, 10 March, 1 May 1851; Herman S. Colton, William P. Hendrick, and William Beardsley to Secretary, 29 April 1851, AHMSC.

5. Flavel Bascom to Secretaries, 18 June 1851, Miscellaneous Letter, no. 279, (n.d.) 1851, AHMSC; *North Western Gazetteer*, 27 February 1851, cited by the *American Missionary* O.S. 5 (April 1851), 44; *Annual Report*, American and Foreign Anti-Slavery Society (1851), 64; Oliver Emerson to George Whipple, 15 April 1851, AMAC.

6. *The Christian Era*, 24 February 1851; *Western Citizen*, 25 March 1851; Milton Badger to Albert Hale, 21 April 1851; see: David Coe to J. G. Porter, 1 May 1851, Letter Book, vol. X; Albert Hale to Milton Badger, 9 May 1851; Milton Badger to William Carter, 21 April 1851, Letter Book, vol. X, AHMSC.

7. *Home Missionary* 24 (May 1851):2; Andrew Benton to S. S. Jocelyn, 9 June 1851, AMAC.

8. William Kirby to Milton Badger, 23 May 1851, AHMSC; *Prairie Herald*, 27 May, 3 June 1851; J. A. Reed to Milton Badger, 19 June, 23 September 1851; William Carter to Milton Badger, 24 May 1851; William Kirby to Milton Badger, 23 May 1851; William Carter to Milton Badger, 24 May 1851, AHMSC.

9. *Prairie Herald*, 10 June 1851; *Independent*, 3 July 1851.

10. *Western Citizen*, 18 March 1851; Charles B. Boynton to George Whipple, 7 January 1851, AMAC; *Prairie Herald*, 27 May 1851; *Independent*, 5 June 1851.

11. Jonathan Blanchard to *Western Citizen*, 17 June 1851; *Prairie Herald*, 6 May 1851; *Prairie Herald*, 17 June 1851; I. M. Weed to A. L. Chapin, Chicago, 2 May 1851, ALCC.

12. *Prairie Herald*, 1 July 1844; *Minutes of the Christian Anti-Slavery Convention, 1851* (Chicago: Western Citizen, 1851), 25; *Western Citizen*, 2 September, 15 July 1851; *Prairie Herald*, 22 July 1851; J. A. Wight to Milton Badger, 22 July 1851, AHMSC.

13. *Western Citizen* cited by *Independent*, 3 July 1851; *Independent*, 24 July 1851; Calvin Clark to Milton Badger, 27 June, 10 July 1851; Dexter Clary to Milton Badger, 19 June 1851; Aratus Kent to Milton Badger, 3 July 1851, AHMSC.

14. Milton Badger to Calvin Clark, 2 July 1851; Badger to Aratus Kent, 14 June 1851, Letter Book, vol. Y, AHMSC.

15. William Kirby to Milton Badger, 7 July 1851; R. M. Pearson to Secretaries, 11 July 1851; G. F. F. Savage to Milton Badger, 5 August 1851; Aratus Kent to Milton Badger, 12 July 1851; Dexter Clary to Badger, 8 September 1851; A. B. Rich to Executive Committee, AHMS, 15 July 1850, 23 September 1851, AHMSC; Badger to A. B. Rich, 1 November 1851; Badger to Aratus Kent, 17 December 1851; Badger to Dexter Clary, 18 December 1851, Letter Book, vol. Y, AHMSC.

16. *Prairie Herald*, 16 December 1851; Frederick Kuhns, "Slavery and Missions in the Old Northwest," *Journal of the Presbyterian Historical Society* 24 (December 1946):206.

17. J. C. Holbrook to Secretaries, 8 Janaury 1852; J. S. Clark to Charles Hall, 14 January 1852; Clark to Milton Badger, 12 February 1852; Badger to J. S. Clark, 2 February 1852, Letter Book, vol. Y, AHMSC.

18. Myron Tracy to Milton Badger, 2 March 1852, AHMSC; *American Missionary* O.S. 5 (August 1851), 76; Daniel Chapman to George Whipple, 28 August 1851, AMAC; Hope Brown to Aratus Kent, 29 August 1851, attached to Kent's letter to Milton Badger, 25 September 1851, AHMSC; William Beardsley to George Whipple, 28 July 1851; Horace Borros to Secretary, 25 August 1851; Hope Brown to Secretaries, Fox River Union, Committee of Missions, 25 August 1851, AMAC; William Beardsley to Secretaries, 20 April 1852, AHMSC.

19. Records of the Rock River (Genessee) Congregational Association (28 October 1851), 24–25 (Chicago Theological Seminary MSS); William Kirby to Milton Badger, 20 November 1851; M. N. Miles to Milton Badger, 24 February 1851, AHMSC; M. N. Miles to George Whipple, 15 March, 1 July 1851, AMAC; S. G. Wright to Milton Badger, 1 July 1851; L. H. Parker to Milton Badger, 16 December 1851; Milton Badger to L. H. Parker, 8 January 1852, Letter Book, vol. Y. AHMSC.

20. James H. Henry to Milton Badger, 2 September 1851; Charles W. Hunter to Secretaries, 15 September 1851; Levi Spencer to Badger, 5 October 1851; James Longhead to Badger, 7 October 1851; I. A. Hart to Secretaries, 10 October 1851; William B. Dodge to

Secretary, 1 October 1851; Joseph H. Payne to Badger, 28 February 1852; Lucien Farnham to Badger, 15 November 1851; Badger to Lucien Farnham, 18 December 1851, Letter Book, vol. Y; Silas I. Francis to Executive Committee, 31 May 1852, AHMSC; Francis Lawson to Secretary, 8 March 1851; Levi Spencer to George Whipple, 6 June 1851; I. D. Helms to George Whipple, 11 July 1851, AMAC; A. J. Copeland to Milton Badger, 1, 10 March 1852; Milton Badger to A. J. Copeland, 23 March 1852, Letter Book, vol. Y; Samuel Thompson to Secretary, 13 October 1852, 31 March 1853, AHMSC.

21. Aratus Kent to Milton Badger, 25 September 1851, AHMSC; D. B. Coe to A. L. Chapin, 11 February 1852, ALCC.

22. Richard S. Taylor, "Seeking the Kingdom: A Study in the Career of Jonathan Blanchard, 1811–1892" (Ph.D. diss., Northern Illinois University, 1977), 384.

CHAPTER 10

1. *Independent*, 11 September 1851; *New York Observer*, 11 September 1851; Milton Badger to J. A. Reed, 12 September 1851, Letter Book, vol. Y, AHMSC; J. A. Reed to Milton Badger, 23 September 1851, JARC; Jonathan Blanchard to J. P. Williston, 6 September 1851, SWC; *Independent*, 11 September 1851; *New York Observer*, 11 September 1851; *Prairie Herald*, 23 September 1851; *New York Observer*, 11 September 1851; *Independent*, 18 September 1851.

2. Jonathan Blanchard to J. P. Williston, 6 September 1851, SWC; *Prairie Herald*, 2 March 1852; Jonathan Blanchard to J. P. Williston, 6 September 1852, SWC.

3. J. C. Holbrook to J. A. Reed, 10 June, 20 October 1852; Charles Burnham to J. A. Reed, 4 August 1852, JARC.

4. Milton Badger to D. B. Coe, 29 June 1852, Letter Book, vol. 1, AHMSC; Leonard Bacon to Parsons Cooke, 29 September 1852, in Bacon, *Leonard Bacon*, 358.

5. Bacon, *Leonard Bacon*, 361; Oliver Emerson to George Whipple, 11 November 1851, AMAC; *Oberlin Evangelist* (10 May 1852):10.

6. *Christian Observer*, 4 September 1852.

7. Senior, "New England Congregationalists and the Anti-Slavery Movement," 289–90; Truman O. Douglass, *Builders of the Commonwealth: The Patriarchs and Their Associates* (S. Grinnell College, Grinnell, Iowa).

8. Clark, *American Slavery and Maine Congregationalists*, 163; *National Era*, 14 October 1852; *New York Observer*, 28 October 1852; Johathan Blanchard to Wife, 7 October 1852, JBFP; *New York Observer*, 14 October 1852; *Independent*, 14 October 1852; *American Missionary* O.S. 7 (November 1852), 4; Lewis Tappan to George Whipple, 8 October 1852, AMAC; *Congregational Year Book* (1854), 344; Lewis Tappan to Richard D. Webb, 26 October 1852, in *A Side-Light on Anglo-American Relations, 1839–1858*, ed. Abel and Klingberg, 299; Lewis Tappan to George Whipple, 8 October 1852, AMAC; Taylor, "Seeking the Kingdom," 405.

9. George W. Perkins to Editor, *American Missionary* (1852), no. 5389, 5390; George W. Perkins to Secretary, 21 October 1852, AMAC.

10. *American Missionary* O.S. 7 (December 1852), 10; Oliver Emerson to Editor, *American Missionary*, 25 November 1852, AMAC; *American Missionary* O.S. 7 (February 1853), 27; *Minutes of the General Association of New Hampshire* (1853), 7–8, *Independent*, 30 June 1853, *Congregational Year Book* (1854), 137, 157, 191–92; Clark, *American Slavery and Maine Congregationalists*, 164.

11. *Christian Observer,* 14 May 1853; *New York Evangelist,* 11 November 1852; J. C. Holbrook to J. A. Reed, 14 December 1852, 10 January 1853, JARC.

12. *American Missionary* O.S. 7 (February 1853), 31; *Independent,* 5 May 1853; see Jonathan Blanchard's letter, 27 October 1852, in the *Independent,* 9 December 1852; J. C. Holbrook to Milton Badger, 7 December 1852; Samuel G. Wright to Milton Badger, 14 December 1852, 1 April 1853, AHMSC.

13. Dexter Clary to Milton Badger, 3 January 1853, AHMSC.

14. J. C. Holbrook to Milton Badger, 7 December 1852; Samuel G. Wright to Milton Badger, 14 December 1852, 2 February 1853; Milton Badger to S. G. Wright, 14 January 1853; Badger to J. C. Holbrook, 13 January 1853, Letter Book, vol. 2, AHMSC; MGAPC (New School, 1850), 326.

15. Milton Badger to J. C. Holbrook, 13 January 1853, Letter Book, vol. 2, AHMSC; *Independent,* 6, 20 January 1853.

16. *Home Missionary* 25 (March 1853):266, 268-69.

17. Milton Badger to J. C. Holbrook, 21 February 1853; Badger to Samuel G. Wright, 21 February 1853, Letter Book, vol. 2, AHMSC; Samuel G. Wright to Milton Badger, 17 January, 16 March, 1 April 1853; Milton Badger to Samuel G. Wright, 24 March 1853; Charles Hall to Samuel Wright, 1 April 1853, Letter Book, vol. 1, AHMSC; Epaphras Goodman to S. S. Jocelyn, 24 April 1855, AMAC.

18. *Independent,* 25 November 1852; J. B. W. to Editor, *Independent,* 16 December 1852, 2 June 1853; J. B. Walker to George Whipple, 22 May 1853, AMAC; *Independent,* 16 June 1853.

19. J. C. Holbrook to J. A. Reed, 25 February 1853, JARC; *Congregational Herald,* 7 April 1853; J. B. Walker to George Whipple, 14, 25 March 1853, AMAC; J. B. Walker to J. C. Holbrook in *Congregational Herald,* 7 April 1853; *Congregational Herald,* 14 May 1853.

20. H. D. Kitchel to George Whipple, 28 April 1853, AMAC; Harvey D. Kitchel, *An Appeal for Discussion and Action on the Anti-Slavery Question* (Hartford, Conn.: L. Skinner, 1850), 10; H. D. Kitchel to Secretary, 10 May 1853, AMAC; H. D. Kitchel to Milton Badger, 6 May 1853; Milton Badger to H. D. Kitchel, 26 May 1853, Letter Book, vol. 1, AHMSC.

21. *Congregational Year Book* (1854), 224, 234, 238-40; J. B. Walker to George Whipple, 4 June 1853; Epaphras Goodman to S. S. Jocelyn, 1 June 1854; F. E. Lord to George Whipple, 7 June 1853; Lord to Whipple, 20 June 1853, AMAC.

22. *Minutes of the General Association of Congregational Churches and Ministers of Iowa, 1840-1855,* 91; *Minutes of the General Association of Iowa, 1853,* 5; J. A. Reed to Milton Badger, 11 June 1853, AHMSC.

23. Records of the Presbytery of Franklin (1846-60), 1:149, 241 (PHS MSS); Records of the Synod of Michigan (1851-53), 2:286 (UM MSS).

24. Milton Badger to H. D. Kitchel, 26 May 1853, Letter Book, vol. 1, AHMSC; Noah Porter, *Two Sermons on Church Communion and Excommunication, With a Particular View to the Case of Slaveholders in the Church* (Hartford, Conn.: Case, Tiffany and Co., 1853), 4, 12, 22, 27-28; B. P. Stone to Milton Badger, 22 February 1853; Badger to H. D. Kitchel, 26 May 1853, Letter Book, vol. 1, AHMSC; The *Christian Mirror, Vermont Chronicle, Prairie Herald,* and *The Ohio Observer* approved the position of the AHMS. The *Congregational Herald, Christian Press,* and *Oberlin Evangelist* criticized the March statement of the AHMS. See: Milton Badger to H. D. Kitchel, 26 May 1853, Letter Book, vol. 1, AHMSC; *Oberlin Evangelist* 10 (30 March 1853):54; Gerrit Smith to George Whipple and Lewis Tappan, 27 February 1853, AMAC; Lewis Tappan to Gerrit Smith, 14 March 1853, GSP; *American Missionary,* O.S. 7 (April 1853), 45, 46; ARAMA (1853), 7:15.

25. *Thirteenth Annual Report*, American and Foreign Anti-Slavery Society (1853), 117; *The American Home Missionary Society and Slavery* (New York: American and Foreign Anti-Slavery Society, 1853), 3, 4, 6, 7, 8.

26. In August 1851, the friends of free missions had met in Chicago and organized the North Western Home Missionary Association. See: *Western Citizen*, 26 August 1851; Epaphras Goodman to George Whipple, 10 July 1852, AMAC; S. G. Wright, "Home Missions No. 9," *Congregational Herald*, 30 August 1855.

27. *Proceedings of the General Convention of Congregational Ministers and Delegates* (New York: S. W. Benedict, 1852), 77; Williston Walker, *A History of the Congregational Churches in the United States* (New York: Scribner's, 1907), 382–83; Evans, "Abolitionism in the Illinois Churches," 218–19.

CHAPTER 11

1. *New York Observer*, 28 July 1853; *Christian Observer*, 5 July 1853; *New York Journal of Commerce*, 26 July 1853.

2. *New York Journal of Commerce*, 21 July 1853.

3. *Christian Observer*, 23 July 1853; *New York Journal of Commerce*, 11 August 1853; *Home Missionary* 25 (March 1853):266; Robert Gray to Milton Badger, 5 July, 9 October 1852; 3 January 1853; C. A. Marvin to Gray, 22 July 1852, Letter Book, vol. 1, AHMSC.

4. *New York Journal of Commerce*, 20, 24 August 1853; *New York Evangelist*, 14 July 1853.

5. *New York Journal of Commerce*, 1 October 1853; *Southern Aid Society: Its Constitution and Address to the Christian Public* (New York: D. Fanshaw, 1854), 8–9; Ernest T. Thompson, *Presbyterians in the South, 1607–1861*, 3 vols. (Richmond, Va.: John Knox Press, 1963), 1:416–17; *New York Observer*, 10 November 1853; *Southern Aid Society: Its Constitution and Address*, 12.

6. *Christian Observer*, 8, 29 October 1853; *Southern Aid Society: Its Constitution and Address*, 23, 24; *Oberlin Evangelist* 11 (22 November 1854):190.

7. *Southern Aid Society: Its Constitution and Address*, 4, 24; *New York Observer*, 31 May 1855 (see: "General Assembly Debate"); C. P. Wing to Secretary, 7 June 1847; C. P. Wing to Milton Badger, 17 September, 18 October 1847; Charles Hall to C. P. Wing, 4 October 1847, Letter Book, vol. U, AHMSC; *First Annual Report of the Southern Aid Society* (New York: D. Fanshaw, 1854), 18; *New York Observer*, 8 December 1853; *American Missionary* O.S. 8 (January 1854), 22.

8. *New York Observer*, 15 December 1853; *Presbytery Reporter* 4 (1 November 1853): 99–100.

9. *Christian Observer*, 22 October 1853; *Presbyterian Witness*, 17 May 1854.

10. Flavel Bascom to Milton Badger, 9 March 1854, Letter Book, vol. 3, AHMSC; S. S. Jocelyn to Milton Badger, 31 July 1854, AMAC; S. S. Jocelyn to Milton Badger, 1 August 1854; D. B. Coe to S. S. Jocelyn, 3 August 1854, Letter Book, vol. 3, AHMSC; Austin Putnam to S. S. Jocelyn, 5 August 1854, AMAC; *Minutes of the General Association of Connecticut* (New Haven: The Association, June 1854), 10–11.

11. *New York Journal of Commerce*, 1 November 1853; *Presbyterian Magazine* cited by *Independent*, 1 December 1853; *Southern Aid Society: Its Constitution and Address*, 4–5; *Fourth Annual Report: Southern Aid Society* (New York: George F. Nesbitt, 1857), 43; MGAPC (1853), 327, 332, 334–35, 338.

12. *New York Observer*, 13 June 1846, 8 September 1859; *Christian Observer*, 12 June

1846; Henry A. Rowland, *The Church and Slavery: Or the Relations of the Churches to Slavery Under the Constitution* (New York: M. W. Dodd, 1854), 20, 41, 44.

13. *New York Evangelist*, 18 February 1875; *New York Observer*, 9 June 1853; ARACS (1847), 13:31; *Newark Daily Advertiser*, 4 August 1854; A. D. Eddy to Stephen A. Douglas, 29 December 1856, Stephen A. Douglas Papers (University of Chicago MSS).

14. *New York Observer*, 5, 9 June 1847; Samuel H. Cox to Joseph Stiles, 1 December 1853; *Southern Aid Society: Its Constitution and Address*, 19; ARACS (1849), 32:53.

15. *National Cyclopaedia of American Biography*, 10:492; John Q. Adams, *A History of Auburn Theological Seminary* (Auburn, N.Y.: Auburn Seminary Press, 1918), 129.

16. *National Cyclopaedia of American Biography*, 13:592; *Rochester Union and Advertiser*, 19, 20 September 1871; *Rochester Democrat and Chronicle*, 19 September 1871; Franklin B. Dexter, *Biographical Sketches of the Graduates of Yale College* (New York: Henry Holt, 1855–1912), 4:97; John A. Murray to Milton Badger, 10 March 1843, 3 April 1846, 3 May 1854; Aristarchus Champion to J. A. Murray, 25 March 1854; Champion to Charles Hall, 29 January 1849; Hall to Champion, 19 February 1849, Letter Book, vol. 5, AHMSC; H. C. Bowen to Aristarchus Champion, 10 July 1855; Charles Seabody to Champion, 23 January 1855; J. B. Richardson to A. Champion, 26 March 1856, Aristarchus Champion Papers, Rochester, New York Public Library.

17. *New York Times*, 26 January 1866; *New York Journal of Commerce*, 26 January 1866; ARACS (1852), 35:54; *New York Times*, 5, 7 Janaury 1866; *New York Tribune*, 5 January 1866; *New York Journal of Commerce*, 6 January 1866; Gerard Hallock, *History of the South Congregational Church, New Haven* (New York: Tuttle, Morehouse and Taylor, 1865), 19, 44, 47; N. L. Rice, *Lectures on Slavery Delivered in the North Presbyterian Church, Chicago* (Chicago: Goodman and Cushing, 1860), 43; *New York Observer*, 1 October 1863.

18. *Congregational Herald*, 16 November 1854, citing the *New York Tribune*; *American Missionary* O.S. 9 (December 1854), 12; *New York Observer*, 2 November 1854, 7 June 1855; *First Annual Report of the Southern Aid Society*, 4.

19. *Christian Observer*, 25 November 1854; *New York Observer*, 2 November 1854, 7 June 1855.

20. "Circular Letter to the Boston Branch, Southern Aid Society," *Southern Aid Society Constitution and Address* (New York: Day Book, 1854).

21. *Congregationalist* cited by *Springfield Republican*, 11 April 1857; *Christian Intelligencer* and *Christian Observer* cited by *Presbyterian Witness*, 26 May 1857.

22. *Congregationalist*, 29 May 1857; *Presbyterian Witness*, 16 June 1857; *New York Tribune*, 28 May 1857.

23. John E. Todd, *John Todd: The Story of His Life Told Mainly by Himself* (New York: Harper and Bros.; 1876), 88–90; *Springfield Republican*, 24 March 1860; *New York Tribune*, 28 May, 31 October 1857; *Fourth Annual Report of the Southern Aid Society* (1857), 11; *New York Observer*, 5 November 1857.

24. *New York Tribune*, 31 October 1857.

25. ARACS (1850), 33:11, 25; (1853), 36:3, 58; (1855), 38:13; *Southern Aid Society: Its Constitution and Address*, 4.

26. James McChain and Samuel Sawyer to Milton Badger, 24 June 1856; R. P. Wells to Secretary, 8 July 1856, AHMSC.

27. Samuel Sawyer and James McChain to Secretaries, 24 June 1856; W. E. Caldwell to Secretary, 15 June 1856; D. B. Coe to Samuel Sawyer, 31 October 1855, Letter Book vol. 1; Samuel Sawyer to D. B. Coe, 19 October 1855; Timothy Hill to Milton Badger, 14 May 1856; Hill to Coe, 16 September 1856, 5 February 1857; Coe to Hill, 26 February 1857,

Letter Book, vol. 2; Robert Caldwell to Secretary, 9 April 1855; Samuel Sawyer to Milton Badger, 30 March 1855; Benjamin Mills to David Coe, 21 May 1857; J. J. Robinson to David Coe, 20 January 1855; A. H. Boyd to Secretary, 25 September 1855; Milton Badger to A. H. Boyd, 6 October 1855, Letter Book, vol. 1; Timothy Hill to David Coe, 5 February 1857, AHMSC.

28. Milton Badger to S. P. Stone, 31 January 1854, Letter Book, vol. 2; Flavel Bascom to Milton Badger, 9 March 1854, Letter Book, vol. 2, AHMSC.

29. *Congregational Herald,* 29 Janaury 1857; D. B. Coe to Lewis Tappan, 6 February 1857, Letter Book, vol. 2, AHMSC; MGAPC (New School, 1857), 403–6; *Presbyterian Quarterly Review* 6 (September 1857), 246.

CHAPTER 12

1. *Northampton* (Mass.) *Courier,* 14, 21 February 1854; sermon, March 1854, LBP; *Northampton Courier,* 28 February 1854; *Hartford Daily Courant,* 25 February 1854; *Northampton Democrat,* 28 February 1854; *Atlas and Argus,* 27 February 1854.

2. Zephaniah Humphrey, *Memorial Sketches: Heman Humphrey* (Philadelphia: Lippincott and Company, 1869), 160; Heman Humphrey, *The Missouri Compromise: An Address Delivered Before the Citizens of Pittsfield, Massachusetts* (Pittsfield, Mass.: Hull and Peirson, 1854), 32; Eliphalet Nott to Thurlow Weed, 28 January 1854, Thurlow Weed Papers, Rochester University; *Cleveland Daily Plain Dealer,* 10 May 1854; *New York Tribune,* 28 February, 10 March 1854; *Detroit Daily Democrat,* 22 February 1854; see also: *Milwaukee Daily Free Democrat,* 14 April 1854; *Atlas and Argus,* 24 February 1854.

3. *National Era* (Washington, D. C.), 24 January 1854; *New York Daily Tribune,* 25 January 1854; *Congressional Globe,* 33d Cong., 1st sess., 30 January 1854, 281–82; *Cincinnati Daily Enquirer,* 6 April 1854, citing *New York Journal of Commerce;* Ronald D. Rietveld, "The Moral Issue of Slavery in American Politics, 1854–1860" (Ph.D. diss., University of Illinois, 1967), 40.

4. George Fort Milton, *The Eve of Conflict: Stephen A. Douglas and the Needless War* (New York: Houghton Mifflin Co., 1934), 167; Albert J. Beveridge, *Abraham Lincoln 1809–1858* (New York: Houghton Mifflin Co., 1928), 2:221; Edward L. Pierce, *Memoir and Letters of Charles Sumner,* 4 vols. (Boston: Roberts Brothers, 1877), 3:366; Edward Beecher to Leonard Bacon, 16 February 1854, LBP; C. E. Stone to Charles Sumner, 20 February 1854; H. B. Stowe to Charles Sumner, 23 February 1854; Henry Dexter to Charles Sumner, 23 February 1854, CSP; *Congregationalist* cited by *Daily Free Press* (Burlington, N.J.), 18 May 1854; George B. Cheever to Henry Cheever, 17 February 1854, GBCP; Horace James to Charles Sumner, 24 February 1854, CSP; *Northampton Courier,* 21, 28 February 1854.

5. *Daily Free Press,* 18 May 1854; *Presbyterian of the West* (Cincinnati), 30 March 1854, citing *Puritan Recorder;* Henry M. Dexter to Charles Sumner, 8 April 1854, CSP; *New York Evangelist* cited by *Presbyterian of the West,* 30 March 1854.

6. *New York Tribune,* 16 March 1854; *Springfield Republican,* 28 March 1854; *Liberator,* 14 April 1854; *Chicago Tribune,* 28, 29, 31 March 1854; *Chicago Daily Democratic Press,* 29 March, 12 May 1854; John C. Holbrook to Charles Sumner, 1 May 1854, CSP; *Detroit Daily Free Press,* 30 April 1854; Records of the following: Presbytery of Portage, 4:228 (Office of the Presbytery of Cleveland MSS); Presbytery of Pataskala, 2:120 (Wooster College MSS); Presbytery of Alton, 2:109 (MTS MSS); Presbytery of Trumbull: *The Ohio Observer,* 3 May 1854.

7. "S" to Charles Sumner, 15 March 1854, CSP; *Northampton Democrat*, 9 May 1854; *Hartford Daily Courant*, 7 July 1854.

8. John G. Whittier to R. C. Winthrop, 4 January 1854, Robert C. Winthrop Papers, Massachusetts Historical Society; Leonard Bacon to Isaac Toucey, 14 February 1854, in *Independent*, 16 February 1854.

9. *New York Times*, 11 March 1854; *Liberator*, 24 March 1854; *Chicago Tribune*, 30 March 1854.

10. Cited by *National Era*, 2 March 1854; *New York Evangelist*, 12 January 1854; *Christian Press* (Cincinnati) cited by *Free West*, 2 March 1854; *Central Christian Herald*, 13 April 1854; *The Ohio Observer*, 15 February 1854; *Chicago Tribune*, 13 February 1854; *Congregational Herald*, 26 May 1854; *The Iowa Republican* (Iowa City), 29 March 1854.

11. *New York Times*, 20 February 1854; *New York Evangelist*, 26 January 1854; Henry Dexter to Charles Sumner, 23 February 1854, CSP; Leonard Bacon, *The Morality of the Nebraska Bill* (New Haven: Reprint from *New Englander*, May 1854), 4.

12. Sidney E. Mead, *Nathaniel William Taylor, 1786–1858: A Connecticut Liberal* (Chicago: University of Chicago Press, 1942), 585; *Speeches and Other Proceedings at the Anti-Nebraska Meeting, New Haven, Connecticut, March 8 and 10, 1854* (New Haven: John H. Austin, 1854), 13; *Milwaukee Daily Free Democrat*, 17 March 1854; Roland H. Bainton, *Yale and the Ministry* (New York: Harper and Bros., 1957), 158.

13. *Boston Daily Advertiser*, 13 May 1854; see: Samuel A. Johnson, *The Battle Cry of Freedom* (Lawrence: University of Kansas Press, 1954); *Cincinnati Daily Enquirer*, 25 June 1854.

14. Eli Thayer, *A History of the Kansas Crusade: Its Friends and Foes* (New York: Harper and Bros., 1889), 177; Samuel Johnson, *The Battle Cry of Freedom*, 69; *Chicago Daily Democratic Press*, 13 March 1855.

15. Albert Pantle, "The Connecticut Kansas Colony: Letters of Charles B. Lines to the *New Haven Daily Palladium*," *Kansas Historical Quarterly* 22 (1956):3; *Northampton Courier*, 15 April 1856.

16. *Minutes of the Ohio Congregational Conference* (1854), 6; *Minutes of the General Association of Congregational Churches of Michigan* (1854), 14; *Congregational Herald*, 31 August 1854; Records of the General Association of Rock River Congregationalists, 1851–67 (Chicago Theological Seminary MSS), 68; *General Association of Congregational Churches and Ministers of Iowa, 1840–1855*, 101; *Minutes of the General Association of Illinois* (1854), 11; for the action of the Elgin, Medina (Ohio), Council Bluffs, Fox River, Genessee Associations see: *Congregational Herald* (Chicago), 28 April, 23 June, 14 July, 31 August 1854; *Minutes of the Massachusetts General Association* (1854), 12–13; *Minutes of the General Conference of Maine* (1854), 6; for the resolutions of the Hartford North Association see: *Hartford Daily Courant*, 13 March 1854; see records of the following: Presbytery of Franklin (1846–60), 1:215, 224 (Ohio State Historical Society MSS); Presbytery of Crawfordsville (1835–68), 451 (Office of the Synod of Indiana MSS); Synod Of Illinois (1831–55), 1:435–36 (MTS MSS); Presbytery of Indianapolis (1839–63), 1:283 (Office of the Synod of Indiana MSS); Presbytery of Greencastle (1851–60), 1:113 (Office of the Synod of Indiana MSS); Presbytery of Alton (1850–63), 2:122; Presbytery of Elyria (1842–63), 1:233; Presbytery of Cincinnati (1844–70), 2:281–82 (Historical Society of Cincinnati MSS); Synods of Utica and Geneva: *New York Evangelist*, 7 September 1854; Presbytery of Ottawa: Nahum Gould, "History of the Ottawa Presbytery" (TS. MTS, n.d.), 155, 175, 179–80; George Allison, *Forest, Fort and Faith: Historical Sketches of the Presbytery of Fort Wayne* (Fort Wayne: Presbytery of Fort Wayne, 1945), 45.

17. Ralph V. Harlow, "The Rise and Fall of the Kansas Aid Movement," *American Historical Review* 41 (October 1935):4; *Boston Daily Advertiser*, 13 June 1855; *Springfield Republican* (Springfield, Mass.), 18 June, 12 July 1855.

18. Tyack, "The Kingdom of God," 448; James W. Fraser, *Pedagogue for God's Kingdom: Lyman Beecher and the Second Great Awakening* (Lanham, Md.: University Press of America, 1985), 184–86; Horace Mann, "Twelfth Report" in *The Republic and the School; Horace Mann on the Education of Free Men,* ed. Lawrence A. Cremin (New York: Teachers' College Press, Columbia University, 1957), 6; Thomas, "Romantic Reform in America," 659–60; Harlow, "The Rise and Fall of the Kansas Aid Movement," 5–6; *Springfield Republican,* 12 July 1855.

19. Harlow, "The Rise and Fall of the Kansas Aid Movement," 5–6, 9; *Boston Daily Advertiser,* 1 September, 2 October 1855; *Boston Daily Advertiser,* 30 July, 24 August, 2 October, 27 November 1855; Thayer, *A History of the Kansas Crusade,* 124–25, 130–31, 133–36.

20. J. S. Clark to Milton Badger, 20 June 1854, AHMSC; *Milwaukee Daily Free Democrat,* 17 May 1854.

21. Milton Badger to Horace James, 5 July 1854, Letter Book, vol. 1, AHMSC; Samuel C. Pomeroy to Milton Badger, 7 October 1854; Daniel P. Noyes to Horace James, 20 October 1854; Badger to Samuel Pomeroy, 16 October 1854; Badger to S. Y. Lum, 23 October 1854, Letter Book, vol. 1, AHMSC; *Independent,* 26 October 1854; *Home Missionary* 27 (January 1855):217–18; Lewis Tappan to George Whipple, 4 September 1854, AMAC; C. B. Boynton to S. S. Jocelyn, 24 June 1854; Epaphras Goodman to S. S. Jocelyn, 28 May 1855, AMAC; *American Missionary* O.S. 8 (May 1854), 55; James Allen to S. S. Jocelyn, 28 March 1854; E. E. Wells to S. S. Jocelyn, 5 July, 21 September 1854, AMAC.

22. J. P. Williston to Lewis Tappan, 1 January 1848; J. P. Williston to Secretaries, January 1854, no. 52456, AMAC; *Springfield Republican,* 7 March 1855; Thomas H. Webb, *Information for Kansas Immigrants* (Boston: Alfred Mudge and Sons, 1856), 2; Eli Thayer to S. S. Jocelyn, 16 September 1854, AMAC; *Springfield Republican,* 4 June 1855.

23. *American Missionary* 7 (June 1854):58; John H. Byrd to George Whipple, 3 June 1854; John Lowry to S. S. Jocelyn, 18 December 1854; Samuel Curry to S. S. Jocelyn, 16 December 1854; L. C. Matlock to S. S. Jocelyn, 4 January 1854, AMAC; *New York Tribune,* 22 October 1857.

24. Richard R. Wescott, "A History of Maine Politics, 1840–1856; The Formation of the Republican Party" (Ph.D. diss., University of Maine, 1966), 215, 257; *Daily Advertiser* (Portland, Maine), 3 July 1854, 7 March 1855; see: Charles S. Sydor, *The Development of Southern Sectionalism, 1819–1848* (Baton Rouge: Louisiana State University Press, 1948), 129; George Dangerfield, *The Era of Good Feelings* (New York: Harcourt Brace, 1952), 228; Sernett, *Abolition's Axe,* 109; Roy Nicholas, *The Disruption of American Democracy* (New York: Macmillan, 1948), 43, 50; "A Conservative View of the Nebraska Question," *The New Englander* 12 (November 1854):552.

25. J. L. Tracy to Theodore Weld, 24 November 1831, in *Letters of Weld and Grimké,* ed. Barnes and Dumond, 1:57; ARAHMS (1844), 18:106; Horace Bushnell, *Barbarism, the First Danger: A Discourse for Home Missions, 1847* (New York: William Osborn, 1847), 5, 28; Barbara M. Cross, *Horace Bushnell: Minister to a Changing America* (Chicago: University of Chicago Press, 1958), 80.

26. Albert Barnes, *Home Missions: A Sermon in Behalf of the American Home Missionary Society* (New York: William Osborn, 1849), 16; *New York Evangelist,* 10 May 1849; *American Missionary* O.S. 5 (December 1850), 12; Address of Reverend E. L. Cleveland, AHMS Anniversary, 1853, AHMSC; *Independent,* 19 May 1853; *New York Observer,* 19 May 1853; A. L. Brooks, *An Appeal for the Right: A Sermon* (Chicago: Daily Democrat Press, 1856), 8; A. L. Chapin, *A Sermon in Behalf of the American Home Missionary Society* (New York: American Home Missionary Society, 1878), 8.

27. Charles Ellsworth, "The American Churches and the Mexican War," *American Historical Review* 45 (January 1940):313, 315; *Cleveland Daily True Democrat,* 4 October 1850.

28. *New York Herald,* 19 February 1854; *New York Daily Times,* 20 February 1854; Eliphalet Nott to Francis Wayland, 21 March 1854, in *Memoirs of Eliphalet Nott for Sixty Two Years President of Union College,* ed. Cornelius Van Santvoord (New York: Sheldon and Co., 1876), 3, 20; Codman Hislop, *Eliphalet Nott* (Middletown, Conn.: Wesleyan University Press, 1971), 507.

29. *Atlas and Argus,* 25 March 1854; *New York Times,* 15 May 1854.

30. Eden B. Foster, *The Right of the Pulpit and the Perils of Freedom* (Lowell, Mass.: J. J. Judkins, 1854), 36, 68–69; Joseph P. Thompson, *No Slavery in Nebraska: The Voice of God Against National Crime* (New York: Ivison and Phinney, 1854), 22; *Pittsburgh Daily Gazette,* 2 December 1854; *Milwaukee Daily Free Democrat,* 5 December 1854.

31. *Pittsburgh Daily Gazette,* 18 January, 22, 23 February 1856; *New York Times,* 23, 26 February 1856; Victor B. Howard, "The Illinois Republican Party: The Party Becomes Conservative, 1855–1856," *Journal of Illinois History* 64 (Autumn 1971):296–98.

32. See: *Council Bluffs* (Iowa) *Chronotype,* 7 May 1856; *New York Tribune,* 29, 30 May, 18 June 1856; *Wisconsin Messenger* (Delavan), 29 October 1856; *Pittsburgh Gazette,* 20, 30 June 1856; *Newark Advertiser,* 28 May 1856; *National Cyclopaedia of American Biography,* 8:474; *Free Press* (Burlington, N.J.), 3 July 1856.

33. *Newark Daily Advertiser,* 2 June 1856; *Jersey Tribune,* 1 November 1856, cited by *New York Post,* 3 November 1856; *Wisconsin Free Democrat,* 17 September 1856; *New York Tribune,* 31 October 1856; *New York Observer,* 9 June 1853; *New York Tribune,* 2 June 1856; *New York Times,* 2 June 1856; Edward B. Coe, *An Address in Commemoration of Asa Dodge Smith, June 27, 1882* (Concord, N.H.: Republican Press Association, 1882), 30; *New York Times,* 8 November 1856.

34. *Delaware* (Ohio) *Gazette,* 8 August 1856; *Summit Beacon* (Akron, Ohio) 30 July 1856; *Western Reserve Chronicle,* 18 June 1856; *Trumbull Democrat,* 18 September 1856; *Clermont* (Ohio) *Sun,* 10 July 1856; Victor B. Howard, "The 1856 Election in Ohio: Moral Issues in Politics," *Ohio History* 80 (Winter 1971):33–34; A. L. Brooks, *An Appeal for the Right: A Sermon* (Chicago: Daily Democrat Press, 1856), 16–17; A. G. Norton to Lyman Trumbull, 29 March 1856, LTP.

35. John R. Howard, *Henry Ward Beecher* (New York: Fords, Howard, Hulbert, 1891), 88; *New York Times,* 13 October 1856; *New York Herald,* 11 October 1856; *Daily Evening Telegraph,* 28 July 1856; Lyman Abbott, *Henry Ward Beecher* (New York: Houghton Mifflin and Co., 1903), 205; *Daily Free Press,* 8 September 1856; *Atlas and Argus,* 1 October 1856; *New York Tribune,* 3 November 1856; *New York Times,* 21 November 1856; *New York News* cited by *Cincinnati Daily Enquirer,* 30 September 1856; *Detroit Daily Free Press,* 30 September 1856.

36. Robert M. York, *George B. Cheever, Religious and Social Reformer, 1807–1890* (Orono: University of Maine Press, 1955), 135, 144; *Independent,* 25 September 1856; *New York Tribune,* 31 October 1856; *New York Times,* 17, 29 September, 8 November 1856; J. P. Thompson, *Teachings of the New Testament on Slavery* (New York: Joseph H. Ladd, 1856), 16; Joseph Henry Allen, *A Reign of Terror: A Sermon Preached in Union Street Church, Bangor, Maine, June 1, 1856* (Bangor: Samuel S. Smith, 1856), 15; George Thacher, *No Fellowship With Slavery: A Sermon Delivered June 29, 1856, in the First Congregational Church, Meriden, Connecticut* (Meriden: L. R. Webb, 1856), 7, 20; *Cleveland Plain Dealer,* 20 June 1856; *Trumbull Democrat,* 26 June 1856; *Milwaukee Daily Free Democrat,* 22 September 1856; J. M. Sturtevant, Jr., *Julian M. Sturtevant: An Autobiography* (Chicago: Fleming H. Revell Co., 1896), 279–80, 290; *Washington D.C. Daily Union,* 30 July 1856; Taylor, "Seeking the Kingdom," 445–46.

37. A. A. Overton to Secretary, 15 August 1856; Henry Shedd to Secretary, 3 October

1856, AHMSC; for example see: D. C. Curtiss to Secretary, 8 August 1856; James Howell to Secretary, 3 September 1856, AHMSC.

38. Joseph Jones to S. S. Jocelyn, 17 June, 1 November 1856, AMAC; Lawrence Brainard to George Whipple, 24 December 1855, AMAC; *Hartford Daily Courant*, 27 October, 3 November 1856; *Daily Cleveland Herald*, 1 November 1856; G. W. Perkins, *Facts and Duties of the Times. A Sermon Delivered Before the First Congregational Church, Chicago, Illinois* (New York: William S. Dorr, 1856), 25, 30; Seth Partridge to Secretary, 29 December 1856, AMAC; *Ohio State Journal*, 4, 5, 6 August 1856; Howard, "The Illinois Republican Party," 305-6; *Cleveland Leader*, 4 March 1856; Ralph Harlow, *Gerrit Smith: Philanthropist and Reformer* (New York: Holt and Co., 1939), 364; William Goodell to Gerrit Smith, 7 August 1856, American Anti-Slavery Society Letter Books, Oberlin College; Leon Perkal, "William Goodell: A Life of Reform" (Ph.D. diss., City College of New York, 1972), 266; Frederick Douglass to Gerrit Smith, 31 August 1856, GSP.

39. *Worcester Daily Spy*, 22 May 1856; *Springfield Republican*, 23 April, 4 June 1856; *Council Bluffs Chronicle*, 16, 23 July 1856; examples of Eastern clergy who journeyed to Kansas are William C. Clarke, Horace Bushnell, R. H. Seeley, Charles B. Boynton, and H. P. Cutting. See: *Free Press* (Burlington, N.J.), 19 July 1856; *Daily Free Democrat*, 3 November 1855; *Worcester Daily Spy*, 25 January 1856; *Springfield Republican*, 12 April 1856; *Davenport Daily Gazette*, 27 June 1856.

40. Presbyterian examples are: David M. Riddle, William Jessup, Joseph Hornblower, and Benjamin F. Butler. All were officers in the AHMS. See: *Pittsburgh Gazette*, 1 May, 6, 16 September 1856; *New York Tribune*, 17 February 1854; *Montrose* (Penn.) *Democrat*, 23 February 1854; *Susquehanna Register* (Montrose), 30 November 1854; *Independent Republican* (Montrose), 27 March, 23 August 1855; *New York Herald*, 23 September 1856; *Newark Daily Advertiser*, 11 August 1856. Congregational examples are: Professor Benjamin Silliman and Chief Justice Thomas S. Williams. See: *Presbyterian of the West*, 30 March 1854; *Litchfield* (Conn.) *Enquirer*, 12 June 1856; *Hartford Courant*, 25 February 1856; *Northampton Democrat*, 28 February 1854; *Salem* (Mass.) *Register*, 5 June 1856; *New York Tribune*, 24 May 1856; *Boston Evening Transcript*, 30 May, 2 June 1856; *Liberator*, 22 August 1856.

41. *Congregational Herald*, 2, 23 October 1856; *Minutes of the General Conference of Congregational Churches of Maine* (1856), 13; Records of the General Association of Rock River Congregational Churches (1851-67), 103-4 (Chicago Theological Seminary MSS). These associations included the Congregational Association of Middlesex, Connecticut; the Congregational Association of the Western District of Fairfield County, Connecticut; the Somerset Conference of Congregational Churches of Massachusetts; the Congregational Association of Iowa; and the General Association of Congregational Churches of Michigan. See: "Resolutions of the Congregational Association of Middlesex," June 1856, CSP; S. J. M. Merwin to Charles Sumner, 28 May 1856; L. W. Harris to Charles Sumner, 19 June 1856; Sidney Perkins to Charles Sumner, no. 154; W. Salter to Charles Sumner, 16 July 1856; S. Smith Hobart to Charles Sumner, 3 June 1856, CSP; George Hall to Gerrit Smith, 5 June 1856, GSP; Synod of Western Reserve: *Central Christian Herald*, 9 October 1856; Synod of Cincinnati: *Central Christian Herald*, 13 November 1856; Nahum Gould, "History of the Ottawa Presbytery," 182; Records of the following: Synod of Peoria, 1:225, 264-65 (MTS MSS); Synod of Wabash (1851-69), 71 (PHS MSS); Presbytery of Elyria (1842-63), 287; *Minutes of the Synod of Michigan* (1856), 12-13, 19-20; GDD 6 (1832-61):15.

42. *Congregational Herald*, 26 September 1856; *Congregationalist* cited by *Daily Evening Telegraph*, 16 August 1856 and the *Gate City* (Keokuk, Iowa), 3 June 1856; *Daily Free Press*, 8 December 1856; *Religious Herald*, 29 May 1856; *Christian Mirror*, 3 June 1856; see: *New York Evangelist* cited by *Chicago Democratic Press*, 3 September 1856; *Genesee Evangelist*

cited by the *Dixon* (Ill.) *Telegraph*, 11 October 1856; *Presbyterian Witness* cited by *Central Christian Herald*, 31 July 1856; *New York Observer* cited by the *New York Herald*, 27 July 1856; *Christian Observer*, 10 July 1856; *The Presbyterian*, 14 June, 20 September, 25 October 1856.

43. *New York Journal of Commerce*, 2 September 1856; *Chicago Times* cited by the *Wisconsin Messenger*, 8 October 1856; *Weekly Chicago Times*, 3 July 1856; *Cleveland Plain Dealer*, 28 November 1856.

44. Stephen E. Maizlish, *The Triumph of Sectionalism: The Transformation of Ohio Politics, 1844–1856*, 217–18; Richard H. Sewell, *Ballots for Freedom*, 272; Austin Blair to A. T. McCall, 14 April 1855, Austin Blair Papers, Detroit Public Library; Ray A. Billington, "Anti-Catholic Propaganda and the Home Missionary Movement, 1800–1860," *Mississippi Valley Historical Review* 22 (December 1935):363, 384.

45. William E. Gienapp, *The Origins of the Republican Party, 1852–1856* (New York: Oxford University Press, 1987), 92–93, 179. For a convincing account that traces the Whig party decline back to the election of 1848 and the cause of the disintegration to slavery, see: Joseph G. Rayback, *Free Soil: The Election of 1848* (Lexington: University Press of Kentucky, 1970), 303–7; James McPherson, *Battle Cry of Freedom: The Civil War Era* (New York: Oxford University Press, 1988), 138.

46. Richard H. Sewell, *A House Divided: Sectionalism and Civil War, 1848–1865* (Baltimore: Johns Hopkins University Press, 1988), 41; Lee Benson, *The Concept of Jacksonian Democracy: New York as a Test Case* (Princeton: Princeton University Press, 1961), 18–20, 94–95, 114–20, 150; Richard McCormick, *The Second Party System, Party Formation in the Jacksonian Era* (Chapel Hill: University of North Carolina Press, 1966), 11–12, 15, 115–21, 215–20, 265–66, 337–38.

47. William E. Gienapp, "Nativism and the Creation of a Republican Majority in the North before the Civil War," *Journal of American History* 72 (December 1985):534–35. Gienapp argues that the realignment of political parties went through two phases: the first focused on state and local ethnocultural issues and the second on the issue of expansion of slavery.

48. Sewell, *Ballots for Freedom*, 267; Foner, *Free Soil, Free Labor, Free Men*, 233; McPherson, *Battle Cry of Freedom*, 138; *American Jubilee* 1 (New York, March 1855):88.

49. Oscar Handlin, *Boston's Immigrants: A Study in Acculturation* (Cambridge: Harvard University Press, 1941; New York: Atheneum Publishers, 1972), 202; Dale Baum, *The Civil War Party System: The Case of Massachusetts, 1848–1876* (Chapel Hill: University of North Carolina Press, 1984), 27; McPherson, *Battle Cry of Freedom*, 138.

50. V. B. Jones to Editor, 1 March 1855, *Syracuse Wesleyan*, 28 March 1855; John G. Fee to Editor, 16 February 1855, *National Era*, 15 March 1855; J. G. Fee to William Goodell, 23 July 1850, JGFC; John G. Fee, "Berea: Its History and Work," TS. 8, from *Berea* (Ky.) *Evangelist*, JGFC; Muelder, *Fighters for Freedom*, 358–59; Wyatt-Brown, *Lewis Tappan*, 47. In 1850, church membership made up 16 percent of the total population. See: *Yearbook of American Churches, 1859* (New York: National Council of Churches, 1958), 27:294. The total population of the United States was 23,191,876 in 1850; the New School Presbyterians made up 139,797 and the Congregationalists, with 1,595 churhces, were approximately 157,000 of the total number. *U.S. Bureau of the Census, 1860; Minutes of the General Assembly of the Presbyterian Church* (Philadelphia: Presbyterian Board of Publications, 1894), 283; *The Year-Book of the American Congregational Union, 1854* (New York: Congregational Union, 1854), 311.

51. Sewell, *Ballots for Freedom*, 327; Kenneth Stampp, "Race and the Republican Party of the 1850s" in *The Imperiled Union: Essays on the Background of the Civil War* (New York: Oxford University Press, 1980), 116; Stephen E. Maizlish, "Race and Politics in the Northern

Democracy, 1854–1860," in *Race and Slavery in America,* ed. Robert H. Abzug and Stephen Maizlish (Lexington: University Press of Kentucky, 1986), 79–88; Maizlish, *Triumph of Sectionalism,* 220; McPherson, *Battle Cry of Freedom,* 143.

52. Howard, "Anti-Slavery Movement in the Presbyterian Church," 157–59, 171–75, 193–207; Robert C. Senior, "New England Congregationalists and the Anti-Slavery Movement," 374–414.

53. Sewell, *Ballots for Freedom,* 267; Eugene H. Roseboom, "Salmon P. Chase and the Know-Nothings," *Mississippi Valley Historical Review* 21 (December 1938):345; William E. Gienapp, "Salmon P. Chase, Nativism, and the Formation of the Republican Party in Ohio," *Ohio History* 93 (Winter–Spring 1984):28; Michael F. Holt, *The Political Crisis of the 1850s* (New York: Wiley and Sons, 1978), 179; Joshua Leavitt, "American Democracy," *The New Englander* 14 (February 1856):71; Hugh H. Davis, "The Reform Career of Joshua Leavitt, 1794–1873" (Ph.D. diss., Ohio State University, 1969), 343; Ray Billington, *The Protestant Crusade, 1800–1860,* 429; Hammond, *The Politics of Benevolence,* 107, 124–25, 127–29; Dale Baum, "Know-Nothingism and the Republican Majority in Massachusetts: The Political Realignment of the 1850s," *Journal of American History* 64 (March 1978):985; Baum, *The Civil War Party System,* 212, 214; Foner, *Free Soil, Free Labor, Free Men,* 237; for views differing from Foner, see: Stephen E. Maizlish, "The Meaning of Nativism and the Crisis of the Union: The Know-Nothing Movement in the Antebellum North," in *Essays on American Antebellum Politics 1840–1860,* ed. S. E. Maizlish (College Station: Texas A&M University Press, 1982), 179–81; William G. Bean, "An Aspect of Know-Nothingism—The Immigrant and Slavery," *The South Atlantic Quarterly* 23 (October 1924):322; Harry Carman and Reinhard Luthin, "Some Aspects of the Know-Nothing Movement Reconsidered," *The South Atlantic Quarterly* 39 (April 1940):234; Hendrik Booraem, *The Formation of the Republican Party in New York* (New York: New York University Press, 1983), 120–22; Humphrey J. Desmond, *Know-Nothing Party* (Washington: New Century Press, 1905), 86–87.

54. A. D. Eddy to S. A. Douglas, 29 December 1856, Stephen A. Douglas Papers, University of Chicago.

55. Richard S. Taylor, "Seeking the Kingdom," 384; Maizlish, *The Triumph of Sectionalism,* 165–66.

56. *Pittsburgh Gazette,* 18 October 1856; *Rock Island Morning Argus,* 4 July 1856; *New Haven Daily Register,* 29 August 1856.

57. Barnes, *The Anti-Slavery Impulse,* 4–5; James Hastings Nichols, "John Witherspoon on Church and State," *Journal of Presbyterian History* 24 (September 1846):166.

58. Nichols, "John Witherspoon on Church and State," 172; W. W. Henning, ed., *Statutes at Large of Virginia* (Richmond, Va.: George Cochran, 1823), 12:6, 81.

59. Jordan, *White Over Black,* 299–300.

60. Victor B. Howard, "Presbyterians, the Kansas-Nebraska Act, and the Election of 1856," *Journal of Presbyterian History* 49 (Summer 1971):154.

61. Clifford S. Griffin, *Their Brothers' Keeper: Moral Stewardship in the United States, 1800–1865* (New Brunswick, N.J.: Rutgers University Press, 1960), x–xi.

62. Robert Baird, *Religion in America* (1856; reprint, New York: Harper and Bros., 1970), 299–303; David Brion Davis, *The Slave Power Conspiracy and the Paranoid Style* (Baton Rouge: Louisiana State University Press, 1969), 81–84; Hans L. Trefousse, "The Republican Party, 1854–1864," in *History of the U.S. Political Parties,* ed. Arthur M. Schlesinger, Jr., 4 vols. (New York: Chelsea House Publishers, 1973), 2:1151; Eugene Roseboom, *A History of Presidential Elections* (New York: Macmillan, 1964), 166.

63. Timothy L. Smith, *Revivalism and Social Reform: American Protestantism on the Eve of the Civil War* (New York: Harper and Row, 1957), 161; Chester F. Dunham, *The At-*

titude of the Northern Clergy Toward the South, 1860–1865 (Toledo, Ohio: Gray Company, 1942), 35–36.

64. Scott, *From Office to Profession,* 152; Sernett, *Abolition's Axe,* 135.

65. MGAPC (1835), 327, 331–34; *Home Missionary* 25 (March 1853):266–69; F. A. Ross, *Slavery Ordained of God* (Philadelphia: J. B. Lippincott and Co., 1857), 65; MGAPC (1857), 403–6; ARAHMS (1857), 123–29.

CHAPTER 13

1. James Harrison to Milton Badger, 1 January, 30 April, 1 May, 1 October 1855, AHMSC.

2. See: *Oberlin Evangelist* 12 (1 August 1855):125.

3. J. H. Newton to Secretary, 1 May 1856, AHMSC.

4. Thomas Wicks to Milton Badger, 23 June 1856; Henry M. Storrs to Secretaries, 13 July 1856; Milton Badger to Henry M. Storrs, 25 July 1856, Letter Book, vol. 1; J. A. Hart to Milton Badger, 18 July 1856, AHMSC. For example see: Alvah Day to Secretaries, 3 July 1854, AHMSC; *Congregational Herald,* 25 September 1856; Charles Morgan to Secretary, 6 January 1855; Milton Badger to Charles Morgan, 19 January 1855, Letter Book, vol. 2; Charles Morgan to Milton Badger, 3 April 1855; Badger to Dexter Clary, 19 January 1855, Letter Book, vol. 2; Clary to Badger, 27 January 1856; David Coe to Clary, 24 February 1856, Letter Book, vol. 2; Clary to Coe, 26 April 1855, AHMSC; Dexter Clary to Badger, 27 January 1855, AHMSC; Dexter Clary to Miss Martha C. Todd, 11 January 1856, DCP Letter Book, 53–56; Dexter Clary to David Coe, 20 March 1856; Dexter Clary to Milton Badger, 27 January 1855, AHMSC.

5. Dexter Clary to D. B. Coe, 30 October 1856; Aratus Kent to Milton Badger, 9 October 1856. AHMSC.

6. Dexter Clary to David Coe, 26 April 1855, 20 March 1856, AHMSC.

7. ARAMA (1854), 8:11; Oliver Emerson to S. S. Jocelyn, 14 February 1854, 22 March 1854; Oliver Emerson to George Whipple, 29 June 1854, AMAC.

8. Howard, "The Anti-Slavery Movement in the Presbyterian Church," 181–221; Records of the Synod of Michigan, 2:286 (UM MSS); Records of the Presbytery of Franklin, 1:149, 241 (PHS MSS); Howard, "The Anti-Slavery Movement in the Presbyterian Church," 234–35, 247–48.

9. David Coe to Horace James, 13 February 1856, Letter Book, vol. 2; Horace James to Milton Badger, 30 April, 14 June 1856, AHMSC.

10. *Congregationalist,* 11 January 1856; *Home Missionary* 29 (May 1856):5; ARAHMS (1856), 30:79.

11. J. T. Hargrave to Secretary, 21 July 1856; D. P. Noyes to John T. Hargrave, 2 August 1856, Letter Book, vol. 1, AHMSC.

12. *Minutes of the General Association of Iowa, 1856* (Burlington, Iowa: Hawkeye Press, 1856), 7; *Minutes of the Ohio Conference of the Congregational Churches* (Cleveland: Conference Printing, 1856), 8; *Oberlin Evangelist* 13 (2 July 1856):109.

13. *American Missionary* O.S. 10 (October 1856), 91; *Minutes of the General Association of Illinois, 1856* (Peoria, Ill.: Benjamin Foster, 1856), 32; *Minutes of the General Association of New York, 1856* (Albany: J. Munsell, 1856), 11; *Congregational Herald,* 30 October 1856.

14. Richard Hall to Secretary, 28 October 1856; David Coe to Richard Hall, 12 November 1856, Letter Book, vol. 2, AHMSC.

15. *Minutes of the General Association of Iowa* (1856), 7; Oliver Emerson to S. S. Jocelyn,

30 June 1856, AMAC; William Salter to Executive Committee, 29 September 1856, AHMSC; Milton Badger to William Salter, 26 November 1856, Letter Book, vol. 2, AHMSC.

16. *Congregational Herald*, 29 January 1857; D. B. Coe to Lewis Tappan, 6 February 1857, Letter Book, vol. 2, AHMSC.

17. *Minutes of the Annual Meeting of the Evangelical Consociation of the Congregational Churches of Rhode Island, 1855* (Providence, R.I.: M. B. Young, 1855), 7; *Minutes of the General Association of New York, 1856,* 12.

18. William Hosmer, *Slavery and the Church* (Auburn, N.Y.: William J. Moses, 1853), 193.

19. *New York Evangelist,* 14 May 1857; *Chicago Daily Tribune,* 6 June 1853.

20. F. A. Ross, *Slavery Ordained of God,* 65.

21. *Liberator,* 5 September 1856; *Evangelical Repository* 15 (January 1857):481–83; *Presbytery Reporter* 3 (February 1857):431; *New York Evangelist,* 21 May 1857.

22. *New York Observer,* 21 August, 23 October 1856; *New York Evangelist,* 14 May 1857.

23. Records of the Presbytery of Portage, 4:276 (PHS MSS).

24. *Central Christian Herald,* 9 October 1856; Records of the Synod of Western Reserve, 2:251 (PHS MSS); *New York Evangelist,* 14 May 1857.

25. See records of the following: Presbytery of Cleveland (1847–70), 161–64; Presbytery of Elyria (1842–63, University of Chicago MSS, photocopy), 297–99; Presbytery of Grand River, 3:157 (UM MSS); Synod of Wabash (1851–69), 70–73 (PHS MSS); Synod of Indiana, 2:198–201 (PHS MSS); Presbytery of Portage, 4:281–82 (PHS MSS); Presbytery of Huron: R. Braden Moore, *History of the Huron Presbytery* (Philadelphia: William F. Fell, 1892), 189.

26. MGAPC (New School, 1856), 197–211; *New York Observer,* 5 June 1856; Records of the Presbytery of Springfield, 4:5–6 (MTS MSS); Records of the Synod of Illinois, 2:17–18 (MTS MSS); C. L. Watson to D. B. Coe, 11 October 1856, AHMSC; *Central Christian Herald,* 13 November, 19 March 1856; see: Records of the following: Presbytery of Salem, 2:423–24 (PHS MSS); Presbytery of Hamilton (1847–68), 188–90 (PHS MSS); Presbytery of Pataskala, 2:165, 172 (Wooster College MSS); Presbytery of Schuyler (1856–70), 10–11 (MTS MSS); Presbytery of Ottawa: Nahum Gould, *History of the Ottawa Presbytery,* 186–87; Records of the Presbytery of Kalamazoo, 2:114 (UM MSS); Presbyteries of Dayton and Franklin: *Central Christian Herald,* 23 October 1856, 16 April 1857; Records of the Presbyterian and Congregational Convention of Wisconsin, 1:343 (WHS MSS); Elizabeth L. Smith, ed., *Henry Boynton Smith, His Life and Letters* (New York: A. C. Armstrong and Son, 1881), 434.

27. Milton Badger to J. A. Reed, February (n.d.), 1857, JARC; Badger to Edgar Ketchum, 13 April 1857, Letter Book, vol. 2, AHMSC; see Letters to Agents (1857): Milton Badger to Benjamin Tappan; J. F. Stone; Theodore Spencer; John A. Murray; James Newton; Thomas Wicks; Henry Little; Julius A. Reed; Richard Hall, 10, 11 March, Letter Book, vol. 3, AHMSC.

28. *American Presbyterian,* 19 February 1857; *Christian Observer,* 26 February, 12 March 1857; *Congregational Herald,* 12 March 1857; *New York Evangelist,* 19 March 1857; *American Presbyterian,* 5 March 1857; *New York Observer,* 16 April 1857; *New York Evangelist,* 26 March 1857; *Congregational Herald,* 16 April 1857, cited by *American Presbyterian,* 26 March 1857; *Central Christian Herald,* 16 February 1857; *Congregational Herald,* 29 January, 16 April 1857; *American Presbyterian,* 9 April 1857; *Oberlin Evangelist* 14 (15 April 1857):61; *American Missionary* 1 (April 1857):4, 83–84.

29. A. C. Feissell to David Coe, 4 May 1857, AHMSC; *Christian Observer,* 18, 25 June 1857; *New York Observer,* 18 June 1857; J. A. Murray to Secretaries, 18 May 1857, AHMSC, cited by *New York Observer,* 16 April 1857; John Murray to Secretaries, 21 March 1857, AHMSC; Theodore Spencer to Milton Badger, 5 March 1857, AHMSC.

30. A. D. Smith, *Home Missions and Slavery* (New York: John A. Gray, 1857), 4; John

A. Murray to Secretaries, 18 May 1857, AHMSC; *The Protest of the Philadelphia Home Missionary Society, April 28, 1857* (Philadelphia: Henry B. Ashmead, 1857), 3; ARAHMS (1856), 29:103; (1857), 30:101; *American Presbyterian*, 5 March 1857; *Congregational Herald*, 23 April 1857.

31. *New York Evangelist*, 19 March 1857; A. D. Smith, *Home Missions and Slavery*, 46.

32. David Coe to Theodore Spencer, 21 April 1857, Letter Book, vol. 2; Coe to W. H. Goodrich, 28 April 1857, Letter Book, vol. 3, AHMSC; Milton Badger to P. H. Fowler, 30 March 1857; Badger to William Timlove, 10 April 1857, Letter Book, vol. 2, AHMSC; *Congregational Herald*, 14 May 1857; David Coe to James Dewmont, 21 April 1857, Letter Book, vol. 2; David Coe to Dexter Clary, 24 April 1857; Coe to J. H. Newton, 21 April 1857; Coe to J. A. Reed, 24 April 1857; Coe to Aratus Kent, 24 April 1857, Letter Book, vol. 3, AHMSC.

33. Theodore Spencer to Milton Badger, 10 April 1857; Theodore Spencer to Milton Badger, 15 April 1857, AHMSC; Milton Badger to Theodore Spencer, 15 April 1857, Letter Book, vol. 3, AHMSC; *Position of the Southern Church in Relation to Slavery, As Illustrated in a Letter of Dr. F. A. Ross to Rev. Albert Barnes, With an Introduction by a Constitutional Presbyterian* (New York: John A. Gray, 1857), 3, 6, 16.

34. Milton Badger to P. H. Fowler, 30 March 1857, Letter Book, vol. 2, AHMSC; *New York Evangelist*, 16 April 1857; Asa D. Smith, *Home Missions and Slavery*, 28; *Congregational Herald*, 2 April 1857.

35. Milton Badger to P. H. Fowler, 30 March 1857, Letter Book, vol. 2, AHMSC; *New York Evangelist*, 21 May 1857; Joseph C. Stiles, *Modern Reform Examined; or the Union of the North and South on the Subject of Slavery* (Philadelphia: J. B. Lippincott and Co., 1857), iii.

36. D. B. Coe to Theodore Spencer, 21 April 1857, Letter Book, vol. 2, AHMSC; *New York Observer*, 7 May 1857; *American Presbyterian*, 23 April 1857; *Christian Observer*, 23 April 1857.

37. Records of the Presbytery of Genesee, 4:239 (PHS MSS); Daniel Gibbs to D. B. Coe, 9 May 1857, AHMSC; Theodore Spencer to Milton Badger, 22 April, 15, 22 May, 4 July 1857; S. S. Goodman to Secretaries, 18 June 1857; J. A. Murray to Secretaries, 6 May 1857; S. H. Williams to D. B. Coe, 23 June 1857; S. N. Robinson to Milton Badger, 22 June 1857, AHMSC.

38. E. D. Morris to Secretary, 6 May 1857; J. H. Newton to Secretary, 30 May 1857; Warren Jenkins, 9 May 1857; D. H. Coyner, 30 March, 20 April 1857; N. C. Robinson, 13 April 1857; G. G. Rice, 7 May 1857; Henry Little, 28 April 1857; H. B. Holmes, 1 February 1858; Aratus Kent, 10 March, 20 April 1857; Albert Hale, 3 April 1857; A. L. Harrington, 5 April 1857; Milton Badger to P. H. Fowler, 30 March 1857, Letter Book, vol. 2; J. H. Newton to Badger, 30 May 1857; Dexter Clary to Badger, 6, 16 February 1857, AHMSC; *American Presbyterian*, 23 April 1857; see records of the following presbyteries: Alton, 2:90 (MTS MSS); Cleveland (1847-70), 164 (Presbytery of Cleveland MSS); Belvidere (1847-63), 77 (MTS MSS); Franklin, 1:266 (PHS MSS); Madison (1838-57), 390-91 (Hanover College MSS); Logansport, 2:164:65 (Hanover College MSS); Cincinnati, 2:327 (Historical Society of Cincinnati MSS); Indianapolis, 1:327 (Office of Synod of Indiana MSS); Trumbull, 2:231-32 (PHS MSS); Columbus (Wisconsin), 1:33 (WHS MSS); Kalamazoo, 2:115 (UM MSS); Presbyterian and Congregational Convention of Wisconsin, 1:356 (WHS MSS); Presbytery of Ottawa: Gould, *History of the Presbytery of Ottawa*, 186; William Fuller to Milton Badger, 13 May 1857. The question was indefinitely postponed to take up other matters in the presbyteries of St. Joseph and Elyria: Records of the Presbytery of Elyria (1842-63), 296-302; Records of the Presbytery of Detroit, 4: 203, 228 (UM MSS); *New York Evangelist*, 7 May 1857; George Duffield's Diary, vol. 5, 7 February 1848; vol. 6, 3, 14 April 1857, Detroit Public Library; L. G. Vander Velde,

"The Diary of George Duffield," *Mississippi Valley Historical Review* 24 (June 1937):32–33; Evans, "Abolitionism in the Illinois Churches," 128; *American Presbyterian*, 23 April 1857.

39. Horace Hooker to Milton Badger, 14 February 1857; Benjamin Tappan to Badger, 3 March 1857; J. F. Stone to Badger, 4 March 1857; J. S. Clark to Badger, 11 February 1857; Benjamin P. Stone to Badger, 27 January 1857; Milton Badger to C. B. Barton, 11 November 1857, Letter Book, vol. 1; C. B. Barton to Badger, 26 October 1857; Badger to Elisha Jenny, 29 December 1860, Letter Book, vol. 2, AHMSC; Hedge, Elias G., *Sermon . . . Before the Maine Missionary Society and A History of Its First Half Century* (Augusta, Maine: Elias G. Hedge, 1857), 18; Benjamin Tappan to Milton Badger, 24 June 1857, AHMSC; *Minutes of the General Conference of Maine, 1857* (Portland, Maine: Brown Thurston, 1857), 13; E. F. Durer to Milton Badger, 1 July 1857, AHMSC; *Minutes of the General Association of Massachusetts, 1857* (Boston: Crocker and Brewster, 1857), 12; J. J. Dana to Milton Badger, 29 June 1857; M. M. Langley to Secretary, 4 May 1857, AHMSC; General Association of Connecticut: *Puritan Recorder* cited by *Congregational Herald*, 9 July 1857; *Minutes of the General Association of New Hampshire* (Hanover, N.H.: Dartmouth Press, 1857), 7; the Long Island consocation also approved the rule. See: Christopher Youngs to Secretary, 22 May 1857, AHMSC; for example see: Minutes, District Convention of the Presbyterian and Congregational Churches of Beloit (1842–61), 321 (WHS MSS); *Minutes of the Ohio Congregational Conference, 1857* (Cleveland: Ohio Conference Print), 8; *Minutes of the Congregational Churches of Michigan*, 195; *Minutes of the Congregational Association of Iowa* (Burlington, Iowa: Hawkeye Press, 1857), 3; Elizur Andrus to Secretaries, 27 April 1857, AHMSC.

40. J. P. Williston to Secretaries, 10 April 1857; J. A. Reed to Milton Badger, 12 June 1857, AHMSC; E. D. Seward to S. S. Jocelyn, 16 February, 14 May 1857; Elias Hawley to Lewis Tappan, 21 April 1857, AMAC; A. A. Guthrie to Editor, 14 October 1857; Joseph H. Jones to Editor, 1 May 1857; *American Missionary* N.S. 1 (July 1857):160, 1 (November 1857): 253; Oliver Emerson to Milton Badger, 30 August 1861; Badger to Emerson, 6 September 1861, Letter Book, vol. 1; Flavel Bascom to Badger, 22 August 1861; Badger to Bascom, 31 August 1861, Letter Book, vol. 1; J. E. Roy to D. B. Coe, 30 October 1861; Coe to Roy, 21 November 1861, Letter Book, vol. 1; Badger to J. E. Roy, 10 December 1861, 3 January 1862, Letter Book, vol. 2; Roy to Badger, 17, 31 December 1861, AHMSC.

41. Benjamin Mills to D. B. Coe, 21 May 1857, AHMSC.

42. *New York Observer*, 5 November 1857.

43. George D. Phelps to Deacons and Prudential Committee of the Church of the Puritan, 27 December 1855, 2 January 1856, GBCP; Stiles, *Modern Reform Examined*, 119, 121, 145.

44. ARAHMS (1857), 31:129.

45. Cited by *American Presbyterian*, 9 April 1857.

46. *American Presbyterian*, 23 April 1857; *Christian Observer*, 30 April 1857.

47. *Central Christian Herald* (Cincinnati), 28 May 1857.

48. D. B. Coe to Milton Badger, 1, 3 June 1857. AHMSC.

49. MGAPC (New School, 1857), 234, 236–37; *Central Christian Herald*, 28 May 1857.

50. MGAPC (1857), 403–6; *New York Observer*, 18 June 1857; *Presbyterian Magazine* 7 (October 1857):433–39.

51. Milton Badger to S. Hopkins Emery, 30 July 1860, Letter Book, vol. 1, AHMSC.

52. D. B. Coe to Benjamin Mills, 5 May 1857; Milton Badger to L. R. Morrison, 16 February, 10 April 1857, Letter Book, vol. 1, AHMSC.

53. ARAHMS (1857), 21:129; Milton Badger to L. R. Morrison, 10 April 1857; D. B. Coe to Benjamin Mills, 5 May 1857, Letter Book, vol. 1; Benjamin Mills to D. B. Coe, 16, 18 May 1857, AHMSC.

54. Milton Badger to Benjamin Mills, 9 June 1857, Letter Book, vol. 1, AHMSC.

55. Truman Hill to D. B. Coe, 12 May 1857; J. J. Porter to Milton Badger, 2 September 1859, AHMSC.

56. MGAPC (1860), 253, 255, 258; (1861), 468.

CHAPTER 14

1. *Congressional Globe*, 36th Cong., 2d sess., 12.

2. Carl L. Spicer, "The Great Awakening of 1857 and 1858" (Ph.D. diss., Ohio State University, 1935), 223, 224, 231-32, 239-40; Smith, *Revivalism and Social Reform*, 215-16, 223; *New York Times*, 7 April 1857. C. C. Goen contends that the Great Awakening of 1858 did not accelerate sectionalism or contribute to the election of a sectional candidate in 1860 as Timothy Smith argues. Goen has apparently not read Spicer's dissertation. See: Goen, *Broken Churches*, 148.

3. A. M. Colton to A. L. Chapin, 26 March 1857, ALCC.

4. Levi Field, *Crime — Its Causes and Remedy: A Sermon Preached in the Union Congregational Church, in Marlborough, on Fast Day, April 16, 1857* (Boston: Franklin Printing House, 1857), 15-16.

5. N. S. S. Beman, *Antagonisms in the Moral and Political World: A Discourse Delivered in the First Presbyterian Church, Troy, New York, Thanksgiving, November 18, 1858* (Troy, N.Y.: A. W. Scribner and Co., 1858), 35.

6. Dunham, *The Attitude of the Clergy Toward the South*, 62-65; William S. Rollins, "The Northeastern Religious Press and John Brown," *Ohio State Archaeological and Historical Quarterly* 61 (April 1952):131-33.

7. The *New York Observer* censured this practice. See: *New York Observer*, 8 December 1859.

8. *Central Christian Herald*, 8 December 1859; Stephen Oates, *Our Fiery Trial: Abraham Lincoln, John Brown, and the Civil War Era* (Cambridge: University of Massachusetts Press, 1979), 9-11.

9. *Anglo-American*, 5 November, 10 December 1859, cited by Benjamin Quarles, *Black Abolitionists* (New York: Oxford University Press, 1969), 240-41; Joel Schor, *Henry Highland Garnet*, 164; MGAPC (New School, 1846), 4; Joshua R. Giddings to Gerrit Smith, 20 October 1859, GSP; Beriah Green to Wendell Phillips, 29 December 1859, Wendell Phillips Papers, Houghton Library, Harvard University.

10. *Liberator*, 25 November 1859; Senior, "New England Congregationalists and the Anti-Slavery Movement, 401-5; Frank P. Stearns, *The Life and Public Service of George L. Stearns* (Philadelphia: J. B. Lippincott, 1907), 196.

11. *The Principia* (New York), 10 December 1859.

12. John R. Howard, ed., *Patriotic Addresses in England and America* (New York: Fords, Howard and Hulbert, 1887), 207; James Redpath, *Echoes of Harper's Ferry* (Boston: Thayer and Eldridge, 1860; reprint, New York: Arno Press, 1969), 156; for the radical position of Rev. A. M. Milligan on Brown see: *The Chicago Christian Cynosure*, 14 May, 18 June 1885.

13. Timothy Howe to Horace Rublee, 26 October 1859, Horace Rublee Papers, Wisconsin Historical Society.

14. Redpath, *Echoes of Harper's Ferry*, 94; S. L. Emery to John Sherman, 6 December 1859, John Sherman Papers, Library of Congress.

15. *American Missionary* N.S. 3 (December 1859), 279; John G. Fee to Cassius M. Clay, 12 December 1859, JGFC; *Autobiography of John G. Fee* (Chicago: National Christian Association, 1891), 147-49.

16. *New York Times*, 25 November 1859; *National Anti-Slavery Standard*, 10 December 1859; Bacon, *Leonard Bacon*, 58.

17. Carleton Mabee, *Black Freedom: The Nonviolent Abolitionists from 1830 Through the Civil War* (New York: Macmillan, 1970), 327; ARAHMS (1859), 6-8; Elihu Burritt to Thaddeus Stevens, 11 April 1862, Thaddeus Stevens Papers, Library of Congress; John W. Bond, "John G. Fee and Antislavery Agitation in Kentucky" (Masters thesis, Indiana University, 1959), 75-79; Philip W. English, "John G. Fee: Kentucky Spokesman for Abolition and Reform" (Ph.D. diss., Indiana University, 1973), 156-58; Victor B. Howard, "John Brown's Raid at Harper's Ferry and the Sectional Crisis in North Carolina," *North Carolina Historical Review* 55 (October 1978):405-7.

18. Howard, "John Brown's Raid at Harper's Ferry," 420; Tappan, *History of the American Missionary Association*, 10-11; *Galseburg Free Democrat*, 13 March 1860; *Sioux City, Iowa Times*, 20 April 1860; *American Missionary* 4 (February 1860):42; *Weekly Council Bluffs (Iowa) Bugle*, 23 May 1860.

19. Cited by *Rockford (Ill.) Republican*, 9 August 1860.

20. F. D. Parrish to John Sherman, 23 December 1858, John Sherman Papers, Library of Congress; speech of Carl Schurz delivered at a Republican rally, 10 May 1860, Carl Schurz Papers, Library of Congress; *New York Times*, 18 May 1860; *Independent*, 10 May 1860; Carl Schurz, *The Reminiscences of Carl Schurz*, 2 vols. (New York: McClure Company, 1907), 2:174-75.

21. *Congregationalist*, 27 April 1860.

22. *The Rock Island (Ill.) Argus*, 20 January 1860; Howard C. Perkins, "The Defense of Slavery in the Northern Press on the Eve of the Civil War," *Journal of Southern History* 9 (November 1943):527-28.

23. *Chicago Tribune*, 17, 18 May 1860.

24. *New York Herald*, 23 July 1860; Gerrit Smith, *Religion of Reason: The One Test of Character* (New York: Ross and Tousey, 1860), 23.

25. Daniel E. Somes to Gerrit Smith, 27 August 1860: *Liberator*, 5 October 1860; *New York Herald*, 16 October 1860.

26. Thomas Adams, "David Thurston," *Congregational Quarterly* 9 (October 1867):326.

27. *New York Tribune*, 16 July, 30 August 1860; ARAMA (1882), 36:35; *New York Times*, 4 March 1882; *Racine (Wis.) Daily Journal*, 25 August 1860; *Milwaukee Daily Sentinel*, 18, 19 September 1860; *Chicago Daily Democrat*, 19 July 1860; *Baraboo (Wis.) Republic*, 27 June 1866; *Racine Daily Journal*, 28 July 1860; *Chicago Daily Democrat*, 19 July, 2 November 1860; Harold P. James, "Lincoln's Own State in the Election of 1860" (Ph.D. diss., University of Illinois, 1943), 134.

28. *Janesville (Wis.) Morning Gazette*, 24 October 1860; *Racine Daily Journal*, 8, 23 June 1860.

29. *Atlas and Argus*, 5 September 1860; *Burlington (Iowa) Hawk-Eye*, 1 September 1860; *Congregational Herald*, 30 August 1860.

30. N. S. Dickinson, *Slavery, the Nation's Crime and Danger: A Sermon Preached in the Congregational Church, Foxborough, Massachusetts, September 30, 1860* (Boston: George Noyes, 1860), 34-35.

31. William Neal Cleveland, *African Servitude: What Is It, and What Is Its Moral Character?* (New York: D. Appleton, 1861), 20-21.

32. *Independent*, 26 July 1860; *Congregationalist*, June 1860, cited by Durham, *The Attitude of the Northern Clergy Toward the South*, 12; *Congregational Herald*, 30 August 1860.

33. *American Presbyterian*, 9 August, 25 October 1860.

34. *Independent*, 6 September 1860.

35. *Detroit Tribune* cited by the *Elkhorn* (Wis.) *Independent*, 7 September 1860.

36. *Rock Island Argus*, 30 May, 2 July, 1 August 1860; clipping from *Chicago Press and Tribune*, no. 32157, 3 September 1860, AMAC; *Rock Island Weekly Register*, 6 June, 1 August 1860.

37. Henry Shedd to Secretaries, 4 October 1860, AHMSC.

38. John W. Thompson to Secretaries, 1 October 1860, AHMSC.

39. Joseph H. Jones to Secretary, 1 August, 14 September 1860, AMAC.

40. Levin Wilson to S. S. Jocelyn, 3 August 1860, AMAC.

41. Clipping (n.d.), no. 38897, 1860, AMAC.

42. C. H. Eaton to Milton Badger, 25 September, 4 December 1860, AHMSC.

43. John Scotford to Secretary, 20 August 1860, AHMSC.

44. Samuel R. Thrall to Secretary, 11 September 1860; W. C. Merritt to Milton Badger, 1 August, 5 November 1860; J. R. Dunn to Milton Badger, 5 November 1860, AHMSC; John Parry to Secretary, 27 November 1860; H. D. Platt to S. S. Jocelyn, 1 December 1860, AMAC; H. W. Cobb to Secretary, 15 November 1860; Milton Wells to Milton Badger, 6 November 1860, AHMSC; Israel C. Holmes to S. S. Jocelyn, 12 November 1860; G. I. Commins to S. S. Jocelyn, 3 July 1860, AMAC.

45. Muelder, *Fighters for Freedom*, 394; Taylor, "Seeking the Kingdom," 449; *Galesburg Free Democrat*, 2 September 1858, 6 January 1860.

46. J. M. Sturtevant, Jr., *Julian M. Sturtevant*, 286, 288, 296; *Chicago Democrat*, 11 June 1860; Evans, "Abolitionism in the Illinois Churches," 204.

47. *Newark Daily Advertiser*, 17 July, 28 September 1860; *Chicago Journal*, 11 October 1860.

48. *Newark Advertiser*, 9 August, 14 September, 3 October 1860; *Chicago Journal*, 24 September 1860.

49. *New York Tribune*, 28 September, 1, 27 October, 6 November 1860; *New York Times*, 28 September 1860; *New York Tribune*, 6 November 1860; G. E. Legur to William E. Dodge, 5 November 1860, Anson G. Phelps–William E. Dodge Correspondence (New York City Library MSS).

50. *New York Times*, 5 June 1857, 14, 15, 27 June 1860; *New York World* cited by *Cincinnati Daily Commercial*, 24 August 1860; *Daily Free Democrat*, 26 May 1858; *The Daily Wisconsin* (Milwaukee), 10 May 1860; *Boston Evening Transcript*, 31 March 1859; Edward Gilbert to George B. Cheever, 17 October 1860, GBCP cited by James McPherson, *The Struggle for Equality* (Princeton: Princeton University Press, 1964), 19.

51. *Independent* cited by *Rockford* (Ill.) *Republican*, 9 February 1860; *Galesburg Free Democrat*, 10 July 1860; Thomas W. Knox, *Life and Work of Henry Ward Beecher* (Kansas City, Mo.: S. F. Junkin, 1887), 222; *New York Times*, 30 October, 5 November 1860; *New York Tribune*, 12 November 1860.

52. *Cincinnati Daily Commercial*, 30 November 1861; *Congregational Herald*, 28 February 1861.

53. *New York Tribune*, 30 November 1860; *New York Times*, 30 November 1860; Joseph P. Thompson, *The President's Fast: A Discourse Upon Our National Crimes and Follies* (New York: Thomas Holman, 1861), 25.

54. Thomas Adams, "David Thurston," 326; *Independent*, 15 November 1860.

55. *New York Evening Post*, 8 April 1861; *New York Herald*, 22, 23 December 1860.

56. Diary of George Lewis Prentiss (January 1 to December 1860), 7 November, 8 December 1860 (New York City Library MSS).

57. *Daily Evening Transcript*, 30 November 1860; *Springfield Republican*, 4 December 1860.

58. *Christian Observer*, 15 November 1860; *Congregationalist*, 9 November 1860; *Congregational Herald*, 15, 29 November 1860; *Independent*, 29 November 1860.

59. *Christian Observer*, 15 November 1860; *New York Observer* cited by *Presbyter*, 22 November 1860.

60. *Presbyter*, 24 January 1861; *New York Observer*, 31 January 1861; Gardiner Spring, *Personal Reminiscences of the Life and Times of Gardiner Spring*, 2 vols. (New York: Charles Scribner's Sons, 1866), 2:179–85.

61. *Presbyterian Banner*, 27 April 1861; *New York Evangelist*, 16 May 1861.

62. Count Agenor de Gasparin, *The Uprising of a Great People: The United States in 1861*, trans. Mary L. Booth, 4th ed. (New York: Charles Scribner, 1861), 45.

63. C. C. Goen, *Broken Churches, Broken Nation*, 3.

64. Allan Nevins, *The War for the Union* (New York: Scribner's, 1959), 10; Lewis G. Vander Velde, *The Presbyterian Churches and the Federal Union, 1861–1869* (Cambridge: Harvard University Press, 1932), 341; Smith, *Revivalism and Social Reform*, 229; William G. McLoughlin, *Modern Revivalism: Charles Grandison Finney to Billy Graham* (New York: Ronald Press, 1959), 121; Frank G. Beardsley, *A History of American Revivals* (New York: American Tract Society, 1912), 238.

65. James Moorhead, *American Apocalypse: Yankee Protestants and the Civil War* (New Haven: Yale University Press, 1978), 20; Marsden, *The Evangelical Mind*, 185–86, 201; Ronald White and C. Howard Hopkins, *The Social Gospel: Religion and Reform in Changing America* (Philadelphia: Temple University Press, 1976), 19.

66. William W. Sweet, *The Story of Religions in America* (New York: Harper and Bros., 1930), 10; Cole, *Social Ideas of Northern Evangelists*, 223.

67. Cole, *Social Ideas of Northern Evangelists*, 219–20.

68. Marsden, *The Evangelical Mind*, 26.

69. Allan Nevins, *The Statesmanship of the Civil War* (New York: Collier, 1962), 61, 91–92; David M. Potter, "Why the Republicans Rejected Both Compromise and Secession," in *The Crisis of the Union, 1860–1861*, ed. Harmon Knoles (Baton Rouge: Louisiana University Press, 1965), 104–5; Kenneth M. Stampp, "Why the Republicans Rejected Both Compromise and Secession, Comment," in *The Crisis of the Union*, ed. Knoles, 113.

Bibliography

The bibliography is not intended to be comprehensive. All the manuscript material and church records used in this study are contained in this bibliography. The bibliography also contains all contemporary accounts, autobiographies, and pamphlets that were used. As there is no want of extensive bibliographies on the antislavery movement, the bibliography includes only a select list of the most significant and useful newspapers and secondary material. The full and complete listing of all other material used in this study is in the notes.

PRIMARY SOURCES

The correspondence in the American Home Missionary Society (AHMS) Collection constitutes one of the two major manuscript sources for this monograph. The AHMS Collection is a part of the Amistad Research Library housed in the Tulane University Library. The AHMS Collection consists of both incoming and outgoing correspondence. The outgoing correspondence is contained in letter books, and the incoming correspondence is filed alphabetically by the name of the sender, arranged by years and dates. I used incoming correspondence from missionaries, agents, and patrons most frequently. The outgoing correspondence of the Society's secretaries and executive committee was important in determining the evolution of the official position of the Society concerning slavery throughout the antebellum period. The Amistad Research Center also contains the smaller American Missionary Association (AMA) Collection, which was the second major manuscript collection used for this study. The AMA Collection is an antislavery collection of approximately 350,000 manuscript pieces.

Other Manuscript Correspondence and Papers

American Antiquarian Society Library
 George B. Cheever Family Papers
 Abigail Kelly Foster Papers
 Seth Sweetser Papers
Beloit College Library
 Aaron L. Chapin Correspondence

Berea College Library
    John G. Fee Correspondence
Boston Public Library
    William Lloyd Garrison Papers
    Amos A. Phelps Papers
Carroll College Library
    Dexter Clary Papers
Columbia University Library
    Moncure Conway Papers
Detroit Public Library, Barton Room
    George Duffield's Diary
Georgia Department of Archives and History
    Diary of George A. B. Walker
Grinnell College Library
    Truman C. Douglas, "Builders of the Commonwealth: The Patriarchs and Their
    Associates"
    Julius A. Reed Correspondence
Harvard University, Houghton Library
    Wendell Phillips Papers
    Charles Sumner Papers
Indiana Historical Society Library
    Samuel Merrill Papers
Indiana University, Lilly Library
    Hugh McCullock Papers
Iowa Historical Society Library
    James F. Wilson Papers
Library of Congress
    American Colonization Society Papers
    Breckinridge Family Papers
    Carl Schurz Papers
    John Sherman Papers
    Thaddeus Stevens Papers
    Lyman Trumbull Papers
    Elizur Wright Papers
Massachusetts Historical Society Library
    Robert C. Winthrop Papers
Miami Universty Library (Oxford, Ohio)
    Robert Bishop Papers
New York Historical Society Library
    Slavery Manuscripts
New York Public Library
    William E. Dodge Papers
    Diary of George Lewis Prentiss
Oberlin College Library

American Anti-Slavery Papers
Frederick B. Barnes Papers
Henry Cowles Papers
Charles Finney Papers
William Goodell Letters
Presbyterian Foundation Library
Autobiography of Rev. Amasa Converse, 1795–1872
Presbyterian Historical Society
American Sunday School Union Papers
Artemas Bullard Papers
William S. Plumer Papers
Randolph-Macon College Library
John P. Branch Papers
Rochester Public Library
Aristarchus Champion Papers
Thurlow Weed Papers
Syracuse University, George Arents Research Library
Gerrit Smith Papers
Tulane University Library
Charles C. Jones Papers
University of Chicago Library
Stephen A. Douglas Papers
University of Virginia Library
John H. Cocke Papers
Western Reserve Historical Society Library
Peter Hitchcock Family Papers
Wheaton College Library
Jonathan Blanchard Papers
Williston Academy, Easthampton, Massachusetts
Samuel Williston Correspondence
Wisconsin Historical Library
Horace Rublee Papers
Yale University Library
Leonard Bacon Papers
Leonard Bacon Sermons

Manuscript Church Records

Beloit College Library
Records of the Congregational Church and Society of Beloit, Wisconsin, vol. 1
Chicago Theological Seminary
Records of the General Association of Rock River Congregationalists, 1851–67
Cincinnati Historical Society Library
Records of the Presbytery of Cincinnati, 1835–43, vol. 1
Records of the Presbytery of Cincinnati, 1844–70, vol. 2

Hanover College Library
    Records of the Presbytery of Logansport, 1844–70, vol. 2
    Records of the Presbytery of Madison, 1838–57
Historical Foundation of the Presbyterian and Reformed Churches, Montreat, North
    Carolina
    Minutes of the Synod of South Carolina and Georgia, 1833
Louisville Presbyterian Theological Seminary
    Minutes of the Synod of Kentucky, 1802–60
McCormick Theological Seminary Library
    Gould, Nahum, History of the Ottawa Presbytery
    Records of the Presbytery of Alton, 1850–63
    Records of the Presbytery of Belvidere, 1847–63
    Records of the Presbytery of Galena, 1841–63
    Records of the Presbytery of Schuyler, 1856–70
    Records of the Presbytery of Springfield, 1856–66
    Records of the Synod of Illinois, 1831–55, vol. 1
    Records of the Synod of Illinois, 1856–69, vol. 2
    Records of the Synod of Peoria, 1859–63
Office of the Presbytery of Cleveland
    Records of the Presbytery of Cleveland, 1847–70
    Records of the Presbytery of Portage, 1843–63, vol. 4
Office of the Synod of Indiana
    Records of the Presbytery of Crawfordsville, 1835–68
    Records of the Presbytery of Greencastle, 1851–60
    Records of the Presbytery of Indianapolis, 1839–63, vol. 1
Presbyterian Historical Society Library
    Minutes of the Presbytery of Angelica, 1841–56 (New School)
    Minutes of the Presbytery of Cortland, New York, 1825–47
    Minutes of the Presbytery of Niagara, 1842–59
    Minutes of the Presbytery of Rockaway, 1846–51
    Minutes of the Synod of Michigan, 1834–49
    Minutes of the Third Presbytery of New York, 1839–53
    Records of the Presbytery of Chemung, 1836–49
    Records of the Presbytery of Elyria, 1843–63
    Records of the Presbytery of Franklin, 1846–60
    Records of the Presbytery of Genesee, 1839–50, vol. 3
    Records of the Presbytery of Genesee, 1846–70, vol. 4
    Records of the Presbytery of Grand River, Ohio, 1836–48
    Records of the Presbytery of Hamilton, 1847–68
    Records of the Presbytery of St. Joseph, 1845–63
    Records of the Presbytery of Salem, 1843–56, vol. 2
    Records of the Presbytery of Trumbull, 1847–61, vol. 1
    Records of the Presbytery of Utica, 1843–56
    Records of the Synod of Indiana, 1826–45

Records of the Synod of Indiana, 1846–53, vol. 2
Records of the Synod of Wabash, 1851–69
Records of the Synod of Western Reserve, 1846–67
University of Chicago Library
Records of the Presbytery of Elyria, 1842–63 (Photostat)
University of Michigan Library
Records of the Presbytery of Detroit, 1855–69
Records of the Presbytery of Grand River, 1857–70
Records of the Presbytery of Kalamazoo, 1850–65
Records of the Synod of Michigan, 1851–53
Wisconsin Historical Society Library
Minutes of the District Convention of the Presbyterian and Congregational Churches of Beloit, 1842–61
Minutes of the Presbyterian and Congregational Convention of Wisconsin, 1840–61
Records of the Presbytery of Columbus, 1856–65
Wooster College Library
Records of the Presbytery of Chillicothe, 1846–60
Records of the Presbytery of Pataskala, 1848–70
Records of the Synod of Ohio, 1849–69

Published Church Records, Reports, and Convention Proceedings

Address of the Synod of Kentucky on Slavery in 1853. Pittsburgh: United Presbyterian Board of Publications, 1862.
Annual Reports. American and Foreign Anti-Slavery Society.
Annual Reports. American Board of Commissioners of Foreign Missions.
Annual Reports. American Colonization Society.
Annual Reports. American Home Missionary Society.
Annual Reports. American Missionary Association.
Annual Reports of the Board of Managers of the Massachusetts Anti-Slavery Society.
Annual Reports of the New England Anti-Slavery Society.
Annual Reports of the Vermont Anti-Slavery Society.
Exposition of the Object and Plan of the American Union for the Relief and Improvement of the Colored Race. Boston: Light and Horton, 1835.
First Annual Report of the Board of Managers of the Boston Prison Discipline Society. Boston: Boston Prison Discipline Society, 1826.
First Annual Report of the Southern Aid Society. New York: D. Fanshaw, 1856.
Fourth Annual Report: Southern Aid Society. New York: George F. Nesbitt, 1853.
Minutes of the Annual Meeting of the Evangelical Consociation of the Congregational Churches of Rhode Island, 1855. Providence: M. B. Young, 1855.
Minutes of the Christian Anti-Slavery Convention, April 17-20, 1850. Cincinnati: Franklin Book and Job Rooms, 1850.
Minutes of the Christian Anti-Slavery Convention, 1851. Chicago: Western Citizen, 1851.

Minutes of the Congregational Association of Iowa, 1857. Burlington, Iowa: Hawkeye Press, 1857.

Minutes of the Congregational Churches of Michigan, 1857. Ann Arbor: E. B. Pond, 1857.

Minutes of the General Assembly of the Presbyterian Church (New School).

Minutes of the General Assembly of the Presbyterian Church (Old School).

Minutes of the General Assembly of the Presbyterian Church, U. S. A., 1789–1820. Philadelphia: Presbyterian Board of Publications, 1855.

Minutes of the General Association of Congregational Churches of Connecticut, June, 1854. New Haven: The Association, 1854.

Minutes of the General Association of Congregational Churches of Illinois, 1854. Peoria: Benjamin Foster, 1854.

Minutes of the General Association of Congregational Churches of Illinois, 1856. Peoria: Benjamin Foster, 1856.

Minutes of the General Association of Congregational Churches of Iowa, 1853. Burlington: Hawkeye Book and Job Printers, 1853.

Minutes of the General Association of Congregational Churches of Iowa, 1856. Burlington: Hawkeye Press, 1856.

Minutes of the General Association of Congregational Churches and Ministers of Iowa, 1840–1855. Hull, Iowa: Advance Print, 1888.

Minutes of the General Association of Congregational Churches of Maine, 1854. Bangor: Samuel L. Smith, 1854.

Minutes of the General Association of Congregational Churches of Massachusetts, 1851. Boston: Crocker and Brewster, 1851.

Minutes of the General Association of Congregational Churches of Massachusetts, 1857. Boston: Crocker and Brewster, 1857.

Minutes of the General Association of Congregational Churches of Michigan, 1854. Ann Arbor: E. B. Pond, 1854.

Minutes of the General Association of Congregational Churches of New Hampshire, 1853. Hanover, N.H.: Dartmouth Press, 1853.

Minutes of the General Association of Congregational Churches of New Hampshire, 1857. Hanover: Dartmouth Press, 1857.

Minutes of the General Association of Congregational Churches of New York, 1856. Albany: J. Munsell, 1856.

Minutes of the General Conference of Congregational Churches of Maine, 1856. Bangor: Wheeler and Lynde, 1856.

Minutes of the General Conference of Congregational Churches of Maine, 1857. Portland: Brown Thurston, 1857.

Minutes of the General Synod of the Evangelical Reformed Church, 1846–1848. New York: The Synod, 1848.

Minutes of the Massachusetts General Association of Congregational Churches, 1854. Boston: Crocker and Brewster, 1854.

Minutes of the Ohio Conference of the Congregational Churches, 1856. Cleveland: Conference Printing, 1856.

Minutes of the Ohio Congregational Conference. Cleveland: Medill and Cowles, 1854.

Minutes of the Ohio Congregational Conference, 1857. Cleveland: Conference Printing, 1857.

Minutes of the Presbyterian and Congregational Convention Held at Cleveland, Ohio, June 20, 1844. Cleveland: T. H. Smead, 1844.

Minutes of the Presbyterian Synod of Michigan, 1856. Detroit: H. Barnes, 1856.

Minutes of the Presbyterian Synod of New York and New Jersey, 1846. New York: Leavitt, Trow and Co., 1846.

Minutes of the Presbyterian Synod of New York and New Jersey, October, 1847. New York: Leavitt, Trow and Co., 1847.

Minutes of the Western Congregational Convention Held in Michigan City, Indiana, July 30–August 3, 1846. New York: John P. Prall, 1878.

Proceedings of the Convention Which Formed the Maine Union in Behalf of the Colored Race. Portland: Merrill and Byram, 1835.

Proceedings of the General Convention of Congregational Ministers and Delegates, 1852. New York: S. W. Benedict, 1852.

Proceedings of the New England Anti-Slavery Convention. Boston: Garrison and Knapp, 1834.

Proceedings of the Second Convention for Bible Missions, Held in Albany, September 2 and 3rd., 1846. New York: J. H. Tobitt, 1846.

Report of the Executive Committee of the American Union, 1836. Boston: Perkins and Marvin, 1836.

Report of the Proceedings and Views of the Taunton Union for the Relief and Improvement of the Colored Race, May, 1835. Taunton, Mass.: Bradford and Amsbury, 1835.

Southern Aid Society: Its Constitution and Address to the Christian Public. New York: D. Fanshaw, 1853.

Published Documents

Congressional Globe. Washington, D.C.

W. W. Henning, ed. *Statutes at Large of Virginia.* Richmond, Va.: George Cochran, 1823.

Published Manuscripts

Barnes, Gilbert, and Dwight L. Dumond. *Letters of Theodore Dwight Weld, Angelina Grimké Weld and Sarah Grimké, 1822-1844.* 1965. Reprint. Gloucester, Mass.: Peter Smith, 1966.

Dumond, Dwight L., ed. *Letters of James G. Birney, 1831-1857.* 2 vols. New York: D. Appleton, 1938.

Contemporary Accounts, Autobiographies, and Pamphlets

Adams, William. *Christianity and Civil Government.* New York: Charles Scribner, 1851.

Adger, John Bailey. *My Life and Times, 1810–1899*. Richmond, Va.: Presbyterian Committee of Publications, 1899.

Allen, Joseph Henry. *A Reign of Terror: A Sermon Preached in Union Street Church, Bangor, Maine, June 1, 1856*. Bangor: Samuel S. Smith, 1856.

American Mission and Slavery. New York: American and Foreign Anti-Slavery Society, 1853.

Andrews, Ethan Allen. *Slavery and Domestic Slave Trade in the United States*. Boston: Light and Stearns, 1836.

Bacon, Leonard. *The Morality of the Nebraska Bill*. New Haven: Reprint (n.p., n.d.) from *New Englander*, May 1854.

Baird, Robert. *Religion in America*. 1856. Reprint. New York: Harper and Bros., 1970.

Bannard, William. *Memorial of Jasper Corning*. New York: Robert Carter, 1870.

Barnes, Albert. *Home Missions: A Sermon in Behalf of the American Home Missionary Society*. New York: William Osborn, 1849.

———. *The State of the Country, A Discourse Delivered in the First Presbyterian Church, Philadelphia, June 1, 1865 on the Day Appointed as a Day of Humiliation and Mourning in View of the Death of the President of the United States*. Philadelphia: H. B. Ashmead, 1865.

———. *Thanksgiving Sermon: The Virtues and Public Service of William Penn*. Philadelphia: W. Sloanaker, 1845.

Bartlett, David W. *Modern Agitators or Pen Portraits of Living American Reformers*. Auburn, N.Y.: Orton and Mulligan, 1855.

Beckwith, George. *The Book of Peace: A Collection of Essays on War and Peace*. Boston: George Beckwith, 1845.

Beecher, Charles, ed. *Autobiography of Lyman Beecher*. 2 vols. New York: Harper and Bros., 1864.

Beecher, Charles. *The Duty of Disobedience to Wicked Laws*. New York: John A. Gray, 1851.

Beecher, Edward. *Narrative of Riots of Action in Connection With the Death of Reverend Elijah P. Lovejoy*. Alton, Ill.: G. Holton Co., 1838.

Beecher, Henry Ward. *A Discourse Delivered at the Plymouth Church, Brooklyn, New York, Upon Thanksgiving Day, November 25, 1847*. New York: Cody and Burgess, 1848.

———. *Patriotic Addresses*. New York: Fords, Howard, and Hulbert, 1887.

Beecher, Lyman. *Autobiography*. New York: Harper and Bros., 1864.

Beman, Nathan S. S. *Antagonism in the Moral and Political World: A Discourse Delivered in the First Presbyterian Church, Troy*. New York: A. W. Scribner and Co., 1858.

Birney, James G. *The American Churches, the Bulwarks of American Slavery*. Concord, N.H.: Parker Pillsbury, 1885.

Blagden, G. W. *Remarks and Discourse on Slavery*. Boston: Ticknor, Reed, and Fields, 1854.

Bouton, Nathaniel. *The Good Land in Which We Live: A Discourse Preached at Concord, New Hampshire*. Concord: McFarland and Jenks, 1850.

Boynton, Charles B. *Oration Delivered on the Fifth of July, 1847 Before the Native Americans of Cincinnati.* Cincinnati: Target and Gardner, 1847.

———. *Our Country, the Herald of a New Era: A Lecture Delivered Before the Young Men's Mercantile Library Association of Cincinnati, January 19, 1847.* Cincinnati: E. Shepard, 1847.

Braman, Milton Palmer. *The Mexican War: A Discourse Delivered on the Annual Fast Day, 1847.* Danvers, Mass.: Danvers Courier, 1847.

Brooks, A. L. *An Appeal for the Right: A Sermon.* Chicago: Daily Democrat Press, 1854.

Buchard, Samuel D. *Causes of National Solicitude: A Sermon Preached at the Thirteenth Street Presbyterian Church, New York, on Thanksgiving Day, November 25, 1847.* New York: S. W. Benedict, 1848.

Burrows, John Henry. *Henry Ward Beecher, The Shakespeare of the Pulpit.* New York: Funk and Wagnalls, 1893.

Bushnell, Horace. *Barbarism, the First Danger: A Discourse for Home Missions, 1847.* New York: William Osborn, 1847.

Bushnell, William. *Sermon Preached at the Funeral of Hon. William Jackson.* Boston: S. Chism, 1855.

Chapin, Aaron L. *A Sermon in Behalf of the American Home Missionary Society, May 5, 1857.* New York: American Home Missionary Society, 1858.

Child, Lydia Maria. *An Appeal in Favor of That Class of Americans Called Africans.* New York: Allen and Ticknor, 1836.

Crist, A. C. *The History of Marion Presbytery, Its Churches, Elders, Ministers, Missionary Societies, etc.* n.p., 1908.

Clark, Joseph S. *An Historical Sketch of the Congregational Churches in Massachusetts from 1620 to 1850.* Boston: Congregational Board of Publications, 1858.

Cleveland, William N. *African Servitude: What Is It, and What Is Its Moral Character?* New York: D. Appleton, 1861.

Coe, Edward B. *An Address in Commemoration of Asa Dodge Smith.* Concord, N.H.: Republican Press Association, 1882.

Davidson, Robert. *History of the Presbyterian Church of the State of Kentucky.* New York: Robert Carter, 1847.

Davis, Edwin Adams, ed. *Life in the Florida Parishes of Louisiana, 1836-1846, As Reflected in the Diary of Bennet H. Barrow.* New York: Oxford University Press, 1943.

De Gasparin, Count Agenor. *The Uprising of a Great People: The United States in 1861.* New York: Charles Scribner, 1861.

Dexter, Henry M. *Our National Condition and Its Remedy. A Sermon Preached in the Pine Street Church, Boston, June 22, 1856.* Boston: John P. Jewett, 1856.

Dickinson, N. S. *Slavery, the Nation's Crime and Danger: A Sermon Preached in the Congregational Church, Foxborough, Massachusetts, September 30, 1860.* Boston: George Noyes, 1860.

Fee, John G. *Autobiography of John G. Fee.* Chicago: National Christian Association, 1891.

Field, Levi. *Crime — Its Causes and Remedy: A Sermon Preached in the Union Congregational Church, in Marlborough, on Fast Day, April 16, 1857.* Boston: Franklin Printing House, 1857.

Foster, Aaron. *Liberty, the Nation, the Occasion.* Greenfield, Mass.: J. J. Ingersall, 1854.

Foster, Eden B. *The Right of the Pulpit and the Perils of Freedom.* Lowell, Mass.: J. J. Judkins, 1854.

Foster, Stephen S. *The Brotherhood of Thieves or a True Picture of the American Church and Clergy.* Boston: American Anti-Slavery Society, n.d.

———. *Revolution the Only Remedy for Slavery.* New York: American Anti-Slavery Society, 1854.

Galbraith, R. C. *The History of the Chillicothe Presbytery From Its Organization in 1799 to 1889.* Cincinnati: Scioto Gazette Office, 1889.

Garrison, Wendell Phillips and Francis Jackson Garrison. *William Lloyd Garrison.* 3 vols. New York: Century Co., 1876.

Garrison, William L. *Thoughts on African Colonization.* 1832. Reprint. New York: Arno Press, 1969.

Goodell, William. *Slavery and Anti-Slavery.* New York: W. Harned, 1852.

Graham, William. *The Cause and Manner of the Trial and Suspension of the Rev. William Graham by the New School Synod of Cincinnati.* Cincinnati: Privately Printed, n.d.

———. *The Contrast of the Bible and Abolitionism: An Exegetical Argument.* Cincinnati: Atlas Office, 1844.

Hale, David. *Facts and Reasonings on Church Government, Report at a Meeting of the Broadway Tabernacle.* New York: n.p., 1867.

Hallock, Gerard. *History of the South Congregational Church, New Haven.* New York: Tuttle, Morehouse, and Taylor, 1865.

Harrison, W. P. *The Gospel Among the Slaves: A Short Account of Missionary Operations Among the African Slaves of the Southern States.* Nashville: Publishing House of the Methodist Episcopal Church, South, 1893.

Hart, Burdett. *The Mexican War.* New Haven: Peck and Stafford, 1847.

Hatcher, William E. *Life of J. B. Jeter.* Baltimore: H. M. Wharton and Co., 1887.

Hedge, Elias G. *Sermon Preached Before the Maine Missionary Society and a History of Its First Half Century.* Augusta, Maine: Elias G. Hedge, 1857.

Hickok, Laurens P. *The Sources of Military Delusion, and the Practicability of Their Removal.* Hartford: P. Canfield, 1833.

History of the American Missionary Association. New York: S. W. Green, 1874.

Hosmer, William. *Slavery and the Church.* Auburn, N.Y.: William J. Moses, 1853.

Howard, John R., ed. *Patriotic Addresses in England and America.* New York: Fords, Howard and Hulbert, 1887.

Humphrey, Heman. *The Missouri Compromise: An Address Delivered Before the Citizens of Pittsfield, Massachusetts.* Pittsfield: Hull and Peirson, 1854.

Humphrey, Zephaniah. *Memorial Sketches, Heman Humphrey,* Philadelphia· Lippincott and Co., 1869.

James, Horace. *Address of the Rev. Horace James at the Anniversary of the American Home Missionary Society.* New York: American Home Missionary Society, 1856.

Johnson, Thomas G. "A Brief Sketch of the United Synod of the Presbyterian Church in the United States of America." In *Papers of the American Society of Church History.* Edited by Samuel M. Jackson. New York: G. P. Putnam's Sons, 1897.

Jones, Charles C. *The Religious Instruction of the Negroes in the United States.* Savannah: Thomas Purse, 1842.

————. *Second Annual Report of the Missionaries to the Negroes in Liberty County, Georgia.* Charleston: Observer Office, 1834.

Kirk, Edward N. *Our Duty in Perilous Times: A Sermon Delivered in Mount Vernon Church, June 1, 1856.* Boston: S. K. Whipple, 1856.

————. *The Church Essential to the Republic: A Sermon in Behalf of the American Home Missionary Society.* New York: Leavitt, Trow and Co., 1848.

Kitchel, Harvey D. *An Appeal for Discussion and Action on the Anti-Slavery Question.* Hartford: L. Skinner, 1850.

Knox, Thomas W. *Life and Work of Henry Ward Beecher.* Kansas City, Mo.: S. F. Junkins, 1887.

Lafon, Thomas. *The Great Obstruction to the Conversion of Souls at Home and Abroad.* New York: Union Missionary Society, 1843.

March, Daniel. *The Crisis of Freedom: Remarks on the Duty Which All Christian Men and Good Citizens Owe to Their Country in the Present State of Public Affairs.* Nashua, N.H.: Dodge and Noyes, 1854.

Moore, R. Braden. *History of the Huron Presbytery.* Philadelphia: William F. Fell, 1892.

Nelson, Henry. *A Discourse on the Proposed Repeal of the Missouri Compromise, Delivered at Springfield, Massachusetts, Before the Colonization Society of Hampden County, July 4, 1827.* Springfield: Tannott and Co., 1827.

Osgood, Samuel. *A Sermon Delivered at Springfield, Massachusetts, Before the Colonization Society of Hampden County, July 4, 1827.* Springfield: Tannott and Co., 1827.

Patterson, Robert W. *Early Society in Southern Illinois: Address Before the Chicago Historical Society.* Chicago: Fergus Printing, 1880.

Patton, William W. *Conscience and Law or a Discussion of Our Comparative Responsibility to Human and Divine Government.* New York: Mark H. Newman and Co., 1850.

Peet, Stephen. *History of the Presbyterian Congregational Churches and Ministers in Wisconsin.* Milwaukee: Silas Chapman, 1851.

Perkins, G. W. *Facts and Duties of the Times: A Sermon Delivered Before the First Congregational Church, Chicago, Illinois.* New York: William S. Dorr, 1856.

Phelps, Amos A. *Lectures on Slavery and Its Remedy.* Boston: New England Anti-Slavery Society, 1834.

Pierce, Edward L. *Memoir and Letters of Charles Sumner.* 4 vols. Boston: Roberts Brothers, 1877–93.

Pillsbury, Parker. *The Church as It Is or the Forlorn Hope of Slavery.* 2d ed. Concord, N.H.: Republican Press, 1885.

The Political Duties of Christians: A Report, Adopted at the Spring Meeting of the South Middlesex Conference of Churches, April 8, 1848. Boston: Andrews and Prentiss, 1848.

Position of the Southern Church in Relation to Slavery, As Illustrated in a Letter of Dr. F. A. Ross to Rev. Albert Barnes, With an Introduction by a Constitutional Presbyterian. New York: John A. Gray, 1857.

Porter, Noah. *Two Sermons on Church Communion and Excommunication, With a Particular View to the Case of Slaveholders in the Church.* Hartford: Case, Tiffany and Co., 1853.

Protest of the Philadelphia Home Missionary Society, April 28, 1857. Philadelphia: Henry B. Ashmead, 1857.

Redpath, James. *Echoes of Harper's Ferry.* Boston: Thayer and Eldridge, 1860.

Rice, Nathan L. *A Debate on Slavery Held in the City of Cincinnati.* New York: William H. Moore, 1846.

―――. *Lectures on Slavery Delivered in the North Presbyterian Church, Chicago.* Chicago: Goodman and Cushing, 1860.

Rogers, William. *Sermon Preached Before the Massachusetts Home Missionary Society, May 28, 1850.* Boston: James French, 1850.

Ross, Frederick A. *Slavery Ordained of God.* Philadelphia: Lippincott, 1857.

―――. *The Story of Rotherwood From the Autobiography of Rev. Frederick A. Ross, D. D.* Knoxville: Bean, Warters and Co., 1923.

Rowland, Henry A. *The Church and Slavery: Or the Relations of the Churches to Slavery Under the Constitution.* New York: M. W. Dodd, 1854.

Schurz, Carl. *The Reminiscences of Carl Schurz.* New York: McClure Co., 1907.

Smith, Asa D. *Home Missions and Slavery.* New York: John A. Gray, 1857.

―――. *Obedience to Human Law: A Discourse Delivered in the Brainard Presbyterian Church.* New York: Leavitt and Co., 1851.

Smith, Elizabeth L., ed. *Henry B. Smith, His Life and Letters.* New York: A. C. Armstrong and Son, 1881.

Smith, Gerrit. *Religion of Reason: The One Test of Character.* New York: Ross and Tousey, 1880.

Smith, Henry. *The Truly Christian Pulpit: Our Strongest National Defense, A Discourse in Behalf of the American Home Missionary Society.* New York: American Home Missionary Society, 1854.

Smith, Lucius. *The Higher Law, or Christ and His Law Supreme.* Ravenna, Ohio: Star Print, 1852.

Spear, Samuel. *The Law-Abiding Conscience and the Higher Law Conscience.* New York: Lambert and Lane, 1850.

Speeches and Other Proceedings at the Anti-Nebraska Meeting, New Haven, Connecticut, March 8 and 10th., 1854. New Haven: John H. Austin, 1854.

Spees, S. G. *A Discourse on the Great American Idea — Universal Liberty, Delivered in the Second Presbyterian Church, Indianapolis, Indiana, Upon Thanksgiving Day, November 25, 1847.* Indianapolis: Douglas and Elder, 1848.

Spring, Gardiner. *Personal Reminiscences of the Life and Times of Gardiner Spring.* New York: Charles Scribner's Sons, 1866.

Stearns, Frank P. *The Life and Public Service of George L. Stearns.* Philadelphia: J. B. Lippincott, 1907.

Stearns, Oliver. *The Gospel Applied to the Fugitive Slave Law.* Boston: Grosby and Nichols, 1851.

Stiles, Joseph C. *Modern Reform Examined; or the Union of the North and South on the Subject of Slavery.* Philadelphia: J. B. Lippincott and Co., 1857.

Stuart, Moses. *Conscience and the Constitution, With Remarks on the Recent Speech of the Hon. Daniel Webster in the Senate of the United States on the Subject of Slavery.* Boston: Crocker and Brewster, 1850.

Sturtevant, J. M., Jr. *Julian M. Sturtevant: An Autobiography.* Chicago: Fleming H. Revell Co., 1896.

Tappan, Lewis. *History of the American Missionary Association.* New York: American Missionary Association, 1855.

———. *A Letter to a Teacher Among the Freedmen.* New York: n.p., 1867.

———. *Life of Arthur Tappan.* Hartford: E. Hunt, 1850.

Thacher, George. *No Fellowship With Slavery: A Sermon Delivered June 29, 1856, in the First Congregational Church, Meriden, Connecticut.* Meriden: L. R. Webb, 1856.

Thayer, Eli. *A History of the Kansas Crusade: Its Friends and Foes.* New York: Harper and Bros., 1889.

Thompson, Joseph P. *The Fugitive Slave Law, Tried by the Old and New Testaments.* New York: William Harned, 1850.

———. *Memoir of David Hale.* New York: J. Wiley, 1850.

———. *No Slavery in Nebraska: The Voice of God Against National Crime.* New York: Ivison and Phinney, 1854.

———. *The President's Fast: A Discourse Upon Our National Crimes and Follies.* New York: Thomas Holman, 1861.

———. *Teachings of the New Testament on Slavery.* New York: Joseph H. Ladd, 1856.

Thompson, Noyes L. *The History of Plymouth Church, 1847–1872.* New York: G. W. Carleton and Co., 1873.

Thurston, David. *A Sermon Delivered September 25, 1849 at the Third Annual Meeting of the American Missionary Association at Boston, Massachusetts.* New York: William Harned, 1849.

Todd, John E. *The Good Never Die: A Sermon Delivered at Pittsfield, Massachusetts.* Pittsfield: Henry Chickering, 1861.

———. *Memoriam: Rev. Joseph P. Thompson.* N.p., n.d.

———. *John Todd, the Story of His Life Told Mainly By Himself.* New York: Harper and Bros., 1876.

Tolman, Richard. *Evil Tendencies of the Present Crisis: A Discourse Delivered July 4, 1847.* Danvers, Mass.: Danvers Courant, 1847.

Van Santvoord, Cornelius. *Memoirs of Eliphalet Nott for Sixty Two Years President of Union College.* New York: Sheldon and Co., 1876.

Walker, James B. *Experiences of Pioneer Life in the Early Settlements and Cities of the West.* Chicago: Sumner and Co., 1881.

Webb, Thomas H. *Information for Kansas Immigrants.* Boston: Alfred Mudge and Son, 1856.

Wight, W. W. *Semi-Centennial Retrospect, 1844–1894, of the Old White Church.* Milwaukee: Publication Committee, 1894.

White, Theodore F. *The Goodly Heritage: A Sermon, Thanksgiving Day, November 29, 1860.* New York: Thomas Holman, 1860.

Whipple, Charles K. *Relations of Anti-Slavery to Religion.* New York: American Anti-Slavery Society, n.d.

Willy, Austin. *The History of the Anti-Slavery Cause in the State and Nation.* Portland, Maine: B. Thurston, 1886.

Wilson, Henry. *The Rise and Fall of the Slave Power.* Boston: James R. Osgood, 1877.

Woolen, William W. *Biographical and Historical Sketches of Early Indiana.* Indianapolis: Hammond and Co., 1883.

Newspapers and Journals

Newspapers provided an invaluable aid in the research. Of 179 newspapers drawn on as sources, 55 were sectarian and religious journals and 28 were abolitionist, Liberty party, peace, or black journals. The *New York Evangelist,* the *New York Independent, New York Observer, Congregationalist* (Boston), *Boston Recorder, Christian Era* (Galesburg, Ill.), *Herald of the Prairies* (Chicago), and *Watchman of the Valley* (Cincinnati) were the most useful religious journals for the study. The *New York Tribune, New York Times, Chicago Tribune, Boston Courier, Boston Transcript, Cincinnati Gazette, Cincinnati Commercial,* and the *Cleveland Leader* were the most useful political journals. The *Liberator* (Boston), *Emancipator* (New York), *National Anti-Slavery Standard, Western Citizen* (Chicago), and the *American Freeman* (Milwaukee) were the most important abolitionist and Liberty party journals for this monograph.

SECONDARY SOURCES

Dissertations

Thirty-six dissertations were cited in the study.The following list includes the most useful in the research of this work:

Bruner, Charles V. "The Religious Instruction of the Slaves in the Antebellum South." Ph.D. diss., George Peabody College, 1933.

Cook, Lester. "Anti-Slavery Sentiment in the Culture of Chicago, 1844–1858." Ph.D. diss., University of Chicago, 1952.

Coyner, Martin Boyd. "John Hartwell Cocke of Bremo." Ph.D. diss., University of Virginia, 1962.

Davis, E. Bradford. "Albert Barnes, 1798–1870: An Exponent of New School Presbyterianism." Doctor of Theology diss., Princeton Theological Seminary, 1961.

Davis, Hugh H. "The Reform Career of Joshua Leavitt, 1794–1893." Ph.D. diss., Ohio State University, 1969.

Engelder, Conrad J. "The Churches and Slavery: A Study of the Attitude Toward Slavery of the Major Protestant Denominations." Ph.D. diss., University of Michigan, 1964.

English, Philip W. "John G. Fee: Kentucky Spokesman for Abolition and Education Reform." Ph.D. diss., Indiana University, 1973.

Evans, Linda J. "Abolitionism in the Illinois Churches, 1830–1865." Ph.D. diss., Northwestern University, 1981.

Housley, Donald D. "The Independent: A Study of Religious and Social Opinion, 1848–1870." Ph.D. diss., Pennsylvania State University, 1971.

Keller, Ralph A. "Northern Protestant Churches and the Fugitive Slave Law of 1850." Ph.D. diss., University of Wisconsin, 1969.

Loring, Eduard N. "Charles C. Jones: Missionary to Plantation Slaves, 1831–1847." Ph.D. diss., Vanderbilt University, 1976.

MacCormac, Earl. "The Transition from the Voluntary Missionary Society to the Church as a Missionary Organization." Ph.D. diss., Yale University, 1960.

Mattson, J. Stanley. "Charles Grandison Finney and the Emerging Tradition of New Measure Revivalism." Ph.D. diss., University of North Carolina, 1970.

Mounger, D. Mecklin. "Bondage and Benevolence: An Evangelical Calvinist Approaches Slavery — Samuel Hanson Cox." Ph.D. diss., Union Theological Seminary of New York, 1976.

Norton, L. Wesley. "The Religious Press and the Compromise of 1850: A Study of the Relationship of the Methodist, Baptist, and Presbyterian Press to the Slavery Controversy, 1846–1851." Ph.D. diss., University of Illinois, 1959.

Perkal, Leon. "William Goodell: A Life of Reform." Ph.D. diss., City College of New York, 1972.

Senior, Robert C. "New England Congregationalists and the Anti-Slavery Movement." Ph.D. diss., Yale University, 1954.

Spicer, Carl L. "The Great Awakening of 1857 and 1858." Ph.D. diss., Ohio State University, 1935.

Taylor, Richard S. "Seeking the Kingdom: A Study in the Career of Jonathan Blanchard, 1811–1892." Ph.D. diss., Northern Illinois University, 1977.

Willey, Larry Gene. "The Reverend John Rankin: Early Ohio Anti-Slavery Leader." Ph.D. diss., University of Iowa, 1976.

Zikmund, Barbara Brown. "Asa Mahan and Oberlin Perfectionism." Ph.D. diss., Duke University, 1969.

Articles and Periodical Literature

Fifty-eight articles were cited. The following were the most useful for the study:

Billington, Ray A. "Anti-Catholic Propaganda and the Home Missionary Movement, 1800–1860." *Mississippi Valley Historical Review* 22 (December 1935).

Birdsall, Richard D. "The Second Great Awakening and the New England Social Order." *Church History* 39 (September 1970).

Dillon, Merton L. "The Failure of American Abolitionists." *Journal of Southern History* 25 (May 1959).

Elliot, Emory. "The Dove and the Serpent: The Clergy in the American Revolution." *American Quarterly* 31 (Summer 1979).

Ellsworth, Clayton S. "The American Churches and the Mexican War." *American Historical Review* 45 (January 1940).

Griffin, Clifford S. "Religious Benevolence as Social Control." *Mississippi Valley Historical Review* 44 (December 1957).

Harlow, Ralph V. "Gerrit Smith and the Free Church Movement." *New York History* 18 (July 1937).

———. "The Rise and Fall of the Kansas Aid Movement." *American Historical Review* 41 (October 1935).

Kuhns, Frederick. "Slavery and Missions in the Old Northwest." *Journal of the Presbyterian Historical Society* 24 (December 1946).

Ludlum, Robert P. "Joshua R. Giddings, Radical." *Mississippi Valley Historical Review* 23 (June 1936).

MacCormac, Earl R. "The Development of Presbyterian Missionary Organizations, 1790–1870." *Journal of Presbyterian History* 43 (September 1965).

Mathews, Donald G. "Charles Colcock Jones and the Southern Evangelical Crusade to Form a Biracial Community." *Journal of Southern History* 41 (August 1975).

———. "The Second Great Awakening as an Organizing Process, 1780–1830: An Hypothesis." *American Quarterly* 21 (Spring 1969).

Nichols, Robert H. "The Plan of Union in New York." *Journal of Presbyterian History* 5 (March 1936).

Rollins, William S. "The Northwestern Religious Press and John Brown." *Ohio State Archaeological and Historical Quarterly* 61 (April 1952).

Southall, Eugene F. "Arthur Tappan and the Anti-Slavery Movement." *Journal of Negro History* 15 (April 1930).

Staiger, C. Bruce. "Abolitionism and the Presbyterian Schism of 1837–1838." *Mississippi Valley Historical Review* 36 (December 1949).

Williams, Irene. "The Operation of the Fugitive Slave Law in Western Pennsylvania From 1850–1860." *Western Pennsylvania Historical Magazine* 4 (July 1921).

Books

One hundred and twenty-three monographs were cited in the study. The following list includes the most significant works for the research:

Bacon, Theodore D. *Leonard Bacon, A Statesman in the Church.* New Haven: Yale University Press, 1931.

Barber, John W. *History of the Amistad Captives: Being a Circumstantial Account of the Capture of the Spanish Schooner Amistad.* New York: Hitchcock and Stafford, 1840.

Barnes, Gilbert Hobbs. *The Anti-Slavery Impulse, 1830–1844.* New York: Harcourt, Brace and World, 1964.

Clark, Calvin M. *American Slavery and Maine Congregationalists.* Bangor, Maine: Calvin Clark, 1940.

Cole, Charles. *Social Ideas of the Northern Evangelists, 1826–1860.* New York: Octagon, 1966.

Cross, Barbara M. *Horace Bushnell: Minister to a Changing America.* Chicago: University of Chicago Press, 1958.

Cross, Whitney R. *The Burned-over District: The Social and Intellectual History of Enthusiastic Religion in Western New York, 1800–1850.* New York: Harper and Row, 1956.

Dumond, Dwight Lowell. *Anti-Slavery Origins of the Civil War in the United States.* Ann Arbor: University of Michigan Press, 1959.

Dunham, Chester F. *The Attitude of the Northern Clergy Toward the South, 1860–1865.* Toledo, Ohio: Gray Company, 1942.

Essig, James D. *The Bonds of Wickedness: American Evangelicals Against Slavery, 1770–1803.* Philadelphia: Temple University Press, 1982.

Filler, Louis. *The Crusade Against Slavery, 1830–1860.* New York: Harper and Row, 1960.

Fladeland, Betty. *James G. Birney, Slaveholder to Abolitionist.* New York: Cornell University Press, 1955.

Fletcher, Robert S. *A History of Oberlin College.* Oberlin, Ohio: Oberlin College, 1943.

Fox, Early Lee. *The American Colonization Society, 1817–1840.* Baltimore: Johns Hopkins University Press, 1919.

Fraser, James W. *Pedagogue for God's Kingdom: Lyman Beecher and the Second Great Awakening.* Lanham, Md.: University Press of America, 1985.

Friedman, Lawrence J. *Gregarious Saints: Self and Community in American Abolition, 1830–1870.* Cambridge: Cambridge University Press, 1982.

Goodykoontz, Colin B. *Home Missions on the American Frontier.* Caldwell, Idaho: Caxton Printers, 1939.

Goen, C. C. *Broken Churches, Broken Nation: Denominational Schisms and the Coming of the Civil War.* Macon, Ga.: Mercer University Press, 1985.

Griffin, Clifford S. *Their Brothers' Keeper: Moral Stewardship in the United States, 1800–1865.* New Brunswick, N.J.: Rutgers University Press, 1960.

Hammond, John L. *The Politics of Benevolence: Revival and American Voting Behavior.* Norwood, N.J.: Ablex Publishing Company, 1979.

Harlow, Ralph V. *Gerrit Smith, Philanthropist and Reformer.* New York: Henry Holt, 1939.

Hood, Fred J. *Reformed America: The Middle and Southern States, 1783–1837.* University, Ala.: University of Alabama Press, 1980.

Mabee, Carleton. *Black Freedom: The Nonviolent Abolitionists From 1830 Through the Civil War.* New York: Macmillan, 1970.

McKivigan, John R. *The War Against Proslavery Religion: Abolitionism and the Northern Churches, 1830–1865.* Ithaca: Cornell University Press, 1984.

Marsden, George M. *The Evangelical Mind and the New School Presbyterian Experience.* New Haven: Yale University Press, 1970.

Muelder, Herman. *Fighters for Freedom: The History of the Anti-Slavery Activities of Men and Women Associated with Knox College.* New York: Columbia University Press, 1959.

Murray, Andrew E. *Presbyterians and the Negro: A History.* Philadelphia: Presbyterian Historical Society, 1966.

Nye, Russel B. *Fettered Freedom: Civil Liberties and the Slavery Controversy, 1830–1860.* East Lansing: Michigan State University, 1963.

Perry, Lewis. *Radical Abolitionism: Anarchy and the Government of God in Antislavery Thought.* Ithaca: Cornell University Press, 1973.

Quarles, Benjamin. *Black Abolitionists.* New York: Oxford University Press, 1969.

Scott, Donald M. *From Office to Profession: The New England Ministry, 1750–1850.* Philadelphia: University of Pennsylvania Press, 1978.

Sernett, Milton C. *Black Religion and American Evangelism: White Protestants, Plantation Missions, and the Flowering of Negro Christianity, 1787–1865.* Metuchen, N.J.: Scarecrow Press, 1975.

Sesick, Lawrence. *The Lane Rebels: Evangelicalism and Antislavery in Antebellum America.* London: Scarecrow Press, 1980.

Sewell, Richard H. *Ballots for Freedom: Antislavery Politics in the United States, 1837–1860.* New York: Oxford University Press, 1976.

Smith, Timothy L. *Revivalism and Social Reform.* New York: Harper and Row, 1957.

Sorin, Gerald. *The New York Abolitionists.* Westport, Conn.: Greenwood Publishing Corp., 1971.

Staudenraus, P. J. *The African Colonization Movement, 1816–1865.* New York: Columbia University Press, 1961.

Thomas, Benjamin P. *Theodore Weld: Crusader for Freedom.* New Brunswick, N.J.: Rutgers University Press, 1950.

Walters, Ronald G. *The Antislavery Appeal: American Abolitionism After 1830.* Baltimore: Johns Hopkins University Press, 1976.

Wyatt-Brown, Bertram. *Lewis Tappan and the Evangelical War Against Slavery.* Cleveland: Case Western Reserve Press, 1969.

York, Robert M. *George B. Cheever, Religious and Social Reformer, 1807–1890.* Orono: University of Maine Press, 1955.

Index

Abolitionism and church: Albany convention on, 58, 109–15, 117, 118, 119, 120, 122, 124; and American Union, 16–23, 25–27; and Amistad captives, 55–56; attitude to slaveholders, 14; and Brown uprising, 173–75; campaign against Fugitive Slave Law, 94–98; campaign against Kansas-Nebraska Bill, 132–36; vs. colonization movement, 9–16, 32; criticism of AHMS, 43–54, 100–103, 107, 115–18, 119, 156, 157, 159–60; and Dred Scott decision, 172–73; in election of 1856, 151–55; in election of 1860, 175–84; free missions movement in, 92–93, 101, 102, 119–20; impact of Kansas-Nebraska Act, 139, 140–43, 151, 154, 156, 157; and Know-Nothing party, 149–51; and Liberty party, 31–39; Mexican War peace movement in, 73–88, 142; Missionary convention on, 104–5, 107; and missionary societies, 56–62, 104–7 (see also American Board of Commissioners of Foreign Missions; American Home Missionary Society; American Missionary Association, Western Home and Foreign Missionary Association); and missionary spirit, 5, 6–8; mob violence against, 29–30; in political action, 30–39, 77–78, 142–55, 172–84; postmillennialism in, xii, 7–8; and Republican party, 143–49, 151, 154; and sectional differences, 160–71; support for Civil War, 184–89. See also Christian Anti-Slavery Conventions; Congregationalists; Evangelical

movement; Presbyterians; Slavery, extension of
Adair, Robert, 164
Adair, Samuel, 174
Adams, John Q., 56
Adams, Nehemiah, 19, 27, 127, 185
Adams, William, 95
Aiken, Robert, 144
Aiken, Samuel C., 80, 98
Alabama, 26, 123
Albany Atlas and Argus, 178
Albany convention, 58, 109–15, 117, 118, 119, 120, 122, 124
Allen, D. Howe, 145, 167
Alton Observer, 89
American and Foreign Anti-Slavery Society, 29, 59, 62, 73, 98, 102, 119
American Anti-Slavery Society (AAS), 5, 9, 13, 16, 20, 21–22, 29, 57, 62, 95, 97–98, 126
American Board of Commissioners of Foreign Missions (ABCFM), 19, 29, 40, 42, 48, 52, 56, 57, 62, 92, 103, 104, 111
American Colonization Society (ACS), 9, 10, 15–18, 19, 27, 125, 126, 129–30
American Home Missionary Society (AHMS), 9, 14, 19, 22, 24, 27, 29, 57, 60, 61, 79, 81, 83; abolitionism vs. colonization in, 12, 13; and Albany Resolutions, 113–16, 118–19, 122, 124; and American Peace Society, 86–87; and black missions, 24–25; and Brown uprising, 174–75; and charge of sectional prejudice, 70, 71; and Chicago Missionary Convention, 104–5; criticism of position on

CONSCIENCE and SLAVERY

The Evangelistic Calvinist Domestic Missions, 1837-1861

Victor B. Howard

Conscience and Slavery offers a compelling look at the struggle in church and state over the slavery issue and the role it played in events leading to the Civil War. During the antebellum period, Calvinists, more than any other religious group in America, sought to shape frontier communities and especially to prevent the spread of slavery therein. They established the American Home Mission Society to conduct domestic missions in their churches, and developed an uncompromising moral antagonism against the extension of slavery. By the 1850s the Home Mission Society moved completely to an antislavery position.

The driving force behind the Calvinists' stance was the post-millennialist belief that the Kingdom of God would be established on America's virgin soil before the Second Coming of Christ. The evangelical Calvinists were also affected by the revival movement and identified with the philosophy of abolitionism that grew out of revivalism. The vision of Calvinist missionaries in the territories and Northern evangelical churches for a state of holiness led to the development of one separate faction which was more antislavery and to another which sustained domestic missions in the South without regard for the relations Southern churches held with the institution of slavery.

Howard chronicles the history of the domestic missions in the Calvinist churches during the antebellum period and examines the effects of the sectional controversy on